CENTRAL LIBRARY

7/03	· · 5 MAY 2012	**24 JAN 2013**
14 JUN 2007		**-9 MAR 2013**
-8 JAN 2008	3 1 MAY 2014	
-1 AUG 2008		
21 OCT 2008		
-5 MAY 2010		
27 SEP 2010		
19 FEB 2011		
30 MAY 2011		

INVERCLYDE LIBRARIES
CENTRAL LIBRARY
This book is to be returned on or before
the last date above. It may be borrowed
for a further period if not in demand.

Inverclyde L

D0755327

34106 000111232

THE COMPANION GUIDES

*It is the aim of these guides to provide a Companion
in the person of the author, who knows
intimately the places and people of whom he writes, and is able to
communicate this knowledge and affection to his readers.
It is hoped that the text and pictures will aid them
in their preparations and in their travels, and will
help them remember on their return.*

BURGUNDY · THE COUNTRY ROUND PARIS
DEVON · EDINBURGH AND THE BORDERS
FLORENCE · GASCONY AND THE DORDOGNE
GREECE · GREEK ISLANDS · IRELAND · ISTANBUL
KENT AND SUSSEX · LAKE DISTRICT · LONDON
MADRID AND CENTRAL SPAIN · NEW YORK
PARIS · ROME · SICILY
SOUTH OF SPAIN · VENICE

THE COMPANION GUIDE TO

ST PETERSBURG

KYRIL ZINOVIEFF and JENNY HUGHES

914·721

LIBRARIES

COMPANION GUIDES

INVERCLYDE

Copyright © Kyril Fitzlyon and Jenny Hughes, 2003

All Rights Reserved. Except as permitted under current legislation
no part of this work may be photocopied, stored in a retrieval system,
published, performed in public, adapted, broadcast,
transmitted, recorded or reproduced in any form or by any means,
without the prior permission of the copyright owner

First published 2003

Companion Guides

ISBN 1 900639 40 8

*The publishers and authors have done their best to ensure
the accuracy and currency of all the information in*
The Companion Guide to St Petersburg.
*However, they can accept no responsibility for any loss, injury,
or inconvenience sustained by any traveller as a result
of information or advice contained in the guide.*

Companion Guides is an imprint of Boydell & Brewer Ltd
PO Box 9, Woodbridge, Suffolk IP12 3DF, UK
and of Boydell & Brewer Inc.
PO Box 41026, Rochester, NY 14604–4126, USA
website: www.companionguides.com

A catalogue record for this book is available
from the British Library

Printed and bound in Finland by WS Bookwell

Contents

Illustrations

Photographs of The Arcade, 'The Bronze Horseman' and Alexander III in Znamenskaya Square by courtesy of the State Central Archive of Cinema and Photo Documents of St Petersburg; photographs of the Bankovskiy footbridge, the Palace at Pavlovsk and St Nicholas Cathedral by courtesy of Nigel Shakespeare; photographs of the Moika and the Winter Palace by courtesy of Luke Hughes; photographs of Peterhof by courtesy of the State Museum Preserve 'Peterhof'; photographs of the Hermitage Theatre, Palace Square, Summer Palace, Cameron Gallery and Pushkinskaya Metro Station by courtesy of Pavel Demidov and Oleg Trubskiy.

Maps and Plans

Many streets, squares, bridges etc. were re-named after the Revolution. Most of them have now been given back their old names but the process is not finished and visitors should be prepared for a degree of confusion.

Acknowledgements

We must express out great gratitude to Katya Gerasimova and Marina Vershevskaya, whose expertise and constant willingness to help us have made this book possible. We would also like to thank the following for indispensable information, corrections and advice: Lev Baron, Maria Gordeyeva, Alla Yusupova, Vadim Znamenov and some of his staff from the Peterhof Museum Preserve.

We are particularly indebted to Svetlana Bryusova and Inna Dimitriyeva for reading Russian sources aloud to us since these represented certain difficulties, for K. Z. because of his recent blindness, for J. H. because of her ignorance of the language.

We would like to thank Felicity Cave for keeping us in touch with the Tercentenary preparations, Mark Ching for leading us by the hand through our computer problems, Tim Gray of Luke Hughes & Co. for creating the maps, plans and charts, and Ellie Ferguson of Companion Guides for her kindness and patience in the editing process.

Finally we express our deep gratitude to Douglas Matthews for constructing the indispensable Index to our book. And we would like to thank our sons – Luke Hughes and Sebastian Zinovieff-Fitzlyon – for invaluable assistance of many kinds.

Dedication

This book is dedicated to the people of Peter's city whose courage and suffering during the Blockade have added more to the lustre of their city than the finest achievements of its architects.

Kyril Zinovieff

My family's connection with St Petersburg began soon after it became the capital of Russia. The accession of Catherine the Great strengthened the connection since the main instigators of the *coup d'état* which toppled the Emperor Peter III and installed his wife Catherine in his stead were the Orlov brothers. Their mother was the sister of my great-grandfather's grandfather.

From then on, the Zinovieffs were a constant part of the administration of St Petersburg through its various institutions – sometimes as the city's mayor or chairman of its provincial council (*predvodítel dvoryánstva*), as governor, as commandant of its Fortress or, with the introduction of a constitution in 1906, as a member of the Upper House (the Council of State) or the Lower House (*Dúma*). Sometimes, as in the case both of my grandfather and my father, they held several of these appointments in the course of their lives.

None of this entitles me to write a Companion Guide or any other book about St Petersburg. But it does explain my interest in the subject and in the city where I was born in the early years of the last century – which makes my life now equal to almost half the life of St Petersburg as capital of Russia and about a third of its entire existence.

I have transliterated my family name whenever it appears in this book in accordance with the rules set out in the appendix on the Russian language on page 437 i.e. Zinoviev. In referring to myself, however, as co-author of this book, I have kept the transliteration adopted for some reason in the eighteenth century and observed by my family ever since i.e. Zinovieff. The reader should be aware that transliteration systems differ. We have tried to be internally consistent, while making exceptions for names with a generally accepted international form, but there may be variations from other sources.

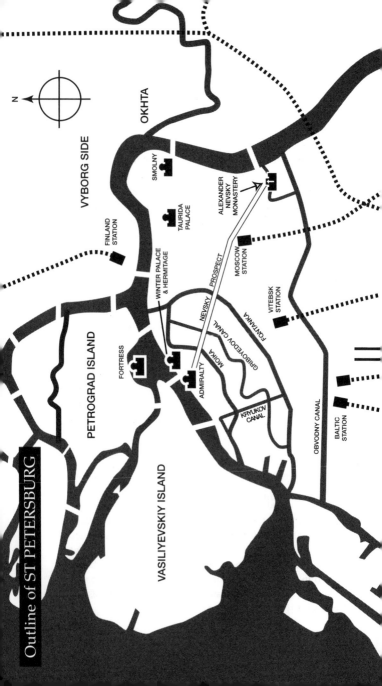

Outline of ST PETERSBURG

N

VYBORG SIDE

OKHTA

SMOLNY

TAURIDA PALACE

FINLAND STATION

WINTER PALACE & HERMITAGE

ALEXANDER NEVSKY MONASTERY

MOSCOW STATION

NEVSKY PROSPECT

VITEBSK STATION

PETROGRAD ISLAND

FORTRESS

MOIKA

ADMIRALTY

FONTANKA

GRIBOYEDOV CANAL

KRYUKOV CANAL

OBVODNY CANAL

BALTIC STATION

VASILIYEVSKIY ISLAND

Introduction

In the late evening of 11 March 1918, a special train bearing the members of the Central Committee of the Russian Communist Party – and of the new Russian Revolutionary Government headed by Lenin – drew up at the Nicholas (now St Petersburg) Station in Moscow. The train had come from the capital, Petrograd (as St Petersburg was known from 1914 until 1924), which it left if not entirely in secret at least without publicity. And now, in Moscow, there were no flowers and no reception committee. On their arrival, Lenin, his wife and his colleagues were whisked away to the *Hotel National* where they spent the night. It was, after all, best not to stress the fact that the Russian authorities did not consider Petrograd entirely safe from a renewed military threat, in spite of the armistice just concluded with the Germans at Brest-Litovsk.

The transfer of the Government to Moscow was regarded at the time as purely temporary, to last while the German troops along the Narva–Pskov line still constituted a serious threat to Petrograd. But, as the French say: '*il n'y a que le provisoire qui dure*' (or, in the English version, 'the provisional is the only thing that lasts'). The day following his arrival in Moscow, Lenin, accompanied by his wife and two friends, went off to inspect the Kremlin. Later that day a telegram was sent to most of the foreign capitals. It read:

> The Government of the Federal Soviet Republic, the Council of People's Commissars and the country's supreme authority, the Central Executive Committee of the Councils of Worker, Soldier, Peasant and Cossack Deputies, have arrived in Moscow. Communications will be addressed to: Council of People's Commissars or CEC of the Councils of Deputies, Kremlin, Moscow.

And so Petrograd gave up its status as the capital city of Russia with as little ceremony as it had assumed it two centuries earlier. In 1712, the royal family had simply 'arrived' and taken up their permanent official residence in St Petersburg. No official proclamation informed the world that the capital had been transferred there from Moscow. In 1918, the arrival of Lenin and his wife to take up residence in Moscow was deemed to have reversed the process. The capital of Russia had swung back to its natural place – so natural that many young Russians with whom I have talked in the last few years find it impossible to believe that it was ever anywhere else. St Petersburg? The capital? Was it really? And there is a sense in which they are right. Was it really? The prime purpose of St Petersburg as conceived by Peter the Great was to be not 'a window on the west' but a door which could be locked against it so that access to Russia through the Baltic Sea would never again be easily obtained by any foreign power. He first gave the name Petersburg not to the city but to the fort which was to guard it from foreign intrusion through the mouth of the Neva. Peter's Fort.

I

The Foundation of the City

MOST VISITORS TO St Petersburg have heard at least four facts about it: that it is 'the Venice of the North'; that a vast number of workmen, perhaps a hundred thousand, died in the early years of its construction; that it was built on uninhabited marshes; and that it was founded on territory which did not and never had belonged to Russia. These 'facts' have one feature in common: none of them is true.

The comparison to Venice was first made as early as 1715 by Prince Alexander Menshikov who was quoted – by the Hanoverian Minister-Resident at the Court of Peter the Great, F. C. Weber – as saying that 'Petersburg should become another Venice to see which Foreigners would travel thither purely out of curiosity'. Menshikov, who in these early years was Peter's *alter ego*, should really have known better. But perhaps it was what he wanted to think and perhaps, indefatigable entrepreneur that he was, he already envisaged the tourist trade – an extraordinary vision for anyone to have had within a dozen years of the foundation of the city. In fact, St Petersburg's only resemblance to Venice is the prevalence of canals – and even they are different in kind and purpose. In St Petersburg they are mostly optional (as on Basil Island – *Vasíliyevskiy óstrov* – which was deliberately canalised because Peter fancied canals rather than streets); they are not the main arteries of the city and are used mainly for barge traffic. Peter himself had a different city in mind: Amsterdam, which he knew and loved, rather than Venice which he had never seen.

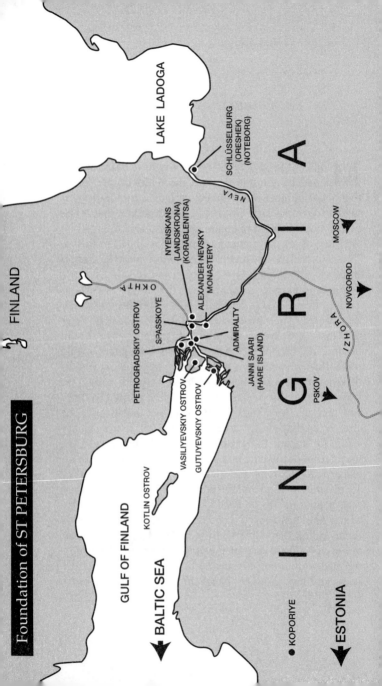

Foundation of ST PETERSBURG

FINLAND

BALTIC SEA

GULF OF FINLAND

KOTLIN OSTROV

LAKE LADOGA

SCHLÜSSELBURG
(ORESHEK)
(NOTEBORG)

NEVA

NYENSKANS
(LANDSKRONA)
(KORABLENITSA)

OKHTA

SPASSKOYE

ALEXANDER NEVSKY
MONASTERY

PETROGRADSKIY OSTROV

ADMIRALTY

VASILIYEVSKIY OSTROV

GUTUYEVSKIY OSTROV

JANNI SAARI
(HARE ISLAND)

I N G R I A

IZHORA

MOSCOW

NOVGOROD

PSKOV

KOPORIYE

ESTONIA

But, though the parallel with Amsterdam is more apt, it obscures the peculiar characteristic of St Petersburg: that it was built entirely in a borrowed idiom, either by architects enticed there from Italy, France, Holland, Denmark, England and almost everywhere else in Western Europe or by native architects sponsored by rich patrons to study abroad. The result was that, in some sense, Peter created a West European city unlike any other city in Russia. But, as the Russian writer Aleksandr Herzen remarked more than a century later, St Petersburg was also unlike any West European city – if only because it was like all of them at once. St Petersburg was an artificial, not an indigenous, creation.

Working conditions were undoubtedly bestial. As well as the normal eighteenth-century hazards of disease, ill-treatment, overwork and inadequate food there were Northern Europe's particular scourges of extreme cold and hungry wolves. (The Petersburg wolves were peculiarly persistent and voracious, hunting in vast packs.) So the legend spread – in songs and poems and letters, until it was held to be an incontrovertible historical fact – that the building of St Petersburg was costlier in human lives than any building project anywhere else. Typical are the much quoted lines of the Russian nineteenth-century poetaster Mikhail Dimitriev:

> A giant built it; lacking stones
> He paved the swamps with human bones.

Peter was, indeed, a giant and he was short of stones. But there is hard evidence – for example, from the lists which survive of conscripted and volunteer workers employed on the Fortress of SS Peter and Paul – that mortality in the workforce was not abnormal for the period and that many names recurred for years.

Nor was the land on which St Petersburg was founded an uninhabited marsh. Forty or so villages and hamlets studded the islands around the estuary – islands big and small, overgrown with hazelwood and alder, copses and woods of pine, birch and fir. Game was plentiful every-where – duck, capercaillies, grouse, snipe. And wild animals abounded – bears, lynxes, foxes, elk, reindeer and hares as well as the hungry wolves. It was new land in the most literal geological sense, which emerged (and is still emerging) only some four thousand years ago, long after the appearance of man in Northern Europe: hence the name of the river *Nevá* (derived from the Old Scandinavian word for 'new').

It was indeed marshy and subject to flooding. There used to be serious floods every five years, when the sluggish current of the Neva was unable to resist the sea, blown upstream by strong south-westerlies, particularly in November. Then the waters rose and, until recently, were still liable to flood the city's lowest-lying districts, forcing their way through the underground channels into base-ments, courtyards and streets. But this did not prevent peasants and fishermen in the seventeenth century from seeking out the highest ground and cultivating it. They used their houses as a kit to be dismantled when a serious flood was expected, breaking them up, tying the boards and logs together and attaching them to a tree to ride out the emergency, while they themselves made a temporary retreat to higher ground further inland. As Peter and his army recovered the estuary islands from the Swedes, they found that the best land to build on was almost invariably land already settled, in the most modest way, by a mixed population of Russian, Finnish and Karelian peasants. And this is why so many of St Petersburg's inhabited districts have been sited where these early villages used to be.

So we come to the fourth untrue 'fact' which visitors may have heard about St Petersburg – that it was founded on ter-ritory which had never before belonged to Russia. Far from being a new acquisition, the territory at the mouth of the

Neva where St Petersburg was built can be said to be the place where Russia began. It was here that the Vikings (Varangians), after crossing the sea from Scandinavia, habitually started their great circular trek south-eastwards – across the Russian plain, following rivers (and sometimes dragging their boats along dry land between them) to the Black Sea, across the Black Sea to Constantinople, through the Mediterranean westwards and back home along the coast of Western Europe. It was known as 'the road from the Vikings to the Greeks'.

In the mid-ninth century, a particular Viking chieftain is recorded by the ancient Russian chronicles as having decided to make a permanent base on the Neva estuary. The chronicles, which date the beginning of Russian history from this moment, tell us that this Viking was called **Rurik** (Ruorigh) and that, in 862, he founded the first 'Russian' dynasty which was to rule the principalities of Russ (including Novgorod and Pskov, Kiev and Muscovy) for some seven centuries through his direct male descendants. Rurik's line ran out with the feeble-minded son of Ivan the Terrible – and the rest is modern history.

The land round the estuary and delta of the Neva, called Ingria, became part of the 'Republic of Novgorod'. But it continued to be the military objective, first of the Teutonic Knights and then of the Swedes (also Vikings in origin), to seize and secure the province of Ingria from the descendants of Rurik. From then until Peter the Great concluded the Peace of Nystadt with the Swedes in 1721, Ingria was disputed territory and the Russian hinterland was exposed. In 1240, the Teutonic Knights invaded the territory of Novgorod and Pskov, capturing Pskov and building a timber fortress at *Kopóriye*,[1] some eighty miles south-west

---

[1] The great castle of *Kopóriye* still stands, battered and largely ruined on its not very impressive hill. Built first in timber by the Teutonic Knights and then in stone by the Russians, restored and strengthened by both sides

of the mouth of the river along the Gulf of Finland. But in the same year, some miles up-river at the confluence of the rivers Izhora and Neva, Prince Alexander of Novgorod (a descendant of Rurik) fought a great victory over a mixed army of Swedes and Teutonic Knights at the Battle of the Neva. The following year, Prince Alexander captured and destroyed *Kopóriye* and that episode in the long dispute was for the time being closed. Some five hundred years later, Peter the Great adopted Prince Alexander (by that time canonised as St Alexander Nevsky) as the patron saint of St Petersburg and brought his bones from Vladímir to lie in a new monastery that he built (the *Aleksándro-Névskaya Lávra*), believing it to be on the site of the Battle of the Neva. (In fact, it is at the confluence of the Neva with another river, now called the Monastyrka.) From Rurik through Alexander to Peter was thus the implied line of descent.

The Teutonic Knights were followed by the Swedes who, in 1330, captured the estuary of the Neva and erected a fort (on the right bank) at the point where the little river *Ókhta* flows into the main river as its tributary. To this first of St Petersburg's predecessors they gave the name of **Landskrona** (Land's End). And, strangely enough, as if prefiguring the debt of its distant successor to Italian architects,

several times in its long history, it was the first prize that had to be won by any Western invader aiming at establishing himself on the Neva delta and the Baltic coast. It was finally secured by Peter the Great, who recaptured and dismantled it in 1703. Peter presented it to Menshikov, his main collaborator at the time and prime minister *avant la lettre*. After Menshikov's disgrace and banishment, it was confiscated by the Crown until, at the end of the eighteenth century, it came into the possession of the Zinoviev family and remained there until the Revolution in 1917. As the castle was uninhabitable, my family built themselves a house near by where my grandfather lived and I used often to stay as a child. This house was burned down by the modern descendants of the Teutonic Knights – a detachment of the German army that occupied the fortress during the siege of St Petersburg. Now there is talk of the fortress being restored by its present owners – the Russian state.

Landskrona too was built by an Italian. **St Petersburg Mark I**, you might say.

This Swedish foothold lasted only a year. It was destroyed by the Novgorod army which replaced it with a settlement right on the river bank whose main function was to provide and service a dock for ships sailing up and down the Neva. So they called it *Koráblenitsa*, from the Russian word *korábl*, meaning ship. Opposite, on the left bank, where centuries later was to be built the famous Smolny Convent, there grew up the Russian village of *Spásskoye*. These two Russian settlements together, *Koráblenitsa* and *Spásskoye*, could with justice be regarded as **St Petersburg Mark II**.

Gradually, the Neva delta, the islands of which it is composed and the territory around it, became dotted with small villages and hamlets belonging to the Republic of Novgorod and populated by a mixture of Russians, Finns and Karelians. To defend these settlements and to impede all future attempts to invade, the Russians built a fortress forty miles further inland, where the Neva flows out of Lake Ladoga. They called it *Oréshek* ('Nut') from the shape of the island on which it was erected. Its name was to change several times.

But Swedish-Russian rivalry could not be resolved by building forts or by taking and re-taking them. It was fundamental. For the Russians, the Neva was the only link entirely in Russian territory connecting Russia with 'the western sea', i.e. the Baltic – the only direct route for commerce with the Hanseatic ports and Western Europe. For Sweden, Russia with her huge potential represented a constant threat; if she could be barred from the Baltic Sea and prevented from spreading her influence along the coast, Sweden would be secure, at least from the east. There followed a series of Russo-Swedish wars in which Ingrian fortresses and settlements continuously changed hands until, by the Treaty of Stolbovo in 1617, the Russians surrendered the whole of Ingria, including the fortresses of *Kopóriye* and *Oréshek* as well as the Neva delta. The Swedish King, Gustavus Adolphus, saw in this victory the hand of God: 'Russia has been deprived of the sea and the Russians, God willing, will find it difficult to jump over that stream.' To make doubly sure, the Swedes destroyed *Koráblenitsa* and built a new fortress of their own. They called it *Nyenskans* ('Neva Fortress'). The Russians shortened it to *Kántsy*.

In the middle of the seventeenth century, *Nyenskans/ Kántsy* was briefly captured by Tsar Alexis (Peter the Great's father) but not for long. And the town of *Nyen*, built by the Swedes under protection of the fortress, continued to grow and prosper. It was a neat and fairly typical Swedish town with carefully planned squares and streets and a Lutheran Church in the centre. Not far from the Lutheran was an Orthodox church to minister to the heterogeneous population. Though there were only some two thousand people in all, each community had its own school. There was also a hospital, standing in a large garden and serving a huge catchment area which included the whole of Finland and the Baltic provinces. Keen to develop *Nyen* as a major port, and particularly as Russia's main export centre for Baltic trade, the Swedish government granted it privileges and immunities with the result that, by the end of the century, it had a commercial fleet of as many as a hundred ships and was well on the way to becoming the most important port on the Baltic coast. *Nyen* and its fortress constituted **St Petersburg Mark III**. As a step along the evolutionary path that was to lead to the real St Petersburg, it was a considerable advance.

Then on to the scene strode two new and enormous figures: **Peter I of Russia** and Charles XII of Sweden. Both were young. Peter took effective possession of his throne in 1694 at the age of twenty; Charles succeeded to his in 1697 at the age of fifteen. Both for various reasons dramatically underestimated each other's abilities. Both, in different ways, were touched by genius. For Peter, there appeared to be an exceptional concatenation of circumstances favourable for a war on Sweden: he himself had just completed his war with Turkey; at the same time, two allies with vested interests in the defeat of Sweden had declared themselves – Poland-Saxony and Denmark; and the King of Sweden was still only eighteen. In August 1700, Russia declared war on Sweden and the Great Northern War began.

Peter's first objective was to shut the door of the Neva estuary in the face of north-western Europe – this time, for ever. His second aim was to open Russia's access to the Baltic and, with it, her commercial and cultural access to Western Europe which had effectively been closed throughout the Renaissance. It was his inspired intuition that, until she could secure this access, Russia would remain – and could no longer afford to be – a backward country. In this enterprise, he found strength in the ancient origins of Novgorod's rule over Ingria and the estuary of the Neva – a claim which, whenever opportunity arose, he reinforced by association with the heroic past.

Before making an assault on the main Swedish base of *Nyenskans,* he decided first to regain the fortress of *Oréshek* (called *Noteborg* by the Swedes), where the Neva leaves Lake Ladoga. But it was not, as Peter said, punning on the Swedish/Russian meaning of its name, 'an easy nut to crack'. After three weeks' siege, he ordered a final assault under the direct orders of a Major Karpov and Prince Mikhail Galitsin. In the light of the courage and brilliance of the Swedish defence, he then called it off. Galitsin is reputed to have refused to obey the order: 'Tell the Tsar', he is alleged to have said to the messenger, 'that I now belong not to him but to God.' The story is probably apocryphal but the mere fact that it is told at all illustrates the extent to which Russians regarded the recapture of Ingria as a sacred duty. What is not disputed is that Galitsin stormed the fortress and, after thirteen hours of bitter fighting, scaled the walls and overcame the garrison.

Peter's joy was overwhelming. *Noteborg* was a key fortress – the key for forces invading Russian territory; the key to Ingria as a whole; the key, most particularly, to the mouth of the Neva and the fortified town of *Nyenskans/ Kántsy*. For this reason, he gave the captured fortress a new name altogether, neither Russian nor Swedish but Dutch: *Sleutelburch(t)* ('key fortress' – later Germanised to *Schlüsselburg*). When the key was ceremoniously presented to him, he ordered it to be hung on the western tower of the fortress – 'the Sovereign's tower' – and a medal to be struck inscribed: 'Was in enemy hands for ninety years'.

The Swedish governor of *Noteborg/Sleutelburch*, General Schlippenbach, was allowed to leave the fortress, together with the garrison's 250 survivors, their wives and four pieces of cannon, and join the forces in *Nyenskans/Kántsy* forty miles west down the river. But it was less than half a year before Peter followed them there and drove this garrison, too, to capitulate. Meanwhile, he had much to do. He appointed Menshikov as governor not merely of *Sleutelburch* but of the whole of Ingria, including *Kopóriye*, though it was still in Swedish hands. For good measure he made him Duke of Ingria.

Then he began to organise the next stage of the re-conquest. Long letters and short notes, sometimes in his impatience written in his own hand, descended on his Duke, his generals, his ministers – anyone, in short, who was to be involved in the forthcoming campaign. They dealt, sometimes in very elementary grammar, with strategy and tactics, logistics and supplies; no detail too small, no issue too large. Existing regiments must be reorganised and new ones formed; please see to it at once. Baked bread must be sent to *Sleutelburch* at the end of Easter week 'at all costs' – enough to last for a fortnight, no more but no less either. Guns are being neglected; cannon balls have arrived but 3,033 of them are missing from the consignment; they must be made up at once. Not an ounce of medicines has been sent by the pharmaceutical services; why? There are not enough medical officers; more must be despatched, even if old or over-age. And the new navy . . . he had just returned from Lake Ladoga where he personally – sometimes as a shipwright – was helping to build ships.

The new **navy** was a central part of his strategy. He realised that it would not be sufficient to drive out the Swedes and bolt fast the gate against them. He must also have a navy to protect and enhance a new Russian presence in the Baltic. And he must be able to build his navy in peace. At this stage, he decided that the place to do so was on Lake Ladoga in the shelter of his new acquisition, the fortress of *Sleutelburch*. He had, moreover, dreamed of building a fleet ever since, as a boy of sixteen, he found an old boat[2] in an outhouse on the Romanov estate of *Izmailovo* near Moscow.

According to one (contested) version, the boat had been a gift from Queen Elizabeth of England to Ivan the Terrible who gave it, in turn, to the brother of his first wife, Peter's great-great-grandfather, Nikita Romanovich Zakharin. Nikita owned the *Izmailovo* estate.

Because of this boat, Peter lost his heart forever to the sea. It led him, many years later, to travel to Holland and to England, gathering knowledge (unfamiliar to Russians) about how to build ships and commission a fleet. It was the reason why, when his new city of St Petersburg began to be built, he was reluctant to allow any bridges over the Neva – people should learn to sail their way around. And it is why the boat itself (whose real name is *Shtandart*) is always referred to as *bótik* (a Russification of the English

---

[2] A replica of the boat is now to be seen in the *Bótny dómik* (Boat House) outside the Cathedral in the Fortress of SS Peter and Paul, *see* Chapter II. The original is in the Central Naval Museum.

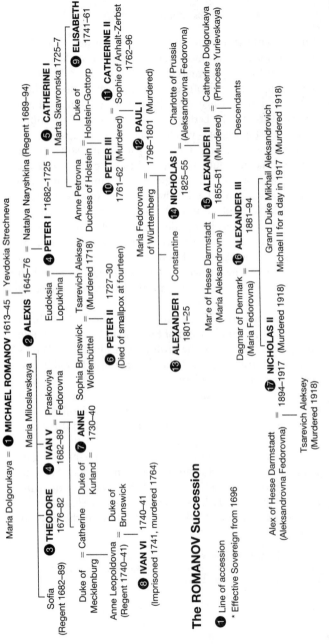

Maria Dolgorukaya = **❶ MICHAEL ROMANOV** 1613–45 = Yevdokia Strechneva

❷ ALEXIS 1645–76 = Natalya Naryshkina (Regent 1689–94)

Maria Miloslavskaya =

❸ THEODORE
1676–82

❹ IVAN V
1682–89 = Praskoviya Fedorovna

Sofia
(Regent 1682–89)

Duke of = Catherine
Mecklenburg

❼ ANNE
1730–40 = Duke of Kurland

Anne Leopoldovna = Duke of Brunswick
(Regent 1740–41)

❽ IVAN VI
1740–41
(Imprisoned 1741, murdered 1764)

❹ PETER I *1682–1725 = Anne Petrovna
Duchess of Holstein

Eudoksia = Tsarevich Aleksey
Lopukhina   (Murdered 1718)

❻ PETER II 1727–30
(Died of smallpox at fourteen)

❺ CATHERINE I
Marta Skavronska 1725–7

Duke of Holstein – Holstein-Gottorp

❾ ELISABETH
1741–61

❿ PETER III = Sophie of Anhalt-Zerbst
1761–62 (Murdered)   **⓫ CATHERINE II**
                        1762–96

Maria Fedorovna = **⓬ PAUL I**
of Württemberg   1796–1801 (Murdered)

Constantine   **⓭ ALEXANDER I**
              1801–25

⓮ NICHOLAS I = Charlotte of Prussia
1825–55

⓯ ALEXANDER II = Catherine Dolgorukaya
1855–81 (Murdered)   (Princess Yurievskaya)

Descendants

Mar e of Hesse Darmstadt = **⓰ ALEXANDER III**
(Maria Aleksandrovna)   1881–94

Dagmar of Denmark =
(Maria Fedorovna)

Grand Duke Mikhail Aleksandrovich
Michael II for a day in 1917 (Murdered 1918)

Alex of Hesse Darmstadt = **⓱ NICHOLAS II**
(Aleksandrovna Fedorovna)   1894–1917 (Murdered 1918)

Tsarevich Aleksey
(Murdered 1918)

The ROMANOV Succession

❶ Line of accession

* Effective Sovereign from 1696

'little boat') and, at the same time, as 'the grandfather of the Russian Navy'.

Peter had Nikita's boat repaired and fitted with sails. And in it he learned to sail – on the river *Yáuza*, a tributary of the *Moskvá*. In particular, he acquired the very necessary skill for anyone intending to sail on a river: of tacking into the wind. This was the moment when he first realised that a Russian fleet might be able to sail down the Neva, out into the Gulf of Finland and the Baltic Sea. If it is true that Queen Elizabeth gave the boat to Ivan the Terrible it is ironic that the sovereign he frightened most when the first ships of his new fleet actually made their appearance at the mouth of the Neva was Queen Anne. The government of England reacted with alarm, duly recorded in Russian diplomatic despatches from London.

On 23 April 1703, Field Marshal Sheremetev left *Sleutelburch* with an army 20,000 strong and advanced towards *Nyenskans*. He halted ten miles from the fortress and began serious preparations for a siege: building a bridge over the *Ókhta*, bringing up artillery for a bombardment. And then, on 26 April, Peter himself appeared. He chose to act in the capacity not of Tsar nor of Commander-in-Chief but in the rather modest rank to which he had appointed himself – bombardier captain. Two days later, he took himself off on a reconnaissance with seven companies of men and sixty rowing boats – passing under the walls of the fortress in the dark and down the Neva to the sea. Having requisitioned some livestock from local peasants, he returned twenty-four hours later but minus three companies which he had left concealed on Basil Island (*Vasíliyevskiy óstrov*) in the estuary to keep watch for enemy vessels. A few hours sleep – he habitually began his working day between three and four in the morning – and he was ready to take part in the assault.

By midday on 30 April, Sheremetev was ready to begin his bombardment. But before they opened fire, the

Russians sent a trumpeter to the Swedish Commandant with a letter 'requesting' his surrender. The trumpeter was away so long that a drummer was sent to fetch him back. At six o'clock in the evening they both returned with the message that the Commandant would defend the fortress with which his King had entrusted him. The Russians gave him another hour to think about it and then opened fire.

They fired all through the night, till daybreak and beyond. Suddenly a roll of drums from the fortress announced that the Commandant was willing to capitulate. Under the terms of his surrender, the garrison was accorded full military honours and left the fortress with four pieces of cannon, men bearing arms, drums beating, flags flying and standards held aloft. *Nyenskans/Kántsy* had become a Russian possession providing the possibility of a clear passage to the Baltic from Lake Ladoga. There was a thanksgiving service and the town's name was duly changed – to the Dutch *Slotburch(t)*. Peter ordered a public celebration of the victory in Moscow and sent the joyful news to his collaborator and drinking companion Admiral Apraksin with instructions: 'Don't fail to remember us to Ivashka.' ('Ivashka' or 'Johnny' was the code used by him with his closest friends to indicate a drinking bout. 'Battles with Ivashka', in which Ivashka 'won', feature frequently in his correspondence.)

But the clear passage to the Baltic was still notional rather than real. Further along the Baltic coast, the Swedish army still continued to threaten the new Russian positions. And off the Neva estuary, a Swedish squadron of nine vessels under the command of Vice-Admiral Nummers was approaching from the west, ignorant of the fall of *Nyenskans*. They were spotted and reported to Sheremetev by the soldiers Peter had left behind on Basil Island so that, when they fired two shots to signal their approach to what they believed to be a friendly garrison, the Russians, rightly guessing this to be a prearranged signal, replied with another two shots. On 6 May, two of the Swedish ships, still in ignorance, sailed on eastwards right into the estuary and cast anchor for the night just off Kanoner Island (*Kanonérskiy óstrov*). This, too, was communicated to the Russians in *Nyenskans* by the Russians on Basil Island. At which point, the Tsar of Russia (or bombardier captain, as it took his fancy) suddenly and impulsively decided on a course of action which, but for extraordinary good fortune, would have cost him his life.

He filled thirty rowing boats with soldiers and, taking Menshikov with him, 'since' (according to Peter's Journal) 'apart from them' – Peter and Menshikov – 'there was nobody who knew anything about the sea', he proceeded down the river as far as the fork in the Neva where the *Málaya Nevá* goes off to the north-east. They took shelter, waiting for the night to give them cover. Dawn, fortunately, was overcast and, as it started to rain, Peter split his little flotilla into two – sending Menshikov and fifteen boats on southward to conceal themselves behind Gutuyev Island (*Gutúyevskiy óstrov*) while his own fifteen rowed slowly and quietly round the top of Basil Island until they were able to ambush the Swedish ships between the two groups of rowing boats. The Swedes opened fire but the Russians were too close to be hit; then they hoisted sail in an attempt to rejoin the squadron but, as they had to tack down the fairway, they made very slow progress. Eight of the Russian boats closed in and were able to board, with Peter himself the first to climb on deck, grenade in hand and using his battle axe to cut down the Swedish sailors surrounding him. By the end of the battle, there were thirteen Swedish survivors out of seventy-eight who began it.

In his letters, Peter described this exploit of 7 May as 'an unprecedented victory'. And so, in a sense it was; however small, it was Russia's first victory at sea and it had been achieved without a single Russian casualty. Whether the Tsar should have been personally involved in it is, perhaps, debatable. But it gave him confidence at a critical juncture. It gave him the confidence, in fact, to found St Petersburg.

He now had a major decision to make: how best to secure the passage to and from Lake Ladoga, forty miles up-river, where he was building his fleet. The Swedes were still in a position to threaten him from the sea and, further west, from the land. It was to take Peter another eighteen years before, in 1721, he could conclude a decisive and permanent peace. So 'a council of war was held', according to Peter's Journal, 'to decide whether to fortify *Nyenskans* or look for another, more convenient place since the former was small, far from the sea and with no great natural defences'. The council decided to look for a new place and, within a few days, found one: an island just off the north (right) bank of the Neva, some three miles downstream from *Nyenskans*, called *Lust Eland* (better known by its Finnish name of *Janni saari* – **Hare Island**). Here, on 16 May 1703, fifteen days after the fall of *Nyenskans*, the foundations of a fortress were laid.

At first, the new fortress – with its earthen ramparts and hastily erected battery – had no name. Peter continued to sign his letters and address them as 'from the camp of *Slotburch*' – his name for *Nyenskans*. Then, on 29 June, being the Feast of SS Peter and Paul, the foundations of a wooden church were laid within the precincts to which Peter referred (in Dutch, of course), then and ever afterwards, as **Sankt Pieterburch**.[3] Peter's name for the church was extended to the fortress and then eventually to the miscellany of buildings that started to grow on the larger island to the north of it, now known as the Petrograd Side (*Petrográdskaya storoná*).

---

[3] It should be explained that 'burcht' is Dutch for 'fortress'. Here, as in *Sleutelburch and Slotburch*, Peter along with every Russian would not have bothered with the final 't' since he would have written in Russian and the appropriate character would have been '*X*' – a hard 'kh'. Peter's Dutch names were later Germanified by his successors. Hence 'burcht' became 'burg'. But it derived from the Dutch for 'fortress', not from the German for 'town'.

So **St Petersburg** was born. It is strange to think that, had it not been for Peter's mania for changing place names and for changing them into Dutch, we might all know it as *Nyenskans*. In more than one sense, St Petersburg is *Nyenskans*, for the Swedish town and its defences were quite literally absorbed by the new Russian one. Not only did its inhabitants – or what remained of them – intermarry and merge with the inhabitants of Peter's new settlement but the very stones of its houses were recycled for the buildings that later were erected on both banks of the Neva. As late as the 1900s, it was still not uncommon to come across the foundations of *Kántsy* houses in the *Ókhta* district of St Petersburg.

The purpose of the Fortress of SS Peter and Paul, then, was to protect the approaches to **Lake Ladoga**. And Lake Ladoga was where Peter intended to build his navy. For the rest of 1703, he was occupied supervising the construction of naval vessels. By the middle of 1704, several had been built and were viewed (with some fluttering in West European chanceries) off the mouth of the Neva. But then, in the autumn, something happened that was quite fortuit-ous and quite unexpected: a storm arose – one of those sudden and violent tempests characteristic of the lake – which destroyed some of the new vessels and dispersed the rest. Building ships on Lake Ladoga now appeared a high risk enterprise and Peter preferred to manage his risks. The shipyards must be moved.

On the left bank of the Neva, opposite Hare Island and within range of the new Fortress's guns, Peter identified a clearing in the swamp. The forest around it was dense and the ground was marshy. But, in the clearing, there was a nameless village of five wooden huts occupied by Finnish fishermen and peasants. Where Finns could live, Peter could build. Here he would place his new shipyard which he was to call *Admiraltéyskiy dom* (Admiralty House, more commonly known as the Admiralty).

Apart from the protection of the Fortress, this – on the face of it unpromising – site had a further attraction: across the clearing led three paths through the forest. The easternmost led to *Nyenskans* or, rather, to the point on the Neva where it must be crossed to reach *Ókhta*. The centre one led southwards, towards Novgorod and eventually to Moscow. The westernmost led to Pskov. Thus from the 'Admiralty', the new shipyard had direct connections with the Russian hinterland, with essential supply routes and with the twin capitals of the old Republic of Novgorod and Pskov. These three paths were the basis of what became known, during the subsequent planning of the city of St Petersburg, as the **Trident**, with its apex at the Admiralty gate. The path to *Nyenskans* was transformed into the *Névskiy prospékt*, striking eastwards across the developing city to *plóstchad Vosstániya*, where it connected with the *Lígovskiy prospékt* which turned south and thus also went to Novgorod. The path direct to Novgorod became the *Gorókhovaya úlitsa*. And the path to Pskov became the *Voznesénskiy prospékt*. Along the river banks on each side of the Admiralty were built the first substantial stone houses: to the west, the *Anglíyskaya náberezhnaya* (the English Embankment) and, to the east, the *Dvortsóvaya náberezhnaya* (the Palace Embankment).

The decision to move the dockyards from Lake Ladoga to the protection of the Fortress of SS Peter and Paul was a military and strategic decision. It happened, as so often in history, to have consequences that were neither military nor strategic but social and aesthetic. It determined the shape of the city of St Petersburg.[4]

---

[4] In 1914, at the start of the First World War, St Petersburg was felt to be too Germanic a name and was changed to Petrograd. After Lenin's death, the city became Leningrad (1924) until 1991, when its citizens voted that it should again be called St Petersburg.

II

The Fortress of SS Peter and Paul

Nearest Metro Station: *Górkovskaya*

IF THE FOUNDATIONS of the **Fortress of SS Peter and Paul** (*Petropávlovskaya krépost*) were laid on 16 May 1703, it did not acquire a name for some time. St Petersburg was born – but not as a city, let alone a capital, simply as a hastily erected barrier against attacks by Swedish forces. Such attacks did indeed follow each other with monotonous regularity for the next five years. Only after his final victory over Charles XII of Sweden at Poltáva in 1709 did Peter feel able to write: 'Now has the foundation stone been truly laid for Sankt Piterburch.'[1] This was when he affirmed his intention, on which he must have been ruminating for some time, of making it his capital.

In private conversation he referred to it as 'Paradise' (again in Dutch: *Paradijs*) though this was not a view of it shared by his entourage – nor by many of those who worked and lived there in the succeeding centuries. Certainly few people in any class of Russian society, high or low, shared the Tsar's enthusiasm. People came to the new city only if compelled by circumstances or physical force – like Prince Mikhail Galitsin who refused to leave Moscow but was brought in chains to St Petersburg and made to build himself a house there at his own expense.

None of the Russians – neither Peter nor his army – had ever before seen the land which, after almost a century of foreign domination, they had now restored to its former

---

[1] The variations in Peter's spelling reflect his usage in his Journal.

Plan of the PETER & PAUL FORTRESS

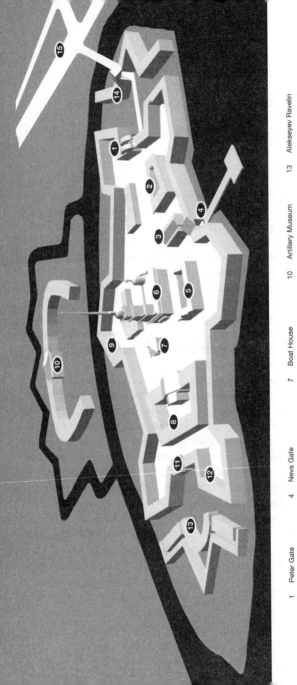

1. Peter Gate
2. Engineers' House
3. Guard House
4. Neva Gate
5. Commandant's House
6. Cathedral
7. Boat House
8. Mint
9. Staff Officers' Wing
10. Artillery Museum
11. Vasiliyevskiy Gate
12. Trubetskoy Bastion
13. Alekseyev Ravelin
14. Ivan Gate & Ravelin
15. Kamenno-ostrovskiy Prospect

allegiance. They saw it, fortunately for them, in one of the best months of the year, before the autumn sea mists had set in or the gales had started blowing, bringing with them – as they all too frequently did – floods and devastation.

The island, which Peter refers to in his Journal as *Lust Eland* but was better known by its Finnish name of *Janni saari* (Hare Island), was selected as the location of his Fortress at the suggestion of a Frenchman, **J. Y. Lambert de Guérin**, whom Peter had appointed General of Military Engineers. Surprisingly little is known of this colourful character, who was working in Poland as an engineer when Peter summoned him on the recommendation of the Russian Ambassador in Warsaw. Few Russian historians mention his name, yet his role in the foundation of St Petersburg was arguably second only to Peter's. He played an important part in the siege of *Noteborg*, organised the siege of *Nyenskans*, and took part in the war council which decided not to refortify it after its capture but to look for another location nearby. He was responsible for suggesting Hare Island as a suitable site and, when the suggestion was adopted, drew up the original plan of the Fortress of SS Peter and Paul. Peter greatly appreciated Lambert and awarded him the highest of all decorations recently introduced by him – the Order of the Apostle Andrew. But Lambert was an irascible man. He killed someone in a duel and quarrelled with his Russian colleagues. A few years later, he was sent to Western Europe to recruit more engineers and refused to return. When, sometime after that, he attempted to regain Peter's favour, he failed and spent the rest of his life outside Russia.

The Tsar had noticed **Hare Island** in the course of his first reconnaissance before the capture of *Nyenskans*. At that time, probably together with Lambert, he measured the fairway and found that it followed the arm of the river known as the Great Neva (i.e. the Neva proper) and passed between Hare Island and the Neva's left bank. So he concluded that the erection of a battery – or even better a fortress – on Hare Island would effectively close to the Swedes the entrance to the Neva and, thence, into Lake Ladoga where at that stage he believed that ships could be built with relative safety. He gave the necessary orders and immediately left for Ladoga without bothering to be present at any ceremony – should there have been one – to mark the foundation of the Fortress.

This version is contested by some authorities and posterity is uneasy with lack of ceremony. So a legend grew up about the foundation of St Petersburg which has charm if not truth. The Tsar, they say, stood that day on Hare Island surrounded by his troops. He took a bayonet from a soldier, cut out two pieces of turf, placed them cross-wise one on top of the other and said: 'Here shall be a city.' Then he took a spade and started digging a trench. At that moment an eagle soared into the sky and spread its wings as it hovered over Peter. When the trench was five feet long, a stone sarcophagus, sprinkled with holy water, was lowered into it. In the sarcophagus Peter placed a golden casket containing the sacred relics of the Apostle Andrew; and over the sarcophagus he put a stone lid bearing the following inscription: 'In the year of the Incarnation of Jesus Christ 1703, the reigning city of St Petersburg was founded by the great Sovereign Tsar Peter Alekseyevich Autocrat of all Russ.' Ornithologists have objected that eagles are unknown in that part of the world. And historians have objected that the very idea of a new city, let alone its name, would not then have occurred to Peter, even if he had been present on that day in Hare Island. But these are details of which legends rarely take cognisance. What mattered was the image: was it not kites, less noble birds than eagles, that were plainly to be seen hovering over the head of Romulus as he laid the foundation stone of Rome?

Just over six weeks after the first sod was turned for the Fortress, another foundation was laid inside it: for a timber church, named after the feast which fell on that day (29 June) of SS Peter and Paul. The name of the church was in due course extended to the Fortress and so the Fortress acquired a name. The building of both proceeded rapidly but only in the form of earthworks (for the Fortress) and timber (for the church). Not until 1706, after the arrival of the architect Dominico Trezzini,[2] did masonry construction begin with the replacement of the earthwork fortifications in stone. And it was eighty years later (in the 1780s) that all the riverside walls of the Fortress were faced in granite.

Timber was plentiful and most building, in those early days of St Petersburg, was in wood or daub and wattle. It was not until 1714 that Peter issued a decree making building in stone or brick obligatory for members of the gentry (though not for others). At the same time, building in stone elsewhere in Russia was forbidden. So that the streets of St Petersburg should be properly paved, everyone entering the area of the city was required to bring with them a stone or stones, the number and weight depending on the form of transport. Boats were obliged to deliver the heaviest stones and the greatest number; carts, fewer and lighter. Even pedestrians were expected to carry at least one stone of decent size. Slowly, the city became covered in granite, stone and stucco. But, as late as the first half of the nineteenth century, enough timber houses remained for smoking in the streets to be prohibited as a cautionary measure against fire – which gave rise, on occasion, to some curious encounters. A well-known Italian singer went walking one day and encountered Nicholas I, who knew and admired

---

[2] Like so many of the Italian architects who worked in St Petersburg, Trezzini came from Tessino, which is now part of Switzerland. The spelling of his Christian name was his own choice.

him. The singer, conscious of the prohibition, hid his cigar up the sleeve of his coat and continued his conversation with the Emperor. Then: *'J'espère que vous me pardonnerez,'* said the Emperor to the singer, *'si je vous préviens que votre manteau est en train de prendre feu du cigare que vous me cachez.'* (I hope you'll excuse me for warning you that your coat is about to catch fire from the cigar that you are hiding from me.)

It took six months, only, to throw up the six bastions of the Fortress on which three hundred cannon were mounted. Each bastion was given the name which it still possesses. Peter assumed direct responsibility for the south-eastern one which has consequently always been referred to as the Sovereign's Bastion (*Gosudárev bastión*). Each of the others bears the name of the individual appointed by Peter to supervise its construction: the southern bastion by Naryshkin; the south-western by Trubetskoy; the north-western by Zotov; the north-eastern by Menshikov; the northern by Golovkin. But in spite of the fact that the war with Sweden continued for many years, the Fortress was never called upon to fulfil the purpose for which it was founded – of defending the Neva estuary and, later, the city of St Petersburg. Instead it was, at first, put to all kinds of humdrum use. Some of its vaulted rooms, the so-called casemates,[3] were taken over by merchants who kept in them stores of wine, vodka and other goods.

In February 1718, however, a grimmer era was inaugurated. The casemates of the Trubetskoy Bastion were emptied of their wares and partisans of Peter's son and heir, the Tsarevich Aleksey, were incarcerated and tortured there. Aleksey was bitterly opposed to Peter's Westernising reforms. He had allies and sympathisers among the Boyars

---

[3] A casemate is an armoured compartment in a fortification (or ship) in which guns are mounted.

and the traditionalists in the Church. He hated Peter's 'Paradise', symbol of everything he disliked, and had declared his intention of moving the capital back to Moscow as soon as he inherited the throne. To escape his father's wrath, he fled to Vienna and, from there, to Naples but was enticed back to Russia on Peter's solemn promise to forgive him if he no longer meddled in politics. The promise was broken almost immediately the Tsarevich stepped onto Russian soil. A judicial inquiry was set up to establish the existence of a conspiracy and to try the conspirators. Aleksey soon found himself in the Trubetskoy Bastion where he was tortured (largely by his father), sentenced to death and, the following day, killed (on his father's orders). Thereafter, the Fortress was used exclusively as a political prison. Prisoners were incarcerated at first in the casemates, later in a small wooden prison constructed within the area of the Alekseyev Ravelin.[4] At the end of the eighteenth century, this was replaced by a stone prison, consisting of twenty cells and known as the 'Secret House'. The 'Secret House' was demolished in the 1890s during the reign of Alexander III. Thereafter political prisoners were held in the Trubetskoy Bastion.

One of the most romantic of the early prisoners was the mysterious and beautiful '**Princess Tarakanova**' (one name among many that she adopted in her short, sad life). Little is known about her beyond the fact that she claimed for herself the throne of Russia when that throne was occupied by Catherine the Great. She had already persuaded people to believe in her claims to be the Sultan's wife, the niece of the Shah of Persia, the Princess of Azov, the Princess of Vladímir – and, now, the daughter of the late Empress Elisabeth of Russia. She distributed 'manifestos' in which she declared her intention of being crowned in Moscow, supporting her claim with copies of a bogus will in which

---

[4] A ravelin is an 'outwork' having two embankments at a salient angle.

the Empress Elisabeth appeared to bequeath the throne to her as her daughter.[5]

But this was one claim too far. Catherine, whose own occupation of the Russian throne was due to a successful *coup d'état*, was in no position to take pretenders lightly. She despatched Aleksey Orlov[6] to Leghorn, where 'Princess Tarakanova' had sought refuge from a storm on her way to Turkey and the southern approaches to Russia. Pretending to fall in love, he made a proposal of marriage and an invitation to celebrate on board his ship. As she stepped aboard, he had her arrested and taken to St Petersburg where she was imprisoned in the wooden prison on the *Alekséyev ravelín* and where, a few months later on Christmas Eve 1775, she died of consumption.

Probably the most famous of all the prisoners in the Fortress were the **Decembrists**, officers and ex-officers of the Guards regiments who staged a revolt on 14 December 1825 at the time of the accession of Nicholas I.[7] Many of them were kept in the harshest conditions of solitary confinement and no communication, even with their gaolers. They were held in cells with neither light nor fresh air and where slime, legacy of the great flood of 1824, covered the floors and walls. They had been interrogated personally by Nicholas I in the Winter Palace before being transferred to the 'Secret House' and Nicholas himself made recommendations to the

[5] Elisabeth would have had a perfect right to nominate 'Princess Tarakanova' as her successor since her father, Peter the Great, abolished the traditional law of succession to the throne of Russia and substituted for it the right of the reigning sovereign to make a nomination. It was not until 1797 that a new law of succession was passed on the Austrian model by Catherine's son, the Emperor Paul.

[6] Aleksey Orlov was the brother of Catherine's former lover, Grigoriy, and had an established track record for eliminating the unwelcome. With his brother, he had been responsible for the murder of Catherine's husband, the Emperor Peter III, and for placing Catherine on the throne.

[7] The Decembrists' Revolt is described in Chapter IV in the section on the *plóstchad Dekabrístov*.

Commandant as to the conditions in which each prisoner was to be held.

In fact, conditions of imprisonment in the Fortress must have varied greatly. Books and writing paper were provided to many prisoners as a matter of course. In 1862, the revolutionary writer **Chernyshevskiy** was imprisoned for two years, in the course of which he was able to write – and to have published – his novel *What is to be Done?* Unreadable now, in its day it probably exerted more influence on radical thought than any other literary work. 'It ploughed me (*perepakhálo menyá*),' said Lenin, conjuring up the image of a field made ready for the sower; and, indeed, he took Chernyshevskiy's title for the first of his own political pamphlets.

In the autumn of 1874, **Peter Kropotkin**, the famous theoretician of Anarchism, was brought to the Fortress and kept there until his escape from the hospital wing eighteen months later. He too could order books and journals (from the library of the Academy of Sciences) and was free to write every day until sunset. When the sun went down, he read, spending Christmas 'laughing and crying' over the Christmas stories of Dickens which had been sent in by his family. But he also left a chilling description of prison conditions in the Fortress at the time: 'Silence, as of the grave, reigned round me', he wrote in his memoirs. For not only were the outer walls five feet thick but the inner walls and floors had been covered by canvas and heavy felt to absorb every sound. 'In vain I knocked on the walls and struck the floor with my foot, listening for the faintest sound in reply. None was to be heard.' Only the bells of the cathedral ringing the *Miserere nobis* at every quarter hour and, at midnight, the anthem 'God Save the Tsar' (which went on for fifteen minutes).

Lenin's brother, Aleksandr Ulyanov, was also a prisoner in the Fortress for a few weeks in the spring of 1887. He was held in cell number 47 of the Trubetskoy Bastion, now open to visitors, before his execution as one of the leaders of the unsuccessful plot to assassinate Alexander III.

On 25 October 1917, the Fortress became the Reserve Head-Quarters of the General Staff who were responsible for the **capture of the Winter Palace** (the Petrograd Military and Revolutionary Committee) and, for a brief moment, it looked as though it was to acquire a military role for the first and only time in its history. It occupied a strategic position on the north bank of the Neva, nine hundred metres across the river. The intention was that the Fortress guns should bombard the Palace from the north while other Bolshevik forces attacked it from the south (across Palace Square). The signal to fire was to be given by raising a lantern with red-tinted glass up the flagstaff of the Naryshkin Bastion but – according to at least one source – many things went wrong that evening. The first was that no such lantern could be found. So the order was finally given by word of mouth. The next was that few of the crew had any idea how to fire the guns. Eventually, two sailors were found to man them and the guns were fired. But, of thirty-five shells, only two hit the immense target – and then only on its cornice. So the Palace was saved from destruction by gunfire.[8]

Thereafter, the Fortress reverted for four more years to its familiar role of **political prison**. This time the prisoners were former government ministers, functionaries and other notables from the Imperial and the Provisional

[8] A more complete account of the capture of the Winter Palace is given in Chapter V. The most trustworthy source, and the one that I have followed, seems to me to be S. Melgunov, that most careful and meticulous of historians, in his *Bolshevik Seizure of Power*, published in Russian by the Editions de la Renaissance, Paris 1933, and in an abridged English translation by the American Bibliographical Centre/Clio Press, Santa Barbara 1972. The official version, on the other hand, does not accept that there was any incompetence; according to this, the red lantern duly signalled; the signal was duly corroborated by a signalling shot; and, at about 23.00, cannon sited on the fortress fired shrapnel shells at the Winter Palace.

Governments. Perhaps at no other time in its history was it used so extensively as a gaol and place of execution. The Grand Dukes Nikolay Mikhaylovich, Pavel Aleksandrovich, Georgiy Mikhaylovich and Dimitri Konstantinovich were probably executed there on 30 January 1919 – shot and buried where they fell, in front of the Mint. The Grand Duke Nikolay Mikhaylovich, who was a distinguished historian, made no secret of the fact that he was in favour of a Republic (as he wrote to the French historian, Masson, in 1917) and was deeply critical of the policies of Nicholas II. It is said that, as he was about to be shot, he took off his boots and threw them to the firing squad: 'Here. You'd better take them. They're royal, after all.' Maxim Gorky travelled to Moscow to argue with Lenin that the Grand Dukes should not be killed. Successful, he returned to the Fortress, only to be told that they were dead. He was, however, in time to save Prince Gavriil Konstantinovich.

In 1921, the Fortress received its last large batch of prisoners: sailors from the naval base at Kronstadt who mutinied in the name of Communism, which they accused the Bolsheviks of betraying by the famine, terror and arbitrary injustice of the new regime. The mutiny was quickly and bloodily suppressed; those survivors who failed to escape to Finland[9] were brought to the Fortress (and other Petrograd gaols) before being executed or sent to concentration camps.

The Fortress then ceased to be used as a prison and became a **museum,** now under the auspices of the Museum of the History of St Petersburg. In the Trubetskoy Bastion there is a permanent exhibition of prison conditions. My grandfather has left a laconic contemporary description of a cell which he occupied for a short time in June 1918,

[9] The last of those who did escape was captured in 1940, at the end of the Russo-Finnish war, brought back to Russia and executed. The Kronstadt mutiny is described more fully in Chapter XIII.

together with two of his sons and a friend.[10] It was probably representative of the average standard – by no means the worst nor, for that matter, the best: 'A vaulted ceiling and a stone floor. A stone wall, an iron bedstead (without a mattress) and a small table, both fixed to the wall. In the corner, an iron basin with water tap. No furniture of any kind – neither chairs nor bench nor straw to lie on.' He seems surprised. But he was former Governor of St Petersburg Province and ought perhaps to have known what it was like.

The Fortress is best approached by the short wooden **Ivan Bridge** (*Ioánnovskiy most*) which leads from Trinity Square (*Tróitskaya plóstchad*) on the Petrograd Side to Hare Island. It is St Petersburg's earliest bridge (originally 1703) but rebuilt and restored many times. Its name commemorates Peter the Great's sickly half-brother Ivan (*Ioann*), who reigned jointly with him for a few years as co-Tsar until his death in 1696. At the end of the bridge stands **Ivan Gate** (*Ioánnovskiye voróta*), with the date '1740' in iron over its arch to mark the year the re-construction of the Fortress in stone was completed. This leads to the gateway to the Fortress itself, a triumphal arch known as **Peter Gate** (*Petróvskiye voróta*), built by Trezzini in wood in 1708 and rebuilt some ten years later in stone. The magnificent double-headed eagle, made of lead by F. Vassu in 1720 and placed directly above the arch, was not taken down after the Revolution. Though a symbol of Muscovite – and, later, Imperial – Russia, it was preserved as forming part of an artistic whole with the main entrance. The wooden panel, which is now above the eagle, belonged to Trezzini's original gateway. It was carved by Karl Osper and represents, in *bas relief*, one of those allegories Peter liked so much: Peter defeating Charles XII of Sweden *alias* Simon the Magician cast down by St Peter, with (to make the point crystal clear) a likeness of Peter the Great himself, crowned with a laurel

---

[10] Aleksandr Zinoviev, *Reminiscences*, unpublished ms. in Russian.

wreath, standing among the characters surrounding the Apostle.

From Peter Gate, a narrow avenue leads to the **Cathedral of SS Peter and Paul** (*Petropávlovskiy sobór*). The modest timber church, erected in 1703–4, was deemed no longer adequate when, eight years later, the Tsar's family left Moscow and took up residence in the new city on the Neva. (The process had been gradual: most of the Government's administrative institutions had by then already been transferred; the arrival of the Household was the last move in the *de facto* transfer of the capital and change in status of the new city.) For a few years the old church was allowed to stand next to the new cathedral. Then it was dismantled (1719) and set up again – this time on stone foundations but without its belfry and re-christened St Matthew – giving its name to the lane (*Matveyévskiy pereúlok*) which now connects *úlitsa Lénina* to *Kronvérkskaya úlitsa*.

Peter wanted his new cathedral to resemble the churches of Moscow as little as possible; he also wanted the height of its spire to surpass that of Ivan the Great's belfry in the Kremlin. The first was achieved partly by design and partly by accident. Trezzini, who was not primarily an architect but an engineer, had spent the previous four years working in Denmark. Hence the Scandinavian and Lutheran feel of the exterior (and hence the three naves of the interior which are also foreign to the Orthodox tradition). The second requirement – superior height – was achieved by the addition of a spire (which the Russians call **iglá** – 'needle') to the belfry, an idea which Trezzini probably borrowed from the much older building of the Exchange in Copenhagen. To establish its supremacy, Peter in fact insisted that the belfry and spire were built before the rest of the church. They rose initially to 112 metres and, finally, to 122.5 metres, indeed ensuring that the cathedral was the tallest structure in St Petersburg, until 1962 when the

Television Tower was built on Apothecary Island (*Aptékarskiy óstrov*) in the north of the Petrograd Side.

But the height of the spire caused no end of trouble down the centuries. In 1756, it was hit by lightning. The belfry was set on fire, the *iglá* fell into the body of the church and a large part of Trezzini's building was destroyed. Nobody knows, for sure, how much of what you see now is true Trezzini. For he left no drawings. The two distinguished architects (B. Rastrelli and S. Chevakinskiy) who were engaged to restore the cathedral had nothing stylistically in common with Trezzini. It is believed, however, on good authority, that they decided in the end to restore the exterior almost as a replica of the original and contented themselves with going to town on the interior. Thus, though the belfry was dismantled in 1760 down to the first storey, when it was rebuilt in 1766 it still looked early eighteenth-century and rather Danish.

During that first fire, the original **iconostasis**[11] was saved by being carried out of the church. Carved in Moscow (1722–6), designed for Trezzini by Ivan Zarudny, painted and gilded, intricate and convoluted, it miraculously accommodates itself to the later Baroque interior that was superimposed on Trezzini's church by Rastrelli. The total effect, it must be admitted, seems more appropriate for a secular feast than for prayer and meditation.

In the early nineteenth century, the *iglá* was covered with gilt copper plates which made it glitter in the sun. But in 1830 it was struck again by lightning. The cross and the angel, above the globe, tipped and threatened to fall. A steeplejack called Tyolushkin cut a hole in the bottom of the *iglá* (which at that time was constructed in wood) and climbed to the top, using the slight protrusions provided by the vertical edges of the copper plates as his only handholds.

---

[11] A wall or screen, covered in icons, which in Orthodox churches separates the sanctuary in the apse from the main body of the church.

He presumably employed a version of what modern mountaineers call a 'prussick loop' to support his feet. When he reached the globe, he found he could not get the rope he was carrying past the curve of it so he tied his feet together underneath it and, leaning out almost horizontal to the ground, threw the rope clear of the curve on to the angel. It is said, and one must hope it is true, that he was rewarded with money and a medal. In the Second World War, the glittering copper provided a directional aid to enemy gunners and pilots. This time, professional mountaineers were sent up to camouflage and protect it with sacking. The *iglá* did suffer some damage (not from the Germans but from some unsuitable paint) and, during the repair work, it was decided to go one better than gilt and to apply real gold. Thirty-six thousand leaves of gold – according to an official statement – were therefore glued on by hand, with the present, magnificent, results. The restorers, however, were more exigent than Tyolushkin and left behind them a note complaining about the terms and conditions of their employment.

Trezzini's Cathedral, even before it caught fire, took a long time to build and was not open for worship until 1733, after Peter's death. Yet, having broken with Muscovite traditions and keen to distance himself from his predecessors in habits and style of life, Peter had no desire to join them in death. So he willed to be buried not in the Archangel Cathedral in the Kremlin but in the Cathedral of SS Peter and Paul at the heart of his new capital. To accommodate his wishes, the funeral service took place in a makeshift wooden structure, erected for the occasion within the walls of the half-finished Cathedral and then carried back across the frozen Neva. There it waited for the Cathedral to be ready to receive it. In 1727, Peter's coffin was joined by the coffin of his wife (Catherine I) and they waited together for another four years until, on 21 March 1731, they could at last be buried in the Cathedral. Peter's grave is to the right of the south door. Fresh flowers distinguish it from the other sarcophagi. The tombstone was replaced in the nineteenth century.

Henceforth, all future Russian sovereigns and their consorts were buried in the Cathedral of SS Peter and Paul – with two exceptions. These were: Peter II, son of the Tsarevich Aleksey and Peter the Great's grandson, who moved the capital back to Moscow and died there from smallpox at the age of fourteen; and Ivan VI, murdered as a prisoner in the fortress at Schlüsselburg. The last Emperor, Nicholas II, was not buried in the cathedral until 17 July 1998, eighty years after he and his family were murdered in the Siberian town of Yekaterinburg. In 1992 their bodies were excavated and flown to Britain where DNA examination established the identity of all the Emperor's family except for his son and one of his daughters.[12] The bones were then brought in coffins to Pulkovo Airport, where I saw them met by a guard of honour and conducted to the Fortress by motorcade, along streets decorated with white, blue and red Russian national flags. To each flag was attached a black ribbon of mourning. The coffins were buried in the presence of President Yeltsin, slightly apart from the other tombs in the **St Catherine Chapel** of the cathedral. On the insistence of the venerable Russian Academician, Professor Likhachov, and of Prince Nikolay of Russia who was also present, the bones of the doctor and the servants who were murdered with the Imperial family were treated with the same honours and buried in the same tomb. Commemorative tablets, with the names of everyone including the missing children, line the walls of the little chapel.

A mystery surrounds the **sarcophagus of Alexander I**, whose army defeated Napoleon when he invaded Russia in

[12] The daughter whose remains have not been found was Marya and not Nicholas's youngest daughter, Anastasia, who was so widely believed in the West to have survived in the person of Mrs Anderson.

1812. There is a belief (most historians would describe it as a 'legend') that his official death in the southern port of Taganrog in November 1825 was fraudulent. He had, it seems, sometimes expressed the wish to abdicate and to finish his life as a pilgrim in Russia and the Holy Land. Some say that he decided to simulate death and escaped in the yacht of the British Ambassador, Lord Cathcart, while, at some point in the coffin's long journey to St Petersburg, the body of a soldier who had recently died was placed in the empty coffin. Meanwhile, Alexander is supposed to have gone in Cathcart's yacht to Palestine and Mount Athos and, eventually, to have returned to Russia under the name of Fedor Kúzmich. There it was said that he led the life of a vagabond and tramp until his real death in 1864 at the age of eighty-seven.

The truth about Fedor Kúzmich, a genuine historical character, remains a mystery to this day. Nothing is known about him until his arrest for vagrancy. His refusal to talk about himself was absolute. But some accounts of his habits, his personality and even possessions (a handkerchief embroidered with a royal monogram, for instance) do suggest links with Alexander I. The Grand Duke Nikolay Mikhaylovich is said to have asked Nicholas II's permission to have Alexander's sarcophagus opened. Permission, granted at first, was later withdrawn. (According to some reports, all the Imperial sarcophagi were opened after the Revolution, when Alexander's was found to be empty. These reports have now been denied.) What is known is that Alexander's coffin was taken, extremely slowly, from Taganrog to Tsarskoye Selo where it was received in March 1826 by the Imperial family, the body by this time in an advanced state of decomposition. There it was transferred from its wooden coffin to a lead one, which was then sealed. Thus it was never seen in an open coffin by the congregation to say their farewells, as is normal at Orthodox funerals.

A side door from the left of the nave leads to the **Burial Vault** (*usypálnitsa*) **of the Grand Dukes**, completed in 1908 (by L. Benois following the designs of D. Grimm). Thirteen of the Grand Dukes and their consorts were buried here in the course of its short pre-Revolutionary history. After 1917, it was not expected that it would be used again. But the collapse of the Soviet regime made the unexpected possible. Three more members of the Imperial family were to be interred in the mausoleum. In May 1992, the body of Prince (self-styled Grand Duke and Pretender to the Throne) Vladímir was brought from Miami, where he died, to St Petersburg, for burial with great solemnity in the vault. In 1995, the remains of his parents, the Grand Duke Kyril and his wife, were brought from Coburg. (After the confirmation of the death of the Grand Duke Mikhail, murdered in Perm in 1918, the Grand Duke Kyril had assumed the role of Pretender to the Russian Throne.)

Opposite the Cathedral stands the most recent, as well as the most controversial, **monument to Peter the Great** in St Petersburg – by Mikhail Shemyakin, a Russian émigré artist in New York. It was unveiled on the rainy afternoon of 7 June 1991, in the presence of a huge crowd. Used to the idealised version of Peter as the heroic 'Bronze Horseman' in *plóstchad Dekabrístov*, people were shocked to see a stiff, ungainly, life-size (albeit 6 ft 7 in. tall) figure of a man in an armchair whose face was cross and rather puffy, whose head was tiny, hairless and bullet-shaped, whose legs were spindly and whose hands were like claws, with a muffler round his neck. Yet the statue repays study. Shemyakin used, as a model for the body, C.-B. Rastrelli's wax effigy made soon after the Emperor's death;[13] the face he modelled from a life-mask of him made half a dozen years before his death, also by C.-B. Rastrelli. (Both effigy and mask are now in the

---

[13] Carlo-Bartolomeo Rastrelli, the sculptor, was the father of the architect, Bartolomeo.

Hermitage Museum and, oddly enough, the mask was also the model for the face of the 'Bronze Horseman'.) It may be as near as we shall ever get to knowing what Peter the Great really looked like. In Deptford, by the Thames, another cast of Shemyakin's statue was recently unveiled on the initiative of Canon Corneck, vicar of St Nicholas, Deptford Green. The local kids who clamber over the chair are oblivious, almost certainly, of the reason why it is there: to commemorate three hundred years since the rebuilding of the church of St Nicholas in 1698 which coincided almost to the day with a visit by Peter to Deptford. He came, as he went almost everywhere, to find out how to build ships and shipyards. He visited the Astronomer Royal (Halley of the comet) and had wheel-barrow races in John Evelyn's garden, of which he made a great mess. No doubt there was a jaunt to the local *avstériya* (hostelry) too.

Just outside the cathedral's west door is an attractive small building, rectangular in shape, with a portico of paired Doric columns supporting a pediment. An archetypically late nineteenth-century female figure, holding an oar and representing Navigation, was placed on the roof in 1891. But the **Boat House** (*Bótny dómik*) itself was built in 1762–6 by R. P. Wiest to contain the dinghy in which Peter learned to sail. In January 1722, as part of the celebrations for the end of the Great Northern War with Sweden, Peter had it brought from Moscow and placed in the fortress at Schlüsselburg. Eighteen months later, he arranged for an offical reception by units of his new Russian Navy at the Island of Kotlin (Kronstadt) off St Petersburg. It was placed in the Fortress of SS Peter and Paul and Peter took it out once more – to meet the galley bringing the remains of St Alexander Nevsky to the newly-built Alexander Nevsky Monastery at the south end of *Névskiy prospékt*. After Peter's death, they built the Boat House for it, next to the Cathedral. When it went out for the last time, in 1836 on the deck of a paddle steamer commanded personally for the occasion by Nicholas I who was reviewing Russia's Baltic Fleet, it was saluted by a roll of drums and a salvo from the warships.

Then in 1940, the *bótik* was transferred to *Vasíliyevskiy óstrov* (Basil Island), where it became part of the permanent exhibition of the Central Naval Museum, demonstrating how it was indeed the 'Grandfather of the Russian Navy' and the part that it played in the early eighteenth century. They were to use it again as part of the tercentenary celebrations of the Russian Navy in 1996 but it was found to be too frail. So an exact replica, flying the Imperial standard, was rowed down the Neva as part of the review. The replica was then placed in the *Bótny dómik* in the Fortress and there it remains. (It is scheduled to make a second appearance at the tercentenary celebrations of the city.)

Almost next to the Boat House stands the simple but charming two-storey building of the **Mint** (*Monétny dvor*). With a long, low, rusticated façade, a shallow pediment over the projecting central section and round squat towers at each end, it was probably built between 1796 and 1805 by A. Porteau (or Porto), who seems to have been involved in only one other building (the Army Medical Academy) in St Petersburg. Some Russian architectural critics have suggested that the Mint was really by A. Voronikhin, but the consensus is against them. And some English writers refer to it as 'English Palladian', comparing it to the Horse Guards in Whitehall. Peter the Great decided to transfer the production of both money and medals from Moscow in 1724 and the coinage was first minted in the Trubetskoy Bastion. Today, the Mint produces some coinage but mostly medals, badges and commemorative emblems. It produced, for example, the emblems which Soviet space rockets have distributed in outer space, depositing them on the moon and the planets Mars and Venus.

Moving round to the river side of the Fortress, there is the two-storey pink and white **Commandant's House**

(*Oberkomendántskiy dom*), built in 1743–6 by the engineer Christophe de Marin. Its original purpose was, as its name suggests, to house the Fortress Commandant – one of whom, in the nineteenth century, was Prince Aleksandr Kropotkin, father of Peter Kropotkin. (An earlier Commandant was an eighteenth-century ancestor of mine, Nikolay Zinoviev. Commandants who died in post were buried in the small cemetery which is tucked between the east wall of the cathedral and the south wall of the Grand Dukes' vault.) It was here that political prisoners in the Fortress were usually brought for interrogation. The large room in which sentence was pronounced on the Decembrists on 12 July 1826 has been meticulously restored to its appearance on that day. A marble slab marks the spot where they stood.

In 1975, a permanent exhibition opened in the Commandant's House on the 'History of the City of St Petersburg up to the Revolution'. It includes material transferred from the Rumyantsev House on the English Embankment (which originally housed the whole museum on the 'History of the City' but is now dedicated to the 'History of the Blockade'). So there are some early exhibits, illustrating a much more remote past of the Neva region and estuary, which impress the viewer with the Russian – or at least Slav – character of the place from time immemorial. Most of the exhibits, however, deal with St Petersburg's economic and municipal development, its social and educational history and its revolutionary past.

The low building to the east of the Commandant's House, also pink and white but only one storey high, is the **Engineers' House** (*dom Inzhenérny*). The architect is unknown. The building was originally workshops put up in 1748–9. It now houses an exhibition of a more light-hearted kind about life in 'Old Petersburg', from early typewriters to shop signs, musical boxes and domestic interiors. A strange venue for it but a pleasant change.

Almost due south of the Commandant's House is the **Neva Gate** (*Névskiye voróta*), between the Naryshkin and the Sovereign's Bastions, the only one of the Fortress's six gates that leads out onto the river. The massive granite portico (N. Lvov, 1784–7) commands a magnificent view of the Palace Embankment on the other side of the Neva with the Winter Palace and the Hermitage to the right; to the left is a row of grand houses which before the Revolution belonged to the great and the good, now mostly scientific and learned societies. But, until the Fortress became a museum, no one passed through the Neva Gate to admire the view. It was the first stage of the journey to execution, or permanent imprisonment, or banishment for those who had survived their grim incarceration in the Fortress of SS Peter and Paul.

The gate leads out to the **Commandant's Pier** from which a cannon has fired every day at noon since 1736, except for the fifty years which followed the Revolution. (The gun is renewed, every now and then; the present one, a 120-millimetre D30, was made in 1978 and installed in April 2002.) The scene here is now peaceful enough, with bathers swimming in the Neva all the year round. One can see them – nicknamed 'walruses' – in the spring and autumn, pushing and kicking away the ice-floes or sitting on them and apparently enjoying themselves. 'The secret', one of these jolly bathers told me as he dried himself with a tiny towel in a piercing wind, 'is not to stay in the water for more than a minute and to start your bathing at the height of summer. Then continue without letting up as the weather gets colder.' He may well be right though, personally, I have not checked.

If you leave the Fortress, as you probably came in, by the Ivan Gate, you will pass through the *Ioánnovskiy* (Ivan) **ravelín**. On the left (follow the signs) you will find a memorial plaque on the wall telling you that in 1932–3 this building accommodated the USSR's first experimental gas-dynamics laboratory for the development of jet propulsion engines. Here, since 1973, is another permanent exhibition – devoted to Russian rocketry, aerospace engineering, engineers and cosmonauts. At the other (south) end of the Ravelin, you might be glad to find a restaurant called the *Avstériya*.

The whole area of the Fortress is now part of the Museum of the History of St Petersburg. It is permanently open. But the Cathedral (a museum since 1924 and used for worship only on rare occasions) and the permanent exhibitions keep regular opening hours. One ticket, sold at the Ivan Gate or the Boat House, covers them all; a separate ticket gives access to the Neva Panorama Walkway, along the ramparts on the river side.

III

Petrograd Island

Nearest Metro Station: *Górkovskaya*

T HE OBVIOUS WAY out of the Fortress leads north-east
across a narrow strip of water onto the mainland of what
the Finns called Birch Island and is now called Petrograd
Island (*Petrográdskiy óstrov*).[1] It is not properly mainland but
one of many islands in the Neva estuary, albeit a very big one,
and runs up to the Kárpovka river (*reká Kárpovka*) in the
north, beyond which lies Apothecary Island (*Aptékarskiy
óstrov*) and Stone Island (*Kámmeny óstrov*).

While the war with Sweden was still in progress (until
1721) and Peter's new Fortress was under construction, the
southern end of Petrograd Island under the protection of the
Fortress's guns was the safest place to build. And, though at
the beginning Peter had no plans to found a city, he needed
to be able to house his collaborators and to provide at least
primitive shelter for his workmen. (Primitive indeed it
was. Contemporary engravings show them living in rows of
timber igloos overhung with birch trees, when they were not
under canvas.) Later on, he needed stores, shops, other
commercial buildings and administrative headquarters. So
Birch Island was the place where civilian St Petersburg began.

---

[1] The early Finnish inhabitants called it Birch Island. As St Petersburg
began to take shape, it was renamed City (*Gorodskoy*) Island. From 1730
to 1914, it was known as Petersburg Island. When, in 1914, St Petersburg
became Petrograd, this part of it became *Petrográdskiy óstrov* and has
remained so ever since. The **Petrograd Side** (*Petrográdskaya storoná*,
which in most maps is stamped across this area) in fact includes not only
Petrograd Island but also Apothecary Island in the north, Hare Island (on
which the Fortress stands) to the south and Peter Island to the west.

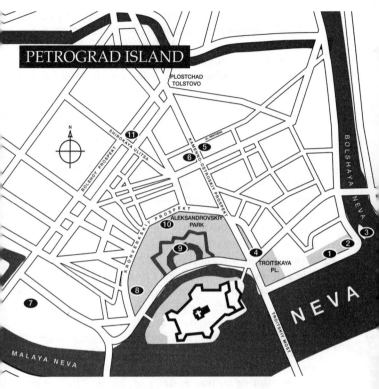

1	Peter I's Cottage	7	Jubilee Palace of Sport
2	Nakhimov Naval College	8	Zoo
3	Cruiser *Aurora*	9	Artillery Museum
4	Kshesinskaya's House	10	*Baltíyskiy dom*
5	Lyceum	11	Yelizarov Apartment
6	Kirov Museum		

Its second major period of expansion came nearly two hundred years later, at the turn of the nineteenth and twentieth centuries, when the *Tróitskiy most* (Trinity Bridge, completed 1903), crossing the Neva from the Palace Embankment, made it possible to respond to the huge demand for housing and factory space generated by Russia's industrial development. Between 1890 and 1910, the population of Petrograd Island alone rose from 75,000 to 210,000. So it developed very early and comparatively late.

The earliest building of all is the *Dómik Petrá Pérvovo* (Peter I's Cottage) at Peter's Embankment, *Petróvskaya náberezhnaya No. 6*. Put up in three days (24–26 May 1703) by soldiers of the Semyonovskiy Regiment on the site of a Finnish fisherman's hut, it is a pine log cabin without proper foundations, unconvincingly painted to resemble brick, forty feet long, eighteen feet wide and eight feet high – just high enough for Peter, who was 6 ft 7 in. tall, not to hit his head against the ceiling. It is roofed in shingle made to look like tiles. Facing the cottage across the embankment are steps leading to the Neva, now guarded by two mythical stone lions (Shin-Tsze), more frog-like than leonine, brought from Manchuria in 1907. From this point, Peter had a clear view of the building operations being carried out at his command on his new Fortress and also on his new port (St Petersburg's first) then being built between his cottage and the *Bolsháya Névka*.

Apart from a small and narrow entrance passage, the cottage contains three rooms: study, bedroom and dining room, fitted out to give the illusion that the host, whose coat is there waiting for him to slip it on, happens to have gone out for a moment. A meticulous restoration of the interior to produce this effect – including displays of Peter's personal possessions, artefacts from domestic life of the period, the original Dutch stove still standing in its corner, early eighteenth-century furniture some of which belonged to or was made by Peter himself – was made during the 1970s. But, for all the care taken to conform to historical accuracy, the restoration has been criticised for making the interior look less modest than it did in Peter's day.

Though it was modest, Peter was well aware of the interest his cottage would present to future generations and had a protective gallery built round it in 1723. The Empress Catherine had it encased in a timber pavilion that in 1846 was re-erected in brick. In 1874, iron railings were added preparatory to the unveiling in the garden of a bronze bust of Peter by P. Zabello (a copy of the contemporary portrait bust by Carlo-Bartolomeo Rastrelli, now displayed in the remnants of Peter's Winter Palace under the Hermitage Theatre. And so, until the Revolution, his memory continued to be held in holy awe. Little by little, the cottage became a place of pilgrimage until, in the 1840s, the Emperor Nicholas I had the bedroom converted into a chapel in honour of Peter's favourite personal icon of Christ the Redeemer. Candles burned in front of the iconostasis and school children – even undergraduates – used to go there to pray for success in their annual exams. The chapel did not, of course, long survive the Revolution but the atmosphere of hagiolatry still hangs about.

Till the spring of 1704, this cottage was the only private house in Petersburg. Compared to the tents and sheds which everybody else had to put up with, it was relatively commodious and so it became known as the 'Fair Mansion' (*Krásnyie khorómtsy* – 'fair', not 'red' as the museum translates it). It remained Peter's only residence until his Summer Palace was finished on the south (left) bank of the Neva in 1712. (The cottage, the Summer Garden and the Summer Palace form part of the same museum.) Peter solved the problem of entertainment in these early years by taking his visitors off to the local pub – the *Avstériya*, now vanished – between his house and the port. The first visiting ship was a Dutchman in 1703, closely followed by an English vessel, and the skippers of both may be presumed to have felt at ease in the *Avstériya*. Peter was clearly at home, a frequent visitor, drinking vodka or beer and smoking his pipe in the company of shipwrights and sailors. It was here that he came the day following his son's death and, as he says in his Journal, 'had a good time'.

Later, even when his Summer Palace was in commission, he still preferred entertaining on the right (north) bank of the river. When occasion demanded something grander than the pub, he sometimes took people to an open-air masquerade in Trinity Square – and that was a nightmare because it was liable to last several days; attendance was obligatory in the absence of a signed medical certificate and the penalty for non-attendance was a fine in the shape of a vast draught of vodka which every malingerer, man or woman, was forced to swallow. More often, he simply commandeered the biggest house in Petersburg at that time, Menshikov's mansion on *Vasíliyevskiy óstrov*.

Following the *Petróvskaya náberezhnaya* (Peter's Embankment) along to the east until it turns north and becomes the *Petrográdskaya náberezhnaya*, you come to the bright blue **Nakhimov Naval College** (*Voyénno-Morskóy institút*), named after Admiral Nakhimov, defender of Sebastopol in the Crimean War. The Imperial Naval Academy, founded in 1715, was on *Vasíliyevskiy óstrov* and it was here (in the Naval Cadet Corps) that Nakhimov himself had been a cadet. The Nakhimov College started life as a secondary school (1910–12 by A. Dmitriev, in spite of its pseudo-Petrine appearance) and was not converted into a naval academy until 1944 but is now the only one in Russia. Boys are accepted at fifteen or sixteen for a two-year course, subject to a fitness test, to having eight years primary and secondary education and to being able to speak some English. Before you turn the corner to the College itself, you pass a large yellow block with statues on top and *bas reliefs* on the side, once an Intourist Hotel by Levinson and Fomin, which now provides the living quarters. As a hotel, it must have commanded one of the most spectacular views in St Petersburg.

From 1948 to 1956, the training ship for the Nakhimov Naval College was the cruiser *Aurora* (*Kréyser Avróra*), anchored just offshore in the *Bolsháya Névka*. Now she is a museum, a monument and a marvel of restoration, having in the 1980s been returned to her original form. Commissioned in 1897, launched in 1903, the *Aurora* served with the Baltic Fleet in the Japanese war of 1905, in the First World War and, after a fashion, in the Second. But she owes her fame to the fact that she was the first ship of the Russian Navy to hoist the Red Flag (in February 1917) and to the part she played in the capture of the Winter Palace from the Provisional Government by the Bolsheviks in October of that year. She did not play it with great efficiency but well enough, as a popular joke has it, to have with one blank shot reduced an immense country to rubble and kept it that way for three-quarters of a century.

The museum that is the *Aurora* in the twenty-first century contains the six-inch gun which, according to the official version, fired that blank shot. But respectable historians are still discussing whether it was really a blank – fired out of respect for the architectural beauty of the Palace and merely as a signal for the assault to begin – or a live shell which was intended to inflict damage but failed to do so because the crew had positioned the ship incorrectly. Whatever the truth of it, there is an upright stone slab (or stele) on the English Embankment (*Anglíyskaya náberezhnaya*) opposite the place in the Neva at which the *Aurora* had been ordered by the Military Revolutionary Committee to drop her anchor before firing. It bears the following not entirely accurate inscription:

ON 25 OCTOBER (7 NOVEMBER) 1917
THE CRUISER *AURORA*,
MOORED OPPOSITE THIS SPOT,
ANNOUNCED BY THE THUNDER OF ITS GUNS
AIMED AT THE WINTER PALACE
THE BEGINNING ON 25 OCTOBER OF
A NEW ERA –
THE ERA OF THE GREAT SOCIALIST REVOLUTION.

Also preserved in the cruiser are the radio room and station from which Lenin made his broadcast to the citizens of Russia announcing the proletarian Bolshevik victory over the bourgeois Provisional Government.

Returning west along Peter's Embankment, we come back to **Trinity Square** (*Tróitskaya plóstchad*), the earliest public square in the city. The first proper building to be erected there was a wooden church, the **Church of the Holy Trinity** (now vanished), to commemorate the foundation of St Petersburg on 16 May 1703 which was Whitsun or the Feast of the Trinity. Although never officially a cathedral, for a long time this was the principal church of the city. As Trinity Square in Peter's time also contained the main market (*Gostíny dvor*), the church – and much else besides – was burned down several times, on the last occasion in 1913. Oddly enough it was restored in 1928 but, five years later in 1933, it was finally de-consecrated and demolished by the city authorities. More generally after 1704 the square became framed by timber houses into which Peter's more important collaborators moved, most of the houses far grander and more substantial than the Tsar's Cottage. To these were added a customs house, the Senate and other administrative buildings as well as a parade of shops, the only retail outlet allowed in the city, which was Peter's personal property.

Nor in Peter's day was entertainment – or what passed for entertainment – neglected in Trinity Square. Public executions, much in vogue then and for some time as entertainment all over Europe, were a fairly frequent spectacle and gallows were assembled and dismantled in the square as occasion demanded. When the market was moved in 1711, to reduce the risk of fire, from Trinity Square to what is now *Sýtninskiy rýnok* on the north side of the *Kronvérkskiy prospékt*, the executions went too.

In the centre of the square there was a pyramid, the start of processions and masquerades and the focal point of fireworks displays. In 1721, it provided a very particular spectacle when one of Peter's courtiers, Petr Buturlin, was married off by order of the Tsar to the widow of another, Peter himself being the guest of honour at the wedding. After the ceremonial supper the newly-weds were accompanied in procession to the pyramid where the bridal bed had been prepared. But holes had been drilled in the wooden walls and the pyramid illuminated from inside, so the couple's first night together became a peepshow for the benefit of the citizens.

On 22 October of the same year, to celebrate the defeat of Sweden and the Peace (after twenty years of war) of Nystadt, the Senate officially bestowed upon Peter the title of Emperor in a ceremony that was duly solemnised in Trinity Church. (The SS Peter and Paul Cathedral in the Fortress was still not finished.) Henceforth Peter and his successors ceased to be Tsars and Grand Dukes of Muscovy and became Emperors of Russia. But Sweden alone, as the defeated power, acknowledged the change in Peter's lifetime.

Thus, Trinity Square in the early eighteenth century. At the beginning of the twentieth, it was alive with very different activity. Factories and industrial housing had mushroomed on the Petrograd and Vyborg Sides (*stórony*) and the square began to attract demonstrators. On Sunday 9 January 1905, a large contingent, which was making its way to the Palace Square to present a petition, assembled in Trinity Square. The officer commanding the police who were attempting to prevent the demonstrators from crossing the *Tróitskiy most* gave the order to shoot into the crowd and some three dozen people were killed. The crowd was halted, but not entirely, and many went on to join the main demonstration. This was '**Bloody Sunday**' and its victims were buried in the 9 January Cemetery, as it was later named in their honour, in the south-east of the city.

On the north-east side of the square, on the corner of *Kronvérkskiy prospékt* and *úlitsa Kúybysheva* (Kuybyshev Street *No. 2*), stands a mansion which is often referred to as a palace. Asymmetrical, two-storeyed, *Style Moderne*, faced in red and grey granite with a balcony overlooking the *prospékt*, it was built (1904–6) for **Matilde Kshesinskaya** by an immensely fashionable architect called Aleksandr Hohen, assisted by the same A. Dmitriev who built the secondary school/naval college. (In Russian characters, 'Hóhen' becomes 'Gógen', which is also the Russian spelling of 'Gauguin', the French painter. Hence the suggestion, which is wrong, that the two were cousins.)

Kshesinskaya was a remarkable woman and her house acquired a remarkable history. First, the woman. She was the only Russian dancer (in fact, she was Polish) to have received the coveted title of *prima ballerina assoluta*. When very young, she became the mistress of the heir to the throne (later, the Emperor Nicholas II). After his marriage to Princess Alix of Hesse (later, the Empress Alexandra), she became the mistress of one of his cousins – the Grand Duke Sergcy Mikhaylovich; then the mistress, and finally the wife, of Grand Duke Andrew. Many years later, when she was writing her memoirs in Paris, the suggestion was made that they should be called 'Sixty Years Under the Romanovs' but, so it is said, was turned down by the publishers as being liable to be taken too literally. Dancers may look frail but they have to be tough. And Kshesinskaya spent her years of exile mainly in Paris providing for her husband and son by teaching ballet in the Russian tradition to the young dancers of Western Europe. She lived to be nearly a hundred and died in 1971, teaching to the end.

Secondly, the house. It had numerous and lavishly decorated reception rooms in which many grand parties were held. In the weeks leading up to and beyond the February Revolution, Trinity Square had become a place much favoured by street orators, where groups of people gathered to be harangued in what came to be known as *mítingi* ('meetings'; a verb was coined – to *mitingovát* – which meant to hold a public gathering of this kind. Such *mítingi*, like a sort of proliferation of Hyde Park Speakers' Corners, were happening all over the city and especially in Trinity Square.) But in spite of the *mitingovaniye* going on below her balcony, Kshesinskaya continued to entertain. On Wednesday 22 February 1917, she gave a dinner for twenty guests which, she thought, was a great success. It was, though she could not have known it, precisely a week before the abdication of the Emperor and with it the end of the *ancien régime*. **Kshesinskaya's House**, seized by mutinous soldiers, became the Headquarters of the Central and Petrograd Committee of the Bolshevik Party (its military organisation).

A month later, late in the evening of 3 April, Lenin arrived back in Russia at the Finland Station (on the Vyborg Side), having crossed enemy territory with German permission in the famous 'sealed train'. An armoured car, provided by his enthusiastic supporters, brought him across the *Sampsónievskiy most* and down (what is now) *úlitsa Kúybysheva* to Kshesinskaya's house, where he went into the reception room which opened on to the balcony (by that time, the room of the Central Committee secretariat). From there he addressed the largest *míting* of them all, on and off throughout the night.

In the intervals, downstairs in the hall on the ground floor, he attended a working meeting of Party officials. And to them, he addressed his even more famous 'April Theses'. One thesis was the argument (much pleasing to the Germans) that the Bolsheviks should withdraw support from the Provisional Government in its attempt to continue the War. Another, in the words of Pravda on 7 April, proceeded 'from the premise that the bourgeois-democratic revolution has been completed and counts on the immediate transformation of that revolution into a socialist one'. The theses came to pass – but not in April.

'In a fairly large hall', recalls an eyewitness,[2] 'were assembled many people: workers, "professional revolutionaries" and ladies . . . It seemed as if all the elemental forces had risen from their lairs and the spirit of destruction . . . circled in Kshesinskaya's hall above the heads of the enchanted disciples.' But the Central Committee voted against the theses and *Pravda* refused to print the speech. Lenin still had work to do and he went off to stay with his sister Anna and her husband, Mark Yelizarov, in *Shirókaya úlitsa* (now *úlitsa Lénina*) further to the north where, according to the Smolny Museum which is responsible for the apartment, he wrote 150 works in three months.

Forty years later, in 1957, Kshesinskaya's house reopened as the Museum of the Great October Socialist Revolution, its nine thousand exhibits – gathered in from the Winter Palace where they had been waiting for a permanent home – spreading over into the adjacent house, *úlitsa Kúybysheva No. 4*, to which it was joined by a connecting gallery. But that lasted only until 1991 when the houses became a more neutral **Museum of Russian Political History**. Permanent exhibitions of considerable interest are now mounted there on themes such as 'Political Parties and Power in Russia from Autocracy to Perestroika' and 'Entrepreneurship in the Second Half of the Nineteenth and Early Twentieth Centuries'. There are also temporary exhibitions, concerts and a little museum of history for children. And there are some exhibits relating to the life of Kshesinskaya herself. But it is still possible, though with an effort, to find your way to the room with a balcony and listen for the ghostly sounds of the *mítingi* down below.

Practically next door to Kshesinskaya's house, to the north of it and also facing on to the *prospékt*, is St Petersburg's

---

[2] Nikolay Sukhanov, a member of the Socialist Revolutionary Party, in *Zapíski o revolyútsii 1922*, quoted by Richard Pipes in *The Russian Revolution 1899–1919* (Harvill/Fontana: London, 1990).

only **mosque** (*méchet*), *Kronvérskiy prospékt No. 7*. Built in commemoration of a recent state visit by the Emir of Bukhara in 1910–14, but not finished until 1920, it was modelled by N. Vasiliyev, assisted by S. Krichinskiy and the ubiquitous A. Hohen, on the Gur-Emir, Tamerlane's beautiful fifteenth-century Mausoleum in Samarkand. It somehow misses the beauty of the original, in spite of a fine blue-tiled dome, perhaps because the ponderous blocks of granite which form its façades are essentially Northern in spirit and alien to the attempt at Eastern fantasy. It stands on the right spot, however, being the actual site of the first *Gostíny dvor* – a Russian version of the Central Asian traders' market.

Kronvérkskiy prospékt now goes off to the left. Ahead, **Kámenno-ostróvskiy prospékt** (Stone Island Avenue) runs for over three kilometres northwards across Petrograd Island, across the Kárpovka river, until it arrives at the eponymous Stone Island. There had been tracks leading to Stone Island for as long as anyone could remember but they had not been dignified by a name until 1831 when a formal plan for the development of Petersburg Island specified a *prospékt* which would link *Kronvérkskiy* at the Neva end with *Bolshóy* further north and intersect with *úlitsa Míra* on the way. This resulted in *Kámenno-ostróvskiy prospékt* running in a dead straight line across the island, intersecting with *úlitsa Míra* at *Avstríyskaya plóstchad* (Austrian Square) and with *Bolshóy prospékt* at *plóstchad Lva Tolstóvo* (Leo Tolstoy Square) before it crossed the Kárpovka. Practically all the buildings on it are nineteenth and twentieth century, those at the southern (Neva) end reflecting the boom times of the *fin de siècle* which flowered just before the Revolution. It is a long road and not entirely rewarding for the pedestrian (as an area it is not unlike St John's Wood in London and was much coveted in the 1930s by Party *apparátchiki*) but here are some highlights which can be seen, with luck, by hopping on and off a bus.

Staying on the same (east) side as the mosque, *No. 1* is a large block of comfortable flats, built 1899–1904 in high *Style Moderne*, Russia's *Art Nouveau*, and decorated with fantastical birds and beasts and large-headed fishes by the great practitioner of the mode, Fedor Lidval (see also the Grand Hotel Europe). *No. 5*, now the *Détskaya muzykál-naya shkóla* (Musical School for Children), used to be the home of **Count Sergey Witte** (1849–1915), famous Russian statesman and President of the Council of Ministers (Prime Minister) until 1906. His house was designed by E. Wirrich in 1898 but reconstructed and largely spoilt in 1980. It is appropriate that this was where Witte decided to live since it was he, as Minister of Transport and later as Finance Minister, who was largely responsible for Russia's economic expansion. As Prime Minister he put Russia on the Gold Standard, concluded an unexpectedly favourable peace treaty with the Japanese (signed in Portsmouth because it was the British who had financed the Japanese), and was one of the authors of the new Constitution which created the *Dúma*. In many ways a symbol of hope and progress, disliked by Nicholas II, he resigned in 1906 and never served as a politician again.

No. 9, built in the Constructivist style in 1932 by G. Simonov, is a Students' Hostel (*Studéncheskoye obstchezhítiye*) but a rather special one. It is – and was, in Soviet days too – the place where Russian and foreign (including British) students stay when they are sent to St Petersburg to learn the Russian language and something about the way Russians live. So successfully that some of the foreigners acquire a Russian in the process.

No. 11, style 'ultra modern' by S. Trofimenko, 1980s, is now the Sports Club of Railway Transport Engineers. Not worth getting off the bus for, you might think. But the site is part of Soviet history. Before the Revolution it was occupied by the huge wooden building of the *Tsirk Modern* (Circus 'Moderne'), later rebuilt in stone (1932) in the shape of the Hammer and Sickle, which in 1917 became a great forum of the Revolutionaries. In June 1917, Lenin spoke there to a vast audience denouncing the follies of the Provisional Government and its 'Imperialist' policy. In October, just before the Bolsheviks seized power, it was the scene of a massive demonstration 'in the bare gloomy amphitheatre, lit by five tiny lights hanging from a thin wire' – perhaps the last and greatest *míting*, as described by John Reed in his *Ten Days that Shook the World*.[3]

Before crossing *Avstríyskaya plóstchad*, there are two sites on the left (west) side of the *prospékt* which should be noted. *No. 2* is a statue of the writer Maxim Gorky standing at the intersection of *Kámenno-ostróvskiy prospékt* and *Kronvérkskiy prospékt*, by the Metro station which carries his name. Throughout the First World War and until 1921, Gorky (1868–1936) lived at *Kronvérkskiy prospékt No. 23* and in 1932 they named the whole street after him. It went back to being *Kronvérkskiy* in the early 1990s.

No. 10 is Film Land. In 1918, the new Soviet Ministry of Education founded some studios run by the Petrograd Kino Committee which in 1934 became the base of the distinguished **Lenfilm** enterprise. Their productions included Kozintsev's *Hamlet* and a *King Lear* with music by Shostakovich. Indeed, for a couple of years in the 1930s, Shostakovich lived in the block next door. Films are still made here but the studios are broken up and leased by various companies, sometimes Russian (for example, Aleksey Balabanov and Aleksey German have worked here), sometimes foreign (the 'South Bank Show' film about Pasternak was made in these studios). The Lenfilm block itself was built in 1934 (by D. Fomichov) especially for 'Workers of the Arts' and has been the home of many leading Soviet personalities in the art world – musicians, writers, painters.

[3] Published by Penguin Books: London, 1966.

There has been a continuity of tradition here. In the nineteenth century, this was the site of the central market. In the 1890s, a merchant called Aleksandrov decided to develop his 'pitch' and opened the immensely popular **Aquarium Pleasure Gardens**. He provided a 'Pavilion of Ice' (skating rink) and a theatre where Chaliapin, who lived further north on *Aptékarskiy óstrov*, made his debut. And on 4 May 1896, he showed the first film ever produced in Russia. Its success was immediate and enormous; cinemas sprouted all over the country – to the indignation of some contemporary Russians who chose to equate cinemas with brothels and gambling dens. Even now, there are Western historians who purport to see in the goings on at the Aquarium a clear sign of Imperial Russia's moral decline.

Beyond *Avstríyskaya plóstchad*, on the east side we come to an intersection with *úlitsa Réntgena*. At *Kámenno-ostróvskiy prospékt No. 21* is the *Aleksándrovskiy Litséy*. The school, now a technical college, began life in 1810 as an annexe to the palace at Tsarskoye Selo and Pushkin was one of its earliest pupils (*see* p. 409). The building to which it was moved had once been a wool factory (1760) and then was bought by Catherine the Great to be converted into a hospital (1768) when she brought to Russia an English physician called Thomas Dimsdale. She required him to vaccinate the heir to the throne, Prince Paul, and then herself, and then a number of other people (including my great-great-grandfather) against smallpox. And she didn't stop there. Her *Ospoprivivátelny dom* (**Vaccination House**) was opened for the citizens of St Petersburg who could walk in, refer themselves and get treatment free of charge. The facilities were advertised. In 1781, it became a House of Social Welfare and in 1803 it was requisitioned as a School for Orphans. Finally, in 1844, the architect Ludwig Charlemagne was commissioned to refurbish the building and make it fit for the Tsarskoye Selo *Litséy* which had changed its name to *Aleksándrovskiy* the previous year.

Almost opposite, on the other (west) side at *No. 26* is the **Kirov Museum** in the block inhabited by the head of the Leningrad Communist Party, Sergey Kirov, from 1926 until his assassination on 1 December 1934. The whole building – comfortable, exclusive and upholstered in red granite – was designed by the Benois brothers (1911–12). The museum (*Apartment No. 20*) has been meticulously restored to its original state by the Museum of the History of St Petersburg with some of the original furnishings from the Smolny Institute and many other items taken back from Kshesinskaya's house. But it is tantalising, this 'museum'. The man who lived here held Leningrad in his hand for eight years (1926–34); he became a member of the Politburo and a secretary of the Party's Central Committee; he was murdered – we now believe by Stalin – and his murder signalled the beginning of the 'Purges' against Party members and the senior ranks of the armed forces (*see* p. 229). What was he really like? What would have happened if he had not been murdered? The memorabilia, gathered here so painstakingly, leave us no wiser.

Plóstchad Lva Tolstóvo acquired its name in 1918. From 1831 until the Revolution, it was called the Square of the Archpriest (its re-christening was thought to be rather a good joke in the light of Tolstoy's much publicised anti-clericalism) after a divine who lived in the time of Peter the Great and enthusiastically supported Peter's move to place the Orthodox Church under the control of the Head of State. The square is dominated by an apartment block built during the First World War in ghastly taste, known as Tower House and loaded with crenellated *motifs* derived from British castles. Immediately beyond it, to the north, is the entrance to the *Petrográdskaya* Metro Station. To the east, along *úlitsa Lva Tolstóvo*, is a gigantic block that opened in 1897 as the Women's Medical Institute. (Medical women in Imperial Russia were well in advance of their Western contemporaries and a significant proportion of surgeons were female, even during the First World War.) It is now the First Medical Institute. Also in the square is a small experimental theatre which opened in 1985 specialising in dissident (now merely satirical) plays.

Towards the south-west, the square sprouts the major highway of the *Bolshóy prospékt* running back to the *Málaya Nevá* where this tributary skirts the north shore of the *Vasíliyevskiy óstrov*. The present *prospékt* dates from 1806 when the area to the west of it began to be developed for civilian housing. Until then, it had been called the Great Garrison Street and had been occupied only by barracks and military billets (hence the closely packed footprint of the streets – soldiers in the side streets, officers along the main road) from the time in the latter part of the eighteenth century when Catherine II gave the entire island to her military-and-security-minded son Paul (*see* p. 296).

The sixth turning to the right (west) is *Shirókaya úlitsa* (Broad Street – changed since the Revolution to *úlitsa Lénina*) where, at *No. 52* (*Apartment 24*), Lenin and his wife, Krupskaya, went to stay with his sister during the three months that followed his return to Petrograd in April 1917. The **Yelizarov Apartment Museum** is (just) within walking distance of the *Petrográdskaya* Metro Station and for those in search of the domestic Lenin (and the historical one too since he did a great deal of crucial work here) it is a necessary visit. Much, much more modest than Kirov's apartment, it gives a hint of what it was like to be fairly poor in pre-Revolutionary St Petersburg. Lenin's sister, Anna Yelizarova, who did not die until 1935, helped to rediscover the contents of the flat – bedsteads, wardrobe, bentwood chairs and coarse woollen blankets. By July, when the Provisional Government had begun to treat the Bolsheviks increasingly as hostile, Lenin and Krupskaya had to go into hiding – moving from flat to flat in northern Petrograd until they arrived, in October, back on the Vyborg side in *Polyústrovskiy prospékt*. Here there used to be another Lenin museum but fashion has eliminated it. So too has it eliminated a museum which used to exist in the flat on the southern embankment of the Kárpovka where, on 11 October, the Bolshevik Central Committee decided that the time had come for Socialism to rise up and overthrow the Provisional Government.

To the left (east) just before *Bolshóy prospékt* hits the river, between *úlitsa Blokhiná* and *prospékt Dobrolyúbova*, rises the rather strange **Knyaz-Vladímirskiy sobór** (Cathedral of Prince Vladímir). Sometimes called St Nicholas of the Wetlands (*Nikóla na Mokrúshakh*), it is a hybrid of Baroque and Classical since it was built over nearly seventy years and involved D. Trezzini (1719), M. Zemtsov (1742), A. Rinaldi (1772) and I. Starov (1789). On the opposite (south-west) side of *prospékt Dobrolyúbova* is the **dvoréts Spórta 'Yubiléyny'** (Jubilee Palace of Sport), built to commemorate fifty years since October 1917. It is one of the largest places of recreation in the city with good ice skating (particularly hockey) and a concert hall which features well-regarded pop-singers.

Prospékt Dobrolyúbova leads eastwards to the point where *Kronvérkskiy prospékt* and *Kronvérkskaya náberezhnaya* diverge, the Prospect arcing to the north and the Embankment running along the south to contain a large area, much of which is green. Within it are the Zoo, the *Kronvérk* itself and the Alexander (*Aleksándrovskiy*, ex-Lenin) Park.

The western end of this area is the territory of the **Zoological Park** (known locally as the *Zo-opark*). The idea of a zoo originated, like so many other things, with Peter the Great who, in 1711, established what was then known as an Animal Yard (*Zverovóy dvor*) near the present Marble Palace across the Neva. He acquired St Petersburg's first elephant, presented by the Shah of Persia, which was taught to bow to the sovereign. The present Zoo was founded in the nineteenth century by an enterprising Dutch woman,

Sophie Ter-Regan who had lived in Russia for the previous twenty years, quietly and judiciously getting married from time to time. Her first successful investment was made in the new and fashionable Alexander Park where she sold waffles *à la hollandaise*; then she embarked on a 'Cabinet of Wax Figures'. By the 1860s she was a Petersburg personality and married to a German zoologist who encouraged her to return to her earlier haunts in the park. There, on 25 February 1865, she opened her Zoological Gardens. Though they occupied a much smaller area than now, they were an instant success. The Emperor Alexander II presented two elephants and Sophie organised a restaurant in a little garden of its own on the banks of the Neva.

Her husband enriched the Zoo with many acquisitions but in the early 1870s he died. The indomitable Sophie, by now about sixty, married yet again. This time, the lucky man was a German carriage-maker and under his influence she introduced some rather more dubious attractions to her Zoo: in the 1880s a few live Zulus and African Pygmies arrived as well as two giants – one Russian and one Chinese; they were joined by acrobats, tightrope walkers, weight-lifters, with the result that serious zoology became somewhat diluted. Sophie had gone over the top and offended against the prevailing notion of human dignity: men and beasts should not be exhibited together. So she returned the Zoo to zoology and turned her own attention to developing a highly successful summer theatre.

Wars and revolutions are bad for zoos. During the Blockade, the Zoo's animal population was all but wiped out by starvation. A hippopotamus is said somehow to have survived on a daily diet reduced from thirty-six kilograms of nourishing food to five kilograms of grass and hay with the balance in steamed sawdust. But perhaps, even so, it was more fortunate than its keepers. It did survive and the Zoo, somehow, kept open – if only during the summer months. Now it is restored and re-stocked, with many more animals than before the war, but it is unlikely that Sophie would approve of the way it, and they, are kept.

Between the Zoological Park in the west and Alexander Park on the east is the *Kronvérk* which gives its name to both the Prospect and the Embankment. With its crown-shaped battlements, it was built in 1705–8 as a protective wall or rampart to provide defence from the north for the Fortress of SS Peter and Paul. Itself it is protected from the south by the narrow *Kronvérkskiy proliv* (Rampart Sound) and from the north by a moat. In fact, it was never used for defensive purposes. It was, however, the place where five of the Decembrist leaders were executed on 13 July 1826. In 1975 to mark the hundred and fiftieth anniversary of their death, an obelisk was erected on the eastern rampart of the *Kronvérk* which carries the inscription: 'On this site, on July 13(25) 1826, the Decembrists P. Pestel, K. Ryleyev, P. Kakhovskiy, S. Muravyov-Apostol and M. Bestuzhev-Ryumin were put to death.' On the far side of the monument is inscribed Pushkin's poem addressed to his Decembrist friends who were condemned to hard labour in Siberia. (The Decembrist Uprising is described in Chapter IV.)

In the 1850s a red brick neo-Gothic building, shaped like a giant horseshoe and pierced with lancet windows, was built on the *Kronvérk* by the architect P. Tamanskiy. It was intended to be the Artillery Arsenal but, within a few years (1868), it became the home of the Artillery & Army Signals Museum (*muzéy Artillérii, Inzhenérnykh voysk i voysk Svyázi*) at *Aleksándrovskiy Park No. 7*. The museum itself was founded in 1703 (by Peter, of course) and was built around the artillery, military vehicles, banners, orders, and medals of the Russian Army which were kept in the 'Memorial Hall' at the Petersburg Armoury. Since 1965, it has included exhibits from the Central Historical Museum of Military Engineering in Moscow. With over half a million artefacts in its possession, it is one of the largest military museums in the world and there are people, quite unmilitary, who find it magical. The swords of early Slav tribes, a fifteenth-century arquebus, a bronze gun cast in 1491, paintings of cavalry battles and wonderful uniforms work on the historical imagination like yeast; the sections devoted to the war of 1812 and to the Second World War (for Russians, the Great Patriotic War) would be substantial, even for scholars. Twice in its life, the museum has moved from passive to active mode. During the Revolution, it became an important centre for the distribution of arms to Red Army units; during the Blockade, part of it was adapted for use as tank repair workshops.

Beyond its moat, to the west, north and east, the *Kronvérk* was originally surrounded by fifty-five acres of empty space, technically known as a glacis which, in accordance with the military science of the time, was to enable the defenders to observe the approach of the enemy and to pre-empt an attack. (This is the area now occupied by the Zoo, the Park and the complex of buildings which stand in the centre of the south side of *Kronvérkskiy prospékt.*) At the edge of the glacis there used to stand a willow tree which survived until the early years of the last century. For two hundred years, it served to remind the citizens of St Petersburg how unpopular the city had been at the time of its foundation. Many were the prophets of doom in the early days who foretold a quick and early disappearance of Peter's 'Paradise' – so many, indeed, that Peter made it a punishable offence to spread pessimistic rumours about the city's future. One such prophet, a familiar figure with a long white beard, used to stand by the willow and declaim:

> The Lord will drown the Anti-Christ's city
> The Heavens will open and rains pour down
> The Neva that day will turn and flow backwards
> Its waters will rise higher than this willow.

There was much in his prophecy[4] but he made the mistake
of being quite specific about the actual day on which
St Petersburg was to disappear beneath the waves. On the
day following the one he had predicted, he was arrested,
chained to the willow and flogged.

By the 1840s, it was finally recognised that no enemy
was going to advance on the *Kronvérk* across the glacis
and that it could be made to serve the public in a more
attractive form. Trees were planted and a park laid out. In
the summer of 1845, on the feast day of St Alexander
Nevsky, it was formally opened and named after the saint:
Aleksándrovskiy park. Just before Lenin's death, it was
re-named after him but has now returned to the original.
The park at once became fashionable. Smart St Petersburg
walked, rode and drove along its avenues as through a
miniature Bois de Boulogne, listened to military bands,
stopped for lunch or coffee at Kremer's, which opened in
1848. But the novelty wore off; Kremer's closed down; the
avenues became neglected; and, by 1914, Baedeker's *English
Language Guide to Russia* dismissed Alexander Park with
a single phrase: 'a favourite resort of the lower classes'.
(There were worse things to be, of course.) The *Górkovskaya*
(Gorky) Metro Station, built in 1963, was placed just inside
the park to make it easier to get to.

Almost opposite, at ***Kronvérkskiy prospékt No. 23*** (built in
1911–12 by Morozov), is the house in which **Maxim Gorky**
had an apartment from 1914 to 1921. It became a centre of
Petrograd's literary and political life with a stream of visitors
including Lenin and Lunacharskiy, Chaliapin, Rachmaninoff,
Mayakovskiy and H. G. Wells. Wells stayed there in September 1920 but they had little in common except a mistress
(not, perhaps, at the same time) – Moura Budberg, who died

[4] The great flood of 1824 was the inspiration for Pushkin's famous poem,
The Bronze Horseman.

in Italy only in 1974, much mourned by her crowds of friends and admirers particularly in England. Gorky was a generous man, helping fellow writers, interceding with Lenin to spare the lives of Grand Dukes, protecting women. On one occasion he sent a note, which may or may not have been true, to an official in charge of food distribution: 'Extra rations are required by . . . since she is now pregnant by me.'

On the same (south) side of the *prospékt*, west of the Metro Station, is a leisure complex which comprises a Planetarium (1959), now containing a very expensive, uninhibited nightclub, the **Baltíyskiy dom** (once the Lenin Komsomol Theatre and today the venue for alternative arts festivals, all-night shows of 'performance art' and gay and lesbian parties) and the *Múzik-khól* (Music Hall).

The *Baltíyskiy dom* and the *Múzik-khól* share the carcass of what was once referred to – and increasingly is again – as **Nicholas II's House of the People** (*Naródny dom*). This had its origins in the fervent belief, popular in Russia at the turn of the nineteenth century, that public entertainment was the way to civilise the masses and wean them from drink and revolutionary activity. 'Houses of the People' sprang up all over Russia, from the Baltic to the Pacific, with these laudable aims. St Petersburg had a second one, founded by Countess Panin in *Tambóvskaya úlitsa* in the south-west of the city which later became the St Petersburg Railway Workers' Palace of Culture. All the Houses of the People were, suitably enough, run by the Russian Temperance Society.

Nicholas II's House was the first in the field. Part of the enormous building was put up in 1899 by G. Lutsedarskiy and in 1911 the great dome was added under the same architect's supervision. This had been dismantled in distant Nizhny Novgorod, where it had been housing an industrial exhibition, transported by rail and re-assembled in Alexander Park – a remarkable feat of engineering, or so it was considered at the time. The premises included lecture rooms, a free public library, a theatre and an opera house. Tickets for the theatre and the opera cost a few pence each – even for the best seats in the stalls. (They were virtually destroyed by fire in 1932 and, on the site, in 1939, was built the Lenin Komsomol Theatre and the Music Hall.)

The whole thing, in spite of the ban on alcohol, was a wild success. Come the Revolution, between 'February' and 'October', Nicholas II's House became the centre of innumerable *mítingi*, including the First Peasant Congress in May 1917. And so it earned its nickname as 'The Hearth of the Revolution', having in a short time changed its purpose from anti-revolutionary to revolutionary.

But the opera never closed. On 25 October 1917, the last evening of pre-Communist Russia, Chaliapin was singing King Philip in Verdi's *Don Carlos*. Rifle and machine-gun fire could be clearly heard by the performers, some of whom tried to disappear as discreetly as their roles permitted but, with difficulty, were brought back to complete the performance. A young girl called Natalya Mestcherskiy attended that performance and travelled home after it – an experience she never forgot though at the time she had no idea of its significance. While she was still in the theatre, she thought she heard the heavy boom of a gun (perhaps the cruiser *Aurora*). Jittery and apprehensive as she left the theatre, she heard the rattle of machine-guns and ran to catch a tram which would take her home over the Neva.

> Then through a window of the tram I saw the Winter Palace: a lot of people, cadets standing in ranks and in groups, camp-fires burning, several camp-fires, and it all looked so clear cut on the background of the Palace wall. I thought I could even distinguish some of the faces of these cadets. I distinctly saw that they were cadets and not just any soldiers. The tram, running rapidly along the bridge, suddenly braked, giving us all a jolt. It looked as if the tram driver in his fright had decided to go back. But a

moment later the tram suddenly jerked forward and reached the Embankment at a dashing speed. As it did so, young faces again appeared, particularly clear and close in the light of the nearest camp-fire. One cadet, in a typically Russian gesture, was slapping himself round the body with his arms to keep warm; the whole group, however, was immobile as if shown by a magic lantern . . .

The next morning there were rumours, of course: what had happened, and how, nobody knew exactly. By the evening, however, we learned that Kerensky and the Provisional Government had surrendered and there was a new government in power. 'It doesn't matter', friends said. 'This won't last long. And who are they, anyway?' Who in our house or among our friends knew then who Lenin was, who the Bolsheviks were, or what their programme was? Practically no one, I should think.[5]

---

[5] N. A. Krivoshayin (*née* Mestcherskiy) in *Chétyrye tréti náshey zhízni* ('Four Thirds of our Life') (YMCA Press, Paris, 1984). She was right about the Provisional Government having fallen but wrong about Kerensky who had made his escape (from Petrograd to Gatchina) before the capture of the Winter Palace.

IV

The Admiralty Glacis

Nearest Metro Station: *Névskiy Prospékt*

THERE IS A BRIEF note in the Journal of Peter the
Great for 5 November 1704: 'Laid the foundation of
Admiraltéyskiy dom and were in the *Avstériya* and had a
good time, length 200 sazhens, width 100 sazhens' (426 ×
213 metres). This was his answer to the storm that had
scattered the new fleet he was building up-river at Lake
Ladoga; the shipyards were to be moved down-river, within
easy reach of the open sea but under the protection of the
guns on the new Fortress on Hare Island. The ships to be
built there for Russia's new navy were, on Peter's instructions, quite small, some sixty to seventy feet long, some
only twenty.

The **Admiralty** (*Admiraltéyskiy dom*) was never a house
nor, at that stage, even a building. It was a heavily fortified
shipyard, designed personally by Peter from a small timber
drawing office which he put up to the west of it, roughly on
the present site of his statue. The 426 metres ran parallel to
the river with two arms projecting northwards to embrace
the docks. (These are still part of the footprint of the present building, though the space between them is now filled.)
To the south were timber bastions and earthworks and an
encircling canal; beyond that again was a vast **glacis**, on a
scale comparable to that which surrounded the new
Fortress itself. This empty space, kept clear to expose any
enemy approaching from the land, extended in Peter's
time all the way from the Neva in the north-west to the
Moika river in the south-east and from what is now the

Decembrists' Square (*plóstchad Dekabrístov*) and St Isaac's Square (*Isaákiyevskaya plóstchad*) in the south-west to the far side of the Winter Palace in the north-east.

It was an enormous vacant area, conserved in the heart of St Petersburg, the apex of the Trident from which the three great roads were driven across the marshes to form *Névskiy prospékt*, *Gorókhovaya úlitsa* (street) and *Voznesénskiy prospékt*. And it provided the ground on which in due course it was possible to build St Isaac's Cathedral – or rather, many versions of St Isaac's Cathedral one of which, eventually, was persuaded to stand upright on the marshes beneath – and to create the expanse of Palace Square (*Dvortsóvaya plóstchad*). If Peter had not decided to protect his Admiralty with a glacis, St Petersburg as you see it now could not exist. No Winter Palace, no Hermitage, no Alexander Column, no 'Bronze Horseman', no Cathedral, no Senate, no Synod. Yet, three hundred years ago, all you could see was a small clearing on the banks of a sluggish river with five huts and three paths crossing the swamp that surrounded them.

Ordinary mortals, however rich or powerful, were by special decree (1717) forbidden to encroach on the area of the glacis (though several had already built themselves mansions on the banks of the Neva each side of the dockyard). But gradually those, great and small, who worked in the shipyards were encouraged to make themselves at home there and were assigned building sites. Peter encouraged *slóbody* (something like self-regulating settlements) of specialist workmen. One, the *Galérnaya slobodá* ('galleys' settlement') grew up when a new shipyard was opened in 1713 for smaller boats, propelled by oars and manned by soldiers or marines, known as *galéry*. For this purpose a new canal was dug (also in 1717) to the west of the Admiralty to join up with the bend of the Moika river in the west. That section, at the western end, is still the *Admiraltéyskiy kanál*. The lane that ran through the settlement is, unsurprisingly, known as *Galérnaya úlitsa*.

Another *slobodá* developed along the northern bank of the Moika, between *Névskiy* and *Voznesénskiy prospékty*, and was known simply as the **Morskáya slobodá** – the 'maritime settlement' – which formed two lanes roughly where the *Bolsháya* (Great) and *Málaya* (Little) *Morskáya úlitsy* (Maritime Streets) now are. There were huts in which both sailors and shipwrights lived; and there were sheds and yards in which materials were kept. But, as the huts were all of timber and the materials (including pitch and tar) were highly inflammable, fires were frequent and sometimes (as in 1736) all-consuming. An impression of the fortified dockyard with its surrounding glacis, and of these early settlements on its edge, can be gained from a plan of 1753 (see below). The fortifications by that time were in stone rather than timber and the entire *Morskáya slobodá* was being rebuilt (its previous occupants decanted south-westwards after the fire). But still it provides a picture that is closer to the Admiralty district in Peter the Great's time than it is to the present.

Also in 1717, the **Kryukov Canal** was constructed to provide a link between the Neva, the Moika and (later) the Fontanka rivers. This intersected with the *Admiraltéyskiy kanál* at what is now *plóstchad Trudá* (Labour Square) and created, more by accident than design, a triangular islet surrounded on all three sides by water (the third side being the Moika). Called *Nóvaya Gollándiya* (New Holland) for luck, it became an invaluable and relatively safe place for storing timber. The only way to see *Nóvaya Gollándiya* is by boat (easily arranged). Built of brick, tall as a tall ship's mast, it is entered through a cavernous arch, straight out of Piranesi. In the nineteenth century, it contained a prison.

So, with the spars safely stored on an island, the preparation of tar and pitch (*smolá*) – the most inflammatory process – was moved to a new site to the north-east as far as possible from habitation, near the old village of *Spásskoye* on the bend of the Neva. So that became known

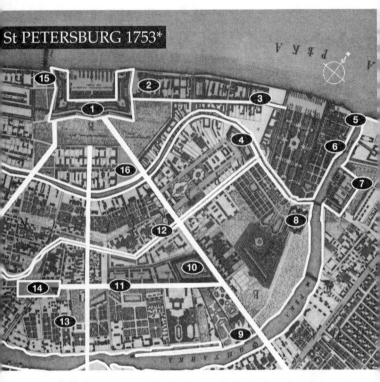

St PETERSBURG 1753*

*Based on M. Makhayev's plan published to commemorate the fiftieth anniversary of the city's foundation. Begun 1746, finished 1749, it in fact relates to St Petersburg as it was just before 1750.

as the Smolny District and in due course gave its tarry name to the convent and girls' school built there by Peter's successors. What the fire-watchers forgot, of course, was the flourishing market (*Morskóy rýnok*) that had moved into the empty space to the east of the Admiralty on the edge of the present Palace Square by the General Staff Building. No markets without fires.

St PETERSBURG 2003

1   Korobov's Admiralty / Zakharov's Admiralty

2   Apraksin's House converted to Winter Palace / Rastrelli's Winter Palace

3   *Milliónnaya úlitsa*

4   Court Stables

5   Peter I's Summer Palace

6   Summer Garden

7   *Partikulyárnaya verf* (Private Wharf) / Salt Warehouse

8   Wooden Summer Palace / Engineers' (St Michael's) Castle

9   Anichkov Palace

10 *Gostíny dvor*

11 *Sadóvaya úlitsa* (Garden Street)

12 Zemtsov's Cathedral of our Lady / Voronikhin's Kazan Cathedral

13 Yusupov Mansion and Garden / Railway Museum & Yusupov Garden

14 Hay Market

15 Second (Mattarnovi) St Isaac's / Bronze Horseman

16 Site of temporary Winter Palace (1755-61) / Chaplin House & Barrikada Cinema

Peter and Menshikov, meanwhile, did not take long to assign themselves building sites on the edge of the glacis. On the west side, Menshikov (in 1710) ordered for himself some clay and wattle sheds from which he conducted a profitable monopoly in maritime and other consumables, more or less where the Senate building stands today. After Peter's death, this part of the glacis was connected during the summer months to *Vasíliyevskiy óstrov*, where Menshikov's main palace was, by a pontoon bridge which was opened to admit big ships. The stone abutments, which were added in the 1820s (by A. Béthencourt), can still be seen on the embankments. In the same year (1710) and in the same area in which Menshikov put up his sheds, Peter attached to his drawing office a single storey wooden church dedicated to his patron saint, St Isaac.

As chief master shipwright, he was also entitled to receive from himself a site for a house; he chose one on the east side of the glacis, just beyond the Winter Ditch (*Zímnyaya kanávka*) and a little inland from the Neva. Here were built the first and second Winter Palaces (1708, in timber, and 1711 in stone – both probably D. Trezzini). Slightly to the north and west of this were built the third and fourth (D. Trezzini and G. Mattarnovi 1716–18) which extended westward into the area now covered by the Hermitage Theatre and had their façade on the Neva. Peter died here. The tantalising and charming remains can be visited on conducted tours (in Russian only) through an entrance on the Palace Embankment.

Fifteen years after its foundations were laid, it was time to embellish the **Admiralty** and make it recognisable across the growing city. A Dutch architect, Herman van Boles, was commissioned to place a spire (*iglá*) on its stumpy wooden bell tower to match the one across the Neva on the belfry of the Cathedral of SS Peter and Paul inside the Fortress. It was fifty metres high, of gilded iron. On top van Boles put a sphere (diameter one metre) and, on the sphere, a sailing ship (height two metres) which acted as a weather vane. Through all the metamorphoses to which the Admiralty has been subjected, the needle and the sphere have remained constant – removed, returned and re-gilded (using forty-three and a half tons of pure gold on the orders of that extravagant Empress, Elisabeth) in 1732 when the architect I. Korobov replaced the timber buildings below it with stone ones (they sent again for Mijnheer van Boles to see it was properly done) and, again, around 1820 when A. Zakharov constructed the present building. But the original ship is no longer there; it was taken off its sphere in 1886 and placed in a museum. What you see now is an exact replica. Of what? It is believed that the model for it was the first naval vessel ever built in Russia. Called *Oryól* (Eagle), twenty metres long, it was built by Peter the Great's father, Tsar Alexis, in 1668, captured on the Volga by a rebel chief called Razin and burned by him, for one reason or another, near Astrakhan.

After a hundred years, the original structure – however improved by Korobov – was deemed no longer suitable. The final version of the Winter Palace – though not of the Palace Square – was now in place to the east. And on the west, the mansions that had arrived on the English Embankment[1] were palatial in all but name. Alongside them, the old Admiralty lacked dignity. At the same time, a growing bureaucracy under Alexander I required there to be a Ministry of the Navy sited near the naval headquarters. It was hoped at first that the venerable Scotsman, Charles Cameron,[2] would design a new Admiralty fit for the nineteenth century but in 1805 the Minister of the Navy decided on the younger Andreyan Zakharov, who had studied in Paris. Building started in 1806 but did not finish until 1823, by which time Zakharov himself was dead (1811).

---

[1] Described in Chapter XI.
[2] Charles Cameron (c.1740–1812), Catherine II's architect at Tsarskoye Selo and Pavlovsk. *See* Chapter XV.

The present Admiralty is High Classical and a quite different affair from the old one though, oddly enough, the front elevation is slightly shorter (406 rather than 426 metres). There is nothing about it that suggests a dockyard, except the symbolism of the decoration – such, for instance, as the high relief on the 'attic' over the main archway which depicts Neptune handing his trident over to Peter while Minerva, goddess of wisdom, stands at Peter's side and Russia, a young girl under a bay tree, rests on the club of Hercules and holds the horn of plenty. Some of the symbolism, indeed, is enough with hindsight to make you weep. But it is a feast of sculpture, prepared at a golden moment for Russian (and they were Russian) sculptors. F. Stchedrin, and his friends and colleagues S. Pimenov, I. Terebenyov and V. Demut-Malinovskiy, contributed most of the fifty-six large sculptures and eleven *bas reliefs*. Monumental groups on each side of the main archway represent the nymphs of earth, air and water supporting the terrestrial and celestial globes while the figures on the corners above the 'attic' represent Classical heroes: Achilles, Ajax, Pyrrhus, King of Persia, and Alexander the Great. Twenty-eight more allegorical statues, one for each of the columns, decorate the top of the smaller cube which supports the needle. (Inside the smaller cube, incidentally, Zakharov enfolded Korobov's tower; and, inside the sphere on the top of the needle, he concealed a box which some say contains all the coins minted in previous reigns, some that it contains documents relating to the reconstruction.) Both needle and sculptures were heavily damaged during the German bombardment (hit by fire bombs and twenty large shells) but restoration was complete by the end of 1990. This time, also, they removed the boat; but they returned it, once more re-gilded, by helicopter.

The interior, unfortunately, cannot be seen by visitors as the building is – and has been since 1925 – in use as the Higher Naval Engineering Academy. The desirable thing to see is said to be the staircase. Externally, the main changes since Zakharov's day stem from the decision in 1844 to stop building ships in the shipyard. The inner canal was filled in and became the *Admiraltéyskiy proyézd*. The outer canal (*Admiraltéyskiy kanál*) was filled in, except for its extreme western end, and became the *Konnogvardéyskiy bulvár* (Horseguards Boulevard). And, in 1871, the area immediately to the south and west of the Admiralty was laid out as a garden cutting across the top of the *Névskiy* and *Voznesénskiy prospékty* so that they no longer met at the main gate. By the 1870s, too, it proved irresistible not to develop the docks themselves as building land – hence the *Admiraltéyskaya náberezhnaya* and the houses on it.

At Lakhta on the Gulf of Finland, a few kilometres north-west of St Petersburg, there was a granite boulder which had been split by lightning (a **grom-kámen** – thunder stone). On to it, according to local tradition, Peter used to climb to survey his new city as it grew. Perhaps. At any rate the boulder was tall enough, being more than forty feet high, to provide a fine view over the estuary. Now it stands on the site of Peter's drawing office in the Decembrists' Square as the plinth from which Peter's monument (the **'Bronze Horseman'** – *Médny Vsádnik*) looks out over the Neva. It has become the emblem of St Petersburg and the source of many legends. In 1812, with Napoleon in Moscow, Alexander I ordered a Major Batunin to see that the statue was taken to safety in the Vologda Province. The Major had a dream (induced, perhaps, by the difficulty of the task he had been given) which he reported to Prince Galitsin who reported it to the Emperor. In his dream, Peter had appeared and accosted Alexander as he was coming out of the Palace: 'Young man,' he said, 'what have you done to my Russia? But so long as my monument is not moved from this place, there is nothing to fear.' The Emperor cancelled the order; the horseman was never disturbed and Napoleon never came to St Petersburg.

The statue, '**To Peter I from Catherine II**', was first mooted in 1766 when the Empress Catherine, through her ambassador in Paris (another Galitsin), consulted Voltaire and Diderot about a suitable sculptor for what must have been one of the first monuments to be erected in the city. They came up with name of Étienne Falconet. Falconet accepted, his terms being an eight year contract paid at half the rate demanded by the competition. (In fact, the project took twice as long.) He was provided with a workshop and living quarters on the site of the Empress Elisabeth's throne room and kitchen in the timber Winter Palace on *Névskiy prospékt* which Catherine had demolished. The entrance was at what is now *Málaya Morskáya No. 11*.

Finding a suitable stone for the plinth was only a beginning. Catherine herself went to examine the *grom-kámen* and decided to advertise a prize for the best suggestion about how to get it on to the site. It appears to have been rolled, like the stones for the Pyramids, along a specially constructed road until it reached the northern coast of the Gulf of Finland. Progress was a few metres a day and the journey took five months. It was then embarked, more than one and a half million kilos of it, and conveyed across the Gulf by water to the point on the Admiralty Embankment chosen for the monument.

Back at the workshop, Falconet was faced with the problem of how, in the days before photography, to capture movement. Two Imperial horses, one called *Brilliant* and the other called *Caprice*, were ridden in sequence up a specially constructed ramp and reined in until they reared at the end of it, while the sculptor stood at the side, sketching and sketching. The finished statue provides three points of support for Peter's horse: his two hind feet and his tail, which rests on a serpent; but *Brilliant* and *Caprice* had no such support and the 'sittings' must have been full of incident.

Peter himself rides on only a bearskin – the bear being the symbol of the Russian people. The model for his body was provided by Melissino, Head of the Holy Synod and a Greek by origin. Peter's head was modelled not by Falconet but by his pupil, Mademoiselle Collot, who succeeded in capturing in one night the likeness that had eluded Falconet for several years, basing it on the life mask made by C.-B. Rastrelli for Peter's statue now in the Hermitage. The serpent was added to the composition by F. Gordeyev, some say primarily to provide the third point of support. All agree that it represents Peter's vanquished enemies but whether foreign (Swedes) or domestic (Boyars, the Church, traditionalists generally depending on your ideological standpoint) no one can be sure. Finally, on 7 August 1782, the whole was unveiled and the glacis acquired its most distinctive feature.[3] Keen-eyed visitors may note how brilliantly the horse's testicles shine after all these years. This is no Petrine marvel but the achievement of cadets from the naval college who regularly celebrate the end of their exams by painting them over and, in the morning, having to polish them clean.

Around this statue, over the next fifty years, the **Decembrists' Square** (*plóstchad Dekabrístov*) was gradually formed at the western end of the Admiralty glacis. When the statue was first commissioned, the glacis was undeveloped. And the area where it was placed was sometimes referred to as Peter's Square (*Petróvskaya plóstchad*). But things were changing, under the new Empress, both institutionally and aesthetically. In 1762, the year of Catherine's accession, the Russian architect S. Chevakinskiy suggested

---

[3] Pushkin's poem, *Médny Vsádnik*, was written in 1833. It was not published until after his death, in 1837. People have been arguing ever since about who was the hero of it – the Tsar or Yevgeny, the little man. The young Pushkin had been an admirer of Peter the Great as a reforming 'Tsar-educator', so it is unlikely that Belinskiy's view of the poem – the little man hero, pursued and crushed by autocracy – is wholly right. On the other hand, there had been Nicholas I and the Decembrists since Pushkin's early admiration for heroic tsars. Among his papers was found a sketch of the bronze horse – looking more like a frightened Arab mare than Falconet's bold stallion, bearskin replaced by an ordinary saddle and, on the saddle, no one.

the idea of a formal square in the Classical style to be laid out west of the Admiralty, closed on the south by a new and grander church of St Isaac (to replace Peter's second attempt to build one on the marshes next to the Neva). No building in fact took place for six years, except for Chevakinskiy's highly Classical cladding for the wooden storage sheds on the *Nóvaya Gollándiya* (the great arch on the Moika side being finished in 1780 but the other two sides, and the circular building of the naval prison, not completed until well into the nineteenth century).

In 1763, however, the Senate moved into a mansion on the river bank which had belonged to Field Marshal A. P. Bestuzhev-Ryumin in the north-west corner of the future square where Menshikov once had his sheds. More than sixty years later, one of his relatives was to be hanged for taking part in the Decembrists' Uprising, in memory of which the square carries its present name. Then, in 1768, A. Rinaldi started work on the third St Isaac's church (now to be a *sobór*, no longer a mere *tsérkov*), this time placing it as Chevakinskiy suggested to the south of the area and facing it in marble. By 1796, at Catherine's death, the building was only half-finished. It was completed in 1801 by V. Brenna, a protégé of Catherine's son, Paul. Paul, who detested his mother, insisted that Brenna remove Rinaldi's marble from her cathedral and deploy it on his own Mikhaylovskiy Castle (now the *Inzhenérny zámok*). The third St Isaac's lasted for less than twenty years.

From 1784 to 1787, that most delightful Classical architect, G. Quarenghi, was set to work on the **Konnogvardéyskiy manézh (Horse Guards' Riding School)** on the south-west corner of the developing square, to serve the Horse Guards' Barracks that had been built a little earlier on the banks of the *Admiraltéyskiy kanál*. Elegant, precise and perfect, like Rusca's tiny masterpiece (the Portico) on *Névskiy prospékt*, it mimics a fifth-century Athenian temple with a portico of eight Doric columns bearing a pediment and *bas reliefs*.

Over the top, perhaps, for a military riding school. But the Horse Guards were special, even among Guards regiments, since the males of the Imperial family usually became officers and were frequently to be found in the vicinity.

On the steps of the riding school/temple stand the statues of two young horsemen, copies from Roman antiques – made for Quarenghi by the sculptor P. Triscornia – of the Dioscuri: Castor and Pollux who were sired by Zeus out of Leda. According to Greek legend, they would appear on the field of battle, riding white horses, and award victory to the side they favoured. Some forty years later, with the nineteenth century in full swing and the Cathedral Chapter of the fourth St Isaac's in full outrage, these two naked heathen gods were removed from their pedestals and placed out of ecclesiastical sight on the gate pillars of the Horse Guards barracks. We owe it to the restorers of Leningrad after the Blockade that they were returned to the steps of the *Manézh* in 1954. The *Manézh* is now the Central Exhibition Hall (*Tsentrálny Výstavochny zal*) and was used as such occasionally even before the Revolution. Never mind the exhibitions; it would be a shame to miss the building.

In 1806, Zakharov started work on the third version of the Admiralty which, in due course, was to acquire a Classical western façade and would form the east side of the square, by now becoming known as *Senátskaya plóstchad* (Senate Square). In 1818, with Paul murdered in his Castle and Alexander I on the throne, the foundation stone was laid of the fourth St Isaac's – which would complete the square to the south. It was to be built on the same site as the third one and to incorporate its foundations (though if this was conceived as an economy measure, it turned out to be the reverse). So it was that there were workmen on the scaffolding of what was to be St Isaac's Cathedral at about eleven o'clock on the morning of **14 December 1825**. They were about to witness an early attempt to overthrow the Russian autocracy.

What they saw was the arrival in the square of some seven hundred troops of the Moscow Regiment, led from their barracks on the Fontanka Embankment by Aleksandr and Mikhail Bestuzhev and Prince Stchepin-Rostovskiy. They were joined by eleven hundred men from the Imperial Naval Guards, led by Nikolay Bestuzhev, two hundred and fifty Grenadiers led by Nikolay Panov and some nine hundred more from the Moscow Regiment under A. Suthof – about three thousand in all. The soldiers formed a square, as for battle, immediately to the west of Peter's monument; the sailors formed a column, south of the monument, between it and the fence surrounding the scaffolding at St Isaac's. Other troops then arrived and were deployed around the square – some nine thousand infantry, three thousand cavalry and thirty-six guns, led by the Emperor himself. A vociferously sympathetic crowd began to gather, in the course of the day growing to 'tens of thousands' – at all events, to many more citizens than there were soldiers in the square. For the next five hours, in the bitter cold, the three thousand faced the twelve thousand while the crowd grew and the Emperor decided what to do.

Before describing what he did do, it is necessary briefly to describe what it was all about. In the élite Guards Regiments of the army, among the more intelligent, talented and influential of the officers, revolutionary ideas had been fomenting since their return from taking part in the occupation of Paris (1814–15). These took many forms ranging from an authoritarian Republic (which would have involved the murder of the Imperial family) to some kind of constitutional monarchy in the English mode. Organisationally, they gave rise to a number of secret societies – some devoted to armed insurrection, some to the abolition of serfdom, some to social welfare and some to constitutional reform. In amongst it all, Freemasonry and clandestine journalism played their part. Two main centres developed: the 'Northern Society' (based in the Petersburg regiments) and the 'Southern Society' (based on the regiments in the Ukraine). For several years, the leaders plotted, quarrelled, reorganised, hesitated.

Then, on 19 November 1825, the Emperor Alexander I died unexpectedly (some say that he spirited himself away), leaving a momentary power vacuum. He would normally have been succeeded by his brother Konstantin but Konstantin (married to a Polish Roman Catholic) had two years before agreed with Alexander to renounce the succession in favour of his younger brother Nicholas. The agreement was secret though copies, witnessed by the Metropolitan, were duly lodged with the Senate and the Holy Synod as well as the Uspenskiy Cathedral in the Kremlin. Nicholas was not consulted (though he was aware of the agreement). He was in two minds. He knew that he was unpopular with the élite regiments in the army so, when the time came, he decided to take the oath of allegiance to Konstantin; furthermore, because he was in Russia and Konstantin was in Poland, he gave the order that such an oath should be administered throughout the empire. The brothers batted the throne between them for a couple of weeks until police reports of revolutionary activity among leading officers in the Guards obliged Nicholas to announce that he would be proclaimed Emperor on 14 December. This meant a second oath of allegiance. It also meant that the military conspirators, who had found it difficult to agree a programme and were far from ready for action, saw an opportunity that they feared might not return.

On the night of 13 December, the members of the 'Northern Society' met just south of St Isaac's at the Moika Embankment (*No. 72*) in the apartment of Kondratiy Ryleyev (a retired officer, prominent Free Mason, radical poet and passionate Republican). At five minutes to midnight, they decided that something, they had no clear idea what, must be done the following morning. Their favoured remedies varied from extreme republicanism to constitutional monarchy. 'Nevertheless we must make a beginning', Ryleyev is believed to have said. 'Something will come out of it.' What came out of it, in the longer run, was a violent check on the movement for reform. What came out of it on 14 December 1825 would have been laughable if it had not also been tragic.

The conspirators had cobbled together a 'Manifesto to the Russian People'. It called for the end of autocracy, the abolition of serfdom, compulsory and universal military service, the introduction of a free press, open courts and a jury system, and the creation of a 'Supreme Assembly' which would decide the future form of government. They decided on a provisional 'dictator' (Prince Sergey Trubetskoy) to lead the post-Imperial state while all this was being arranged. Meanwhile, troops loyal to the cause would occupy the Fortress of SS Peter and Paul and the Winter Palace, arrest the Imperial family, surround the Senate and compel the Senators not only to refuse the oath of allegiance to Nicholas but also to issue their Manifesto.

But so much time was spent prevailing upon their troops (and, it has to be said, confusing them so that many thought they were marching for Konstantin rather than for a Constitution) that, by the time the Bestuzhevs and the first contingent of insurgents arrived on the Senate Square, the Senate had already sworn its oath to Nicholas and gone home while Prince Trubetskoy had got cold feet and taken refuge in the Austrian Embassy. When the Emperor and his twelve thousand arrived, another miscalculation became apparent: the greater part of the Imperial Guard were not going to join the uprising (or, at any rate, not without a greater show of force than the insurgents were prepared to display). If there were two hundred and fifty Grenadiers in the centre of the square, there were ten squadrons on the outside obeying the new Emperor's orders. There was indeed a cavalry charge which the insurgents repulsed. Then the Emperor, reluctant to begin his reign by killing his subjects, sent in mediators to negotiate a surrender. The Grand Duke Mikhail, the Metropolitan, the Governor General of St Petersburg (Count M. Miloradovich) and a Colonel N. Styurler were all involved. But still the two sides faced each other until somebody's nerve snapped. P. Kakhovskiy, an ex-officer from the Yegerskiy Regiment, mortally wounded Miloradovich and Colonel Styurler with a pistol.

All the while, the building workers hurled stones and scaffolding poles from above while the crowd on the square grew larger, louder and more dangerous, shouting for the insurgents to give them weapons so that they could 'turn the town upside down'. (In vain. The revolutionaries of 1825 did not understand how useful the proletariat could be.) Just after four in the afternoon, the Emperor gave the order for the guns to open fire. Three were posted along the western face of the Admiralty, one at the *Manézh*. Seven canisters of grapeshot killed at least eighty and wounded fifty more while the insurgents were pursued across the ice on the Neva. By five it was all over – in St Petersburg. On 29 December, the 'Southern Society', led by Muravyov-Apostol and Mikhail Bestuzhev-Ryumin, staged an uprising in Kiev with the Chernigov Regiment but it was hopelessly compromised by the debacle in the north. It was suppressed on 3 January, its leaders brought to St Petersburg and nearly four hundred men exiled in carts to the Caucasus. The two leaders were hanged.

From north and south, a hundred and twenty-five officers were arrested, imprisoned in the Fortress of SS Peter and Paul and, together with many hundreds more, interrogated over the next six months. The Emperor participated personally and listened attentively to many of the interviews. At the end of June, a specially-convened Supreme Criminal Court sentenced five to be hanged and the remainder to banishment to Siberia, preceded by various penal terms which, for some, included five years in the salt mines, for others enforced service in the Caucasus. Of the Petersburg conspirators, only two – Kakhovskiy, who had murdered the Governor General, and Ryleyev, who had declared himself to be in favour of murdering the Imperial family, neither of whom were serving officers – were condemned to death. Which may go some way to explaining the Emperor's comment to the Duke of Wellington, who was in St Petersburg during that summer, that his clemency would astonish Europe.

It did. And the British press made comparisons with the fate of the five Cato Street conspirators, executed in 1820 for plotting to murder the Cabinet and declare a republic. To Lord Liverpool's nervous and reactionary Government, a government which had appeared to condone the 'massacre of Peterloo' and repressed public meetings and the distribution of literature, the Decembrists' Uprising appeared to call for the utmost severity. It was ten years after the defeat of Napoleon, and only thirty-three since the King of France had lost his head. The revolutionary ideas which were tumbling around in the 'Northern' and 'Southern' societies had been shared with, and indeed were still shared by, the leading writers of the day: Griboyedov, whose bitter comedy, *Woe from Wit*, had just been censored by Miloradovich, was frequently to be found breakfasting with Ryleyev on rye bread, raw cabbage and vodka; Pushkin, whose poems were found in the papers of every prisoner, would, as he told the Emperor, have been without doubt in Senate Square himself had he not already been in some sort of exile in the country. At the time, he was writing the fifth chapter of *Eugene Onegin*. On a page of it he sketched two corpses hanging from a rope (two were hanged on the first attempt; for the other three the rope had broken). Below, there was another sketch – of five little stick bodies hanging from a gibbet. 'Poor Russia', Muravyov-Apostol is said to have remarked before they hanged him for the second time. 'We cannot even hang properly.'

At the time, Nicholas's triumph seemed complete. But, though all future generations of Russian revolutionaries considered themselves to be the heirs of the Decembrists, it was Nicholas's son and heir who reversed the roles. Alexander II dedicated his reign (1855–81) to the introduction of reforms which met many of the demands in the 'Manifesto to the Russian People', including the emancipation of the serfs,[4] the introduction of trial by jury, the democratisation of compulsory military service and its reduction from twenty-five years to six. The revolutionaries, on the other hand, dedicated most of their energies to trying to murder him and, after seven attempts, finally succeeded on 1 March 1881. It is difficult to say what further Decembrist aims would have been realised if Alexander's life had not been cut short. Limitation of the Emperor's autocratic powers was next on his list; the final draft of a tentative and limited system of elective representation (the 'first steps to a constitution', as he himself is said to have described it) was found in the pocket of the uniform he was wearing when he was killed. It was to be published the following day. His heir, Alexander III, forbade publication and suppressed the draft.

A hundred years after the failure of that first attempt and eight years after the October Revolution, the Soviet Government renamed *Senátskaya plóstchad*. They called it **plóstchad Dekabrístov**. It is one of the few name changes not to have been changed back again after 1990.

Before leaving the square, two more buildings must to be mentioned that completed its Classical make-over. The first is the formidable triangular structure on the west side of St Isaac's and the corner of *Admiraltéyskiy prospékt*.

---

[4] Alexander's emancipation of the serfs was criticised even at the time (by Alexander as well as others) for conveying too little land to them and for imposing redemption payments on them at too high a level – though these, in fact, were never paid in full and were abolished altogether in 1905. Alexander was never able to overcome the landlords' opposition to his reforms; hence their limitations.

Almost unbelievably, it was built as a private **mansion for Prince Lobanov-Rostovskiy** in 1817–20 by Auguste de Montferrand, the French architect who was engaged to complete the fourth version of the St Isaac's Cathedral. The main façade, with portico and eight Corinthian pillars, faces north on to the Admiralty and the stairs are guarded by a pair of marble lions. It is on one of these that Pushkin's Yevgeny perches while he shakes his fist at the 'Bronze Horseman': 'All right then, builder of marvels! Just you wait.' The bronze figure turns its head, the bronze horse leaps the railings, Yevgeny scrambles off the lion's back and is pursued through the streets by the sound of the horse's '*tyazhólo-zvónkoye skakánye*'.[5]

The final project in *plóstchad Dekabrístov* (it can hardly be missed) is Carlo Rossi's monumental re-housing of the **Senate** (*Senát*) which he conjoined with the **Synod** (*Sinód*) in twin buildings linked by an arch (1829–34) along the west side of the square, facing Zakharov's new Admiralty. The Bestuzhev-Ryumin house on the corner by the Neva, which had housed the Senate hitherto, and a substantial merchant's house to the south of it were demolished while Rossi crowned the success of his double arch into Palace Square (completed in 1829) by defeating some half-dozen distinguished competitors to win the prize which entitled him to design the complex. Whether the Senate was, by that time, of sufficient importance to justify such an important-looking building is doubtful. It had been conceived by Peter the Great as the body to whom he would entrust the government of Russia whenever he was abroad. Now, and particularly after the changes introduced by Alexander I, its powers were confined to a revisionary function applicable only to past legislation. The Synod was the Department of State under the Emperor

---

[5] All my life I have tried, and failed, to translate this passage to my satisfaction. An inadequate, if literal, translation would be: 'the horse's ponderous gallop ringing on the cobble-stones of the shaking roadway'.

responsible, since Peter, for administering the Church and, in particular, for Church appointments. The entire building is now home to the Central State Historical Archives.

Before having a serious look at St Isaac's, it is worth a walk along *Admiraltéyskiy prospékt* to *No. 6* on the corner of *Gorókhovaya úlitsa* (of which it is *No. 2*) to visit a house by Quarenghi with a very ugly history. In the mid-nineteenth century it became the office of the Chief Commissioner of the City Police (*Gradon achálstvo*, not the Secret Police – *Okhrána* – who were quartered on the Fontanka River). In 1918, it was made the head quarters of the St Petersburg Branch of the Communist Secret Police – Felix Dzerzhinskiy's 'Cheka' (the commission for suppressing counter-revolution and sabotage) and subsequently of the OGPU.[6] Now it has turned the other cheek to become the **Museum of the History of the Political Police** (nineteenth and twentieth centuries). It means what it says: 'the displays reconstruct the history and methods of the secret police, its agents-provocateurs . . . and eminent figures involved in police surveillance'.

Forty years passed between the foundation stone of the fourth and last church of St Isaac's[7] being laid (1818) and the present **St Isaac's Cathedral** (*Isaákiyevskiy sobór*) being open for worship (1858). There have been few years since when repairs have not been in progress. Petersburgers will some-times tell you that the work was needlessly prolonged because of a belief that the Romanov dynasty would fall when work on the church of St Isaac's ceased. But there are plenty of better explanations: Auguste de Montferrand, the architect chosen for the project, was young and inexperienced; the exquisite drawings that won him the competition turned out

[6] The *Ob-yedinyónnoye* (United) *Gosudárstvennoye* (State) *Politícheskoye* (Political) *Upravléniye* (Administration). And for 'Administration', read 'Police'. Subsequently the NKVD, MVD and later still the KGB.
[7] The first St Isaac's, 1710, in timber; the second, by Mattarnovi, 1715, in stone; the third, 1768–1801, Rinaldi/Brenna.

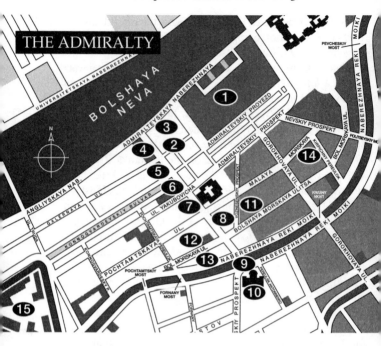

1	Admiralty	9	Blue Bridge
2	Decembrists' Square	10	Mariinskiy Palace
3	Bronze Horseman	11	Hotel Astoria/Angleterre
4	Senate	12	Nabokov Museum
5	Synod	13	Architects' Club
6	Horse Guards' Riding School	14	Fabergé
7	St Isaac's Cathedral	15	*Nóvaya Gollándiya*
8	Nicholas I		

to contain so many mistakes and miscalculations that he was required to make another set which were not ready until 1825; the ground, even at the south end of the square, was too marshy to support the massive structure (the cathedral can hold fourteen thousand people and is believed to weigh three hundred thousand tons. The forty-eight columns which support the porticoes weigh a hundred and thirty tons each. Montferrand eventually resolved the problem by sinking thousands of piles, variously estimated as eleven and twenty-four thousand); Nicholas I was a fidgety and difficult employer; and there were too many fingers in the pie.

Was it worth it? For Montferrand, the enterprise consumed his life – as it consumed the lives of many of the workers who helped to build it. He died a month after the cathedral opened, having asked to be buried in the crypt – a request refused by Nicholas on the grounds that he was not an Orthodox.[8] He left behind an album of water-colours depicting the various stages of construction which are at once delightful and awe-inspiring. Both inside and out, the eye was to be delighted by a profusion of colour and texture – bronze for the doors, the statues, the bases and the capitals of the columns; rose granite for the columns themselves and grey granite for the walls; galvanised iron (a process invented in 1838) on the pediment *hauts reliefs*; gold leaf on the domes; on the internal walls, six hundred metres of mosaics and some twenty paintings by Russian masters; on the iconostasis, white marble and lapis lazuli and brilliant green malachite. No wonder the story got about, in the terrible famine years of the late 1920s and early 1930s, that Stalin, who had been selling the country's ecclesiastical and art treasures to raise foreign currency, was now going to flog the whole of St Isaac's to the Americans, lock, stock and barrel; it was to be dismantled taken to the United States and rebuilt (a rather magnificent version of Korda's 1935 film, *The Ghost Goes West*).

Posterity has given it a mixed reception. It is presently much admired, as a result perhaps of the contrast it

---

[8] His widow was allowed to arrange for the coffin to be carried round the Cathedral before being conveyed to a Requiem Mass at the Catholic Church on *Névskiy prospékt*. Montferrand was buried in France.

provides to the bleakness of Soviet architecture. Young Russians coming to St Petersburg for the first time seemed filled with wonder at St Isaac's. But the artistic establishment a hundred years ago thought pretty poorly of it. The critic, V. Kurbatov (in *Péterburg. 1913*), described it as an 'inkpot', criticising in particular the proportions of the dome in relation to the drum on which it sits. And 'inkpot' was the least of the insults it attracted though nobody had yet thought of 'carbuncle'. St Isaac's has not returned to being a cathedral, though services are occasionally held there, and remains what it became in 1937, a museum. It is now, in essence, a museum of itself. It also provides perhaps the best view of the centre of St Petersburg from its upper colonnade.

South of the cathedral, another square was formed on the old glacis, which runs down to the Blue Bridge (*Síniy most*) on the Moika Embankment and is crossed by *Bolsháya Morskáya úlitsa*. In the middle of **St Isaac's Square** (*Isaákiyevskaya plóstchad*), facing the south portico of his cathedral, is the **Monument of Nicholas I**. Petersburg sculptors often adopt a more honest relationship with their patrons than would be thought appropriate in other cities. Trubetskoy's feelings for Alexander III were not reverential – and they showed. P. Klodt had no love for Nicholas (who caused him a great deal of trouble with his horses on the Anichkov Bridge) and they say he showed that too, particularly in his treatment of the face. In any event, it was perhaps tactless to place his monument so close to the square of the Decembrists. The events of his reign, depicted in *bas reliefs* on the four sides of the plinth, are also pretty chilling: his personal appearance during the Uprising; his appearance in *Sennáya plóstchad* during the cholera riots;[9] the presentation of a code of laws and the opening of a railway bridge. The first two, at least, were

---

[9] See the description of *Sennáya plóstchad* in Chapter X.

some kind of tribute to his courage. Higher up, on the pedestal, are four female figures in bronze – Justice, Power, Faith and Wisdom – in which contemporaries recognised the features of his wife and three daughters. The statue is mostly remarked for the fact that it has only two points of support – the horse's hind legs; the distant views of it are very elegant.

On the west side of the cathedral, *Isaákiyevskaya plóstchad No. 7*, is the house in which **Griboyedov** lived while he was trying to arrange for the publication of his famous play, *Woe from Wit*. He stayed for nearly a year (1824–5) in the eight-room apartment of his friend Prince Aleksandr Odoyevskiy, a cornet in the Horse Guards and a Decembrist sympathiser. In that apartment, *Woe from Wit*[10] was read aloud by Griboyedov and copied by young officers who distributed it among their comrades all over Russia, in spite of the censor. It is unclear whether Griboyedov actually joined the Northern Society and he was out of town during the time of the Uprising. But he was arrested and interrogated from February to May 1826 when he was released 'with a certificate of innocence' back to the Foreign Service and briskly posted abroad.

No. 9 next door to the south across the *Pochtámtskaya úlitsa*, is the oldest surviving house on the square (1760s), built originally for L. Naryshkin and generally known as the **dom Myátleva**. There is a plaque on the wall of this house which announces that Diderot lived there (1773–4), while he was negotiating the sale of his library to Catherine the Great. The plaque is still there though it was recently discovered that Diderot stayed somewhere else – in a different house belonging to a different Naryshkin. In the nineteenth century, the house belonged to Myatlev, a courtier, a minor

---

[10] Griboyedov's play, *Woe from Wit*, was finished in the winter of 1823–4 but the censor only agreed to the publication of the third act and part of the first. It was not played in its entirety until the 1860s.

but amusing poet and a host to 'everybody', including Madame de Staël. After the Revolution, it was occupied by various institutions.

No. 11 (on the corner of *Bolsháya Morskáya*, of which it is *No. 41*) is, together with the Astoria Hotel on the opposite side, the last building to be put in place on St Isaac's Square (1911–12) – designed by **Peter Behrens**, construction supervised by **Mies van der Rohe** just before he opened his own office in 1913. On the site of a merchant's house of the 1740s, reconstructed by V. Stasov in 1815, it had become the German Embassy in the 1870s. In 1911, the request had come for permission to pull the house down and build a new one altogether (perhaps provoked by the Italian Embassy moving in next door to *Bolsháya Morskáya No. 43* and apparently without reference to the gathering storm over Europe). The result seems more appropriate to Albert Speer's Berlin than to Nicholas II's St Petersburg and strangely ponderous as the product of two founder members of the Bauhaus. As an embassy, it did not have long to live. The Germans put statues on the roof, mediaeval knights on war horses, for which they had not asked permission and which they would certainly not have been given. So they erected them clandestinely, behind scaffolding. By the time the scaffolding came down, it was 1914. In July, a wildly patriotic crowd swarmed on to the roof and pulled the knights out by their roots, then turned its attention to the interior. After 1990, the building briefly became the Dresdner/BNP Bank and is now occupied by various Russian institutions. It attracts a great deal of interest from German visitors.

South again, across *Bolsháya Morskáya, No. 44* is the twin of the house opposite on the east side of the square (*No. 42*). They frame Klodt's statue of Nicholas I and were built in 1803 (N. Yefimov) as the Ministry of State Property (which became the Ministry of Agriculture); here Moussorgsky was employed during the time that he was writing the music for *Borís Godunóv*. Beyond them is the widest bridge in St Petersburg, so wide (ninety-nine metres) that it is hard to realise it is a bridge. Called the **Síniy most** (Blue Bridge), from the time when it was made of wood and had red and green neighbours over the Moika river, it really forms part of St Isaac's Square which is completed, on the south side, by the **Mariinskiy Palace** (*Mariínskiy dvoréts*) across the bridge.

On the site of a house which once belonged to a grandee of Catherine's court, it was almost entirely rebuilt by A. Stackenschneider between 1839 and 1844 as a wedding present for the daughter of Nicholas I, Maria, who married the grandson of Napoleon's Josephine, through her first husband, the Vicomte de Beauharnais, and thus became the Duchess of Leuchtenberg. The marriage appears not to have been a success and she fell in love with Count Stroganov who, until the chaise longue could be replaced by the double bed, was frequently concealed in the Mariinskiy Palace. Stackenschneider produced his usual florid, mid-nineteenth-century extravaganza with a grand white marble staircase, embellished with white marble warriors, leading to a white marble rotunda – though, because Maria suffered from a deformation of her hip, many of the staircases in the palace were in fact built as ramps.

When eventually her husband died and she was able in 1852 to marry Stroganov, they moved down the road to his palace on *Névskiy prospékt*. The Mariinskiy stood empty until 1884 when it was taken into the possession of the state and occupied by the State Council. In February 1917, it served as the seat of Kerensky's Provisional Government and, later, of the *Pred-parláment* – the pre-parliamentary consultative assembly. In October, the Bolsheviks drove out the pre-parliamentarians and, in December, Lenin and the Bureau of the Supreme Economic Council met there to pass the decree which nationalised the banks.

The Mariinskiy is now the seat of the St Petersburg City Council.

Returning northwards up the eastern side of St Isaac's Square, footsore visitors will come with some relief to the **Hotel Astoria** (*Bolsháya Morskáya No. 39*, though its main entrance is on St Isaac's Square) – a delightful and expensive watering hole, architecturally Eclectic but predominantly *Style Moderne*. Until 1907 there were private houses on the site which was bought to be developed as a hotel (F. Lidval, opened in 1912). An apartment, with bath, then cost four roubles (roughly 40 p) – good value even in those days for a hotel that was always elegant. In 1990, it was fundamentally refurbished and connected to its neighbour, which now serves as a slightly cheaper annexe (the Angleterre Annexe). The ballroom of the Astoria was chosen by Hitler as the venue for a banquet to celebrate the fall of Leningrad – invitations were printed, and are preserved in the Central Historical Archives, which specified the time and the day though not the date of this event. But Hitler's social secretary must have had difficulty communicating with his naval High Command which, on 29 September 1941, had received a rather different instruction: 'The Führer has decided to wipe the city of St Petersburg from the face of the earth. After the defeat of Soviet Russia, there will be no reason at all for the further existence of this large inhabited area.'

Moving on, then, northwards to the corner of *Málaya Morskáya*, the Astoria annexe (*No. 24*) was once the Hotel d'Angleterre. The new management and new décor have made it impossible to identify the most famous room in this building – where the poet **Sergey Yesenin** was found in 1925, having apparently slashed his wrists and hanged himself after writing in his own blood a verse that began: 'Goodbye, my friend, Goodbye'. He could well have committed suicide, which is the official story; a man of extreme charm and talent, four times married (his third wife, whom he married in 1922, was the dancer Isadora Duncan),[11] in trouble with the authorities. Or, as his niece has recently alleged, he could have been murdered by the Cheka. In which case, they would have to have written his last poem.

Across the southern edge of the Admiralty glacis runs *Bolsháya Morskáya úlitsa* (Greater Maritime Street), from *No. 69* on the north side, built originally as a guard house on the western approaches to the city, and *No. 58* on the south side (built by Bosse as a Protestant church, completely rebuilt in the 1930s in Constructivist style and now the Palace of Culture for communications workers) across *Isaákiyevskaya plóstchad*, across *Gorókhovaya úlitsa*, across *Névskiy prospékt* and under Rossi's triumphal arch at the east end through which it issues into *Dvortsóvaya plóstchad* (Palace Square). It is a street worth spending time in, containing something of Mayfair, of Bond Street, of Piccadilly and the City. At the same time, it was a street in which people very actively lived.

This whole area, including *Málaya Morskáya úlitsa*, was transformed in the four years that followed the great fire of 1736 from a haphazard shanty town – almost entirely built of wood and occupied by people engaged in the dockyard – to a rigorously planned inner suburb of, mostly, modest stone houses. A triumvirate of distinguished Russian architects (Yeropkin, Zemtsov and Korobov) planned and supervised 'exemplary' housing construction. Numbered plots were sold off in the late 1730s and early 1740s.

In *Bolsháya Morskáya úlitsa*, some were sold to prosperous artisans (a tailor at *No. 35*, a tapestry weaver at *No. 17*, jewellers at *Nos. 13, 10* and *8*), some to merchants (*No. 19*, built by a merchant, was soon bought by Catherine's banker, Richard Sutherland, who was eventually caught with his hand in the till), some to architects (Zemtsov, for

---

[11] Isadora Duncan herself died dramatically, in Nice in 1927, strangled by her scarf which became entangled in the wheel of her drop-head coupé.

instance, owned as well as designed *No. 31*), a few still to people connected with the navy (*No. 22* to the Captain of the galley fleet, *No. 33* to Admiral Kruis's daughter), some, rather fewer, to the nobility.

Most were enlarged (at any rate by an extra storey) in the latter part of the eighteenth century. Almost all were reconstructed in the nineteenth century, sometimes leaving traces of the earlier house, sometimes root and branch. As early as 1827, *No. 40* was acquired by Russia's first insurance company. In the 1830s, Montferrand found relief from his tribulations on St Isaac's by making massive 'improvements' to *No. 43* (later the Italian Embassy) which included the bosomy caryatids supporting the balcony, and to *No. 45* which he bought himself. Later on in the century, and into the early 1900s, banks and insurance companies moved into the area, particularly east of St Isaac's, enlarging, re-facing, sometimes demolishing and rebuilding (*Nos. 48, 40, 37, 35, 34, 32, 18, 17, 15, 5* and *3* all became at one time banks or insurance companies). Several of these houses were acquired by the post office and communications industry. About some of them, there are more amusing things to tell.

Starting at the far (west) end, on the north (odd) side, *No. 61* began life in the 1730s as the site of the public baths. In 1756, Lomonósov had an exceptionally large house built here (at the time, with fifteen rooms, it was the largest in the street).[12] Unusually, it had a front garden which contained the workshop where he experimented with mosaics. In the 1840s, it was rebuilt to serve as the first staging post for long-distance coaches to Moscow. When the railways put stagecoaches out of business, the house was occupied by successive Imperial Ministers of the

[12] Mikhail Lomonósov (1711–65), son of a fisherman, was poet, grammarian, physicist and astrologer. He also revived the art of mosaics. The museum devoted to him on *Vasíliyevskiy óstrov* is described on p. 324.

Interior, including the last of all – D. Trepov. It is now the head office for Communications in Leningrad Province.

On the same side, *No. 55* was built as a single storey house in 1740 and occupied by Catherine the Great's Russian teacher, A. Adadurov.[13] Gutted and refurbished in the 1850s, after the Revolution it became the Society for the Study and Protection of Old Petersburg, of which the first president was P. N. Stolpyanskiy.[14] It is now a Russo-Finnish joint venture company.

The footprint of *No. 47* goes back to the 1740s but, both outside and in, it now owes almost everything to its purchase by the parents of **Vladimir Nabokov**[15] who was born there in 1899. In 1901, a third floor was added and the whole of the street façade covered over (the first in the street) with *Style Moderne* motifs of an unusually delicate variety. In the pantry on the ground floor is arranged a permanent exhibition (a 'museum') relating to both the house and the writer, built round Nabokov's personal effects which were given by his son. More fun is to wander over the more or less empty house, which now contains the editorial offices of the journal *Névskoye Vrémya* (Neva Times). With *Speak, Memory* in one hand, it is not difficult to glimpse and even to smell the quality of cultivated Petersburg life at the turn of the century. In the pantry, there is a photograph of Nabokov with his mother. She looks very much more beautiful than Madame Proust.

No. 45 was acquired in 1780 by Count Musin-Pushkin. In 1812, the Musin-Pushkin library, the largest in Russia,

[13] Catherine came to Russia from Germany in 1744 at the age of fifteen and, at the time, spoke no Russian.
[14] P. N. Stolpyanskiy was the author of *Petersburg – How Sankt Piterburch Arose, was Founded and Grew*, which was first published before the Revolution and is still a most valuable source of information.
[15] V. Nabokov, author of *Speak, Memory, Lolita, The Gift* etc. and also distinguished lepidopterist. Born St Petersburg, 1899, died Switzerland, 1977.

was burned during the destruction of Moscow. In 1834 Montferrand bought and rebuilt it and in that form it has remained. After the Revolution it became an apartment house where the poets Klyuyev and Yesenin lived and were much visited by other poets. It is now the **House of Composers** (*dom Kompozítorov*).

On the opposite (south) side of the street, *No. 52* was the grandest house of all. By 1762, it belonged to French merchants. In 1793, Louis XVI went to the guillotine and his brother, the Comte d'Artois came to live here until he returned to France in 1820 to become Charles X. The house acquired its Late Classical façade in 1835. And from 1869 it belonged to Senator Polovtsov, Financial Secretary. He founded, and became the first president of, the Russian Historical Society and he started to edit a Russian Dictionary of National Biography. (It was halted in 1917 after only twenty-five volumes had appeared – but another six were recently found ready for press and have been published.) He married a very, very rich wife and their son, Aleksandr Polovtsov played an important part in preserving St Petersburg's art treasures after the Revolution.[16] Since 1934, the house has been occupied by the **Architects' Club**, which contains an excellent restaurant, the *Nikolay*, open to the public.

Across *Isaákiyevskaya plóstchad* to the east, *No. 38* (south side) once belonged to Catherine's Head of Chancery, I. P. Yelagin, who owned and gave his name to Yelagin Island. From the 1870s, it was the centre of the city's artistic life becoming, in 1882, the **Imperial Society for the Encouragement of Art**. Inspired by V. V. Stasov, it encouraged among many others the New Realist school of Russian painting whose members were known as the *peredvízhniki* ('movers', because they displayed their work in travelling exhibitions) and the early Cubists (such as Vrubel).

[16] See Chapter XV.

A famous school of drawing was attached (the equivalent of the Academy Schools), under the directorship from 1906 to 1917 of N. Rerikh (or, in German, Roerich, to whom there is a commemorative plaque). The school had many remarkable features: half the students were able to attend without fees; there were special classes of interest to women; the teachers included I. Bilibin (who later came to England), V. Stchuko and A. Stchusev. There was a library and a museum of modern Russian art, the contents of which were sold off in 1929. The house is now occupied by the **St Petersburg Union of the Artists of Russia** with 3,500 members. There is an exhibition centre and the museum has been reconstituted; it now possesses ten thousand works covering Russian art throughout the twentieth century and provides advice to people and institutions who wish to form their own collections.

No. 36 was rebuilt in 1873 and, in 1910, opened as the **New English Club** (not to be confused with the English Club which opened for the younger members of the nobility on the Palace Embankment in 1770). The members of the New English Club were the (male) members of the English colony and their chairman was the British Ambassador.

Across the street on the north side, *No. 31* had been designed and built by Zemtsov in the 1730s, rebuilt in 1852 and, in 1903, became the **Imperial Yacht Club** – the club for the fathers of the members of the English Club. It had nothing to do with yachts and everything to do with influential networking; it was an indispensable source of news. If you needed to find out what was going on, you went to the Yacht Club. The day after Rasputin was murdered, they all went to the Yacht Club – including the murderers. (I remember my father coming home one day from the Club and telling my mother how he felt that someone had been eavesdropping on his conversation. He looked up but the 'listener' was buried in a newspaper. He looked again

and saw that the newspaper was upside down. My parents
thought it was very funny. But I was puzzled: how could the
man read it – upside down?)

In 1802, *No. 29* was the house of **Count L. Razumovskiy**,
who had won his wife at cards from Prince A. Galitsin. Far
from objecting, Princess Galitsin decided she preferred the
new arrangement, divorced her feckless husband and lived
happily ever after at *No. 29*. After Razumovskiy's death, she
gave a party at which Pushkin asked an Englishman to act
as his second at the fatal duel with D'Anthès. The
Englishman wisely refused. The original house was pulled
down in the 1970s and rebuilt according to 1850 designs.

No. 27 was bought by the architect V. Brenna at the turn
of the eighteenth and nineteenth centuries, while he was
working on the third St Isaac's and the palace at Pavlovsk.
At the beginning of the twentieth century, it returned to
architectural hands when Lidval's mother lived there.

The site of *No. 25*, on the north-west corner of *Bolsháya
Morskáya* and *Gorókhovaya úlitsa*, was given to the German
Comedy Theatre by the Empress Elisabeth in 1742. By the
nineteenth century, there were apartments to let above
ground floor shops and **Aleksandr Herzen** came to lodge
there in 1840 after six years of exile in Siberia.[17] While
there, he wrote to his father criticising the police, a letter
which was intercepted. This time they sent him to
Novgorod. So his stay was brief – but long enough to give
his name to the street which, after the Revolution, became
úlitsa Gértsena. (As it was only recently changed back to
Bolsháya Morskáya, it features as *Gértsena* in many maps).

[17] Aleksandr Herzen (1812–70), who shared a common ancestor with the
Russian royal family, was a radical and very rich Russian journalist, author
of memoirs of great literary and historical value entitled *My Past and
Thoughts*. He finally left Russia, living in London, Paris and Italy, during
which time he edited and published a magazine called *The Bell* (*Kólokol*)
which was so accurate about affairs in Russia that several members of the
Russian Government subscribed to it to keep themselves informed.

Some things, however, do not change. In the eighteenth century there was a fruit shop on the ground floor of *No. 25*. There is still a fruit shop there today.

Across the road, at *No. 24*, is the building which housed the last and smartest shop of **Fabergé**, the court jewellers. The family were originally Huguenot refugees to Germany and it was not until 1842 that Peter Gustav Faberg (without the final '*é*') came to St Petersburg and opened a workshop with three assistants on the ground floor of *Bolsháya Morskáya No. 11*, later expanded into *No. 16*. His grandson, Karl Peter, by this time with an '*é*' on the end of his name and an international clientèle, bought *No. 24* from a major-general in 1898. By 1900 he had reconstructed it in a cross between *Style Moderne* and Gothic Revival, providing himself with shop, workshop and an apartment of fifteen rooms. In 1918 he and the firm left for Paris, where he had already opened a branch. Now the Fabergé Arts Foundation plans to restore *Bolsháya Morskáya No. 24*, providing a museum and library of the jewellery arts, space for contemporary craftsmen and an outreach education programme.

Opposite, at *No. 21*, there once lived a rich merchant, Aleksey Zhardimirskiy, who had a very beautiful wife, Lavinia. She was unhappy in her marriage and attracted the attentions of Nicholas I. Rather than become his mistress, she ran away with Prince S. Trubetskoy but the pair were caught. He was at first imprisoned in the 'Secret House' in the Fortress of SS Peter and Paul; on release he was stripped of his title and rank and despatched to the Caucasus. She went to live at his house in the country and waited for him. In due course he came back, and, Zhardimirskiy having died in the interim, they married and, it is believed, lived happily ever after.

Across *Kirpíchny pereúlok, Bolsháya Morskáya Nos. 16* and *11* on the east corners mark the outer edge of the Empress Elisabeth's temporary Winter Palace. *No. 11* had been the throne room which the Empress Catherine gave to

Falconet as a workshop in which to model his monument to Peter the Great. Diderot, the French *philosophe* who had recommended him to Catherine and who was in St Petersburg in 1773, often came there to watch him and to talk. Catherine came too. In 1778, Falconet returned to France and the studio was sold to the German consulate which, in 1837, sold it on to Paul Jacquot, the architect, to build his own house while he was working on the Catholic Church on the *Névskiy prospékt* round the corner. From then until the Revolution, the ground floor was handed from one French restaurateur to another. In the opposite corner, at *No. 16*, there used to be the smartest and best restaurant in St Petersburg: *Cubat*, frequented sometimes by Rasputin, drunk and demanding a *cabinet particulier*.

Bolsháya Morskáya No. 9 (also on the Winter Palace site, on the corner of *Névskiy prospékt – No. 15*) contained another haunt of Griboyedov. In November 1817, Count Aleksandr Zavadovskiy had a large apartment there. Just after entering the Foreign Service, Griboyedov went to live with him and walked into a major scandal. There was a ballet dancer (Istómina), her ex-lover (Count V. Sheremetev), Zavadovskiy (who slept with Istómina), Griboyedov (who introduced the lovers) and a bellicose friend of Sheremetev, Aleksandr Yakubovich. One way or another, it ended up with a *partie carrée* (four-handed duel) in which Zavadovskiy killed Sheremetev. The survivors were all punished, Griboyedov being posted on his first diplomatic tour to Persia. But Istómina went on dancing – most beautifully: 'Then, with a half ethereal splendour/ bound where the magic bow will send her/ Istómina, thronged all around by Naiads, one foot on the ground,/ twirls the other slowly as she pleases . . .' (Pushkin). On the ground floor of this building is now a book shop called *Mir* (World) and a theatrical suppliers called *Masque*.

Before crossing *Névskiy prospékt*, it is worth going one block to the north and turning back westwards, into

Málaya Morskáya, where there are three houses of particular interest. *Málaya Morskáya No. 10*, still an eighteenth-century Baroque mansion, was during the nineteenth century inhabited by an old woman, Princess Natalya Galitsin. She was the model for the Countess, Anna Fedorovna, in Pushkin's short story, *The Queen of Spades*, who possessed the secret of the three winning cards and who, from her coffin, appeared to wink at Hermann, causing him to place his bet on the Queen rather than the Ace. Pushkin's diary records that the story was popular – 'gamblers are punting on the three, the seven and the Ace'. In fact Princess Galitsin did not get into her coffin until after poor Pushkin. She lived to be ninety-seven by which time she was known, with good reason but without much affection, as 'Princess Moustache'.

Across the road, at *No. 13*, is the house in which **Tchaikovsky** died, in his brother's apartment, after drinking infected water. It is now thought that this was unintentional and not a deliberate act of suicide, as was earlier supposed.

Two houses further west is *No. 17*, the reason why this street was re-named *úlitsa Gógolya*. In a small flat, looking out on to the courtyard, lived **Nikolay Gogol** for three years from 1833. It was early in his writing life and here he wrote *The Nose*, *The Portrait*, *Diary of a Madman* and the play *The Government Inspector* which was performed at the Alexandrinskiy Theatre in April 1836. He felt passionately then, and on almost all subsequent occasions, that the play was misunderstood by both actors and audience. He left St Petersburg for Rome a couple of months later. Many years afterwards, in Moscow in 1851, Turgenev heard him read *The Government Inspector* aloud: 'It was only then that I realised how wrongly, how superficially [the play] is usually performed, the actors being anxious only to get quick laughs out of the audience. I sat there overcome with joyful emotion.' By February 1852, Gogol was dead. Turgenev had been a student of his at Petersburg University: 'I can still see his thin long-nosed face tied up in a black silk handkerchief . . . he was born to be the instructor of all his contemporaries but not for a University Chair.'

Back to *Bolsháya Morskáya* and across the *Névskiy prospékt*, there is not much that is any longer of interest. But *Nos.* 3 and 5 are an important part of the Post Office – the city's Public Telephone Exchange. If you have a difficult call and you cannot get through, it is worth trying to phone from here. It often works. The building is 1912–13 by Lidval. In the nineteenth century, *No.* 3 was the *Hôtel Belle Vue*. Turgenev stayed there in 1880. And in 1899, Jerome K. Jerome was a guest, delivering himself of a judgement on St Petersburg which his English fans might find surprising: 'The people's patience is coming to an end and there is going to be a revolution soon. And it will be bloody and terrible.'

V

Palace Square

Nearest Metro Station: *Névskiy Prospékt*

THERE ARE TWO HUNDRED and twenty-five metres between the double arch which now forms the eastern end of *Bolsháya Morskáya* and the southern façade of the Winter Palace. The southern façade of the Winter Palace is nearly two hundred metres long. And it faces a continuous curve, broken only by the archway and its flying chariot of Victory, which sweeps for nearly six hundred metres from east to west across the southern side of this square with an area of sixty thousand square metres. Figures in themselves do not tell much of a story. But how else does one convey the immensity of the space which is the heart of St Petersburg? Another thing must be conveyed as well: the family who lived above this space for a hundred and fifty years were the autocratic rulers of their Empire in a sense that no British sovereign has ever been. It must have felt very different – more vulnerable as well as more powerful, more responsible as well as less constrained – to look out from the windows of the Winter Palace than ever it did from a royal palace in England.

Like many architectural arrangements in St Petersburg that look so planned, **Palace Square** (*Dvortsóvaya plóstchad*) was assembled, large piece by large piece, over a period of more than a hundred years and incorporates many visions. Peter I died, as it were to the right of the picture, in his third Winter Palace on the site of what is now the Hermitage Theatre. He was succeeded for two years by his second wife, Catherine I (1725–7), who continued to live in Peter's

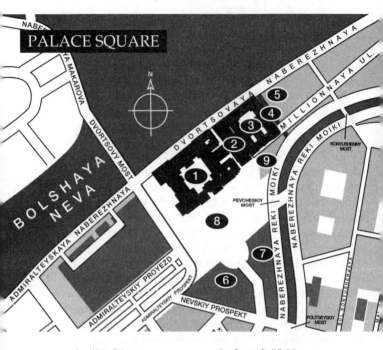

1	Winter Palace	6	General Staff Building
2	Small Hermitage	7	Hermitage Extension (M. of F. Affairs)
3	Large Hermitage	8	Alexander Column
4	Winter Ditch	9	Guards' Corps Building
5	Hermitage Theatre		

palace, and then by his eleven-year-old grandson (the son of the Tsarevich Aleksey), who went to Moscow for his coronation and never came back but died there of smallpox in 1730. The crown then passed to Peter I's niece, Anna Ioannovna (daughter of Peter's half-brother), who wished to take her court back to St Petersburg but did not fancy the relative modesty of Peter's palace. Fortunately for her – and perhaps for all of us because it was the seminal building of

Palace Square – she inherited a huge house on the banks of the Neva just east of the Admiralty, across what is now the *Dvortsóvy proyézd* and was then a watery inlet from the Neva which formed a protective canal around the dockyard. This house had belonged to one of the few people to whom Peter would have granted the right to build there – Mikhail Apraksin, who was appointed in 1705 to command the embryonic Russian fleet. Apraksin at first made do with a timber house until, in 1716, he commissioned (probably) J.-B. Le Blond to build him, in stone, by far the grandest house on the south bank of the river. In his will, he left it to Peter I's young grandson, Peter II, and thus to the crown.

On her accession in 1730, the Empress Anne let it be known that she regarded **Apraksin's house** as hers; it was to be repaired, enlarged and improved. She would come and live there (which she did until her death in 1740) and would return the centre of government to St Petersburg. She much enjoyed the hunting still to be had on both sides of *Névskiy prospékt*, particularly in the marshes south-east of what is now the Griboyedov Canal. There was, in all probability, some shooting to be had from the windows of her Winter Palace for in those days it looked southwards across a meadow which covered about two-thirds of the original Admiralty glacis and stretched from what is now St Isaac's Cathedral in the west to the Winter Ditch (*Zímnyaya kanávka*) which ran along the side of Peter's palace in the east. Until the accession of the Empress Elisabeth, it provided pasture for the milch cows of St Petersburg of which, at the time, there were a good number. Then the Empress appropriated the meadow for the royal farms and tried to put it down to oats.

They went on enlarging, repairing and (sometimes) improving Apraksin's house for more than twenty years. Bartolomeo Rastrelli was in charge. Enlargement took the form of acquiring (by forced purchase and by simple confiscation) the houses that had grown up to the east, demolishing them and building an extension to Apraksin's house that more than doubled its size. But no amount of repairing and improving could disguise the extreme cold of this, the fourth Winter Palace, with water on two sides of it – sometimes, due to the faulty plumbing, inside as well – and smoke seeping out of the cracked stoves. The Empress Elisabeth (who succeeded in 1741 and who did not suffer discomfort lightly) endured it for more than ten years and then sent for Rastrelli. He was to start again, build her an almost entirely new and even grander palace, placing it slightly further east (away from the dockyard), knocking down as many other houses as might be necessary to achieve perfection.

The foundation stone of the fifth **Winter Palace** (*Zímniy dvoréts*) was laid in 1754. Rastrelli was by that time fifty-four and at the peak of his career. He had arrived in Russia at the age of sixteen with his father, the sculptor Carlo-Bartolomeo, and brought with him an Italian flare and passion for Baroque which suited the taste of both Anne and Elisabeth. It did not suit the Empress Catherine II who sent Rastrelli away, with the result that he was never able to finish the interior. Externally, the new palace has hardly changed over the years. It has three floors – unlike Apraksin's house which had two – and columns play a major (if perhaps not always successful) part in breaking up the expanse of the façade. The top two floors are united by giant order columns which rest on a cornice supported by the ground floor colonnade. The stucco round the window frames that is almost Rococo in its intricacy, the azure blue of the walls, the detailing of the corners, the free standing statues on the attic cornice – they are all devices to please the eye and break the monotony. Yet they do not entirely succeed in disguising the fact that the cornices are two miles long and the façades are very straight. It must have been a strange sight in the last years of the Empire when, for reasons which were said to be of economy, the walls were painted blood red.

The Empress Elisabeth did not live to see the completion of Rastrelli's masterpiece. She died – a few months before it was habitable – on Christmas Day 1761, still in the wooden Winter Palace on *Névskiy prospékt* that she asked Rastrelli to build for her as a temporary refuge in 1755.[1] The new Emperor, Peter III, and his wife, Catherine, made haste to get out of the timber palace and into the real thing. Inside, the builders were still at work. Outside was worse. The meadow had become a builders' tip, littered with the eighteenth-century equivalent of portakabins, tents, abandoned bricks, untidily stacked timber and the rest. The Emperor Peter, whose intelligence quotient was always limited, could not find his way through the debris into the palace. He apparently solved the problem by advertising the fact that the citizenry were for a night free to help themselves. They did and the next morning the 'meadow' was empty.

But the outlook from Peter's apartments in the southeast corner of the first floor left a good deal to be desired. Beyond the meadow, down in the southern corner of the glacis where *Névskiy prospékt* intersected *Bolsháya Morskáya*, there had for many years been a thriving market (the source of the great fire of 1737). There were pubs and bare-fisted boxing matches and a good many other disorderly activities. *Bolsháya Morskáya* itself carried straight on northwards, around the outer edge of the meadow, until it met what is now *Milliónnaya úlitsa* and was then called *Lugováya* (Meadow) *Milliónnaya úlitsa*. To the east, with their gardens running down to the Moika river, there had grown up an assortment of substantial private houses. Peter III did not survive long enough to do more than tidy

---

[1] *See* Chapter VII. Rastrelli took less than a year to create it and Elisabeth lived there from 1756 until her death at the end of December 1761. The future Emperor Peter III and the future Empress Catherine II also lived there until January 1762.

up the entrance to his new palace. By 29 June 1762, he had been forced by the Orlov brothers to sign an unconditional abdication ('driven from the throne as a child is sent to bed', according to Frederick the Great) and by 3 July he was dead, throttled in his country estate at Ropsha.

For the new Empress, his wife and widow Catherine, there must have been weightier matters on her mind than architecture. But already she was clear that she did not like Baroque and that the hallmark of her reign would be Classical. By 1763, men were at work embanking the Neva in granite along the north side of the Winter Palace under the supervision of her architect, Yu. Felten.[2] In the following year, Vallin de la Mothe started work on the Small Hermitage to the east of it. And, by 1770, Felten was designing the north ('Old') section of the Large Hermitage, to the east again. In 1779, in furtherance of Catherine's expressed desire for some 'magnificent' houses to face the palace, the Academy of Arts launched a prize – won by Felten – to develop the area between *Bolsháya Morskáya* and the Moika. One of these houses was presented to Catherine's new favourite, Aleksandr Lanskoy. But, more importantly from the architectural point of view, Felten placed them and their Classical façades in a sweeping curve which was adopted and adapted by Carlo Rossi some forty years later when he designed the General Staff Building (*Generálny shtab*) for Catherine's grandson, Alexander I, in 1819.

On 28 March 1811, before Napoleon's advance into Russia, Alexander decreed that all sections of the army general staff be brought together in a single building near the Palace. For the next seven years, the defeat of Napoleon and the allied occupation of France took priority. But, after

---

[2] Yuri Felten's father was a German, employed at the Palace to maintain the stoves, and spelt his name with a 'V' which Russians transliterate with an 'F'. Yuri was born in Russia and studied architecture there, in Italy and in France.

1815, as the Russian High Command returned from the wars, the Crown purchased three of the Felten houses (one of which by that time belonged to Senator Molchanov) and commissioned Rossi to design the new headquarters. The intention was to commemorate Napoleon's retreat from Moscow and the Russian victory in 1812.

Rossi's **General Staff Building**, shaped in a sweeping curve which imparts a partly circular appearance to the 'square', is split into two equal wings by a majestic triumphal arch. And the arch itself is topped by a high-prowed chariot driven by a winged Goddess of Victory and drawn by six horses. The idea that there should be such a monument came from Alexander I's younger brother, Nicholas I, who succeeded in 1825. The overall design was Rossi's (when the Emperor questioned the structural soundness of the arch, so the story goes, Rossi offered to stand on the chariot as the supporting scaffold was removed) and the sculptors were Demut-Malinovskiy and Pimenov, fresh from decorating Zakharov's new Admiralty with powerful nymphs and ancient heroes. The chariot and its troupe received a good deal of maintenance during the nineteenth century but, from 1906 until the turn of the millennium, nobody had much time for them. Now they have been saved from 'likely disintegration' (the words come from the Hermitage Museum) in time for the city's tercentenary in 2003.

Impressive though it is, in length and mass, the General Staff Building is not much more than a façade and, on the first floor, a series of magnificent halls one room thick. Behind, and running down to the Moika, there are courtyards and relics of the original eighteenth-century structures, unified again on the Moika embankment side. To the west of the arch, the General Staff was accommodated; in the centre, behind the arch, the Ministry of Finance; and, to the east, the Ministry of Foreign Affairs. (The eastern wing was in fact completed after the death of Alexander and repeated Felten's curve in a mirror image. Restoration of the interior of that wing is now well advanced.) Through the middle, Rossi pulled *Bolsháya Morskáya*, twisting it slightly eastwards and threading it through his double archway which perfectly frames the view northward across the two hundred and twenty-five metres to the Winter Palace.

But – and this is a personal, probably unrepresentative, opinion – this breath-taking architectural achievement was in some sense marred by the column of rose-pink granite that was placed in the centre of the square on 30 August 1832. The **Alexander Column** (*Aleksándrovskaya kolónna*), designed by the newly-arrived French architect, Auguste de Montferrand, is carved out of a single block of granite which needs, apparently, no support but is kept erect by its own weight. It may or may not have been part of Rossi's original conception.

It is seductive to believe that Rossi planned an unimpeded view from one side of the square to the other across the magnificently empty space, for Montferrand's column has the effect of diminishing the perceived size of that space – the reason why Venetians have always refused to have a statue or any other monument in the middle of the Piazza San Marco. Napoleon's description of that Piazza as the largest drawing-room in Europe may have become a cliché; without the Alexander Column, St Petersburg's Palace Square might have qualified as the largest ballroom. In fact it often served as a parade ground. Nowadays, paved as it is with smooth granite setts, it is used more often for roller-skating and, occasionally, by military cadets who hold their passing out parades there. (The sapper cadets make a speciality of throwing their caps in the air and catching them again while they march across the square.) Once a year, on 9 May, there is a full-scale military occasion when, in a ceremony which still brings a catch to the throat, the Petersburg garrison recalls the end of the Great Patriotic War. An officer addresses each corner of the square in turn, congratulating the troops assembled there on their victory over Fascist Germany. He shouts his congratulations; there is a pause, while the words carry; then back across the square come three 'hurrahs'.

But, if the column has stolen the limelight from the square, it may yet be admired for its simplicity and for the sheer bulk of its seven hundred and four tons, hewn from a single block from the same quarry on the Gulf of Finland as the columns of St Isaac's. Like Rossi's arch, it commemorates the defeat of Napoleon and the successful campaign against him by the coalition of European states headed by the Emperor Alexander I. The *bas relief* on the Palace side of the plinth represents Russian troops pursuing Napoleon's. When it was hauled into position – with the aid of sixty 'machines', four hundred workmen and two thousand veterans of the Napoleonic Wars – Alexander's column could claim, probably correctly, to be the highest monument in the world and, specifically, to be 11 ft 6 in. higher than the Vendôme Column in Paris, thus symbolising the defeat of Napoleon's *Grande Armée* to which the Vendôme Column was dedicated. (Strange that the Russian monument was designed by a Frenchman.) But the world record lasted for only ten years when Alexander was overtaken by Nelson in Trafalgar Square (1842), to whose monument Nicholas I, on a state visit to Queen Victoria, is believed to have made a handsome contribution.[3] Alexander's column is crowned not by the image of the victor but by an angel bearing a cross, the work of the Russian sculptor B. Orlovskiy, who was said (though this is not apparent from close-up photographs) to have given his angel the features of the Emperor.

In 1837, after a cataclysmic fire, Aleksandr Bryullov was at work on restoring the interior of the Winter Palace for

---

[3] Alexander: 156 ft plus 19 ft of angel v. Nelson: 167 ft 6 in. plus 17 ft 4 in. of Nelson.

Nicholas I. At the same time, he was commissioned to reconstruct another of Felten's houses – at the eastern end of what
had now become recognisably a square – and incorporate it
in a **Guards Corps Building** (*Shtab Gvardéyskovo Kórpusa*).
This took him six years and resulted in a four-storey structure, each floor rather shallow and with Ionic columns unit-
ing the top two, which has grace and no pomposity. It
happily completes the ensemble to the east and was the
penultimate piece of Palace Square to be assembled. Current
plans are to make this building into a museum of the Guards
regiments.

At the west end of the square, the vista is still open,
across to what remains of the Admiralty Meadow (now the
Admiraltéyskiy sad – garden). By that time, houses had
grown up along *Névskiy prospékt* and joined with the western end of Rossi's building. So the last piece of architectural
activity on Palace Square was performed by I. Chernik in
1845 to 1846 when he wrapped Felten's *Névskiy prospékt
No. 2* into the east end of the General Staff Building.

It was tempting to write 'final' instead of 'last'. But it
would have been wrong. Under the **Greater Hermitage
Programme**, it is planned to reorganise Palace Square. The
Hermitage Museum, which already administers the Winter
Palace, the Small Hermitage, the Large Hermitage and the
Hermitage Theatre, has taken over the whole of the east
wing of Rossi's building on the south side of the square.
The restoration of Victory in her chariot and of the interior
of the east wing (where there are now two major permanent exhibitions – 'Under the sign of the Eagle: Imperial
Art' and pictures from the Hermitage collection by
Bonnard and Maurice Denis) is intended to be only the
first stage of creating 'around Palace Square, a cultural
centre of unique scale'. This is to include not merely further
exhibitions of Hermitage treasures but 'entertainment and
shopping centres' – maybe a hotel, a theatre, a cinema,
restaurants. Care will be taken, or so it is said, to preserve

the outer appearance of Rossi's masterpiece. One must hope so but it may turn out to be difficult – and tempting not to. Meanwhile, the western wing of Rossi's building continues to be occupied by the military and there are no plans to turn them out. It is currently the Headquarters of the Leningrad Military District which is responsible for the whole of north-west Russia.

In the centre of the south side of the Winter Palace is the Grand Entrance, a triple arch which supports a balcony on the first floor. This balcony was normally never used. But on **20 July 1914**,[4] the day after the declaration of war, the last Russian Emperor, Nicholas II, appeared on it to greet the vast crowd assembled in the square below him. They carried icons, banners, portraits of the Emperor himself. Then, in an outburst of monarcho-patriotic fervour, they knelt and sang the Russian national anthem, *Bózhe Tsaryá Khraní* (God Save the Tsar). Yet the war was to destroy both Emperor and people. Four years later almost to a day, on 17 July 1918, the man on the balcony was murdered with all his family. A few months earlier, in December 1917, the Russian people under Lenin's leadership had concluded a separate peace with Germany. It is perhaps interesting that contemporary photographs of July 1914 show the crowd held well back from the Palace, in the southern two-thirds of the square, and Nicholas standing alone without his family in the corner of the balcony close to one of the columns. It was a moment of spontaneous warmth – but also of tension. Contemporary prints on the other hand show the crowd gathered round the foot of the balcony, the tension airbrushed out.

The French ambassador, Maurice Paléologue, was present then and had also been present on a previous occasion, on **9 January 1905**. He recalled that earlier crowd, 'the working masses of St Petersburg, led by the priest Gapon

[4] 2 August, Western style, see p. 436.

and preceded, as now, by sacred images . . . assembled, as they were assembled today, before the Winter Palace'. It was another, irreparable, tragedy. By 1905, the population of St Petersburg had grown to nearly two million, from one million in 1890. This exponential growth stemmed from the economic and social reforms of Alexander II in the 1860s and 70s which made possible the development of the textile and steel industry, much of it involved in the manufacture of arms on the outskirts of St Petersburg, and drew into the city peasants and recently liberated serfs from the countryside. The conditions under which these new workers were employed compared – probably unfavourably – with conditions in Britain before labour legislation began to be introduced in the 1840s; the conditions in which they lived, crammed into tenements in the back courtyards of eighteenth century buildings or into cheap new housing, though the subject of Russian fiction, had no chronicler like Henry Mayhew and was disastrously ignored by the Imperial bureaucracy.[5]

There were two other important ingredients in the situation which resulted in the tragedy of '**Bloody Sunday**', 9 January 1905. First, assassination by (a few) revolutionary terrorists had become a successful method of eliminating figures of authority, indirectly another by-product of Alexander II's reforms. (Terrorists were much encouraged when one of the newly-constituted juries refused to bring in a verdict of guilty against Vera Zasulich, who had manifestly shot and gravely wounded the Chief of Police.) The Chairman of the Council of Ministers formed in October of 1905, Count Witte, wrote in retrospect: 'I would not be candid if I did not voice the impression, perhaps an entirely groundless one, that at the time public figures were

[5] Henry Mayhew, *London Labour and the London Poor* (Griffin, Bohn and Company: London, 1861–2), republished by Constable and Co. Ltd in 1968, and by Penguin, ed. Victor E. Neuburg, in 1985.

somewhat frightened of the bombs and the Brownings which were much in use against people in power.'[6] The second ingredient was a complete lack of understanding about how to control crowds. In St Petersburg, at this time, there were some three thousand ordinary police on whom, with the sometimes ambivalent support of mounted Cossacks, the burden of first-line crowd control fell. Once that failed, there was only the army (of which there has always been a strong presence in St Petersburg) and they had not been trained to do anything but shoot people. Finally, it must be remembered that, a year earlier, the Japanese fleet had attacked the Russian naval base at Port Arthur and Russia was at war with Japan.

This was the scene. The main actor was a young priest called **Georgiy Gapon** who had studied at the Theological Academy of the Alexander Nevsky Monastery. In 1903 he had founded the Assembly of Factory and Mill Workers, with the express intent of helping labour to organise in ways that did not involve violence and were not in conflict with the authorities. The Minister of the Interior approved Father Gapon's Assembly; the Chief Commissioner of Police of St Petersburg, I. Fullon, was photographed visiting a meeting. Then, in December 1904, the management of the Putilov armaments factory sacked four workers who belonged to the Assembly and, by 8 January, over a hundred thousand workers were on strike throughout the city. St Petersburg was without electricity and newspapers. There is no doubt that Father Gapon encouraged the strike nor that he had grafted into his workers' demands for higher wages and shorter hours many of the politico/constitutional aims of the Liberation Movement.

On Thursday 6 January, he had announced there would be, on the following Sunday, a procession to the Winter Palace to hand in a petition to the Emperor. 'If you do not

---

[6] Witte: *Vospominaniia*, Vol. III, p. 110.

respond to our pleas,' it concluded, 'we will die here in this square before your palace . . . we have nowhere else to go.' The authorities took fright. On 7 January, the Governor appealed to the workers to stay away; and, on 8 January, an order went out for Gapon's arrest. The procession, nevertheless, went ahead. In an orderly fashion, some 140,000 marchers gathered at six assembly points which included the *Tróitskaya plóstchad*, on the north bank of the Neva, and the Narva Gate, in the south-west of the city in the direction of the Putilov factory. As Maurice Paléologue had observed, they carried icons and sang hymns; many of those who watched crossed themselves and took off their hats; the churches tolled their bells. It had been decided to allow the march to take place but to contain it and, above all, to prevent it reaching Palace Square. So, as the police fell back, the marchers encountered the troops. To begin with, some of the soldiers fired into the air. But, soon, the authorities lost their heads. Troops were ordered to fire without discrimination into the crowd, sometimes hitting onlookers as well as marchers. At the Narva Gate, where Father Gapon was leading the procession, forty people were killed and many wounded. In Palace Square, where several thousand marchers eventually got through, many more were killed and wounded. Nobody can agree on the figures but the best estimate now seems to be about a thousand casualties in the city, of which two hundred were fatal.

Father Gapon's role remains obscure. He went into hiding, and then into exile, to avoid arrest. But he returned the next year and, on 10 April 1906, was 'executed' by a group of Socialist Revolutionaries who hanged him from a coat hanger at a cottage in *Ozerkí* in a northern suburb. The authorities thought he had become a revolutionary; the revolutionaries thought – or chose to think – that he was an *agent provocateur*. He was probably neither. What was not at all obscure was the damage done to the perception of the Emperor as father of his people. In fact, as the organisers of the demonstration well knew, the Emperor had left St Petersburg and was with his family in Tsarskoye Selo. So he could not have received the petition, even if he would have. On the evening of Bloody Sunday, he wrote in his diary: 'A painful day. Serious disorders took place in Petersburg when the workers tried to come to the Winter Palace. The troops have been forced to fire in several parts of the city and there are many killed and wounded. Lord, how painful and sad this is!' He was writing about an event which precipitated the first Russian revolution and was 'the dress rehearsal', as Lenin called it, of the Bolshevik Revolution twelve years later.

In **October 1917**, Palace Square was once again invaded by a crowd. But this time there was no longer an emperor. Nicholas II and his family were in Siberia, dispatched there in August by the Prime Minister of the Provisional Government, Aleksandr Kerensky. And, on 1 September, Kerensky, acting alone and without consulting his cabinet, had declared Russia a 'Socialist Republic'. Now the crowd, reinforced by mutinous troops, was intent on entering the Palace in which, by this time, Kerensky himself was installed and where the Provisional Government held its meetings. There was little opposition, as young Natalya Mestcherskiy, who had caught the tram home from the opera that night, saw in the light of the bonfires by which the soldiers were warming themselves (*see* p. 65). The young officer cadets guarding the Palace had been partly withdrawn, partly overwhelmed and partly persuaded to disarm. The northern façade of the Palace, facing the Neva, suffered very little – either from the Fortress guns or from the guns of the cruiser *Aurora*, moored downstream at the Nicholas (now Lieutenant Schmidt) Bridge, though both were intended to play a part in the assault. Nor was much damage inflicted on the rest of the exterior.

I remember, as a child, being taken for a walk to Palace Square on the day after the Palace was captured and feeling

vaguely disappointed at seeing the walls intact and
unscathed, save for being pitted with holes from machine
gun and rifle fire and for some plaster lying around. None
of which prevented the great Russian film producer,
Eisenstein, from dramatising the event some years later
more in keeping with public expectation and the requirements of propaganda.[7]

The damage to the interior of the Palace, through
destruction by the mob which invaded it a few hours later,
was more serious. The mob included a group of American
journalists, among them John Reed, author of *Ten Days
that Shook the World*, who described the 'shattered rooms'
and the looting (in which Reed appears to have participated) while the old Palace servants, still in their gold, blue
and red uniforms, wandered about and tried to protect the
rooms formerly in their care by repeating listlessly from
time to time: 'You can't go in there, Sir. It's not allowed.'
A Protection Committee was soon formed to impose some
restraint. It did so but not with uniform success. Reed, for
instance, got smoothly away with a jewel-studded sword
hidden under his coat, by feigning indignation when questioned by a guard – an incident revealed by Reed's biog-
rapher which did not feature in Reed's best-seller.

It was essential that neither mob nor journalists should
succeed in looting the wine cellars. And to this end, the
Protection Committee found it necessary to refuse a
Swedish offer of several million gold roubles (at ten roubles
to the pound sterling) for the cellars' contents because it
could not devise a mob-proof method of transporting the
bottles to a waiting boat. Rather than risk a gigantic
drunken orgy, every bottle was destroyed by rifle fire.

[7] Accounts of the capture of the Winter Palace by the Bolshevik forces,
and the role played by the Peter and Paul Fortress and the *Aurora* are as
numerous as they are unreliable and as fanciful as they are contradictory.
As mentioned in Chapter II, footnote 8, we believe that the most trustworthy source is S. Melgunov.

Somehow, the wine must have found its way out into the Neva since, according to one witness, the river acquired for a short time 'all the colours of the rainbow'. Thereafter, the Palace cellars have never again been used to store wine. Many years later, for a short and exceptional time, they were put to a use undreamt of by Rastrelli or the Empress Elisabeth. During the Blockade and bombardment of Leningrad in the Second World War, they were, together with the cellars of the other Hermitage buildings, adapted to serve as underground homes for the Museum staff and their families, some two thousand people in all.

VI

The Hermitage

Nearest Metro Station: *Névskiy Prospékt*

FIVE BUILDINGS AT PRESENT house the **State Hermitage** (*Gosudárstvenny Ermitázh*): the Winter Palace (*Zímniy dvoréts*), built for the Empress Elisabeth, and first occupied by Peter II and his wife, Catherine (later Catherine II or Great), by Bartolomeo Rastrelli, 1754–62; the Small Hermitage (*Mály Ermitázh*), built for Catherine the Great by Yu. Felten and J.-B. Vallin de la Mothe, 1764–7; the Large Hermitage (*Bolshóy Ermitázh*), of which the 'Old' (*Stáry*) part on the Neva side was built for Catherine by Felten with the assistance of Giacomo Quarenghi, 1771–87 and the 'New' (*Nóvy*) part, on the side of *Milliónnaya úlitsa*, was built for Nicholas I to the designs of Leo von Klenze and executed by V. Stasov and N. Yefimov, 1839–52; and the Hermitage Theatre (*Ermitázhny teátr*), built by Quarenghi for Catherine, 1783–7. (The Hermitage Museum also now owns part of the General Staff Building on the south side of Palace Square, in which it has mounted two exhibitions, and has a separate exhibition in the Menshikov Palace on *Vasíliyevskiy óstrov* for which there are different entrance arrangements.)

Until 1917, the **Winter Palace** was the home of the Russian Imperial family – where they lived their sometimes complicated lives, where some of them died, where they entertained and where they celebrated state occasions. It did not become a site for the self-conscious display of art until it was placed by the Leningrad Soviet under the jurisdiction of the State Hermitage (*Gosudárstvenny Ermitázh*) in 1945.

So what you will see in the Winter Palace (particularly on the first floor)[1] is sometimes primarily of interest for the interior decorations, the formal function or the private history of the rooms themselves; sometimes it is of interest only for the art displayed there, as in the south-east wing of the second floor where pages and maids of honour used to sleep in a warren of little rooms which currently house perhaps the most famous pictures in the Hermitage Museum – French Impressionists and post-Impressionists which in fact never formed part of any Imperial collection but were brought into public ownership after the Revolution with the 'nationalisation' of two great private collections.

The entrance is from the Palace Embankment (*Dvortsóvaya náberezhnaya No. 36*), in the centre of the north (Neva) front of the Winter Palace. Tickets, to be bought at the Ticket Office on the courtyard side of the entrance hall, will admit you to everything in the Hermitage Museum except the 'Golden Rooms' (one of which, called the Treasure Gallery, is in the south-west corner of the Winter Palace Ground Floor) and 'The Winter Palace of Peter I' which has been excavated under the stage of the Hermitage Theatre and has a separate entrance at *Dvortsóvaya náberezhnaya No. 32*, immediately to the east of the Winter Ditch (*Zímnyaya kanávka*). 'Timed Entry' tickets for these can also be bought at the main Ticket Office.

The first occupants of the Winter Palace, early in 1762, were Peter III and his wife Catherine. From their day to this, the exterior has barely changed. Neither the Revolutionary guns of the *Aurora* and the Peter and Paul Fortress in 1917, nor bombardment by the Germans from 1941 to 1944 inflicted permanent damage. Remarkably, and in spite of all war-time difficulties, restoration began in

---

[1] Throughout, floors will be referred to in English style: ground, first, second. Russian style, like American, describes the ground floor as first etc.

1942 while the Germans were still at the gates and, by the end of 1945, some seventy rooms were once again open to the public.

The serious damage was sustained by the interior when, more than a hundred years earlier in December 1837, a fire broke out on the second floor of the Winter Palace. It destroyed a great part of the interior which had been created for two Empresses (Elisabeth and Catherine) and two Emperors (Alexander I and Nicholas I) and had involved at least seven distinguished architects.[2] Seven thousand people, as well as the Imperial family, had to be evacuated (permanent inhabitants of the Palace, other than the Imperial family, were granted compensatory pensions for life). But the reigning Emperor, Nicholas I, was determined to have the Palace back in working order within a year. He, or rather the architects he appointed to achieve the impossible – Vasiliy Stasov and Aleksandr Bryullov – had completed the restoration of the State Rooms by Easter 1839, employing up to ten thousand workers at a time. They tried to preserve as many of the original features as possible or, at least, to respect the original style. But most of the public rooms on the first floor of the Winter Palace are in fact the work of them or their assistants and date from 1838.

How you tour these rooms will depend partially on your inclinations and partially on the guide to whom you attach yourself. Guides tend to take you to the left from the Entrance along what is called the Rastrelli Gallery to the Jordan Staircase and thence up into the middle of the State Rooms. It is without doubt the most impressive introduction to the Winter Palace but, when you get to the top of the staircase, it may make more sense historically and architecturally to find your own way quickly through the State Rooms to the south-east corner of the Palace where

[2] For Elisabeth: Rastrelli; for Catherine: Felten, de la Mothe, Rinaldi and Quarenghi; for Alexander and Nicholas: Montferrand and Rossi.

Catherine the Great had her private apartments for thirty-four years. This is the starting – and ending – point of the tour that this Guide will take round the **first floor of the Winter Palace**. (If you decide to dispense with an official tour, or even to flit from one guide to another, remember always that people have been known to get lost. Note down on a piece of paper the number of the room from which you set out so that you have some point of reference.) We will give the Museum's official numbers of the rooms we describe (which are not, by the way, the same as the numbers in the Hermitage Virtual Tour available on the Internet) and also (*see* p. 128) a floor plan.

But, first, the **Jordan Staircase**. It is one of the few creations of Rastrelli to survive Catherine's dislike of Baroque and the fire of 1837. Even so, it has certainly been touched up and toned down by Stasov's reconstruction of 1838. Vast and magnificent, twin curves of white Carrara marble, abundant gold mouldings on white plaster, a ceiling apparently upheld by atlantes (supporting columns in the form of male figures) *en grisaille* while three-dimensional caryatids overhang the hall; even the windows are not what they appear since some of them are mirrors and look in not out – if Rastrelli had to abandon his *chef d'oeuvre*, then at least he left a worthy reminder. In Catherine's day, the staircase was used by foreign ambassadors attending Imperial audiences and so was known as the Ambassadors' Staircase. Later it was renamed the Jordan Staircase because it was the route by which the Emperor led his family to attend the annual service of the Blessing of the Waters on 6 January in commemoration of Christ's Baptism in the river Jordan. On these occasions, a temporary pavilion was set up on the ice of the Neva at a point opposite the northern (and now the main) entrance to the Palace. The Metropolitan of St Petersburg dipped a cross in a hole made in the ice and referred to as 'Jordan'. A small cup was then lowered into the hole and presented to the Emperor who took a sip of the water and handed the cup back to the Metropolitan. Charles Heath, former tutor of the last Emperor, Nicholas II, was English and Protestant and had no belief in the purifying power of a church service. He found the ceremony repellent and warned his ex-pupil against it on grounds of hygiene. But his well-meant advice was ignored and no ill effects seemed to follow the drinking by the Sovereign of the Neva's undubitably polluted water. After the water had been blessed, the Imperial family returned to the first floor by the way it had come.

Catherine's private apartments in the south-east corner of the first floor (*Rs. 263–81*) had in the first instance been occupied by her husband Peter III and his mistress, Yekaterina Vorontsov, whom he intended to marry when he had got rid of his wife. In the event, it was his wife – or, rather, her supporters – who got rid of him. After her coronation in September 1762, she took over the apartments and lived in them during the winter until her death. Here she rose every morning at five o'clock. Here she played with and supervised the education of her grandsons, two of whom became emperors of Russia. Here, on 5 November 1796, she suffered a massive stroke from which, after thirty-six hours, she died. Her lovers (she very seldom had more than one at a time) were invariably accommodated on the floor below in a room connected to her apartments by a private staircase which is still there and still, unofficially, referred to as *Favorítskaya léstnitsa* (Favourites' Staircase). In a drawer of the writing desk, a hundred thousand roubles would be discreetly waiting for them.

Some years later, these apartments became the Second Reserve Suite (*2-ya Zapasnáya Polovína*) for distinguished, but not the most distinguished, visitors. In the late nineteenth century, they were occupied by the Grand Duke Vladímir, brother of Alexander III, while he was waiting for his new house in *Dvortsóvaya náberezhnaya*. Now, some of the rooms (*Rs. 263–6*) are used to display German fifteenth- and sixteenth-century portraits (including works by Cranach, Dürer and Holbein). Some (*Rs. 267–8*) display German applied art and later paintings. Some (*Rs. 275–81*) display the earlier works from the great collection of French seventeenth- and eighteenth-century art (Le Nain, Poussin, Claude Lorrain).

Moving westwards along the south wing of the Palace, on the courtyard side is a display of French applied art (*Rs. 290–7*); on the side of Palace Square, we arrive at Watteau (*R. 284*), Boucher (*R. 285*), Falconet – of the 'Bronze Horseman' – in *R. 286*, Chardin in *R. 287*. The *pièce de résistance* of this room is Chardin's *Still Life with the Attributes of the Arts* which had been commissioned for the newly-founded Academy of Arts for its Conference Hall but which Catherine kept and hung in her Hermitage. (This picture was sold by Nicholas I in 1854 and bought back, by the Commission for the Improvement of Children's Lives in Leningrad, in 1926.) In the same room is Houdon's statue of Voltaire in old age. Greuze and Fragonard are in *R. 288*. Before the Revolution, these rooms were used as the First Reserve Suite for really distinguished visitors such as Heads of State.

So we arrive at the **White Hall** (*Bély zal, R. 289*) and the beginning of the **apartments occupied by Alexander II and his wife, Maria Aleksandrovna.** The White Hall itself, barrel-shaped and full of light, was designed by Bryullov, as was the rest of the suite, for their wedding in 1841 but, sadly, is the only room left with decorations from that period. The others were re-worked during the rest of the century. *Rs. 304–7* were assigned to Maria on her arrival from Hesse-Darmstadt as a very young bride, before her husband succeeded to the throne (1855). These she occupied until her death in 1880. The most admired of her rooms, but also the most florid, is the **Gold Drawing Room** (*R. 304, Zolotáya gostínaya*). In 1853, V. Schreiber refurbished Bryullov's original and partly gilded the walls. But that did not prevent it being done over again, some ten

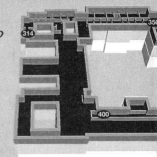

Floor plan of
THE HERMITAGE
SECOND

314
350
400

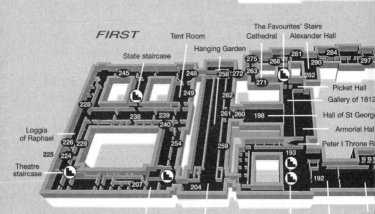

FIRST

State staircase

Tent Room

Hanging Garden

The Favourites' Stairs
Cathedral   Alexander Hall

245
248
258 272
275 263 268 281 290 284 297
271 282

249

262

Picket Hall
Gallery of 1812

228

238   239
240

261 260 198

Hall of St George

254

Armorial Hall

Loggia
of Raphael

226 229

259

Peter I Throne R

225 224

193

Theatre
staircase

207

204

192

Council staircase

Pavilion Hall

Jordan staircase
Fore Hall

Nichola
Hall

GROUND

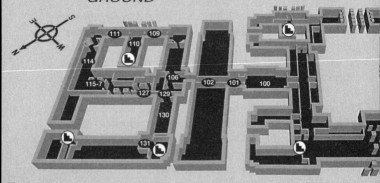

111   109
110
114
115-7   106
127   129
130
131

102 101 100

NEVA RIVER

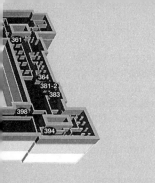

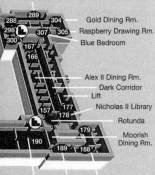

White Hall

Gold Dining Rm.
Raspberry Drawing Rm.
Blue Bedroom

Alex II Dining Rm.
Dark Corridor
Lift
Nicholas II Library
Rotunda
Moorish
Dining Rm.

Malachite Hall
Concert Hall   White Dining Rm.

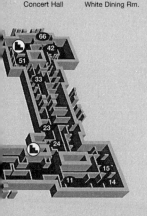

years later, by the fashionable and (especially in Royal circles) sought-after Andreas Stackenschneider. This time, the walls were gilded all over and much of the ceiling too. A century later, when the room was being restored in 1961, some of this excessive gilding was removed but enough still remains to justify 'gold' as in 'drawing room'. It now contains an exhibition of French and Italian cameos. The **Raspberry Drawing Room** (*R. 305, Malínovaya gostínaya*) and the **Boudoir** (*R. 306, Buduár*) were entirely renovated from 1956 to 1961. The **Blue Bedroom** (*R. 307, Sínyaya spálnya*), at the end of the Empress's suite, now contains a display of Fabergé *bijouterie* and artefacts which had been made for the Imperial family.

Most of the centre of the west wing on the first floor (*Rs. 161–74*) consists of rooms that were the **private apartments of Alexander II**, which he occupied on his marriage and in which he died. They are of particular interest in the history of Russia since it was here that some of his most momentous reforms – beginning with the emancipation of the serfs in 1861 – received his signature and set Russia on the path of rapid economic and social development. In post-Communist Russia, there is a growing appreciation of his achievements and there are plans to reconstruct some of these rooms, particularly the bedroom in which he died, as they were during his time.

Alexander survived seven attempts on his life, one in 1880 when Stepan Khalturin, a member of the terrorist wing of the revolutionary People's Will Party, disguised himself as a workman and placed a charge of dynamite under the Emperor's dining room (*R. 161* on the courtyard side). The explosion wrecked the room and killed nineteen people, wounding forty-eight others. But the Emperor was not among them for he was late for lunch.

Khalturin was not among them either. He managed to leave the Palace in time and unnoticed, eventually making his way to Odessa. There, two years later, his luck gave out.

He was caught and executed after taking part in another – this time successful – political murder. In spite of his failure to kill the Emperor, and in spite of the number of innocent victims of his attempt, he was honoured on the first anniversary of the Revolution in 1918 by having the street which runs up to the eastern approach of the Palace renamed *úlitsa Khaltúrina*. But it was one of the first to return to its pre-Communist name and become *Milliónnaya úlitsa* again. On 1 March 1881 came the eighth and final attempt on the life of Alexander II.[3] Alive but unconscious and with his legs blown off, he was brought back to the Winter Palace and died an hour later in his own bedroom (*R. 171*).

Between *Rs. 174* and *176*, on the side facing the Admiralty, there is a lift which, as we shall see when we reach the second floor, played an important part in the private life of Alexander II.

Carrying on northwards up the west wing, we come to the **Rotunda** (*R. 156, Rotónda*), a meeting of several ways in the north-west corner of the Palace, originally designed by Montferrand, redesigned by Bryullov after the fire. Its walls between the pillars used to be hung with velvet; on the velvet used to hang portraits of emperors and empresses, stretching from floor to gallery. The busts of Peter I and Menshikov, executed by the sculptor Carlo-Bartolomeo Rastrelli (father of the architect), used to be here but are now in Peter I's Winter Palace next door. Later emperors and empresses have been moved into a Gallery of their own.

You can arrive at and leave the Rotunda in many ways: up some stairs from the ground floor; out of the Dark Corridor (*R. 303*) which runs down the middle of the west wing; from the long thin room which runs along the courtyard side of the northern State Rooms and which was once a winter garden but has recently been given over to the displaced Imperial portraits (*Rs. 151–3*, now *Galeréya Románovyk*,

---

[3] *See* Chapters VII and XI.

the Gallery of the Romanovs); or from the Moorish Dining Room.

In Imperial days, the Rotunda was one of three places from which champagne buffets were served during balls at the Palace. Great blocks of ice held tubs filled with champagne; there were cakes, *petits fours*, fruit, and ices on tables decorated with palms and flowers. Many years later, during the Blockade of Leningrad, it served a very different purpose. Food rations, including of course for the Hermitage staff, were below starvation levels; at their lowest point, they were reduced to a hundred and twenty-five grams (about two slices) of bread a day. People who worked at the Hermitage supplemented their rations with furniture glue (itself made from old bones) and heated the rooms by burning old display screens and the contents of cabinet-makers' workshops. Starvation claimed many more victims than bombardment and some of the cellars of the Small Hermitage were turned into a mortuary. Museum experts began to fear that their specialised knowledge might die with them. So Boris Piotrovskiy (who became Director of the Hermitage Museum) and Andrey Borisov (a distinguished orientalist) decided to solve the problem for their respective directorates by meeting in the Rotunda to give lectures, each on his own particular subject. It was the best chance, they felt, of making sure that their knowledge did not die with them.[4]

The **Moorish Dining Room** (*R. 155, Arápskaya stolóvaya*) lies between the Rotunda and the Malachite Hall and derives its name not from its décor but from the 'Moors' (*Arapy*) who guarded the entrance to the Malachite Hall. They wore turbans; their uniforms were magnificent and their shoes, like the Moor in *Petrushka*, had curly toes. At the time of Nicholas II, one was a Christian Abyssinian and one an American.

---

[4] Geraldine Norman, *The Hermitage: The Biography of a Great Museum* (Jonathan Cape: 1997).

Nicholas II and his family disliked the Winter Palace as a home, considering it pompous and impersonal. They also found the political situation in St Petersburg too tense for comfort. So, in 1904 on the advice of the security services, they decided to take up residence outside the capital and established themselves in the Alexander Palace at Tsarskoye Selo (now Pushkin), some twenty-five kilometres south of the city. Thereafter they paid only occasional visits to the Winter Palace. When they did so, they occupied apartments (*Rs. 176–88*) on the north-west corner of the first floor, beyond Alexander II's apartments, which face on to the Admiralty and the Neva with beautiful views across to *Vasíliyevskiy óstrov*. Some of these rooms now house an exhibition called 'The Artistic Decoration of the Nineteenth-Century Russian Interior', each room arranged with furniture and artefacts appropriate to the style of a decade from the early 1800s until the Revolution and each room suggesting a different function – music room, smoking room, nursery, etc. This exhibition has, apparently, surprised the Museum by its popularity. But there was an earlier precedent for it.

In 1922, these rooms – the private apartments of the last Emperor and his family – were restored, with the aid of photographs, from the state in which the looters had left them in 1917. The number of new Soviet citizens who came to see them grew and grew until the new Soviet authorities, fearing monarchist influences at work, closed them in August 1926. They almost certainly confused the symptoms of curiosity with the symptoms of affection. It is perhaps a shame that some of the other private rooms in the palace, of which only photographs are now extant, were not also put on view. Pictures from the 1920s of Nicholas I's bathroom, for instance, with two wooden chairs and a tin bath six inches deep, and of the camp bed in his stark study-cum-bedroom, are reminiscent of Franz Joseph's iron bedstead in the Hofburg; both say something more interesting than the grander and more opulent rooms about the problems, for certain temperaments, of being an Emperor. The British delegation to the coronation of Nicholas's son, Alexander II, was taken on a conducted tour of the Winter Palace: 'One of the most interesting things we saw was the little bedroom in which Nicholas lived and died. It is an entresol and not bigger than our day nursery; a small wire bedstead without any curtains, a hard wooden chair or two and a wash-hand stand the only furniture; two or three wretched pictures of opera girls, such as you see in the Burlington Arcade, stuck against the walls, and the black hair brushes and dirty tooth brush just as it was when he died.'[5]

Nicholas II's Library (*R. 178*), heavy with late Gothic Revival, used to house one hundred and fifty thousand volumes, collected by him and now dispersed. The core of it was the purchase, in 1908, of the Lobanov-Rostovskiy library and it included some *incunabula* (rare fifteenth-century editions). The Soviet Government sold 757 volumes to the US Library of Congress for $3,131 – not much more than £1.00 each – but most of the collection has been recovered and is now in the National Library in St Petersburg and Moscow.

The last room (*R. 188*) in Nicholas II's suite is known as the **White Dining Room** (*Bélaya stolóvaya*) or the Small Dining Room (*Málaya stolóvaya*). It was the setting for the final act of the last pre-Bolshevik government and has, so they say, been preserved exactly as it appeared at the time. It is the evening of 25 October 1917. The 'Provisional Government' of the so-called 'Socialist Democratic Republic of Russia' (declared such by its Prime Minister, Aleksandr

---

[5] Unpublished letter from Colonel George Ashley Maude to his wife, July 1856. The 'wretched opera girls' on Nicholas's walls were presumably reproductions of portraits of the great ballerinas – such as Taglioni and Istómina – so popular at the time. Maude was the uncle of Tolstoy's first English translator, Aylmer Maude. A few years after this visit, he became Master of the Horse to Queen Victoria.

Kerensky on 1 September) is meeting as usual in the adjacent Malachite Hall. That room, which faces north across the river, comes under fire from the guns of the Peter and Paul Fortress (not, as we have seen, very effective fire but frightening to ministers, nevertheless). The ministers take refuge in the White Dining Room and continue their deliberations, sitting round its white marble table. And there, says the officially accepted version, still sitting round it, they are arrested at precisely 2.10 a.m. on the morning of 26 October by a detachment of Bolshevik troops and taken to the Fortress of SS Peter and Paul. Kerensky, however, was not among them. He had left the capital some hours previously and had made his way to Gatchina on the city's outskirts.

Beyond the White Dining Room begin the **State Rooms**, following on in two 'Enfilades' or suites at right angles to each other. The **Neva Enfilade**, along the north (river) front of the Palace, meets the **Great Enfilade** (*Bolsháya anfiláda*) at the top of the Jordan Staircase in the north-east corner of the Palace. The Great Enfilade ends, as we shall see, in the Palace chapel, known as the Cathedral.

The Neva Enfilade begins with the **Malachite Hall** (*R. 189, Malakhítovy zal*) which, in Kerensky's time (1917), was the Cabinet Room of the Provisional Government. The hall was refashioned after the 1837 fire by Bryullov, who made extensive use of the green malachite (known as 'silken') recently discovered in considerable quantities in the Urals. Pillars and pilasters, as well as standard lamps, the two fireplaces and other furnishings are made from it. To these have been added a collection of other malachite objects of early nineteenth-century Russian workmanship.

For receptions, grand processions and for one, the largest, ball of the year, the Imperial family assembled here as they came out of their private apartments. Only relatives of the Emperor were admitted. Members of the Court used to gather in the adjacent State Rooms, where they waited for the procession. The doors of the Malachite Hall, guarded by the two gigantic, turbaned 'Moors', were flung open; there was a hush and the royal couple were announced. Then the procession passed, in crocodile formation, through the two Enfilades on their way to the Cathedral: Emperor and Dowager Empress at the head, followed by the Empress Consort with the Grand Dukes and Grand Duchesses proceeding behind them, two by two 'like a team of well-trained, well-groomed poodles, to parade in front of a crowd at a fair' as Nicholas's sister, the Grand Duchess Olga, described it. She disliked all official ceremonies.

From the Malachite Hall, they passed into the **Concert Hall** (*R. 190, Kontsértny zal*) which is now hung about with objects by Russian silversmiths from the seventeenth to the early twentieth century. Standing among them, sixteen feet high, is one of the most remarkable silver monuments in the world. Certainly one of the largest.

It consists of two silver *sarcophagi*, an outer and an inner one. The inner sarcophagus was made by Russian craftsmen in 1695 on the orders of Peter the Great as a **reliquary for the remains of St Alexander Nevsky** which, in 1724, were transferred from Vladímir to St Petersburg and placed in the church at the Alexander Nevsky Monastery (*Lávra*). Peter was following in an ancient tradition. Byzantine emperors, many centuries before him, had also found themselves faced with the problem of ruling an Orthodox population, with an ingrained veneration of holy relics, from a new, relic-free purpose-built capital – in their case, Constantinople. They, like Peter, felt it expedient to sanctify the place and bestow on it an antiquity, however artificial. So they brought in relics and distributed them among the city's churches. Peter's choice of Alexander Nevsky to sanctify St Petersburg was particularly fortunate. Not only was he a highly popular saint but his victories on the Neva and in adjacent territories many centuries before the foundation of the city provided a link with Russia's past and gave the new capital some semblance of historical roots.

Winter Palace

Location	What to See	Room Nos.	Earlier use
Ground Floor			
West	Neolithic & Bronze Age Russia	11–14	
	Altaic People & Scythians	15–23	
	Iron Age Eastern Europe	24 & 33	
	Golden Room	42	
	Caucasus, Transcaucasus & Golden Horde	51–66	
North-East Corner	Rastrelli Staircase		As now
East	Egyptian	100	
First Floor			
South-East	German 15/16th century portraits and later paintings	263–268	Catherine the Great's
	French 17th century paintings	275–281	apartments
	Alexander Hall	282	As now
South on Palace Square	French 18th century paintings	284–288	First Reserve
South on Courtyard	French 18th century applied art	290–297	apartments
	White Hall	289	As now
South-West on Courtyard	British paintings	298–300	
South-West on Palace Square/Admiralty	Empress Maria Aleksandrovna's apartments	304–307	As now
West	Russian Culture 17th & 18th centuries (167–177)	157–177	Alexander II's apartments
	Nicholas II's Library	178	As now
North-West	Russian 19th century interiors	179–188	Nicholas II and Empress Alexandra's apartments
North	Malachite Hall	189	As now
	Neva Enfilade	190–192	As now
	Gallery of the Romanovs	151–3	Winter Garden
East	Great Enfilade	193–8	As now
	Western European Porcelain	270–1	Cathedral
Second Floor			
South-East and South	French Impressionists and Post-Impressionists	314–350	Bedrooms of pages and maids of honour
West	Chinese Art	351–364	Princess Yourievskaya's apartments
	Byzantine Art	381–382	
North-West	Persian Art	383–394	Nicholas I's rooms, later used by Alexander III and Kerensky
North	Numismatic Collection	398–400	

In 1746 Peter's daughter, the Empress Elisabeth, commissioned a German painter, Christopher Grooth, to design a second silver sarcophagus of the greatest possible magnificence to contain the relatively modest one. Grooth had only recently settled in Russia. His fantasy required one and a half tons of silver, which Elisabeth's government found difficult to obtain, and took over six years to make. Its pyramidical structure consists of silver sheets stretched over an oak carcass and an attendant array of battle scenes, in high relief, as wells as angels, shields, arms, two great candelabra and, over it all, a crown.

After the Revolution, the double-skinned sarcophagus was moved from the *Lávra* to the Concert Hall in the Winter Palace. And there it still is – but only just. In the late 1920s, the outer casing was to have been melted down and its bullion sold in Western markets to raise hard currency. It was saved, at the last minute, by the astuteness of Sergey Troynitskiy, Director of the Hermitage Department of Applied Art, which had assumed responsibility for the reliquary. Troynitskiy asserted, untruthfully, that the reliquary contained less silver than appeared at first sight and, furthermore, that the country would be deprived of 'an effective tool of anti-religious propaganda'. He did not explain how the monument could serve anti-religious propaganda. But the order to melt it down was rescinded – though other treasures were melted down and disposed of in its stead, including the iconostasis of Kazan Cathedral.[6]

Before the First World War, two or three times a year, in January and February during the 'social season', balls were given in the Concert Hall. But they were more modest (seven hundred guests) than those that took place, if only rarely, in the huge room next door. The **Nicholas** or **Great Hall** (*R. 191*, *Nikoláyevskiy* or *Bolshóy zal*), designed by Stasov, is the largest in the Palace. It was the venue for the first ball of the season which, in Nicholas II's time, was opened by the Emperor and the wife of the doyen of the diplomatic corps to the strains of a polonaise. The Great Hall can accommodate

[6] I have followed Geraldine Norman's account of the Alexander Nevsky reliquary, including her attribution of its design to Grooth rather than to B. Rastrelli, as Troynitskiy would have it. *See* Geraldine Norman, *The Hermitage: The Biography of a Great Museum*, pp. 183–5.

five thousand people in its 1,150 square metres. For the most famous ball of all, on 22 January 1903, two thousand five hundred guests were bidden to appear in the Court dress of their mid-seventeenth-century ancestors. It was a memorable social occasion (repeated shortly afterwards in the Sheremetev mansion on the Fontanka). It was also the last. The Russo-Japanese war, the 1905 Revolution, the political turmoil that preceded the First World War and the war itself made festive life at Court no longer appropriate.

One important – and, as it turned out, fateful – event took place in the Great Hall in the early days of Nicholas II's reign. In January 1895, the new sovereign received there a delegation from the Province of Tver which had come to offer congratulations on his marriage. Into their Loyal Address they had slipped a reference to the desirability of some form of constitutional government. The Emperor seems at first to have raised no objections. But, by the time he came to deliver his official reply, he spoke of the 'senseless dreams' of those who favoured a constitution and of his own unswerving adherence to the principles of autocracy. Eleven years later, on 27 April 1906, the 'senseless dreams' became reality. In another room of the Palace, the **Hall of St George**, he was obliged to read an address of welcome to the assembled members of the Lower House (the State *Dúma*) of the newly instituted Russian Parliament.

Nowadays, the Great Hall and the rooms on each side of it are used for temporary exhibitions, including those of distinguished collections on loan from foreign countries.

So, on ceremonial occasions, the Imperial procession moved on towards the Cathedral, through the **Fore Hall** (*R. 192, Avanzál*), across the top of the Jordan Staircase and turning right (south) into the first room of the Great Enfilade. This is the **Field Marshal's Hall** (*R. 193, Feldmárshalskiy zal*) where the Cossack Lifeguards would be on duty and where the Emperor would be greeted by the city mayors and by the merchants of the First Guild. The original, designed by Montferrand, perished in the flames of 1837, along with the portraits of Russian field-marshals which adorned it and from which it got its name. It was restored by Stasov, on similar lines but without the portraits.

The next room is **Peter the Great's Throne Room** (*R. 194, Petróvskiy Trónny zal*, also sometimes called the Lesser – *Mály* – Throne Room), again by Montferrand, restored by Stasov. Stasov kept as close as he could to the original decoration, with its lavish use of silver, its dark red silver-embroidered velvet wall coverings, silver tables of Danish eighteenth-century workmanship and silver chandeliers. An oak and silver-gilt throne, made in London in 1731 by Nicholas Clausen, stands in a niche on a platform. Over the throne hangs the portrait by the Venetian painter Jacopo Amigoni of 'Peter the Great accompanied by the Goddess of Glory'. An extra touch of silver was added after the Second World War, when a silver candelabrum was substituted for its bronze predecessor; this had crashed to the floor when a bomb exploded in the Armorial Hall next door.

The **Armorial Hall** (*R. 195, Gerbóvy zal*), designed by Stasov, has an eventful history of which the German bomb was only the last instalment. With an area of over a thousand square metres, it is the second largest room in the Palace. It derives its name from the shields, displaying the coats-of-arms of the provinces of Russia, which are attached to the bronze candelabrum. Paired Corinthian columns in white and gold support a gallery which encircles the room.

On the death of Catherine the Great in 1796, her son, the Emperor Paul, decided to avenge the death of his putative father, Peter III, who was murdered thirty-four years before. He caused Peter III's coffin to be brought from the Alexander Nevsky *Lávra* and placed in the Armorial Hall for a belated and gruesome lying-in-state. The coffin was opened but, as the body had not been embalmed, all that was visible were some bones and the sleeve of a uniform. The Imperial crown had been brought from Moscow and the terrified courtiers were required to perform the ceremony of obeisance. Then Peter's surviving murderer, Count Aleksey Orlov, was ordered to pick up the crown and carry it on a gold cloth at the head of a procession which bore his victim's remains to the Cathedral in the Peter and Paul Fortress. There they were re-interred in a tomb next to Catherine, his widow, whose ambitions had cost him his throne and his life and by whom he now rests in perpetuity. The new Emperor, his family and the entire court followed the coffin on foot across the frozen Neva to the Fortress in bitter cold.[7]

During the First World War, the Armorial Hall was stripped of most of its decorations and transformed into a ward for wounded soldiers. Now it is entirely devoted to eighteenth-century military themes: paintings of battle scenes by A. Kotzebue, regimental standards and flags, uniforms of Peter the Great and Field Marshal Suvorov and the like.

The **Picket Hall** (*R. 196*, *Pikétny zal*) was where the lesser Court officials, accompanied by their wives, greeted the Imperial family on ceremonial occasions as they proceeded to the Cathedral. Guard duties in this hall were, at such times, carried out by the Grenadiers. Now the hall is filled with exhibits relating to the 1812 campaign against Napoleon on Russian soil: the personal belongings of Field Marshal Kutuzov; Napoleon's personal weapons; swords and uniforms abandoned by Napoleon's marshals and captured in Russia; Russian weapons and army uniforms.

The procession would then turn into the **Cathedral** (*R. 271 – sobór*), which was damaged comparatively little by the 1837 fire and retains most of Rastrelli's Baroque ebullience. Now de-sanctified, it contains a display of Western European porcelain. Before the Revolution, it contained a number of relics greatly venerated by Orthodox believers

---

[7] The story is to be found in various sources. But a convincing description of it is by Madame Vigée le Brun who watched the procession from her window. She is quoted by Suzanne Massie in *Pavlovsk* (Hodder and Stoughton by arrangement with Little Brown & Company: 1990).

though, it has to be said, of Roman Catholic provenance: the left arm of the Holy Martyr St Marina and the right arm of St John the Baptist, both in a golden casket; and a Florentine icon of the Virgin reputedly painted by St Luke, the Evangelist. The icon and St John's right arm were presented to the Emperor Paul by the Knights of Malta when he became their Grand Master in 1798 (although he was married and Orthodox and not, as their statutes demanded, a bachelor and Roman Catholic).

The Emperor and Empress went into the church, followed by the Grand Dukes and Duchesses, the high dignitaries and the Mistresses of the Robes. The rest of the procession remained in order in the adjoining rooms. 'This', according to the last head of the Court Chancellery, 'was the most delicate moment for the Masters of Ceremonies, for they were supposed to repress every attempt to speak aloud or to smoke.' This last temptation appeared to be the greatest, even with the Grand Dukes who had a tendency to slip 'quietly out of church, knowing where they would find certain back staircases which made improvised smoking-rooms during divine service . . . The Masters of Ceremonies took care not to go near these "smoking rooms" or the main conservatory of the Palace, where the old generals obstinately went to smoke, in spite of all orders.'[8]

Before you reach these 'improvised smoking-rooms', which were probably where we started this tour in Catherine's apartments, there are two more State Rooms. The **Gallery of 1812** (*R. 197, Galeréya 1812-vo góda*) is a long, narrow room which flanks the Armorial Hall, entirely devoted to portraits of the military leaders who defeated Napoleon in 1812 and drove him out of Russia – three hundred and thirty of them, all painted by the British artist, George Dawe, who had previously painted the portraits of

---

[8] *Memoirs of A. A. Mossolov: At the Court of the Last Tsar* (Methuen and Co.: 1996). Edition of 250 copies.

British generals at the Battle of Waterloo. The Gallery is dominated by three equestrian portraits – of the Russian Emperor, Alexander I, and of King Frederick William of Prussia (both by Franz Kruger) and of Emperor Francis I of Austria by Peter Kraft. Here, in the reign of Nicholas II, another champagne buffet used to be served, complementing the facilities in the Rotunda and the Fore Hall.

The Gallery of 1812 opens into the **Hall of St George** (*R. 198, Geórgievskiy zal*). The third largest room in the Palace, with an area of eight hundred square metres, it is also perhaps the most magnificent, being originally designed by Quarenghi for Catherine the Great and opened, shortly before her death, on St George's Day, 1795. At the far end stands the Imperial Throne which was used for great occasions of state such as the reception of the Diplomatic Corps and other distinguished guests. It was here, in April 1906, that Nicholas II read his address of welcome to the newly-elected members of the *Dúma*. Here, also, on 20 July 1914, he read out the Manifesto declaring war on Germany which, in four years almost to the day, resulted in the death of himself and his family and brought his dynasty to an end. In the process, the Palace lost its identity as the centre of Imperial power and became a museum.

After the Revolution, the throne was moved into the Lesser (Peter's) Throne Room and replaced by a vast mosaic map of the USSR, twenty-seven metres square and made of precious stones: rubies to mark the frontiers of the fifteen constituent republics, rubies again to spell out the name 'Moscow', rubies making up the Soviet Union flag which marked the position of the North Pole, ruby stars to pin-point the location of every republican capital, emeralds to spell out their names, diamonds for the Hammer and Sickle. In the 1970s, the rubies and the emeralds and the diamonds were dismantled and found a new home in the Museum of the Mining Institute on *Vasíliyevskiy óstrov*. The throne returned in the 1990s.

So we come back to Catherine the Great's apartments on the south-east corner. From here, you can either take a modest wooden staircase (next to *R. 269*) to the second floor or cross into the Small Hermitage by *R. 272*. We will stay in the Winter Palace and go up to **the southern wing of the second floor** (*Rs. 314–50*), where works by nineteenth- and twentieth-century West European and American artists are displayed in rooms that have been temporarily constructed for the purpose, within the attics of the Palace. The most distinguished works on show here were collected by two great industrialists, **Sergey Stchukin** and **Ivan Morozov**.

Collecting assumed American proportions among Russia's new tycoons. What distinguished them from Western collectors was a complete confidence in their own taste and a refusal, therefore, to work through agents, dealers or other 'experts'. They were guided entirely by their personal appreciation, without regard for present or potential value, and by the desire, as patrons of the arts, to develop collections which would eventually become the nuclei for public museums. Turn-of-the-century Russian taste, encouraged by Diaghilev and the *World of Art*[9] movement, inevitably inclined them towards contemporary French Art.

Stchukin, who began to collect French paintings in 1890, was an extremely early patron (to the tune of twenty-nine paintings) of Matisse, who visited him in Moscow (*Rs. 343–5*), and of Gauguin (*R. 316*) and Picasso (*Rs. 346–7*). It is characteristic of Stchukin that, at a time

[9] The *World of Art* movement was led by Sergey Diaghilev from the editorial chair of a magazine called *Mir Iskússtva* (*World of Art*), with the participation of many of the leading artists and art critics of the day (such as Benois, Bakst, Dobuzhinskiy, Lanceré, Somov and Kurbatov). It began in the 1890s and ended, with the final closure of the magazine, and the departure of many of its members for Europe, in 1924. At the start, the main influences on it were the European Symbolists and turn-of-the-century Romanticism which led its practitioners into a renewed interest in Old Petersburg. There were almost annual exhibitions of art in various locations and, towards the end, the *Ballets Russes*.

when Picasso had few admirers in the West, he could state with absolute conviction that 'this is the future'[10] and go on collecting Picassos – from his Blue, from his Rose and from his Cubist periods. Morozov, a much younger man, was to some extent influenced by Stchukin but also showed independence of judgment. He started by collecting contemporary Russian artists, among them Marc Chagall who was totally unknown at the time and unable to find buyers. After assembling some four hundred Russian canvasses, he moved on to French Impressionists and post-Impressionists including, particularly, Cézanne (*R. 318*). The importance of his Cézanne collection lies not so much in the number of canvasses as in their quality and in the fact that they represent practically all his different styles. In this sense, Morozov's collection was unique. When you are on the second floor of the Winter Palace, it is sobering to realise that you are looking at only half the Stchukin–Morozov collection. The other half has remained in Moscow.

Both men emigrated after 1917 and their collections were 'nationalised'. (Stchukin, who lived in Paris until he died in 1937, commented that, as it had always been his intention to bequeath his collection to the nation, the Soviet Government was merely giving effect to his own plans.) The pictures were placed, initially, in a Museum of Modern Western Art in Moscow (which became the Pushkin Museum of Fine Arts). In 1948, the combined collection was split between Moscow and Leningrad. Now there is another move afoot – across the square to the General Staff building where it is intended that purpose-built galleries, comparable to those already provided for Bonnard and Denis, will be created to house them. The Hermitage collection of French paintings as a whole is one of the largest and finest in the world, with over fifteen hundred

---

[10] B. W. Kean, *All the Empty Palaces: The Merchant Patrons of Modern Art in pre-Revolutionary Russia* (Barrie & Jenkins: London, 1983), p. 203.

pictures by French masters, of which seven hundred belong to the seventeenth and eighteenth centuries, and over eight hundred to the nineteenth and twentieth.

Also on this, second floor, along the west wing, is now to be found Chinese Art from the sixth to the eighteenth centuries (*Rs. 351–64*), the Culture and Art of Byzantium (*Rs. 381–2*) and the Culture and Art of Persia (*Rs. 383–94* in the north-west corner).

But it was not always thus. In the nineteenth century Nicholas I, his son Alexander II, and his grandson Alexander III all had a presence on the second floor, which was otherwise occupied by pages and maids of honour, in waiting at Court. Nicholas's suite was in the north-west corner. Alexander III had his suite in the same area whenever he stayed at the Winter Palace but he and his wife preferred the Anichkov Palace where they had lived during his father's reign and to which, and to Gatchina, he returned whenever he could. In 1917, Kerensky moved himself into Alexander III's rooms and chose to sleep in his bed.

Alexander II's connection with the second floor was more touching and more tragic. He installed his beautiful mistress, Princess Yekaterina Dolgorukaya, and their children in apartments centring on what is now *Room 359*. Her bedroom was next to the lift which descended to his own official apartments on the floor below, between *Rs. 174* and *176*. The ailing and neglected Empress used to complain to her friends that she was not so much disturbed by the noise made by the Dolgorukiy children overhead as she was hurt and annoyed by this constant reminder of her husband's double family life. When the Empress died in 1880, Alexander – as he had promised – immediately married his mistress, thus legitimising his second family. But he was assassinated eight months later on 1 March 1881. Princess Yekaterina Yourievskaya, as she became after her marriage, survived her husband for over forty years, dying in France at the age of seventy-five as a refugee from the Soviet Union.

Her great-grandson and only direct descendant in the male line, Hans-Georg, runs a software company in Europe. For the brief period of his stay in the Winter Palace, Kerensky installed his adjutants in her apartments.

So far, we have ignored the Museum displays on the **ground floor of the Winter Palace**. If, at the main entrance, you turn right and not (as we did) left, you will find yourself in rather empty and magical rooms reserved for the early civilisations of Russia and Eastern Europe, of the Russian Far East, Central Asia, the Caucasus and the Golden Horde, the Altaic peoples and Scythians. There is to be found a sixth-century BC Scythian stag (*R. 22*) and, in the same area, a fourth-century BC pile carpet, the oldest in the world and utterly desirable, discovered at perma-frost level underneath a burial mound in the Altai mountains. Hard to miss is the huge two-ton bronze cauldron with an eight foot diameter, made for Tamerlane in AD 1399 in the city of Turkestan (*R. 48*). If, on the other hand, you turn right but skirt the Jordan Staircase, you will enter the Department of Oriental Culture and Art, starting with Egyptian Antiquities of which the earliest dates from 4000 BC. The **Hall of Ancient Egypt** (*R. 100*) is the ground floor link into the Small Hermitage.

As so much else, the first so-called 'Hermitage' in Russia was built by Peter the Great in imitation of a fashion then in vogue in Western European royal and aristocratic circles. The purpose of these 'hermitages' – in theory, at least – was to give their owners the opportunity to entertain guests with less formality and in simpler dress than etiquette demanded for receptions in great palaces. They were set in the parks of country estates to give the illusion of rustic isolation. Peter's tiny 'Hermitage' – a pavilion eleven metres high – was erected for him in the park of Peterhof, which was being built a few miles west of St Petersburg. Some twenty years later his daughter, Empress Elisabeth, followed suit and had her 'Hermitage' built in the park of Tsarskoye Selo, a few miles to the south. Considerably

Hermitage

Location	What to See	Room Nos.
Ground Floor – Small Hermitage		
	Egyptian Antiquities	100
	Roman Antiquities	101–2
Ground Floor – Large Hermitage		
West (southwards)	Roman Antiquities	106–9, 127–9
West (northwards)	Etruscan Antiquities	130–1
North-west corner	Council Staircase	
South-east	Greek Antiquities	110–14
	Archaic and Early Classical Vases	111
Centre	Black Sea Coast Antiquities	115–17
First Floor – Small Hermitage		
	Corridor from apartments of Catherine II	272
South end, west wing	Netherlands	258, 261–2
West wing (northwards)	Western European Applied Art	259
North end	Pavilion Hall	204
Centre	Hanging Garden	
First Floor – Large Hermitage		
South wing	Flanders	245–48
West wing	Holland	249–54
West – Centre	Spain	239–40
Centre, east on courtyard and north	Italy (Early)	207–24
	Italy 16th–18th centuries	229–38
East wing on Winter Ditch	Loggia of Raphaël	226–28
Bridge over Winter Ditch		225
Hermitage Theatre	Interior of theatre	
East of Winter Ditch	Remains of Peter I's Winter Palace	

larger than her father's, it was nevertheless a relatively modest structure.

It was only natural for Catherine to follow in her predecessors' footsteps but she did it with a difference. Her 'Hermitage' (which did not immediately acquire that incongruous name) was to be built not in a secluded spot but in the heart of the capital as part of the main Imperial residence. The entertainment of her guests was kept well in mind, of course, but the immediate purpose was to display the pictures she already possessed and those she was intending to acquire – instead of them being enjoyed, as she said, 'only by mice and me'. In 1764, she entrusted the task to J.-B. Vallin de la Mothe, only recently arrived in Russia, and to Yuri Felten, who, though well trained, had little practical experience. These two architects took three years to create the long and relatively narrow building that adjoins the east wing of the Winter Palace and is known as the **Small Hermitage** (*Mály Ermitázh*). In Catherine's time, the only entrance to it was through the long corridor (now *Rs. 272* and *258*) from the Empress's private apartments.

At the door, she appended ten Rules, still to be found there, demanding informal behaviour of all her guests:

One
On entering, titles and rank as well as hat &, especially, sword will be left behind.
Two
Pretensions based on prerogatives of birth, pride & other similar sentiments will also have to remain outside.
Three
Be cheerful, but do not break or spoil anything.
Four
Sit down, remain standing, walk about, do whatever you please without paying attention to anyone.
Five
Talk with moderation & not too much so as not to bother others.
Six
Argue without anger or rancour.
Seven
Banish sighs and yawns so as not to bore or be a drag on anyone.
Eight
Innocent games suggested by one of the guests must be accepted.
Nine
Eat quietly and with appetite; drink with moderation so that you find your legs on leaving.
Ten
Leave all quarrels behind on entering. What goes in one ear must go out of the other before you cross the threshold.

There were penalties for infringement, too, likewise devised by Catherine. The severest was reserved for failure to observe Rule Ten: the culprit was never to be invited again. The others, in descending order of severity, were: learning by heart six lines of Tredyakovskiy's exceedingly dull poem *Telemachus*, reading aloud a page of the same poem or, the lightest of punishments, drinking a glass of cold water. Catherine strictly followed her own rules, particularly Rules One and Two, and had no place reserved for her at table if supper was served. Any of the guests could find themselves sitting next to her. People seem to have enjoyed themselves at her Hermitage parties. She found my great-great-grandfather, Vasiliy Zinoviev, so amusing that – so she said – his conversation would one day make her die from laughing.

Catherine's enthusiasm for collecting soon outgrew the capacity of her Hermitage and a new building, connected to the Small Hermitage, was commissioned (Felten, 1771–87) later referred to as the **Old Hermitage** (*Stáry Ermitázh*). Felten was assisted by G. Quarenghi, who added a gallery along the eastern wall to run alongside the Winter Ditch (*Zímnyaya kanávka*). Known as the **Loggia of Raphael** (*Lódzhii Rafaélya*), it is a fairly faithful reproduction, by the lax standards of the time, of Bramante's gallery built in the Vatican at the beginning of the sixteenth century with murals by Raphael's pupils, executed under his supervision. These murals were copied (1778–86) for Quarenghi on to canvas by a group of artists working under the Austrian painter Christopher Unterberger.

The interiors of Felten and Quarenghi, though not the Loggia, were radically altered by Stackenschneider in the 1850s and there is practically nothing left of them now. They were, perhaps, more akin to private, if extremely grand, drawing and reception rooms rather than rooms in a picture gallery, thus emphasising their original purpose. And, indeed, receptions and Court festivities continued to be held in the Hermitage throughout most of the nineteenth century.

Catherine's successors continued to collect with the result that, by the mid-nineteenth century, the Imperial collection again outgrew its premises (part of which, in any case, began to be used for other institutions. In the late 1820s, Nicholas I assigned rooms on the ground floor of the Old Hermitage to the State Council and the Committee of Ministers, which later gave Stackenschneider the excuse for inserting the white Council Staircase in the north-west corner. Their sessions continued to be held there until 1885.) So, in 1839, the distinguished German architect, Leo von Klenze, who had created the Glyptothek and Pinakothek art galleries in Munich, was invited to design yet another building. Klenze provided the designs but did not come to Russia himself and the New Hermitage was erected by Stasov and N. Yefimov, back to back on the south side of the Old Hermitage, the whole becoming the **Large Hermitage** (*Bolshóy Ermitázh*). The most admired feature of the New Hermitage is the entrance porch on *Milliónnaya úlitsa*, supported by ten muscular atlantes of grey granite by Aleksandr Terebenyov who, unfortunately, drank himself to death a few years later.

The **New Hermitage** was the first purpose-built Russian art gallery. Nevertheless, for twelve years after its official opening (1852), the rule requiring visitors to be 'properly dressed' (morning coat or uniform for men) was still rigorously enforced, except for artists coming to study or copy works of art. The abolition of the 'dress' rule in 1864, and of the requirement that visitors must apply for authorisation from the Winter Palace, led to immediate popularity. By the First World War, there were 160,000 visitors a year. Not the present-day millions but a lot for those days. The number of paintings on show has now reached some fifteen thousand; of sculptures, twelve thousand; of prints and drawings six hundred thousand.

A few of these things had been collected by Peter the Great and a few by his daughter, Elisabeth. But nothing systematic was undertaken until Catherine began her collection in 1764 with the acquisition of two hundred and twenty-five pictures put together by the Berlin dealer, Johann-Ernst Gotzkowski for Frederick the Great of Prussia which Frederick, in financial difficulties, was unable to pay for.[11] They were mainly of Flemish and Dutch masters and included Franz Hals's *Portrait of a Young Man Holding a Glove* and two magnificent Rembrandts, *A Polish Nobleman* and *Joseph accused by Potiphar's Wife*, which, two centuries later, the Soviet Government sold to Andrew Mellon. The Gotzkowski acquisition was soon followed by purchases in Brussels of the collections of Count Karl von Cobenzl and the Prince de Ligne; then there was the even more prestigious collection belonging to the heirs of Saxony's spendthrift Chancellor, Count Heinrich von Brühl.

This wholesale purchase of private collections continued into the 1770s. In 1772, Catherine acquired eleven paintings from the Duc de Choiseul and the entire collection of **Louis-Antoine Crozat**. The latter was the richest in France after that of the Duc d'Orléans and included masterpieces from almost every school – not only several Rembrandts but also some of the great painters of the Italian Renaissance: Giorgione (*R. 217*), Raphael (*R. 229*), Titian (*R. 221*), Veronese (*R. 222*), never before seen in Russia. (Some of these were also sold to Mellon.) The Crozat sale raised a storm in France, mainly directed against Diderot who, as one of Catherine's artistic advisers, had negotiated it. He was judged to have humiliated France. For Russia, on the other hand, it was a hugely successful deal which laid the

[11] This must have given her a wry pleasure for it was Frederick the Great who misguidedly suggested to the Empress Elisabeth that the fifteen-year-old Catherine might be a suitable bride for Elisabeth's nephew and heir, Peter.

foundation of the Hermitage's great collection of seven-teenth- and eighteenth-century French paintings.

In 1779, the Russian ambassador to George III bought on Catherine's behalf a substantial part of **Sir Robert Walpole's famous collection**, including a dozen Van Dycks, from Walpole's grandson, the third Earl of Orford, at a bargain price of £40,000 for 204 pictures. The English reaction was no more favourable than that of the French to the Crozat sale. The *European Magazine* of the time described 'the removal of the Houghton Collection of pictures to Russia' as 'perhaps one of the most striking instances that can be produced of the decline of the empire of Great Britain, and the advancement of that of our powerful ally in the north'.

The ambassador was proud of his coup but Catherine judged otherwise. She decided that a low price could only mean low quality and, when the Van Dycks arrived in St Petersburg, she never bothered to have them unpacked. What Lord Orford thought about it is uncertain. He named his next greyhound bitch 'Czarina', whether in token of his pleasure at the sale or by way of reference to the Royal purchaser's morals was never clearly established. (In the autumn of 2002, the Hermitage sent the Walpole Collection, on loan, back to the United Kingdom in an exhibition sup-ported by the Open Russia Foundation entitled 'Painting, Passion and Politics'.)

The last of the large-scale eighteenth-century purchases took place in 1783, when Catherine acquired the collection of the Comte de Baudouin. This she supplemented by com-missioning new paintings from artists such as Boucher (*R. 285*) and Chardin (*R. 287*). She likewise commissioned a painting from Sir Joshua Reynolds who showed himself to be a consummate flatterer by producing *The Infant Hercules strangling the Serpents* (now in *R. 199*). It symbolised – so he said – the growing might of Russia, youngest of European empires and yet so obviously increasing in strength that she needed no assistance to strangle her enemies.

Catherine's interest was not limited to paintings. She acquired numerous engravings and she fully shared the eighteenth-century passion for jewellery and precious stones. The stones were given, as was the custom of all European courts of the time, usually set in rings or encrusted in snuff boxes, to artists in token of Royal admiration; they were showered on Royal favourites (Potemkin's hat, on one occasion, being studded with so many diamonds that he found it too heavy to wear and had it carried behind him by an attendant); they adorned civil and military decorations and the miniature portraits of the Sovereign which were allowed to be worn as a mark of particular Royal esteem.

In the nineteenth century, the pace of Russian Imperial acquisitions slackened but Alexander I's purchase of several paintings from Empress Josephine's Malmaison collection must be mentioned, if only because a few more Rembrandts were thereby added. Nicholas I was able to introduce some Spanish masters by acquiring several paintings from the collection of the Dutch banker Coesvelt. This last also included the so-called 'Alba' *Madonna* by Raphael, formerly the property of the Spanish Duke of Alba. Nicholas paid the equivalent of £14,000 for it – a record price at the time. (A century later it was sold for another record – US$ 1,700,000 – to Andrew Mellon.)

Purchases of individual paintings continued throughout the nineteenth century and included such important works as Leonardo da Vinci's *Madonna and Child* (the *Madonna 'Litta'*, now in R. 214) and Raphael's *Madonna and Child*, known as the 'Conestabile' *Madonna* from the name of its former owner. The acquisition of entire collections took place more rarely but there were two which were particularly important: the collection of the Palazzo Barbarigo in Venice; and, in 1861, the collection of Classical antiquities of the Marchese Campana. Campana had ruined himself by his passion for collecting and was saved by the Russian purchase, in the nick of time, from twenty years hard labour to which the Papal authorities had sentenced him. The Russians, too, were delighted. Through this purchase, they felt, the museum acquired a European significance.

In the twentieth century, the Imperial collection in the Hermitage was greatly enriched on at least four occasions. The first dates back to not long before the First World War when the Semyonov-Tyanshanskiy collection of Flemish and Dutch masters was added to it. The second came about after the 1917 Revolution, not this time by purchase but by the transfer of paintings (many of which were subsequently sold to America) from the private galleries of the Yusupov, Stroganov, Shuvalov, Naryshkin and other aristocratic families into public ownership. The third occasion, at the same time and by the same method, was the 'nationalisation' of the paintings assembled by the two great industrialists, Stchukin and Morozov (Winter Palace *Rs. 314–50*). The fourth occasion occurred as a result of the Second World War. In 1995, the art world was startled by the Hermitage announcement that for the last fifty years it had kept hidden a very considerable collection of paintings, drawings and pastels (a total of 98 items) mainly by French Impressionists and post-Impressionists. Long reputed to have been lost or destroyed during the war, they had in fact been requisitioned by the Soviet military authorities in Germany in 1945 and taken to the USSR. The haul included works of the highest quality by such masters as Cézanne, Courbet, Daumier, Degas, Gauguin, Manet, Matisse, Monet, Picasso, van Gogh and Toulouse-Lautrec. Most of them had belonged to a German industrialist, Otto Krebbs, who died in 1941. They are intermittently exhibited at the Hermitage though the Krebbs family have claimed them back and their future is still undecided.

The twentieth century, however, conspired to rob the Hermitage of more than it acquired in the course of it, certainly in terms of quality. The economic collapse that followed the Revolution had disastrous results for Russia's capital assets, including, of course, its art treasures. Stringent measures were taken to conceal from the public the sales, to Western buyers for hard currency, of pictures, jewellery, porcelain and antiques of various kinds from national collections (mainly in Petrograd-Leningrad). The sales began at the end of 1918. Ten years later, the trickle became a flood. Among collectors, the main purchasers were the (then) U.S. Secretary to the Treasury, **Andrew Mellon** and the oil magnate, **Calouste Gulbenkian**. Between them, they managed to obtain ten Rembrandts (still leaving the Hermitage with twenty-six including *Flora* in *R. 254*), ten Van Dycks, four Rubens and a lesser number of paintings by Raphael (including *St George and the Dragon*), Jan Van Eyck, Titian, Botticelli, Veronese (*The Finding of Moses*) and many other artists, as well as antique (mainly French eighteenth-century) furniture, sculpture, gold and silver articles – and more.

The Mellon purchases, all of them made between April 1930 and April 1931, consisted of twenty-one paintings which laid the foundation of the Metropolitan Museum of Art in New York. With the exception of the 'Alba' *Madonna*, the prices paid were not high – not high enough, as Gulbenkian himself warned the Soviet authorities 'to produce large enough sums [significantly] to help the finances of the State'. The world-wide economic depression was taking its toll of rich men's fortunes and, when the Soviet Government offered for sale both its remaining Leonardos, one of the two canvases believed to be by Giorgione and a great many French Impressionsists from the Stchukin-Morozov collections, it set the price too high for the market. So these paintings remained in the Soviet Union and, happily, in the Hermitage.

Though the sales were by the Government, and therefore official, it was decided that the public should not know of them. So paintings and other, more awkward, objects, had sometimes to be smuggled out of the Hermitage at dead of night. A curator, Tatiana Chernyavina, remembers being ordered, one day in 1930, to stay in the museum after the other members of staff had gone. She was then to detach Jan Van Eyck's *Annunciation* (a Mellon purchase) from the wall, re-hang the remaining paintings to conceal the gap and deliver the Van Eyck that same night to a member of the Soviet Foreign Office. Only at the end of the 1980s was the embargo on the story of these sales partially lifted and the press allowed to mention them. According to Geraldine Norman, the losses sustained by the Hermitage were so great that they nearly destroyed it. In her view, they demoted it from being 'the greatest collection in the world' to being 'one of the greatest'.

Ten years later, the German invasion brought with it an even more formidable threat: the rapid advance of the Germans towards Leningrad made it essential to evacuate as many of the Hermitage treasures as possible in the shortest possible time if they were to be saved from looting or destruction. The staff was mobilised to strip the shelves, the walls, the show-cases and the floor stacks and to pack the exhibits into crates for shipment by train beyond enemy reach. The chosen destination was Sverdlovsk (now again Yekaterinburg) in Siberia beyond the Urals. Large pictures were taken out of their frames and off their stretchers, to be wrapped round special rollers; smaller ones were left on their stretchers (and three – Leonardo's 'Benois' *Madonna* and the *Madonna* 'Litta', as well as Raphael's 'Conestabile' *Madonna* – were not even taken out of their frames). Packers were allowed two hours sleep in every twenty-four and managed, in surprisingly few days, to fit 1,118,000 objects (about half the total) into 2,254 crates which went to Sverdlovsk in two train loads.

But only just in time. A third train was waiting for more crates when, on 30 August 1941, the evacuation had to stop. The German army had reached the suburbs of Leningrad and was less than eleven miles from Palace Square. The rail-way no longer connected the city with the rest of the country. Thirty-one crates with their precious cargo remained piled in the main entrance to the Winter Palace, to be stored eventually with the remaining exhibits in the various cellars and bomb shelters of the Palace until the end of the war.

Curiously enough, by sending the crates to Sverdlovsk, the Soviet authorities unwittingly restored the link between the Hermitage collection and the Russian Imperial family. One of the three buildings in Sverdlovsk to which the crates were distributed was the Ipatiev House which, in 1918, had been confiscated by the local authorities and designated 'House of Special Purpose'. The 'purpose' was the internment of Nicholas II, his wife, children, doctor, and a few of his servants. There they stayed for a few months until, at about two o'clock in the morning of 17 July 1918, they were all shot in the cellar.

The Hermitage treasures all came back to Leningrad in October 1945 without, so it is said, having suffered any damage, on the journey out, on the journey back or while they were in storage. Less than four weeks later, by 4 November, a sufficient number of rooms in the Hermitage had had their pictures re-hung and other exhibits restored to them for a group of selected guests to be invited to view them and for the Director of the Museum to end his speech of welcome with the words: 'The Hermitage is open'.[12]

But it was a somewhat different Hermitage from the one which had closed four years previously. Just before the war ended, a decree of the Leningrad Soviet dated 6 January 1945 placed the Winter Palace under the jurisdiction of the Hermitage, whose annexe it became. It thus reversed the original roles. Nearly two hundred years before, the Palace had created the Hermitage and made it part of itself. Now the Palace had become part of the Hermitage.

[12] S. Varshavskiy and B. Rest, *Pódvig Ermitázha* (Leningrad, 1969).

'At the end of the Palace', wrote the Comte de Ségur, French Ambassador to Catherine's Court, 'is a beautiful theatre, a reproduction in miniature of the ancient theatre in Vicenza. It is semi-circular in shape: it has no boxes but rising tiers of seats arranged to form an amphitheatre.' The **Hermitage Theatre** (*Ermitázhny teátr*) was built by Quarenghi (1783–7) on the site of Peter the Great's third Winter Palace on the far (east) bank of the Winter Ditch. It was Catherine II's private theatre to which there was no access except through her second (later called 'Old') Hermitage which was connected to the theatre by a gallery over a hump-backed bridge – reminiscent of the Bridge of Sighs in Venice. It is modest in size, designed to seat a maximum of four hundred spectators. Statues of Apollo and the Nine Muses stand in niches, flanked by marble Corinthian columns which march round the auditorium. Quarenghi, with justifiable pride, thought it his finest architectural achievement.

So keen was Catherine to see her theatre in action that she invited friends to a performance in November 1785, before the place was finished. They were treated to the (then and, indeed, later immensely popular in Russia) Russian opera *The Miller: Sorcerer, Cheat and Matchmaker*, music by M. Sokolovskiy (not Fomin, to whom it is sometimes attributed), libretto by A. Ablesimov. The official opening, when finishing touches were still being made, took place almost a year later on 17 September 1786 with Giuseppe Sarti's opera *Castor e Polluce*.

Catherine's enthusiasm for her theatre never waned and she had plays – some of which she wrote herself with her secretary's help – performed in it 'almost daily', according to Ségur. 'Twice a month', he adds, 'the Empress invites the diplomatic corps and persons privileged to have access to the Court. At other times, the audience is limited to no more than a dozen.'

Towards the end of the nineteenth and in the early twentieth centuries, the theatre was no longer used exclusively by the Imperial family and its friends, though it remained the private property of the Sovereign. In 1909, the Grand Duke Vladímir Aleksandrovich made it possible for Diaghilev's touring version of *Borís Godunóv*, which was to take Paris by storm with Chaliapin in the title role, to rehearse in the Hermitage Theatre. The following year, it was planned to use the theatre as the base for the *Ballets Russes* when they were preparing for their first expedition to Western Europe. But, just as rehearsals began, the Grand Duke died and the company had to move to the Catherine Hall on the Griboyedov Canal.

Just before the curtain came down on the last of Catherine's successors, the theatre witnessed for a brief moment the revival of a custom dear to Catherine's heart. To celebrate the hundred and fiftieth anniversary of its foundation, in 1914, it was decided to perform a play by the Emperor's cousin, the poet Grand Duke Konstantin. The play was called *The King of the Jews* and, because it dealt with the life and death of Christ, the Synod of the Russian Orthodox Church had objected to its performance in a public theatre. The Emperor objected, too, on the grounds that it might lead to a wave of anti-semitic pogroms but suggested that it might be privately performed in the so-called Chinese Theatre in Tsarskoye Selo. The idea of a private performance was adopted but the Hermitage, not the Chinese, Theatre was chosen. So, as in Catherine's time, the performance was attended only by the Imperial family and their guests and, as in her time, supper was afterwards served in the Hermitage itself. By all accounts, it was a highly successful party – and the last of its kind.

For the next three-quarters of a century, the theatre was no longer a centre of special occasions and became a lecture hall for students of dramatic art. Then suddenly, seventy-seven years after the *King of the Jews*, it came to life again. In 1991, the Kirov ballet company inaugurated its restoration as a working theatre with a performance of music and dance for foreign (mainly British) tourists, followed by sandwiches and tea or coffee in paper cups.

VII

Nevsky Prospect

Metro Stations: *Névskiy Prospékt / Gostíny Dvor* and
Plóstchad Vosstániya / Mayakóvskaya

LIKE A SPINAL CORD *Névskiy prospékt* runs through
the body of St Petersburg. But it was first conceived
simply as a road along which essential materials could pass
from the Russian interior to the shipyard on the Neva
where Peter the Great was building his new Baltic fleet.

Begun in 1712, as the **Great Perspective Road**, it runs
some three miles more or less east from the Admiralty to
connect with what was the road to Novgorod and is now
Lígovskiy prospékt at *plóstchad Vosstániya* (Uprising Square).
There it kinks to the south-east because the monks, just
settling in to their new monastery and working from the
east end, failed to meet the Swedish prisoners and military
engineers who were working from the west. Much of it –
including the bridges – was constructed of timber because
of the shortage of stone; part of it was painstakingly paved
with large rounded cobble-stones, proof against frost but
clatteringly noisy.

Lack of indigenous stone was not the only difficulty. Most
of the terrain, particularly between the Moika and Fontanka
rivers, was a dense, impenetrable, tree-covered swamp.
Travellers labouring under the burden of stones which Peter
insisted they bring for the streets of St Petersburg, or the five
thousand specialist stonemasons conscripted from the hinterland and encamped with their families in sheds along the
road, had wolves to contend with which hunted in packs and
are reported to have eaten sentinels, soldiers, peasants
and priests. As late as 1819, in *plóstchad Vosstániya*, a wolf
attacked a lamplighter at Christmas time.

By 1721, the western end of the Great Perspective Road had become an avenue. Four rows of neatly-trimmed trees grew along it. But there were only two proper houses: one built for a Dutchman, Admiral Kruis, on the north-west corner where the road crossed the Moika; one, built on the opposite, north-east, corner for a Frenchman, Peter the Great's Architect-General for a few years, Jean-Baptiste Le Blond.

Peter himself ordered a park to be planted, with a grove of birch trees, a good deal further east along the road on the same (north and even) side, which ran down to the Fontanka on the east and to what is now *Sadóvaya úlitsa* on the west. He planted it for his wife, the future Catherine I, and cherished it so much that he passed a law condemning to death by hanging any unfortunate who cut down a tree. (His wife persuaded him to rescind the law before he had time to put it into practice.) In this park, sometime after Peter's death in 1725, there was built in timber a (third) Summer Palace which became a favourite base for the Court for the next thirty years. It had wonderful gardens, parterres and fountains (*Sadóvaya úlitsa* means 'Garden Street'). This was where Catherine II, as the young wife of the Empress Elisabeth's heir, was delivered of her first child, the future Emperor Paul. Elisabeth removed the baby the day it was born and took charge of it herself. Eight years later, in June 1762, it was to this same now-vanished palace that, having dethroned her husband, Catherine made her triumphal entry to St Petersburg to be acclaimed Empress (in her own words) 'by all people of rank and importance', including (particularly important) her son.

During the 1720s, Peter began the great drainage operation of the little River Krivusha that resulted in the construction of the Griboyedov Canal between the Moika and the Fontanka and the embankment of both those rivers. Once again, he used Swedish prisoners to clear the forest, shift the earth and dig the channel, requiring them for good measure

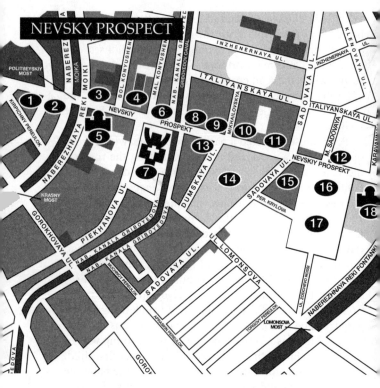

NEVSKY PROSPECT

1	Chaplin House	13	Old City Hall
2	Barrikada Cinema	14	Gostiny Dvor
3	Dutch Church	15	National Library
4	Lutheran Church	16	Ostrovskiy Square
5	Stroganoff Palace	17	Pushkin Drama Theatre ('Aleksandrinka')
6	Dom Knigi	18	Anichkov Palace
7	Kazan Cathedral	19	Beloselskiy-Belozerskiy Palace (Tourist Centre)
8	St Catherine's R.C.Church	20	Anichkov Bridge
9	Grand Hotel Europe	21	Uprising Square
10	Armenian Church		
11	*Passázh*		
12	Yeliséyev's		

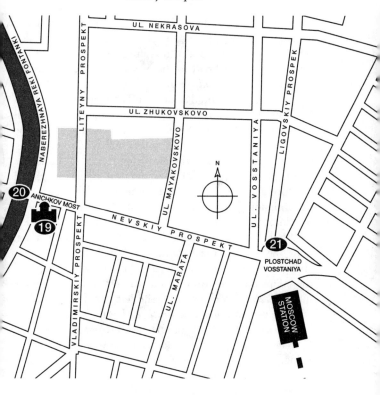

on Saturdays to sweep the Great Perspective clean – a job which, in the mid-nineteenth century, was sometimes performed by prostitutes under the supervision of the police who had arrested them on the previous night. Peter died before the work was finished and, in the 1730s, the area was still so wild that the Empress Anne declared it 'a hunting ground for chasing and shooting deer, wild boar and hares' which she used to shoot herself from the windows of the palace.

In 1736, however, the fire that devastated a large part of the area around the Admiralty glacis, and the Commission that was then appointed to impose some order on the city's development, had important consequences for the Nevsky. First, and least important, it changed its name from the Great Perspective Road to the Nevsky Perspective (shortened in 1783 to *Névskiy prospékt*). Next it ordained that the centre of the city should not be – as Peter had intended and Le Blond had planned it – on *Vasíliyevskiy óstrov* (Basil Island) but on the south bank of the Neva and should be based on the Trident formed by the three roads converging on the Admiralty. On the south and east, it should be bounded by the Fontanka. In recognition of the role played by foreigners in the development of the city, the Commission granted West European churches the right to be allocated plots along the *Névskiy prospékt*.

When these plans were drawn, there were only seven buildings between the Admiralty and the Fontanka. Things changed when Peter's second daughter, Elisabeth, deposed the infant Emperor Ivan VI and seized the throne. On the night of 25 November 1741, she left her own palace on what is now *Milliónnaya úlitsa* and was escorted to the headquarters of the Preobrazhenskiy Guards, where the Nevsky crossed the Fontanka over the wooden Anichkov Bridge. There she was acclaimed the new Empress and, with the Guards, proceeded westward along the Nevsky towards the palace on the Neva of the Regent Anna and her baby son. It was (at that stage) a bloodless coup. On the site of the Preobrazhenskiy barracks, she commissioned Zemtsov to build her a palace named after the Colonel who constructed that wooden bridge and, sixteen years and three architects later, presented the Anichkov Palace to her lover of the moment (perhaps also her husband), Aleksey Razumovskiy.

Elisabeth was determined to transform Peter's relatively modest city into a fit and proper place for an Imperial capital. In 1745, she passed a decree under which all those who possessed a plot of land should build on it and, as prescribed by the Building Commission, build in 'stone'. (Most of the 'stone' buildings in St Petersburg are, by the way, stucco-covered brick which is then painted; hence the lovely colours of the city when it is cared for; hence the shabbiness, when it is not. Very early houses made of wood were often painted to imitate brick.) The first to respond to Elisabeth's decree was her new lover, Ivan Shuvalov who built himself a palatial mansion, set in its own grounds, which stretched from the Nevsky to *Italiyánskaya úlitsa* (where its entrance is to be found at *No. 35*) along *Málaya Sadóvaya* with, at that time, an unobstructed view down to the Fontanka (S. Chevakinskiy, 1753–5). On the same huge plot, Shuvalov built for rent two houses facing on to the Nevsky (on the site of *Nos. 52* and *54*). He was, as well as the Empress's lover, a great patron of the arts, a setter of aesthetic style and the first President of the Academy of Arts, so this was an influential development.

While Elisabeth waited for her new Winter Palace on the Neva, she moved to the temporary timber palace which Rastrelli put up for her in a few months on the south (odd) side of the *Névskiy prospékt*. It occupied an empty site which ran from *Málaya Morskáya* to *Bolsháya Morskáya* and from the Nevsky to what is now *Kirpíchny pereúlok* (lane). Here the Court spent most of the next six years. Elisabeth died here on Christmas day, 1761 and Catherine (at first with her husband, Peter III) moved almost immediately into the new Winter Palace on the Neva. Within three years, substantial houses began to grow along Peter the Great's supply road and it became the main street of St Petersburg.

All plots in the city are numbered. In the eighteenth century they were numbered according to their police district and without reference to the street in which they stood; in 1834 they acquired street numbers, with the odd on the left and the even on the right; in 1858 the arrangement was reversed. So, on *Névskiy prospékt*, they are lined

up on each side (odd to the south or right as you walk away
from the Admiralty, even to the left or north) along a
notional line known as the '*krásnaya líniya*' (red line), 'red'
in this context having nothing to do with politics but being
a term at that time which meant fair or pleasing. (The same
applies to 'Red' Square.) So the *krásnaya líniya* meant a fair
or pleasing line. The houses marched along it. The
churches – and, later, the squares – could be set back from
it within their courtyards (but even there, the church
houses on each side of the courtyards had to conform to
the line). Only the two great palaces, the Anichkov and the
Stroganov (though the latter was not properly a palace
since it was not a royal residence) were exempt. This was in
the tradition of Peter the Great who had discouraged, in
fact and by example, the building of grand houses set,
Moscow fashion, in their own grounds – *usádby*.

We will follow the numbers on one side down to a
natural break – Moika, Griboyedov, Fontanka – at which
point we will go back to the beginning on the other side. It
is inadvisable to cross the road anywhere else.

By the early twentieth century, the west end of *Névskiy
prospékt*, together with the east end of *Bolsháya Morskáya*,
had become the financial centre of St Petersburg. The present building at *No. 1* dates from 1910 to 1911 and was a private commercial bank; the first *No. 1* was built for a German
officer in 1777. (Until then, no one had been allowed to
build on the Admiralty glacis which reached to the Moika.)
Nos. 7 and *9* were reconstructed (M. Peretyatkovich,
1911–12) for the Swedish banker Vavelberg. Known as the
Vavelberg House, it sits heavily on the corner of *Málaya
Morskáya*. But in its day it excited a great deal of attention
in its attempt, elaborate if not successful, to mimic the
Quatrocento, all covered over with rusticated granite
brought by Vavelberg from his native Sweden. It now houses
the St Petersburg office of Russian Airlines (as well as the
Saigon Discoclub and the Society of Russian Authors).

On the opposite corner, on the ground floor of *No. 11* (1898, by L. Benois), there is a food shop, *gastronóm* (not to be confused with *Gastronóm No. 1*, now again Yeliséyev), which used to supply rare or high quality food against special ration cards to senior officers and civil servants. It displayed no name but was universally referred to as 'The Generals" (*Generálskiy*). It sometimes still is.

No. 13, the **Chaplin House**, was built for that family on the corner of *Bolsháya Morskáya* in the first quarter of the nineteenth century by the Italian architect, V. Beretti, and is almost unchanged. In the second half of the nineteenth century Tolstoy's long-suffering publisher, Maurice Wolff ('the King of Russian Books'), had his offices and a bookshop on the ground floor. Up and down the street, publishers had their offices and, next to their offices, very often a bookshop and, next to the bookshop, a café or restaurant where writers, rich and poor, could meet, read the latest journals for free, smoke, talk, and – if they could afford it – eat.

No. 15, known as the **House with Columns** (which it has in profusion), or the **Chicherin House**, stands on a plot with perhaps the most colourful history in the street. For many years now it has been a cinema, the *Barrikáda*.

On this site, between 1716 and the great fire of 1736, there was a market for naval and dockyard stores. For the next twenty years, the ground lay empty waiting, as it were, for Rastrelli to place his temporary Winter Palace on it in 1755. It was from the windows of that palace that Catherine, not yet the Second nor the Great but just the unhappy and neglected wife of the Empress Elisabeth's nephew and heir, first saw a very young, very tall and very handsome Guards officer in the street below and fell in love – with incalculable consequences for herself and for Russia. Grigoriy Orlov became her lover for twelve years, a record of constancy that Catherine never achieved again. He and his dashing brother conceived and executed the plot which installed her on the throne and cost her husband his life.

After Catherine became Empress, she gave part of the old Winter Palace site – including the throne room – to her Chief Commissioner of Police, N. Chicherin. This, in 1768–71, was where the present *No. 15* was built, two sedate tiers of columns marching round its corner and along its main façade on the Nevsky, commissioned probably from the French architect Vallin de la Mothe, with the participation of Kokorinov, Felten and Kvasov. On another part of the site, on the corner of *Málaya Morskáya* and *Kirpíchny pereúlok*, the Empress Elisabeth had built a theatre, the first to be devoted to Russian comedy and tragedy. The earliest audiences were invited (friends and Court officials) but, on 5 May 1757, the first public performance took place and the professional Russian theatre was born. The players – at that stage, amateurs from the city of Yaroslavl – came to St Petersburg under the direction of Fedor Volkov, the first Russian professional actor.

When Catherine presented the site to Chicherin, in 1767, she closed the Empress Elisabeth's theatre and had it refashioned as an apartment for Falconet, the French sculptor of the 'Bronze Horseman'. Next door, still on the same site (entrance in *Málaya Morskáya*), was his studio and workshop where *Brilliant* and *Caprice* modelled for the stallion and Diderot came to gossip. After Chicherin's death, *No. 15* came to be owned by a merchant called Péretz, who owed his fortune to being the purveyor of salt to the Imperial family. *Péretz* in Russian means 'pepper'. So it must have been the work of a moment for him to devise the advertisement which famously linked his name with his product: '*Gdye sol, tam y Péretz*' or 'Where there is salt there is Pepper'. Salt and Pepper invested in *No. 15*.

By the end of the eighteenth century, the first musical club in St Petersburg was giving concerts there, one of the composers being B. Ortnyanskiy. In the 1800s, Quarenghi lived there on the first floor when he arrived from Italy. In the 1810s, V. Stasov added a solid stone extension which fronted on to *Bolsháya Morskáya* and there, in the 1820s, the satirical playwright Griboyedov had an apartment before his last posting to Teheran as Minister Plenipotentiary. The ground floor, at that time, was occupied by the famous French publisher and bookshop, Pluchard. The café attached to Pluchard's – *Talon* – was the favourite venue of Pushkin's hero, Eugene Onegin (Pushkin himself preferring Wolff and Béranger, farther down the street).

Then, in 1858, the house was bought by the Yeliséyev family. Their story is fabulous – a fable of the evolution of a new class of Russian capitalist. Yeliséyev was a serf, tied to his master not by his labour but by the payment of 'quit-rent' which left him free, provided he paid the rent, to seek his fortune elsewhere. He seeks it in St Petersburg, around 1810, and goes to work as a docker in the port. Soon he is a foreman. In 1846, he opens a shop and, when he is rather richer than his owner, he buys himself out. By 1858, he can buy the House of Columns. And by 1902, his descendants are so wealthy and so powerful that they persuade the city authorities to let them buy *No. 56* as well, pull it down, and replace it with something ostentatiously out of character with the street.

For the time being, they contented themselves with making a few alterations to *No. 15*. The Russian architect Grebenka was hired to turn ground floor columns into pilasters and change oval windows into square ones. Popular tradition still has it that, during the changes, the family concealed their gold in the walls and that, somewhere in the recesses of the *Barrikáda*, is treasure beyond imagining. In spite of Stasov and Grebenka, *No. 15* remains essentially a fine and early example of Russian eighteenth-century Classicism.

In 1862, a chess club opened here, organised by a left wing critic of the government, N. Chernyshevskiy, as a meeting place for dissidents, progressives and even serious revolutionaries. But it was closed within six months and

replaced by a rather more respectable club – or gathering –
of civil servants and officers who enjoyed literary and
musical evenings. Writers, who included Turgenev, liked to
go there to read their works aloud. Then came the
Revolution. And, in 1919, on the initiative of Maxim
Gorky, the House with Columns became the House of Arts,
providing shelter for many writers, among them Aleksandr
Blok and the poet Osip Mandelstam who, twenty years
later, was to die in one of Stalin's concentration camps.

Having reached the Moika, we will go back to the
beginning of the street and follow the houses on the even
(north) side. You will not find *No. 2* because it was
wrapped up in to the south-west corner of the General
Staff building by I. Chernik in 1845–6. For eighty years,
however, it provided a home for the **Free Economic
Society**, founded at the secret instigation of Catherine the
Great. Founder members included leading West European
intellectuals as well as powerful members of Catherine's
Court. She intended it to think the unthinkable and, in its
second year, with her secret encouragement the Society
sponsored a competition for the best paper on whether
serfdom in Russia should be abolished. The issue was felt to
be so unthinkable that the papers were circulated to members in locked boxes. But the winning entry (by Grigoriy
Orlov) argued in favour of abolition and was published.
Sadly, Russia had to wait for nearly a hundred years before
the serfs were in reality emancipated by Catherine's great-
grandson, Alexander II. The Free Economic Society moved
in the 1840s to *Moskóvskiy prospékt No. 33*, where there is
now a centre and museum dedicated to the Marxist revolutionary Georgiy Plekhanov.

Nos. 2, 8 and *10* were all built in 1765 (architect
A. Kvasov) for an English family called Perkins – one was a
lawyer, one a merchant. Together with *Málaya Morskáya
No. 12*, they are the earliest residential houses to have
survived intact and provide a fair idea of the Nevsky's

frontage in the early years of Catherine's reign. *No. 8*, sold by John Perkins to Safonov (the **Safonov House**), was altered in 1830. It now contains a showroom and shop for Petersburg artists (the scarves and pottery in particular being interesting and reasonably priced). *No. 10* (the **Weimar House**) forms the focal point for the end of *Málaya Morskáya* and its elegant façade is original.

No. 14 was built by the Soviet architect B. Rubanenko just before the last war and is almost the only post-Revolutionary building west of the Fontanka. Now **School 210**, it carries a famous plaque, advising the citizens of Leningrad that 'during the artillery bombardment this side of the street is the more dangerous'. Indeed it was, because the German heavy artillery was located in a village south-east of the city. In memory of the Blockade, they still place flowers under the sign.

The first house on the site of *No. 18* was built in 1705 and belonged to **Admiral Kruis** whose story could only have happened in the Petersburg of Peter the Great. An officer in the Dutch merchant navy, he arrived on the Neva with other officers, sailors and shipwrights, was invited by Peter to join the vestigial Russian Fleet – and did. By 1713, he was Admiral of the Fleet in the Gulf of Finland with Peter himself choosing to serve as a midshipman under his command. Unfortunately for the Admiral, he ran aground while pursuing two Swedish vessels for which, and for allowing them to escape, he was court-martialled. Midshipman Peter sat on the court-martial which condemned Kruis to death. But his sentence was commuted to exile in Kazan from which he was brought back in 1719 to become Vice-President of the Admiralty (the equivalent of a junior Minister for the Navy). At this point, he got rid of his house on the Nevsky and moved up the road to one next door to Admiral Apraksin on the Neva.

In 1741, Kruis's old house came into the hands of Johann Neumann, a tailor and one of the many purveyors of goods and services to the Imperial Court who became immensely rich. Neumann had just commissioned the distinguished architect Mikhail Zemtsov to build him a house on the other side of the street – at *No. 17* – which he sold, while still under construction and no doubt at a handsome profit, to the Stroganovs. Then he asked Zemtsov to rebuild the Admiral's house at *No. 18*. The result was extremely grand, by the standards of the day, being in three separate blocks united by gateways and pavilions. What you see now is a re-modelling (by V. Stasov) for the merchant family, Kotomin. Stasov took the Baroque blocks of Zemtsov's mansion and turned them into a seamless Classical whole by the Doric colonnade which unites them on the ground floor.

Some years later, there flourished here Pushkin's favourite confectioner and café, **Wolff and Béranger**, whose present entrance is on the Moika. Here, on 29 January 1837, Pushkin called to collect his second, Danzas, on his way to his last and fatal duel. At the Nevsky entrance, in 1985, there opened the *Literatúrnoye kafé*, with a rather less élite clientèle and a deliberately florid appeal to tourists.

You cross the Moika by what, at the time of writing, is the *Zelyóny most* (Green Bridge), which has changed its name at least five times and which, for most of its life, was known as the *Politséyskiy most* after the office of Catherine the Great's Chief Commissioner of Police which is now incorporated in the western wing of the Dutch Church. This house, next to Le Blond's, had belonged to Yákov Dolgorúkiy, a supporter of Peter's murdered son Aleksey. Confiscated by Peter in 1720, it was given to a much-feared Police Commissioner called Devier (another Dutchman) who was charged with enforcing the law and some kind of order in the wild conditions of early St Petersburg. From this north-eastern corner of the Nevsky, where it crosses the Moika, you can now take a canal boat which is one of the most delightful ways of seeing the city.

Crossing the bridge, we will stay on the even (north) side as far as the Griboyedov Canal. The sites allocated to West European churches included space not just for the church but for a courtyard and two 'church houses' to enable the churches to generate their own revenue. In the case of the **Dutch Church**, *No. 20*, which was not built until 1830 to 1839 (by the French architect P. Jacquot), the site had become cramped from the north and the whole *ensemble* – church as well as houses – was built along the 'red line'. So it forms a single, large building which ends in two wings, one returning along the Moika at the western end, the other along *Bolsháya Konyúshennaya*. The whole three-storey façade is Classical and minimal, except for the south front of the church which declares itself with some clarity by an impressive four-column portico running the full height of the building. An ugly fourth storey was added above the cornice to the western house.

At the time that the church was built, the area around was known as the Dutch quarter. An early tenant was A. Krayevskiy, editor of *Otéchestvennye Zapíski* (*Homeland Notes*) which was at the time the focus of Russian intellectual life. In this office, Vissarion Belinskiy had his first job as literary critic. Later, in the 1860s and 70s, the poet Nekrasov became editor and the satirical novelist Saltykov-Stchedrin one of its main contributors. The church is now the Aleksandr Blok library with a delightful reading room – little green lights and separate tables. There is also an antique shop.

The **Lutheran Church of St Peter**, at *Nos. 22* and *24*, was begun much earlier and extends more deeply back from the street. A large site was marked out for it between *Bolsháya Konyúshennaya* and *Málaya Konyúshennaya*, shortly after the marshes were drained. But it was still a wild place. Poor Pastor Kreuz complained of being 'in fear of water shortages [sic], malefactors, murderers, thieves and all sorts of misadventures that happen to those so far from their neighbours'.

In 1730, a modest stone church with a spire was placed towards the back of the site and, along the 'red line', two symmetrical houses were built on each side of the courtyard. Behind this early church, was the **Peterschule** (founded in 1710, the oldest school in the city). The present school dates from 1760 to 1762 and, in spite of alterations and extra floors and all the other adaptations necessary to keep a great school viable, you can still detect the fine lines of the early Baroque building. It was *Alma Mater* to the architect Rossi, the composer Moussorgsky, the paediatrician Dr Rauchfuss and on and on – scientists, poets, novelists. It is now School 222.

The original church was pulled down and rebuilt (1832–8), with a smart new flavour of nineteenth-century Romanesque, by the Russian architect Aleksandr Bryullov whose brother, Karl, painted the altarpiece of the Crucifixion. (Karl Bryullov lived, for a time, at *Névskiy prospékt No.* 6 where Gogol, among others, used to sit for him. His painting of *The Last Days of Pompeii*, now in the Russian Museum, had an international success and was exhibited in London where it inspired Bulwer-Lytton to write his novel of the same name.) The school was enlarged, the houses remodelled (two more floors were added in the early twentieth century) and into the western wing moved the bookseller and publisher, Smirdin. In the eastern wing, there opened a restaurant – *Dominique* – the eating and meeting place of many writers, including Chernyshevskiy and Dostoyevsky, who went there mainly to read the free journals in its reading/smoking room. *Dominique* closed in 1917. There is now a café which sells ices (*morózhenoye*) which, because of the colour of its furniture, is referred to as the 'Frog Pool'. In the 1860s, another bookshop moved into the ground floor, this time with a library attached; it became the centre for the revolutionary Society of Land and Freedom (*Zemlyá i Vólya*). In the 1950s, the Church of St Peter became a swimming pool. It is now re-consecrated, restored and returned to ecclesiastical hands under a German bishop.

Architecturally, *No. 28* was a new departure – *Art Nouveau* or, in the Russian idiom, *Style Moderne*. Commissioned from P. Syuzor by the Singer Sewing Machine Company, it was completed in 1907 with a cast iron frame which made possible the giant ground floor windows at which girls sat sewing away and attracting a crowd of people in the street outside. The corner of the building, on the Canal, is easily identifiable by its elongated dome, topped by a tilted glass sphere which, in turn, is held aloft by a monumental male and a monumental female. The sphere was lit at night to advertise the wonders of electricity. After the Revolution, when the Singer Company had gone, their headquarters became the 'cradle', as the Soviet guide books described it, of 'literature' for children. Its present name, however – *Dom Knígi* or the **House of the Book** – owes more to the fact that it is now the largest bookshop in the city.

Back, now, to the Moika and down the south (odd) side of the street as far as the Canal. The **Stroganov Palace**, at *No. 17*, is one of the grandest buildings in the Nevsky, commissioned by one of the richest families in Russia from arguably the greatest architect to work in St Petersburg. All the same, it is not a palace and, when it was built, it was called a house (*dom*). In the sixteenth century the Stroganovs had conquered the Mongol tribes inhabiting Siberia and presented half a continent to the Tsar, raising their private army to do so and financing it by their revenues from salt and furs (hence the sables and the bear's head displayed in their coat of arms). Even they, however, in the 1740s, were required to conform to the prevailing 'architectural design' and accept the relatively modest version made by Zemtsov for Neumann, the tailor. So they bought the corner site from Neumann and hoped for the best. The best duly came, in 1751, in the form of a fire which burned the Neumann/Zemtsov house down and with it – probably – *No. 19* next door. This belonged to the Master Cook to the Imperial Household, a man called Shestakov whose house had been conceived as a pair with the tailor's but not, one may be sure, with the house the Stroganovs now hoped to build.

In 1752, Sergey Stroganov was free to commission Rastrelli to build him an uninhibitedly Baroque mansion (though even that, one should note, conforms to the 'red line' of the street). Sergey's son, Aleksandr, was a collector and patron of the arts, succeeding Ivan Shuvalov as President of the Academy of Arts. He built up one of the greatest, in quality as well as quantity, collections of pictures in private hands in Russia. Until the Revolution, the public had access to the collection although the family continued to live in the house until 1917.

Fire came again to *No. 17* in the early 1790s and largely destroyed Rastrelli's interior. Aleksandr commissioned A. Voronikhin, probably his illegitimate son, certainly until 1785 his serf, brought up in the house with Aleksandr's own family, to redecorate the interior and provide a suitable setting for his pictures and his innumerable guests. This, Voronikhin's first essay into Classicism, was completed in 1793. The pictures long since have gone to the Hermitage (those not sold on to Andrew Mellon) and the mansion was badly damaged by artillery bombardment during the Blockade. Ten years ago, it was made a branch of the Russian Museum which has begun, slowly, to restore it. You can now go in; some of Voronikhin's rooms are on view; there is a café, coffee in the courtyard and a souvenir shop. Also a permanent exhibition of wax figures, moved from the *Passázh* down the street, and some temporary exhibitions of pictures. A separate ticket is required but will admit you to the Engineers' Castle (*Inzhenérny zámok*) and the Marble Palace (*Mrámorny dvoréts*) as well.

The present **Cathedral of Our Lady of Kazan** (*Kazánskiy sobór*) was built by Voronikhin between 1801 and 1811, just after the assassination of the Emperor Paul. But it was Paul's conception and he intended it to be associated with Russia's military victories – the receptacle of the keys of captured cities and surrendered standards, of the bodies of great generals and, most venerated of all, of the miraculous icon of Our Lady of Kazan. It is sometimes dismissed as a heavy copy of St Peter's. But in fact the great colonnaded wings which frame the *Kazánskaya plóstchad* serve a vital architectural purpose in that they provide a High Classical disguise for a long and otherwise tedious northern flank of the church which, like all important churches, had to face east/west. The colonnade sweeps across the North Chapel at a tangent and in parallel with the street, so the great doors in the centre of it – exact copies of Ghiberti's for the Baptistery in Florence – were never intended to be used as the main entrance. Voronikhin's entrance was at the west end where he created a semi-circular piazza girded by particularly fine wrought-iron railings (1812) and where, in 1935, the fountain of Thomas de Thomon (executed in 1803) was brought from the Pulkovo Road on the way to Tsarskoye Selo. Today, visitors enter through a small door in the east end.

From the time of Empress Anne there had been a stone church here dedicated to The Nativity of Our Lady (Zemtsov, 1733–7). With the shift of urban gravity from the north bank of the Neva to the south, under the Empress Elisabeth, this quickly became the focus for religious and ceremonial life. Like the present cathedral, it had a square facing on to the Nevsky. And this square seemed, like its successor, to invite political demonstrations – though the first recorded demonstration was for, rather than against, the throne.

On 28 June 1762, the future Catherine II was woken at Peterhof by Aleksey Orlov (brother of Grigoriy) and taken by him and Prince Baryatinskiy to the barracks of the Izmailovskiy Regiment and thence to the barracks of the Semyonovskiy. Thus escorted by two regiments of foot guards, they repaired to Zemtsov's Kazan Cathedral where the Horse Guards 'made their appearance in transports of joy' (Catherine's description). Two days later, having despatched her husband to captivity, she went to church where 'the *Te Deum* was sung to the thunder of cannon'. Another bloodless (for the time being) coup – though these coups had a way of ending in murder.

Why Kazan? In the eyes of the faithful of the Orthodox Church, the holiest object in the Cathedral was the copy of the **icon of Our Lady of Kazan** which Peter the Great ordered to be made and sent to him in 1708 from the Cathedral of the same name in Moscow.[1] The icon had a tradition of miraculous victories to its credit; the copy in Moscow had been brought there by Kazan troops attached to the Russian army, under the command of Prince Pozharskiy, which fought against the Poles when they were finally expelled from the Kremlin in 1612.

Peter originally placed his icon in the small timber chapel attached to his quarters on the Petrograd Side and then moved it into the stone church there which replaced the chapel. It was moved again by the Empress Anne in 1737, when Zemtsov finished the Cathedral of the Nativity of Our Lady. And there it remained, save for a minimal removal from Zemtsov's cathedral to Voronikhin's, when the latter was completed in 1811. But nobody knows where it is now. Nor does anybody know where are the many further copies that were made and displayed in Moscow and St Petersburg. The Revolution seems to have swept them all away – though the Moscow icon was seen there as late as 1934.

---

[1] There is some dispute about whether it was a copy, the Russian ecclesiastical authorities insisting that the icon in St Petersburg was the original from Kazan. Professor Likhachov, perhaps the most distinguished Russian historian, was in no doubt that the icon obtained by Peter was not from Kazan but a late seventeenth-century copy of the copy that was taken to Moscow in 1612. In any event, authentic copies are believed to attach the miraculous properties of the original to themselves.

It was not the Revolution, however, but a burglar called Chaykin who removed the original from its safe haven in the convent built specially for it in the city of Kazan on the orders of Ivan the Terrible. Chaykin stole the original icon and went to prison for it in 1904. He claimed till his dying day that, having stolen it, he suddenly realised it was too famous to be profitably disposed of and so burned it. As he was a professional stealer of church valuables, perfectly aware of the difficulty of disposing of them, nobody much believed his story – except the police. The Teetotallers' Society certainly didn't for they offered a reward of three hundred roubles (about £30) when they read of the theft in the press. The mystery rumbled on, through the last days of the Empire, through the First World War, through the first days of the Revolution until, in 1954, precisely fifty years after the theft, an icon, claimed to be the original from Kazan, appeared in a London suburb. (It had travelled *via* Poland, where it had been seen at a fair, and Germany.) There it was seen, among others, by me.

Somebody, at least, thought it might be genuine for the Russian Orthodox Archbishop of San Francisco tried (and failed) to raise the half a million dollars that was the asking price for it in the United States. It is a strange twist to the story that this great Orthodox icon, whose sanctity and fame owe so much to its part in the defeat in 1612 of the Catholic forces of Poland, has now (1970) been found a home by the Uniat[2] Church in the famous Catholic shrine of Our Lady of Fátima in Portugal.

One of the victories with which the icon has been associated was the retreat of Napoleon from Moscow. As **Field Marshal Kutuzov** was leaving that city, to vanish with his army as the French entered it, he went into the Church of Our Lady of Kazan, took Pozharskiy's copy of the icon and put it for temporary safe-keeping under his great coat.

[2] The Roman Catholic Church of the Eastern Rite.

When he died in Bunzlau the following year, having
harried the French across Russia and into Silesia, it is said
that he expressed a wish that his body should be buried in
Russia but that his heart should be buried 'with my
soldiers, sons of the Fatherland', so that they could see that
'as far as my heart is concerned, I have remained with
them'.[3]

Something indeed may have been buried in Tilendorf,
three kilometres from Bunzlau, for a monument was erected
there. Kutuzov's embalmed body was brought back to Kazan
Cathedral for a state funeral and interred in the crypt under
the North Chapel. To the right of the entrance, on the wall,
is an epic depiction of the defeat of the Poles in 1612. Below
the picture is inscribed:

Prince
Mikhail Illarionovich
Golenistchev-Kutuzov
of Smolensk
Born in the year 1745
Died 1813
in the city of Bunzlau

It sounds straightforward. But here too there is mystery.
The rumours about the Field Marshal's heart persisted
until, in 1913, the Russian Society of Military History was
considering whether steps should be taken to bring
Kutuzov's heart back from Silesia. Much later, the story fea-
tured as a fact in the Soviet Encyclopaedia. In 1933, a
Special Commission seems to have been set up to open
Kutuzov's tomb and examine the contents of his coffin. It
issued an official declaration, signed by the Director and
Financial Secretary of the Museum of Religion and
Atheism (which the Cathedral had become in 1932) and a

[3] Kutuzov's words as reported in a Polish Learned Journal.

representative of the local branch of the state secret police, OGPU. This stated:

> The tomb in which Marshal Kutuzov is buried has been opened . . . At the head, on the left hand side, was discovered a jar [*banka* – not an obviously appropriate container for such an illustrious object] which contains an embalmed heart.

There, for the time being, the matter rests.

To celebrate the twenty-fifth anniversary of the rout of Napoleon's army, two monumental statues by the sculptor B. Orlovskiy were erected on each side of the *Kazánskaya plóstchad*, one of Kutuzov and one of General Barclay de Tolly. Barclay de Tolly was a senior Russian general of Scottish descent who had served under Kutuzov at the Battle of Borodino and became Commander in Chief of the Russian army in Europe after Kutuzov's death.

Between the statues lies the great square (***Kazánskaya plóstchad***), scene through the years of much civil unrest. The first workers' demonstration took place here in 1876, when the crowd was roused to a frenzy by a twenty-year-old student from the Institute of Mining who addressed the first political demonstration in Russia. (Georgiy Plekhanov led the Land and Freedom organisation until he had to leave Russia four years later. In 1885, in exile in Geneva, he founded the first Russian Marxist revolutionary movement. On his return to Russia in 1917, he sided with the Mensheviks against the Bolsheviks and was attacked by Lenin for doing so. He died in May 1918.) The authorities hastened to plant a formal garden in the *Kazánskaya plóstchad*. But in vain. Students demonstrated here in 1897, in protest at the conditions which led their fellow student Maria Veltrova to commit suicide in prison. There was another major incident in 1901, and again during the revolutionary year of 1905. In February 1917, crowds gathered here from up and down the Nevsky in an explosion of revolutionary enthusiasm.

After the Revolution, the Cathedral of our Lady of Kazan suffered exceptional punishment. In 1922, its silver icon-ostasis was ripped out, melted down and sold for the price of its bullion. In 1932, it became the Museum of Religion and Atheism with some pretty unsavoury exhibitions. It was badly damaged in the Blockade. But, in 1950, its cupola (originally iron) was re-covered and is a wonderful green copper. More extensive repairs were carried out in 1968. And then, in 1991, the Museum (with the Religion but without the Atheism) was moved to *úlitsa Pochtámtskaya No. 14*. The Cathedral has now been re-consecrated and Mass is celebrated there on a regular basis.

We will cross the Griboyedov Canal by the *Kazánskiy most*, the first stone bridge in the city. We will then cross the *Névskiy prospékt* back to the north (even) side and stay there until the Fontanka. *No. 30* is now the **Mály zal Filarmónii** (the Lesser Philarmonia Hall), not to be con-fused with the Great Hall which is down *Mikháylovskaya úlitsa*. It started life as a dwelling house in about 1790. From the beginning of the nineteenth century, concerts were per-formed here by the Petersburg Philharmonia, one of the most remarkable being the first complete performance of Beethoven's *Missa Solemnis* (described in the programme as the Great Oratorio) on 26 March 1824. (Composed for the installation of the Archduke Rudolph as archbishop of Olmütz, it was not completed until 1823, three years after the event. As a result it was not given a complete perform-ance in Vienna, being somewhat overshadowed by the Ninth Symphony.)

In 1830, *No. 30* was rebuilt by P. Jacquot for a wealthy patron of music, V. Engelhardt, by whose name the house is often known. Liszt and Berlioz played for him here; Johann Strauss and Wagner conducted. Scenes from Lermontov's *Masquerade* (which had not amused the censor) were per-formed. The building received a direct hit during the Blockade; in the course of reconstructing it, they incorporated an entrance to the Metro (*stantsiya metro Névskiy Prospékt*) within it, which is convenient – particularly for those who like listening to chamber music in which the Hall now specialises.

Nos. 32 and *34* are the symmetrical houses which frame the *ensemble* of **St Catherine's Roman Catholic Church**. The bottom two floors were designed by Pietro Antonio Trezzini as early as 1739. (The top two floors were a rather clumsy addition in 1893.) It was also P. A. Trezzini's design to place the church far back from the street and deep in its courtyard. This was followed by Vallin de la Mothe when he actually built the church between 1762 and 1783. The church was altered in 1828 and, again, in 1840. It contains the tomb of Stanislaus II of Poland, Count Poniatowskiy, one-time favourite of Catherine II, through whose influence he acquired the throne of Poland and also lost it, after the third partition of that country by Russia, Prussia and Austria. He died in St Petersburg soon afterwards.

The **Grand Hotel Europe** (*Yevropéyskaya gostínitsa*) whose address is *Mikháylovskaya úlitsa Nos. 1–7*, occupies the corner site which includes *Névskiy prospékt No. 36*. Purpose-built from 1873 to 1875 as a hotel by L. Fontana, its interior re-done *de luxe* by F. Lidval between 1908 and 1911, its outside Eclectic and its inside *Style Moderne*, and yet . . . it is without doubt the most delightful hotel in St Petersburg and must be visited even if you can't stay there. It was successfully refurbished in the 1980s by a Russo-Finnish consortium.

Built on the site of the Empress Elisabeth's private stables, the *ensemble* of the **Armenian Church** (*Nos. 40* and *42*) forms one of the most enchanting groups on the Nevsky. An early (very early, 1771–80) example of Russian Classicism – light and elegant in its blue and white with graceful sculpture – it was financed by a wealthy Armenian philanthropist, E. Lazarev and realised by Yu. Felten. Lazarev was a jeweller by appointment to Catherine the

Great who personally granted him permission to build; he was also a leader of the movement to liberate Armenia from Turkey. The church has now been fully restored and re-consecrated and has a fine choir. (The Armenians claim to be 'the first Christian nation', having adopted Christianity as their state religion in AD 298 when their king was converted by St Gregory the Illuminator.)

The eastern church house (*No. 42*) was completed in 1775, consisting of only two floors and a high basement. (It was re-modelled between 1835 and 1837.) The poet F. Tyutchev, who was a *protégé* of Lazarev, lived there when he arrived from Moscow and worked on Pushkin's *Sovreménnik* (*The Contemporary*) which was later to become a rival to *Homeland Notes*. The western church house was built twenty years later, by an unknown architect.

The *Passázh* (Arcade) at *No. 48* was ceremoniously opened on 22 May 1848, a 'French novelty' introduced to St Petersburg by Count Yakov Stenbock-Fermor. Newspapers wrote at the time that 'the size' (it is much larger than the Burlington Arcade) 'the noble look of its ornate design and its beautiful style make our *Passázh* a pearl among European Arcades'. Mid-century hyperbole, perhaps, but still its arrival in the *Névskiy prospékt* must have been quite an event. It runs for nearly two hundred metres from its entrance on the street to *Italiyánskaya úlitsa* at the back and, for most of its length, has a glass roof.

In the basement, they used to sell wine. On the ground floor, there were shops – rather smart ones, a good deal more up-market than the stalls in the *Gostíny dvor* across the street. On top there were apartments for rent, an echo perhaps of the Central Asian market where traders came from afar and needed somewhere to sleep. There was also a concert hall which doubled as a theatre, on the site of the present *teátr Komissarzhévskoy*. Here were held literary evenings where writers (Turgenev, Dostoyevsky, Goncharov and Ostróvskiy prominent among them) gave lectures and read or performed their work, often donating the proceeds to the Literary Fund. This society, founded in 1859, was modelled on the British Royal Literary Fund and was open to writers of both sexes, dedicated to helping them travel or just to survive.

In 1901, the *Crédit Lyonnais* Bank put some money into the *Passázh* and it acquired a startling new entrance with a portico, electric light and a lift. The concert hall became a fully-fledged theatre with a box office on the ground floor. For three years from 1904, the most successful company was led by the great actress Vera Komissarzhevskaya who played Chekhov (notably *The Seagull*) and Gorky to great, and sometimes politically disturbing, effect. She died in 1909, leading her company on tour in what is now Uzbekistan. A theatre bearing her name was resurrected in the *Passázh* during the last war and is still playing to full houses. And there were other, more frivolous, attractions: gypsy bands, exhibitions of wax figures, a mechanical theatre, a Diorama and a Panorama – not to mention the pretty models who worked in the dress shops and the confectioners, a magnet for the young men.

In 1961, the *Passázh* was turned by the city authorities into 'an examplar of a Department Store', the only one in the Soviet Union to sell things exclusively for women. Now it has acquired 'Western partners' in the fashion business who sometimes sell at concessionary prices which can be good value for Westerners.

No. 56, on the corner of *Málaya Sadóvaya*, with its enormous steel-framed windows and a top storey like fondant icing, was built (1902–7 by G. Baranovskiy) for the brothers Yeliséyev (whose ancestor had bought *No. 15*), to be a food shop. A touch of Harrods Food Halls, a touch of Fortnum and Mason and a touch of something entirely Russian. A food shop, through thick and thin, it has remained for over a hundred years. Even the Revolution failed to destroy it for it re-opened as *Gastronóm No. 1* – open, however, only to higher party officials and senior civil servants. The new name never took on and it is with relief that Petersburgers can call it **Yeliséyev's** once again. Baranovskiy's *Style Moderne* interiors have just been luxuriously restored, including the restaurant on the first floor and the theatre (the Academic Comedy Theatre) on the second. But, eighteen years after he had finished building it, Baranovskiy himself starved to death in the famine year of 1920. (Before his death, he designed two other buildings for the Yeliséyev brothers, including one on the Moika. He was also responsible for the Buddhist Temple at *Primórskiy prospékt No. 91*.)

But in 1881, a different house had stood on the corner of *Málaya Sadóvaya*. In January, some members of the People's Will Party (*Naródnaya Vólya*), a terrorist organisation, hired the premises at the back of *No. 56* (which had an entrance at *Málaya Sadóvaya No. 8*) with the intention of assassinating the Emperor Alexander II. They opened a shop, which they called the Kobzevy shop, and used it as a base from which to dig a great hole in the road. In the hole they planted what was later described as an *ádskaya mashína* (**infernal machine**), some kind of explosive device capable of detonating nitro-glycerine. The terrorists were in a hurry. They wanted the assassination to coincide with the twentieth anniversary of Alexander II's liberation of the serfs and the security forces were closing in. Furthermore, only fifteen members of the People's Will Party were still at large.

The hole was duly dug and the machine planted on this corner of the *Névskiy prospékt* over which the Emperor regularly passed on a Sunday morning on his way to see the parade at the *Manézhnaya plóstchad*. But on Saturday 28 February, the hole and the machine were discovered by the security services. One of the leading conspirators, Zhelyabov, was arrested (at *Névskiy prospékt No. 66* on the corner of the Fontanka) and the Emperor was advised to give the Sunday parade a miss. He rejected the advice.

And this time they got him – not on the corner of the Nevsky but half way down the Griboyedov Canal, on his way home. Zhelyabov, who had hired the shop, was the lover of the other main conspirator, Sophia Perovskaya. Perovskaya was not arrested on that occasion and so was free, on the following day, to direct the eighth – and final – attempt to assassinate Alexander II.[4]

We return to the Canal and come back to the Fontanka on the odd (south) side. Until 1783, there was an old Association of Merchants, and make-shift market stalls associated with it, on this section of the street (*Nos. 31* and *33*). Then there was the inevitable fire and Quarenghi was commissioned to design a new complex which would include permanent stalls and a Western-style City Hall. By 1787, the *Serébryanyie ryadý* (**Silver Rows**) were completed, much as they are now. They still contain jewellers, including a well-known and expensive one called *Ananov*.

The new *Gorodskáya Dúma* (**City Hall**) was not, in fact, built by Quarenghi but by D. Ferrari, who followed Quarenghi's plans. Ferrari also designed and built the pentagonal tower (known as the **Duma Tower**) which stands on the corner of the Nevsky and the *Dúmskaya úlitsa* (1799–1804). The City Hall, which was the seat of the Town *Dúma* (or Council) looked originally very like the Silver Rows and must have had charm. But time and the nineteenth century have been unkind to it – also, of course, the swelling demands of city administration. In the 1840s, it was thoroughly reconstructed (N. Yefimov) and acquired several halls for deputies. Yefimov also 'modernised' the façade, built a third floor and changed the windows. Between 1913 and 1924, two more floors were added. At the time of the Revolution, Kalinin (a member of Lenin's Cabinet) was Chairman of the Council, a fact that is commemorated in a plaque on the façade.

---

[4] *See* p. 243.

The Duma Tower, however, did not change except that its original purpose – to give much-needed notice of fires – was further elaborated by the addition of a signalling turret which, by a species of illuminated semaphore, enabled the Imperial palaces to communicate with one another and also with Warsaw. You can still see an answering turret and rotating frame on the roof of the Winter Palace.

At the foot of the Duma Tower is an entrance to the Metro (*stantsiya metro Gostíny dvor*). Next to it is a delicious remnant of another row of merchant stalls, the *Perínnaya líniya* (Feather Rows, where they sold pillows, eiderdowns, mattresses). The Rows have vanished but the **Portico** (L. Rusca, 1802–5) which used to lead to them was dismantled when they were building the Metro station and then reconstructed stone by stone. Theatre tickets can now be bought here.

The *Névskiy prospékt* then spreads to its widest – sixty metres. Here, at *No. 35* where four roads meet, was built the first 'stone' **Gostíny dvor** (Merchants' Yard), designed and begun by Rastrelli in 1753, completed by Vallin de la Mothe thirty years later. If there is a faint flavour of Central Asia in the *Passázh*, here its presence is strong. The name literally means the place where traders would come with their camels or their horses and their merchandise and would stay, in a great courtyard at a crossroads, until they had finished their business. There had been such courtyards in St Petersburg since its beginning but, until this one, fire had finished them all.

The *Gostíny dvor* used to be an anarchic place, with separate stalls, goods thrown in a heap on the floor and customers left to rummage. Outside each stall there would be a crier who shouted its attractions and also a bench, marked out as a draughts board, where people could sit and play while other people stood round and cheered them on. At the end of the nineteenth century, the building was largely reconstructed and, while the arcades on the ground floor still contained some two hundred shops, the shoppers and the process of shopping became rather more stately.

In 1941, the *Gostíny dvor* was badly damaged by a fire bomb. While they were clearing the debris, workmen uncovered eight large and exceptionally heavy bricks. Hosed down, they turned out to be a hundred and twenty eight kilograms of pure gold, left in a jeweller's shop before the Revolution and never discovered by looters. In 1967, the Metro station (*Gostíny dvor* again; there are two entrances) was incorporated. And, now, it is a more or less conventional department store organised as in the West with franchised boutiques.

Cross *Bolsháya Sadóvaya* with care and you come to the corner of *plóstchad Ostróvskovo* (Ostrovskiy Square). In London, one would do a great deal to avoid descent into the subway. But in St Petersburg, subways can be a surprise: puppies for sale, kittens, snakes (who for a price will crawl up your arm) and posies from cottage gardens – mottled pansies, bachelors' buttons, Star of Bethlehem, grasses, lilies of the valley. So perhaps the best thing to do is to cross by the subway. When you re-emerge, counting numbers has to be abandoned. Stay on the south side.

On the corner of the *Bólshaya Sadóvaya* and the square (*plóstchad Ostróvskovo Nos. 1–3*) is the **Russian National Library**. Founded in 1795 by Catherine the Great, it was first housed in the building on the corner (E. Sokolov, 1796–1801) where the *Sadóvaya* intersects the Nevsky; there it opened for public use as the Imperial Public Library, with one reading room and forty-six seats. During the Soviet period it was known as the Saltykov-Stchedrin Library, after the novelist Saltykov whose *nom de plume* was Stchedrin.

It is one of the largest and most distinguished libraries in the world, containing over thirty million volumes. It possesses Catherine's purchase of the libraries of Voltaire and Diderot, together with the latter's collection of manuscripts.

(These were scattered after the Revolution but have recently been gathered together again.) There are Old Slavonic manuscripts, the Ostromirovo Gospel (eleventh century), the only copy in the world of the Chasóvnik (sixteenth-century Breviary), a great collection of Chinese books and manuscripts and a collection of revolutionary works published before 1917, either abroad or underground in Russia. In addition, of course, it has the right of all national libraries to have all the books published in its native country deposited there and enjoys reciprocal agreements with other national libraries. In 1857, a 'Cabinet of Faust' was constructed in imitation of a monastic library; and, from 1893 to 1895, Lenin regularly used a particular room as a *rendez-vous* with colleagues from underground revolutionary movements.

In the second decade of the nineteenth century, the development of the library down the west side of *plóstchad Ostróvskovo* was part of a grand design by Carlo Rossi. At that time, the grounds of the Anichkov Palace (*Névskiy prospékt No. 39*) extended all the way to the *Sadóvaya*, with orangeries, hot houses, fish ponds and stables as well as formal flower gardens and parterres. Some time before 1818, Rossi was commissioned by the Imperial family (who then owned the Palace) to enclose the grounds. This he did with two pavilions joined by railings (1818) on the east side of what is now the square. The occasion of this commission was probably the marriage of the future Emperor Nicholas I to Princess Charlotte of Prussia. Nicholas and his bride lived in the Anichkov until their accession in 1825 but their association with *plóstchad Ostróvskovo* lasted for the whole of their reign.

Rossi then developed the idea of creating a formal public space in the part of the Anichkov grounds that he had railed off. So, in 1828, he started simultaneously on a new wing for the library on the west side of what was going to be the square and on a theatre at the rear of it. The theatre, named in honour of the (by that time) Empress, was the *Aleksandrínskiy teátr* and took Rossi only four years to complete.'(The new library wing took him six.) He crowned it with four galloping horses, reminiscent of the chariot which topped his arch in the General Staff Building but driven, this time, by Apollo, God of Arts and Beauty. The main façade was decorated by statues of the Muses, made in the first instance of clay, and girded with a frieze of theatrical masks and garlands. In 1840, the Petersburg climate proved too much for one of the Muses; she fell off, nearly killing a passer-by; so all statues were removed until a major refurbishment in 1932 when new ones, made from Rossi's drawings but more securely fixed, were installed.

The theatre opened in 1832. Nicholas and Aleksandra were treated to an overture by Glinka, a tragedy based on the life of Prince Pozharskiy and a ballet *divertissement* called *A Spanish Holiday*. Future fare was not always so bland nor were the audiences so gracious. In 1836, there was the first performance of Gogol's comedy, *The Government Inspector*, the reception of which upset the author so much that he left St Petersburg. It was played for laughs which, on the whole, did not come, but the Emperor, realising the significance of its biting sarcasm, said, as he rose to go, 'c'est une leçon'. In 1872, the first performance of Turgenev's *A Month in the Country* was also badly received, while the first night (in October 1896) of *The Seagull* was described by the critics as 'catastrophic, a spectacle truly unprecedented in the history of the theatre'; though Komissarzhevskaya played Nina and Chekhov attended the (scanty) rehearsals, the play was jeered until the players became inaudible. (When it was revived by Stanislavsky at the Moscow Arts Theatre, its success was so great that the theatre adopted the seagull as its device.)

The tradition of great drama survived, however. On the centenary of Pushkin's death, in 1937, the theatre was re-named the **Pushkin Academic Drama Theatre** (*teátr Drámy im. Púshkina*) which it still is – though often referred to more affectionately as the *Aleksandrínka*.

Rossi himself had always thought it would be agreeable to have a statue in the middle of his square. This had to wait until 1862 when work began on the monument to Catherine the Great (oddly enough, the only one in St Petersburg) by M. Chizhov. Nearly four and a half metres high, and with the great figures of her reign supporting the plinth, it took nine years to complete.

The **Anichkov Palace**, *No. 39*, changed architects many times from the day in 1741 when the Empress Elisabeth commissioned Zemtsov to build it. (She later presented it to her lover, Razumovskiy.) Zemtsov died in 1753 and was followed by G. Dmitriev who died shortly after, and Rastrelli took over. At that stage, the building faced east on to the Fontanka; visitors arrived by boat up a little canal. All this was changed between 1803 and 1811, when first Quarenghi and then Rusca adapted the east front to accommodate the Imperial Chancery (*Kabinét*) which blocked off the palace from the river. Then in 1818 came Rossi's new entrance from the west.

There were also a good many changes in owners. After Razumovskiy, the mansion reverted to the Imperial family. Catherine gave it, in 1776, to her favourite, Prince Potemkin, probably at the end of their physical affair. But Potemkin, who never liked to be too far away from her, moved straight back into the Winter Palace and used the Anichkov briefly for entertaining and for housing his library. This did not deter him from commissioning I. Starov (who later built the Taurida Palace for him) to 'improve' it after the Classical fashion. Whereupon, having given a few parties, he mortgaged it to his banker, Shemyakin. Catherine paid off his debt, as she often did, and returned the house to him. But on his death in 1791, it passed back to the Romanovs where it remained until the Revolution. The last private inhabitant of the Anichkov Palace was the Dowager Empress who, having

lived there as a bride, returned after the death of her husband
Alexander III and remained until 1917. What remained of
Rastrelli's interior was subsumed into three hundred study
rooms and is now the 'Palace of Young Creativity' (*dvoréts
Tvórchestva Yunykh*).

Cross the Fontanka by the Anichkov Bridge. At this
point, you leave the city as planned by the Building
Commission of 1738 and there are fewer houses of historical note. So we will take them in numerical order from
here until *plóstchad Vosstániya*.

The **Anichkov Bridge** (*Aníchkov most*) in its present
form, pink granite and iron railings, dates from 1841 and is
remarkable only for the four magnificent statues of stallions being tamed (or perhaps not). They were commissioned by Nicholas I from the sculptor P. Klodt and,
originally, were just a single pair repeated at each end of the
bridge. They were so much admired that Nicholas insisted
on giving a pair to his father-in-law, the King of Prussia,
and they were replaced on the bridge by a pair made of
gypsum painted to look like bronze. Then he decided to
give the other pair to the King of Naples. But Klodt, by this
time having had nearly enough of his royal patron, decided
to make a second, different pair and to cast all four statues
again in bronze. Rumour has it that the Emperor's face is to
be found, grotesque and unflattering, on the testicles of
one of the stallions. True or not, the statues were much
prized and were buried during the Blockade in the grounds
of the Anichkov Palace. On 30 April 1945, they were disinterred and replaced on the bridge to great rejoicing.

The **Beloselskiy-Belozerskiy Palace**, *No. 41*, was built at
the beginning of the nineteenth century by an heiress whose
arrival in the Beloselskiy family made it one of the richest in
Russia. She bought a small house on the south eastern
corner of the Fontanka, knocked it down and commissioned a mansion from the architect Thomas de Thomon.
The new wealth went to the heads of the Beloselskiys who,

in 1846, employed Stackenschneider to change the eleva-
tions and over-decorate the interior. So lavish were the
parties given in the 1870s that a substantial part of the
family's fortune was consumed and, in 1884, Prince
Konstantin Beloselskiy was obliged to sell his house on the
Névskiy prospékt to the brother of Alexander III, the Grand
Duke Sergey, whereupon the Grand Duke had the interior
done again (1888). At this point (and not before, since only
houses lived in by the Imperial family are 'palaces'), the
house became the Sergiyev Palace.

The Grand Duke was assassinated in 1905 and his wife,
Ella (sister of the reigning Empress and grand-daughter of
Queen Victoria), was murdered in 1918 by being thrown
down a mineshaft with other members of her family. This,
perhaps, is why 'palace' has attached itself to Beloselskiy.
The Romanovs to whom it last belonged were all dead. The
Palace now contains the **City Tourist Information Centre**
(*Gorodskóy turístsko-informatsiónny tsentr*).

Just south of the Beloselskiy-Belozerskiy Palace along
the Fontanka at *No. 46* stands the Countess Karlov House,
dom Grafíni Kárlovoy, acquired from the Zinoviev family
by the Countess's husband, the Duke of Mecklenburg-
Strelitz, when he was obliged to leave the Mikháylovskiy
Palace by Alexander III in the 1890s (*see* p. 245). During the
Duke's lifetime, the house became a musical centre and
was renowned for its private concerts. Built originally in
timber in the 1740s, re-made in stone with a Baroque
façade in the 1760s, it was reconstructed, greatly enlarged –
and aesthetically ruined – by Nikolay Zinoviev and the
German architect Wilhelm Langwagen in the early 1840s.
The exterior remains unaltered. The Duke died in 1909
and, after the Revolution, the house was nationalised.
Now it is home to the British Council and to an excellent
Anglo-Russian library – the Galitsin Library – founded a
few years ago in memory of George Galitsin, grandson of
the Duke, by his English widow and his daughter.

Back across the Nevsky, on the north side is *No. 68*, a
house with a radically different story. **Lopatin's House** was
built in the second half of the eighteenth century but, in the
mid-ninteenth century, it was known with good reason as
the 'Literary House'. The man they all came to see was the
critic V. Belinskiy who lived in this house for four years in
three different apartments. Belinskiy was by that time working on *The Contemporary*. He was visited by Nekrasov and
Pisarev from the rival journal and by the writers he encouraged – Dostoyevsky, Goncharov, Lermontov and, whenever
he was in Russia, Turgenev who described Belinskiy as a
'man not deceived by appearances or surroundings,
instantly recognising the beautiful in the hideous, the true
in the false, and pronouncing his verdict with fearless
courage'. In May 1848, a year after the death of his three-
month-old son to whom Turgenev stood godfather,
Belinskiy died in a sombre, damp room on the ground floor
of *No. 68*, facing on to the Fontanka. Turgenev bought his
library and asked to be buried beside him.

At *No. 84* the poet, V. Zhukovskiy lived, when he came
from Moscow to St Petersburg to become tutor to the
future Alexander II. Zhukovskiy was also the devoted
teacher of Pushkin. Later, in the 1820s, he lived further up
the street at *No. 64*. Wherever he lived, he gathered round
him other writers.

Next door is one of the most striking houses in the
Nevsky. It was built by G. Fossati in the 1820s for the
Yusupov family who abandoned it for their even larger
house on the Moika (*see* p. 278) and gave it as a home for
actors. Before they left, however, in the 1860s, it was the
venue for wonderful musical performances by
Moussorgsky and Rimsky-Korsakov. It has remained in
theatrical hands and, since the Revolution, has been the
headquarters of the **Union of Theatre Workers**.

At *plóstchad Vosstániya* (Uprising Square), *Névskiy
prospékt* really comes to an end – that is, in its serious

purpose of linking the Admiralty with the supply road from Novgorod. For, there, the road to Novgorod goes off to the right, in the form of the *Lígovskiy prospékt*, and the Nevsky continues towards the Alexander Nevsky Monastery. Until the mid-nineteenth century, this was a bleak and unfriendly place, surrounded by wasteland on which, in an attempt to civilise it, they built the Church of Our Lady of the Sign (*Známenskaya tsérkov*). And so, until the uprising that gave it its new name, the square was called *Známenskaya plóstchad*.

VIII

From Uprising Square to the Alexander Nevsky Monastery

Metro Stations: *Plóstchad Vosstániya / Mayakóvskaya* and
Plóstchad Aleksándra Névskovo

A T THIS POINT *Névskiy prospékt* broadens into a
square which lies well outside the eastern extremity of
the original city, an unfriendly part of town where workers
from the nineteenth-century industrial suburbs had
been in the habit of expressing their discontents. In
February 1917, it was the scene of crucial clashes between
Government forces and demonstrators.

By 24 February, 200,000 people were on strike from the
gigantic armaments factories in the south of the city or
crowding in from the new housing estates across the river
to the north, thronging the streets and squares of the
centre, shouting for higher wages, for food and – later – for
the end of the war and the fall of the Emperor. To control
them were some 3,500 police and some noticeably reluctant Cossacks (whose traditional role it was to reinforce the
sparse ranks of the police when they were controlling
crowds). On 25 February in this square, then called
Známenskaya plóstchad, for the first time Cossacks actively
obstructed the police when they charged to disperse the
crowd and a mounted Cossack killed a police officer with
his sabre. That evening Nicholas II, still at the Front, gave
orders that the demonstrations must stop. The garrison
commander, General Khabalov, interpreted this as orders
for the army to shoot if necessary. On 26 February, he

called out the garrison and imposed a curfew. But by midday the crowds were back, particularly dense in this Square which linked *Lígovskiy prospékt* and *Névskiy prospékt*. They refused a police demand to disperse and a company of the Volýnskiy Regiment opened fire, at first into the air but then into the crowd, killing forty people in the Square and ten in *Suvórovskiy prospékt* round the corner.

This was the point when the strikes and the riots became revolution. The Fourth Training Company of the Pavlovskiy Regiment was ordered to take up positions on the Griboyedov Canal near *Névskiy prospékt*. Appealed to by the crowd, fresh into uniform and unenthusiastic about going to the Front, they voted to disobey orders and started to shoot at the police – the first time regular army units actively sided with the citizens and against the forces of order. Nineteen of these soldiers were arrested and carried off to the Trubetskoy Bastion in the Fortress – the last pre-Revolutionary prisoners to be detained there. The remainder ran away and hid themselves in the Summer Garden. (The Pavlovskiy Barracks are close to the Summer Garden along the west side of *Mársovo pólye*; built by Stasov from 1817 to 1819, they are now offices.) There they found other soldiers from their barracks also hiding. Eventually an officer took command and, within twenty-four hours, they had prevailed on almost the entire Petersburg garrison to mutiny. By 27 February, St Petersburg was beyond the control of Government forces. An officer was killed, prisoners released from the Peter and Paul Fortress, a policeman beaten to death. The Revolution had begun. On 2 March, the Emperor abdicated. It was in memory of these events that the Square was later given the new name of *plóstchad Vosstániya* (The Square of the Uprising).

The Square has other claims to fame. In the 1730s, somewhere on this plot of wasteland, the Empress Anne decided to place the first aviary in St Petersburg. In 1851,

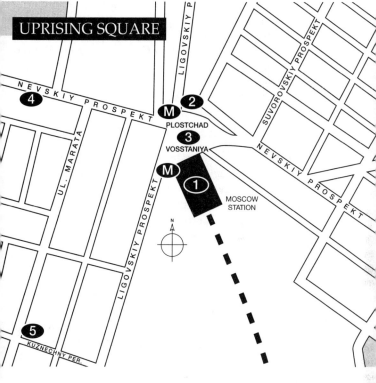

1   Moscow main-line station
2   October Hotel
3   Obelisk
4   Sheraton Nevsky Hotel
5   Museum of the Arctic and Antarctic

the first long-distance railway entered St Petersburg here, connecting the new with the old capital of Russia and terminating in the *Nikoláyevskiy vokzál* (Nicholas Station – since 1924, the Moscow Station) that had its identical twin in Moscow. At that point, the Square was still called after

the church, built at the turn of the eighteenth and nineteenth centuries by F. Demertsov and dedicated to Our
Lady of the Sign – *Známenskaya tsérkov*.

Exactly ninety years later, in 1941, work began – but was
immediately stopped by the war – on St Petersburg's first
underground system. Begun again in 1945, the line (which
crosses the Neva to the Vyborg Side) was completed in
1950 and connected the Moscow, Finland and Baltic
Stations. It was 'given the unique honour of the great and
sacred name of Lenin', and the *Plóstchad Vosstániya
stantsiya* was opened on 20 November 1955 on the site of
the Church of the Sign, which had been demolished in
1940 to make way for it. (Old people, mainly women, can
sometimes still be seen making the sign of the cross to the
flag on the Metro station.) Thus the junction of *Névskiy
prospékt* and the road to Novgorod (now *Lígovskiy
prospékt*) remains a crucial point in St Petersburg's
communications.

The **Moscow Station** building (*plóstchad Vosstániya
No. 2*) on the south side is another First – the first example
in St Petersburg of a style of architecture that has been
variously called Early-Russian Revival or Neo-Russian.
Designed by a great practitioner of the style, K. A. Thon
(who worked mostly in Moscow), and taking six years to
build (1845–51), the façade (recently repainted pink and
white) with a two-tier clock tower at the axis is all that
remains of the original after radical reconstruction in the
1950s. In the main hall there is now a bust of Peter the
Great. But this is a recent acquisition; it was preceded by a
huge bust of Lenin by L. Mess. Lenin was removed from his
pedestal, with a certain public outcry, by Mayor Sobchak
in 1993.

The railway itself, however, is a purely Tsarist creation.
The engineers charged with constructing it included the
father of Whistler the painter (and thus, presumably, the
husband of '*Whistler's Mother*'). They went to ask Nicholas I

for permission to lay the line across land between St Petersburg and Moscow. The Emperor sent for a ruler and proceeded to draw the shortest distance between the two points (with, incidentally, the unfortunate consequence that several towns along the old road lost a large part of their trade from through-traffic). The story is that the point of the Imperial pencil followed round the Imperial thumb as it held the ruler steady, thus indicating a detour which in their anxiety to do exactly what they were told the engineers duly followed. (Whatever the explanation, the line, which is otherwise straight as a die, to this day makes a strange deviation in the District of Bologóye.) It was along this line and from the Nicholas Station, on 11 March 1918, that Lenin, his wife and his cabinet travelled to take up residence in Moscow, thus ending St Petersburg's role as the capital of Russia.

On the north side of the Square, on the corner of the northern arm of *Lígovskiy prospékt*, is a building that was once upon a time *Névskiy prospékt No. 118* and is still known by old Petersburgers as *dom Fréderiksa* but whose proper name since 1932 is the **Oktyábrskaya gostínitsa** (October Hotel). In the mid-eighteenth century, the site had belonged to the Imperial family and was known as the Elephant Yard. Indeed it was a yard where fourteen elephants lived, presented by the Shah of Persia to the Empress Elisabeth who opened her own zoo in this area in the 1740s. (The street that is now *Suvórovskiy prospékt* was once called *Slonóvaya* – Elephant– *úlitsa*, being the road along which the elephants were led to drink from the river Neva.)

Elephants made various appearances in eighteenth-century St Petersburg and their expectation of life was fairly short – Peter the Great got through two in less than twenty years. So perhaps it was wise of the keepers of these elephants to proclaim that they could not possibly survive the Petersburg climate simply on water from the Neva. What they needed was vodka. At all events, vodka was observed entering the premises of *No. 118* not in bottles but in pails for the benefit, according to the keepers, of the elephants. And, though the remedy was not effective and these elephants too soon died, the supply was said to have continued undiminished for some time thereafter.

In 1845 the then owner of the site, Baron Frederiks, sold it to Count Stenbock-Fermor (the first owner of the *Passázh* in *Névskiy prospékt*) for development as a railway hotel which, by 1860, was in business as the *Známenskaya*. Names do not matter much in the life of a hotel – this one has changed its name five times. Three times it has been enlarged (1900, 1961 and 1980) until it now has 680 rooms and nearly 1300 beds. It has even changed its address (to *Lígovskiy prospékt No. 10*). But, though there are many stories about it (some, to our knowledge, authentic), not one suggests that visitors would be sensible to stay there. It has perhaps just three claims to fame: in May 1942, it became a refuge for people dying of starvation during the Blockade; in February 1944, with the liberation of Estonia from German occupation, it was briefly the seat of the Government of the Soviet Republic of Estonia. And, from time to time in the course of 1905, Lenin Slept – or at least conspired – There.

In the centre of the Square now stands a great **obelisk** (architect A. Alimov and sculptor V. Pinchuk), erected on 9 May 1985 for the fortieth anniversary of the victory over Germany to commemorate the city's suffering during the Blockade. The inscription reads: 'To the Hero City of Leningrad'. But until the 1930s, the Square was dominated by a brooding statue of Alexander III by Paolo Trubetskoy, slouched on his horse, apparently the representative *par excellence* of brutal autocracy. When autocracy was overthrown, Alexander's successors left him there for a bit but superimposed a mocking epitaph ('*Púgalo*' – Scarecrow) on his plinth. Then in 1937 he was removed and, rather oddly, preserved *incommunicado* behind a wooden fence outside the Russian Museum where the curious could glimpse him through the chinks. He has now been resurrected, but without his plinth, and set up *en plein air* in the front garden of the Marble Palace (*see* p. 301) in place of the armoured car that brought Lenin from the Finland Station to Kshesinskaya's mansion in April 1917. The 'Scarecrow' may be on his way to rehabilitation.

So the elephant yard has become an elephantine hotel. The Church of Our Lady of the Sign has become a metro station. The bust of Lenin in the Station Hall has ceded to a bust of Peter the Great. The equestrian statue of Alexander III has been succeeded by an obelisk and Lenin's car has made way for the equestrian statue of Alexander III. How they play Musical Chairs in St Petersburg.

On down the last part, sometimes called *Stáry* (Old), of *Névskiy prospékt* – it used to be the shabby and more disreputable end but is becoming, in patches, quite smart – to *Nos. 177* and *190*. These were originally part of the monastic complex but were rebuilt by I. Starov at the end of the 1780s to frame the entrance from *Névskiy prospékt* of his new **plóstchad Aleksándra Névskovo** (Alexander Nevsky Square).

On the left (north) as you enter the Square from Nevsky is the Metro station, tucked into the curved bulk of the **gostínitsa Moskvá** (Moscow Hotel), built in the 1970s and even larger than the *Oktyábrskaya*. Opposite is the narrow entrance to the **Alexander Nevsky Monastery** (*Aleksándro-Névskaya Lávra*), between the Tikhvin and the Lazarus cemeteries and over the little *Chórnaya réchka* (Black Stream) – now renamed the *Monastýrka* – as it flows into the Neva from the west. Here at the beginning of the eighteenth century was a Finnish village called *Fikhtula*, built along one of the paths across the swamp towards Novgorod. After Peter the Great captured the Swedish town of *Nyenskans* on the opposite (east) bank of the Neva in 1703, he noted down the village's name as *Viktori* and, according to his Journal of July 1710, ordered a monastery to be built there which would commemorate his own

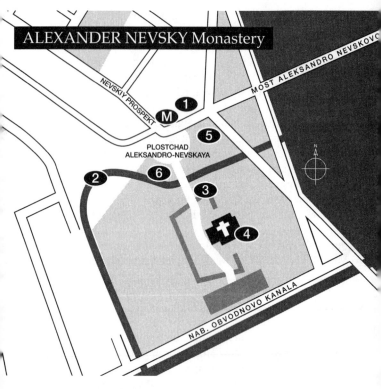

ALEXANDER NEVSKY Monastery

1 Hotel Moskva
2 Monastyrka River
3 Church of the Annunciation (Museum of City Sculpture)
4 Trinity Cathedral
5 Lazarus Cemetery
6 Tikhvin Cemetery

victory and that of St Alexander Nevsky over the Swedes in the Battle of the Neva in 1240, though this in fact took place further up the Neva at its confluence with the river Izhora (*see* p. 6). At one stroke he would thus establish heavenly credentials for his new city and identify his own victorious campaign with that of his illustrious predecessor. So he appointed Archimandrite Theodosius to be head of the putative monastery and the Archimandrite planted his pastoral staff into the earth on the left bank of the river *Chórnaya/Monastýrka*, declaring that 'in the name of the Father, Son and Holy Ghost, by order of the Tsar's Serene Majesty, a monastery is to be erected on this spot'. To be going on with, a temporary chapel was put there and, soon afterwards, a timber Chapel of the Annunciation.

In 1715, the architect Dominico Trezzini received Peter's commission to produce a project for the whole monastic complex. It was intended to be the most important monastery in all Russia (though, in spite of being promoted to *Lávra* in 1797, it never became more important than Kiev).[1] Engravings of this project, which remained the blue print for all subsequent construction within the monastery, were sent by Peter as promotional material to impress the relatively civilised courts of Europe. In 1717, Trezzini started to build in stone on the right bank of the *Chórnaya*. By 1722 he had completed the little double church to the left of the entrance that was to become the permanent **Church of the Annunciation** (*Blagovéstchenskaya tsérkov*) and, above it, the **Church of St Alexander Nevsky**. There, on 30 August 1724 (the third anniversary of Peter's final victory over the Swedes) the relics of the saint were brought from their previous resting place in Vladímir. Just in time, before Peter's death the following year.

Nearly thirty years later, the Empress Elisabeth imperialised the relics still further and had them encased in 1500 kilograms of silver, representing the entire first year's output of the Kolyivan silver mines. In 1790, bones and reliquary

---

[1] A *Lávra* is an Orthodox monastery of the first class, seat of a Metropolitan Archbishop and containing a theological academy. There are currently three in Russia, one in the Ukraine (Kiev), one in Sinai, one in Jerusalem and one on Mount Athos.

were transferred to the Empress Catherine's newly completed Cathedral of the Trinity within the complex where
they remained until after the Revolution, when all holy
objects were dispersed from the Monastery. The reliquary
was taken to the Winter Palace where, much tarnished, it is
displayed in the Concert Hall (*R. 190*); the relics went to
Kazan Cathedral as an exhibit in the Museum of the History
of Religion and Atheism. (The Museum, having dropped
'Atheism' from its title, has moved to *Pochtámtskaya úlitsa
No. 14/15* and the relics have returned to the *Lávra*.)

The lower Church (of the Annunciation) was intended
originally as a crypt where members of the Romanov and
(later) other prominent families, distinguished statesmen
and military leaders could be interred. Peter's favourite
sister, Natalya, who died in 1716 before the stone church
was built, is buried in the Lazarus cemetery just outside.
The tomb of Field Marshal Suvorov (1730–1800) is inside,
simply inscribed: '*Zes Lezhít Suvórov*' ('Here lies Suvorov').
It has been said that the Field Marshal composed his own
epitaph but that is not quite how it was. Standing next to
the poet laureate of the time, Derzhavin, at some official
function, the Field Marshal by way of making conversation
asked the poet what kind of an epitaph he would in due
course be composing for his grave. 'I shall use very few
words', the poet replied. 'Something like: Here lies
Suvorov.' 'Yes', said the Field Marshal. 'Yes. Just that.' And so
it was.

In the 1930s, the Church of the Annunciation became,
and still remains, a **Museum of the City's Sculpture**.[2]

---

[2] Services are no longer held in the Church of the Annunciation. But an
exception was made in 2001 when a memorial service was held for the
repose of the soul of my great-great-great-aunt Yekaterina Zinoviev, wife
of Grigoriy Orlov. In 1781, at the age of twenty-three, she died of consumption in Lausanne where there is a mausoleum for her in the
Orthodox Cathedral. But it is believed that her remains were later brought
home to St Petersburg and interred in the Church of the Annunciation.

It includes the funeral monuments of the great who lie in the Lazarus and Tikhvin cemeteries to the north of the *Lávra* and also in the *Literátorskiye mostkí* some way to the south (*see below*). Many of the exhibits are original pieces of memorial or monumental art collected and kept safe from around the city; some are original maquettes, including Klodt's models for his horses on the Anichkov Bridge. The Museum is responsible for the preservation and restoration of all the city's monuments and is well worth a visit – partly for its contents but, more importantly, because it is one of the earliest buildings still to be seen in Petersburg. Altered and added to by Rastorguyev in the 1760s, the façade and cupola of the Church of the Annunciation nevertheless remain as designed by Trezzini three centuries ago.

The most imposing building at the heart of the Monastery functions again as a church: the **Cathedral of the Trinity** (*Tróitskiy sobór*). Part of Trezzini's original project, started by him and finished by Schwertfeger, the walls of this first cathedral started to crumble and it was mostly demolished in 1755. Some of it was incorporated in the present church which is an example of early Russian Classicism as favoured by Catherine the Great and built by Starov (between 1776 and 1790). The Cathedral has a fine choir; a gilded canopy to the right of the iconostasis is suspended above a more-or-less copy of the original silver reliquary. Starov was also responsible for the **Gate Church** of Our Lady, the Joy of All Mourners (1783–5) and he reconstructed the miscellaneous accretion of buildings on the left bank of the *Chórnaya* river, creating in the process a formal approach and entrance Square.

All around the Monastery, except on the west, are cemeteries laid out in what was once the Metropolitan Archbishop's garden. The earliest, the **Lazarus Cemetery** (*Lázarevskoye kládbistche*), on the left of the entrance to the Monastery just before you cross the river, is mainly eighteenth-century and contains the graves of the great polymath Lomonósov, of Starov himself, of Voronikhin and Rossi. To the right the **Tikhvin Cemetery** (*Tikhvínskoye kládbistche*), mainly nineteenth- and early twentieth-century, includes the graves of writers Zhukovskiy, Krylov and Dostoyevsky; Tchaikovsky dominates a distinguished gathering of musicians including Rimsky-Korsakov, Borodin, Anton Rubinstein and Glinka; among sculptors there are Shubin and Demut-Malinovskiy.

The entrance to this cemetery was for a time guarded by a very fine pair of bulls made by Demut-Malinovskiy in 1827 for the Petersburg slaughterhouse on the *Moskóvskiy prospékt*. In the 1930s they were moved to a new meat factory on the outskirts of the city that, in 1941, was absorbed into the front line of the battle for Leningrad. At this point they were taken to the Monastery to be buried for safe keeping but nobody had the strength to do it and so, for the rest of the war, they stood at the cemetery gates. It is said that, before he died and was buried in the Tikhvin cemetery, Malinovskiy dreamt that his slaughterhouse bulls came to visit him – and so they did, a hundred years later, to guard his grave. They are now back on guard in front of their meat factory.

On the east of the Monastery, between the Cathedral and the Neva, lies the Nicholas Cemetery (*Nikólskoye kládbistche*), less carefully tended and full of more ordinary people. In the centre of the courtyard, in front of the Metropolitan's house, is the 'War' Cemetery, so called because it contains a number of Soviet airmen buried, apparently, with their propellers. It also contains some veteran revolutionaries including Eino Rahja, the Estonian detailed by the Bolsheviks to be Lenin's bodyguard. These cemeteries are not part of the Museum. The third – and perhaps the most interesting – of the Museum cemeteries lies about a kilometre to the south: the *Literátorskiye mostkí*, a part of the Orthodox cemetery which derived its name (in the 1880s) from the duck-boarding which was put down to protect the paths to the graves as, increasingly, the illustrious were buried and venerated there. Its official address is *Rasstánnaya úlitsa No. 30*. In fact, it is best reached by bus from the Moscow Station, and along the *Lígovskiy prospékt*.

It is here that you will find Turgenev, brought home (in 1883) from Madame Viardot's house near Paris and buried, as he had asked, next to Belinskiy who predeceased him by thirty-five years. Here also are Pisarev, Saltykov-Stchedrin, Garshin, Goncharov and Russia's greatest symbolist poet, Aleksandr Blok (who died in 1921). Here are the scientists Mendeleyev, Popov, Pavlov; here is the ballerina Vaganova (the great choreographer Petipa is in the Tikhvin); here is Georgiy Plekhanov, the first Russian Marxist; and here is most of Lenin's family: his sister Olga (1891), his mother Maria (1906), his other sister Anna (with whom he stayed in 1917) and her husband (1935). Some say that, should he ever be moved from Moscow, Lenin himself should be buried here too. Visitors will come with their own short list and will be able to orientate themselves by calling in at the **Church of the Resurrection** (Starov, 1782–5) which is also part of the Museum of the City's Sculpture and which houses an exhibition devoted to the graves and their occupants.

This cemetery is part of a much larger burial ground called the *Vólkovskoye kládbistche* (Volkovo Cemetery) that dates back to pre-Petersburg days. In the seventeenth century about forty villages were scattered through the Neva estuary and many of them, like *Fikhtula*, were inhabited by non-Russians. One of them sprawled across the little river *Vólkovka* (now filled in and running north and south through the middle of the cemetery). The inhabitants of Vólkovo were Lutheran. It so happened that they were buried somewhat superficially in the ground near their church, giving off so vile a smell that it was sometimes impossible to hold services there. By the 1740s, the defects in the burial arrangements of the Petersburg area had come to the attention of the Empress Elisabeth who ordered that they be reviewed and improved. Ten years and a great deal of argument later, the Senate decreed (1757) that there should be three public cemeteries in three separate parts of the city, one of which was to be sited at Vólkovo. This was now to provide primarily for the Orthodox but Lutherans (and Catholics) were to be accommodated too. Indeed, the Lutheran part of the Volkovo Cemetery became the property of the Lutheran Church at *Névskiy prospékt No. 22*).

It is not easy to get back to the centre of the city from the *Literátorskiye mostkí*. One way is to follow *Rasstánnaya úlitsa* out into *Lígovskiy prospékt*, turn right and walk or tram back to *plóstchad Vosstániya*. Where the Prospect intersects the *Obvódniy kanál*, on the northeast corner (*Lígovskiy prospékt No. 128*) you can see the strange shape of the **Church of the Elevation of the Cross** (*Krestovozdvízhenskaya tsérkov*), one of the first of the pre-Revolutionary buildings that you will encounter on the bus into town from Pulkovo Airport. This church is mid nineteenth-century by Ye. Dimmert (a pupil of Starov) but it incorporates parts of a much older (1748) building. Also on the site is the building of the Tikhvin Church (1760s, rebuilt in 1844 and 1939).

A less tiring way home may be to turn left down *Lígovskiy prospékt* to *plóstchad Moskóvskiye voróta*, from where you can take the Metro or a tram right into the centre at *Sennáya plóstchad*. This way, you cannot avoid another landmark passed on the way in from the airport: the **Moscow Triumphal Gate**, *Moskóvskiye voróta* (V. Stasov, 1834–8), erected to commemorate the return of the Russian troops in 1829 at the end of the Russo-Turkish war. The remarkable fact about this arch is that it is made entirely of cast iron; at the time it was the largest cast iron object in the world. In 1936 it was dismantled but somewhere preserved so that in 1941 its cast iron blocks were deployed in the southern outskirts as anti-tank defences. Thus it earned its restoration and, in 1960, it was re-assembled. The place where it stands was originally a guardhouse and checkpoint on one of the southern entrances to the city.

IX

North of the Nevsky Prospect

Nearest Metro Station: *Chernyshévskaya*

A GREAT DEAL of history has been played out in the area that we have chosen to cover in this chapter, north of *Névskiy prospékt*, east of the Griboyedov Canal, and *Smolénskiy rayón* (south and west of the Neva). Much of it is connected with four political murders: the murder of the Tsarevich Aleksey by his father, Peter the Great, in 1718; the murder of the Emperor Paul by a conspiracy of Guards officers in 1801; the murder of Alexander II by the People's Will Party in 1881; and the murder of Sergey Kirov, boss of the Leningrad Communist Party and member of the Politburo, by Leonid Nikolayev in 1934. Each of these murders changed the course of Russian history. Arguably the last two, at least, changed the history of the world.

Litéyny prospékt, which runs north and south through the middle of this area, acquired its name from the *Litéyny dom* (Foundry House) built, at first in timber, on the site of what is now the south abutment of the *Litéyny most* (bridge) in 1711 for James Bruce. Bruce was a Scottish mechanical engineer, hired by Peter the Great to create an arsenal for the manufacture of guns for the new Baltic Fleet. He set up the *Litéyny dvor* (foundry works) where *Nos. 1–4* of the present street now stand (they later extended all the way to the Fontanka) and cast his first cannon in 1713. The choice of site, just as *Nóvaya Gollándiya* had been selected for the storage of timber, was indicated by Peter's desire to keep the most inflammatory parts of his armament business far away from the most inflammable. In those days, *Litéyny prospékt* was a dead end. Until 1851, when the Foundry House was demolished to make room for the bridge, there was no link to the other side of the Neva and most of the buildings, such as they were, were of wood.

The next significant development in the area was the arrival of the **Tsarevich Aleksey**. He chose to set up house on the unoccupied stretch of land between what is now the Liteyny Bridge and Peter's tar yard (*Smolyanóy dvor*) to the east, on the bend of the Neva. Here, he felt, between foundry and tar yard, was as far as he could get from his father's eagle eye and as near as he could get to a swift escape route. He was followed by some of his supporters, most notably the *boyar* (noble), Aleksandr Kikin, one-time companion of Peter and now head of procurement for the Admiralty, who built himself (1714) a mansion at the far (east) end, on the corner of what is now *Shpalérnaya úlitsa* and *Stavrópolskiy pereúlok*. For Kikin, this had the double advantage of being near the Tsarevich and near the tar, which was transported down river to his shipyards.

But Aleksey was to be watched by his father, even in this remote spot. Peter asked his favourite sister, Natalya, to build herself a house next to his son's. The two dowager Tsaritsas (widows of Peter's two half-brothers) were also persuaded to settle along the *Shpalérnaya*, as were other court officials. In 1730, there arrived a factory (at *No. 29*) which made wall coverings for the Court and which eventually (in 1858, when the factory closed) gave its name (*shpaléra* – wallpaper) to the road. So, gradually, the road filled up on the south side (the north side was often lapped by the Neva which was not yet embanked) – in spite of the violent removal in 1718 of the Tsarevich and Kikin to the Fortress of SS Peter and Paul for interrogation, torture and death.

The Tsarevich's well-known hostility to his father's reforms, his declared intention of destroying St Petersburg and of returning the centre of government to the heart of

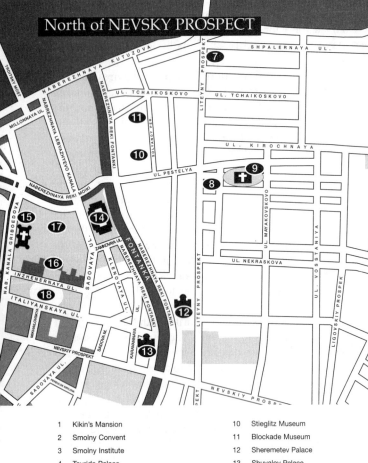

North of NEVSKY PROSPECT

1	Kikin's Mansion	10	Stieglitz Museum
2	Smolny Convent	11	Blockade Museum
3	Smolny Institute	12	Sheremetev Palace
4	Taurida Palace	13	Shuvalov Palace
5	*Gorodskóy Détskiy park*	14	Engineers' (St Michael's) Castle
6	Suvorov Museum	15	Saviour on the Blood
7	*Bolshóy dom*	16	Russian Museum
8	Muruzi House	17	Mikhaylovskiy Garden
9	*Preobrazhénskaya plóstchad*	18	Arts Square

Old Russia in Moscow – above all, the discovery of the depth of support for such a move among the *boyars* and leaders of the Church – led Peter to a fateful decision: to abolish the long-standing convention that the son of the sovereign should succeed his father and to substitute for it, by decree, a right for future occupants of the Russian throne to appoint the successor of their choice. Hard cases

217

making very bad law, this decree was the cause of great turbulence for the Russian throne throughout the rest of the eighteenth century until, for his own reasons, the Emperor Paul rescinded it and replaced it with a succession law based on the Austrian model.

Kikin's Mansion (*Kíkiny paláty*), painted red, still stands on the left (north) side of the street and set back a little in a garden. Since its careful restoration in 1956 after damage done to it during the bombardment, it now looks very like its early eighteenth-century self. On the death of Kikin, it was confiscated by Peter and used for a few years to display his *Kúnstkamera* – Chamber of Curiosities – which he had begun collecting for his own interest and stored in his Summer Palace at Smolny. The philosopher, Leibniz, persuaded him of its educational value and that it should be shared with the public. When he housed his curiosities in the Kikin Mansion, Peter turned down a suggestion that he should charge for admission. Instead, the 'curator' was given an annual budget of four hundred roubles to provide vodka and coffee to all comers and to encourage them 'to study how human and animal bodies were made'. And they were encouraged not merely to study but to contribute to the collection. By a decree of 1718 – 'About Monsters' – Peter required everybody in every town of Russia to bring him such human and animal 'monsters' as might come their way. They should be assured that monsters were not the work of the Devil but resulted from natural – physical, psychological, chemical – causes; since parents were sometimes ashamed, their names would be kept secret; they should be paid (immediately) and allowed (immediately) to go home after delivery of their curiosity. There was a detailed tariff: a hundred roubles for a live human monster, be it giant or dwarf, ten for a dead one; fifteen for a live animal (a two-headed lamb, for example), five for a dead one. The Kikin Mansion, one of the earliest buildings to be seen in St Petersburg, has now become, after many metamorphoses, a school for children's music and a resource centre for music teachers. Peter's collection of monsters found a permanent, purpose-built home on *Vasíliyevskiy óstrov* but it was not completed until 1734.

Beyond Kikin's house, next to the tar yard, Peter had built a palace with a garden for his wife, who became Catherine I; he named it *Smolyanóy dom*. Like all the best sites, it had already been occupied – by a Swedish fort called Sabina, built by a General Kronjort as a defensive outpost of the Swedish stronghold at *Nyenskans* across the river and demolished after *Nyenskans* fell to the Russians in 1703. Peter must have abandoned interest in it in the early 1710s, when Trezzini finished his Summer Palace on the corner of the Fontanka and the Neva. So *Smolyanóy dom* lay neglected until it caught the attention of the Empress Elisabeth.

On her accession in 1740, she became the next major player in this area. First, always mindful of the need to cultivate the Imperial Guard, she gave Kikin's Mansion to the Horse Guards, for a headquarters, church and hospital. Then, for reasons real or tactical, she decided (probably about 1745) to let it be known that she was intending to abdicate and become a nun. There were plenty of convents in Russia but none in St Petersburg. So she selected the Smolny Summer Palace and asked B. Rastrelli, who was permanently engaged in propping up her own Winter Palace, to rebuild it as a convent (*Smólny monastýr*) with an appropriately splendid cathedral (*Smólny sobór*) on the site of the tar yard. He started in 1748 but, by 1764 – when Elisabeth (whose vocation had been noticeably short-lived) was dead, Catherine II had declared her distaste for Baroque and Rastrelli had been made to pack his bags and leave the city – it was by no means finished. The Imperial coffers were empty, partly as a result of Elisabeth's extravagances, partly drained by the Seven Years War; and Rastrelli's two-storey convent buildings, which surround his Cathedral in an indented square, were left without their western towers. These were supplied, a hundred years later in 1860. But the great belfry, which Rastrelli had designed to complete the convent ensemble and to be the highest in St Petersburg, was never built; nor did the Cathedral ever acquire a Baroque interior but was demurely finished by V. Stasov in 1835. There are other beautiful and unfinished cathedrals but none more alluring from the outside than this fantastical mix of Russian and Italian, left suspended in mid-construction.

Catherine staunched the flow of funds into it. She allowed the convent to open but insisted that it share the cell accommodation with an 'Enlightenment' project of her own – a school for the daughters of the gentry, to which she gave the name '**Smolny Institute**'. (She planned this project with her Minister of Education, Ivan Betskoy, who had been her mother's lover when they had been in Sweden together and was said by some to be Catherine's own father; at all events he was the only man for whom she habitually rose when he entered the room.) The school cohabited with the nuns until after Catherine's death and the convent itself was closed (1797), when the last nuns departed and the whole building was taken over by the Institute. Meanwhile, in 1765, Catherine commissioned Felten to build a second 'institute' (the 'Alexander', for daughters of the bourgeoisie) in a new wing to the north of the convent. In 1806, it was decided to enlarge the school for the gentry and provide it with a home of its own. Catherine's grandson, Alexander I, commissioned G. Quarenghi to design the Classical building now known as the Smolny Institute to the south of the convent, and it remained a girls' school until it was closed in August 1917.

Towards the end of the eighteenth century, there arrived in the area the huge presence of **Prince Potemkin** – lover, friend and possibly husband of Catherine II, certainly the only serious statesman and military leader among all her lovers. In 1783, in gratitude for his military and diplomatic triumphs in Georgia and the Crimea (*Tavrida*), the Empress allocated one hundred thousand roubles to the building of a house for Potemkin. The result was the two-storey central block of what is now the **Taurida Palace** (*Tavrícheskiy dvoréts*), on the south side of *Shpalérnaya úlitsa*, a little further west than Kikin's Mansion. The exterior, even after the addition of the wings which project to the street (in 1786 and 1789), is extraordinarily restrained, even severe, except for the softening effect of the yellow and white. Ivan Starov was a master of the Classical style which, strangely for such an exuberant personality, was Potemkin's (as well as Catherine's) preferred aesthetic. The interior was another story.

There were two remarkable features of the mansion which Potemkin called the **House of the Horse Guards** (*Dom Kónnoy Gvárdii* – the ground in this part of the *Shpalérnaya* being designated the *slobodá* of the Horse Guards regiment). The first was its Winter Garden, equal in size to the rest of the Palace and running right across the back of it; the second was the 'English Garden' which extended the vista of the Winter Garden out into the country beyond. Both were the creation of Potemkin's famous gardener, William Gould (a Scotsman, not an Englishman, but a pupil of Lancelot 'Capability' Brown). Since the **Taurida Park**, or at any rate its skeleton (now the *Gorodskóy Détskiy park*), is still there and has given pleasure to generations of Russian families, it is worth quoting a description of a typical Brownian landscape: 'It is characterised by its simplicity – broad sweetly contoured expanses of grass, stretching between the uncluttered front of the house and an adjacent lake or stream; the lake or stream, winding in the valley, made to appear of some size, often majestic; and gently curving plantations [. . .] enclosing the boundaries, providing a continually changing setting for a walk or drive round the grounds.'[1] A quite new formula for gardens in St Petersburg which, hitherto, had tended to the formal and the grand in the Dutch-French style. And a difficult one to realise on ground in north-east St Petersburg which was by nature as flat as a pancake.

Neither Gould nor Potemkin was often in town. They were occupied, the one in subduing the Turks and extending the Russian Empire to the south and east, the other in creating instant gardens wherever the conquering commander decided to pitch camp. But in December 1790 there was a major victory (and a terrible massacre) when Field Marshal Suvorov, under Potemkin's command, captured the near-impregnable fortress of Izmail in Bessarabia. In January, an elated Catherine paid Potemkin nearly half a million roubles for his House of the Horse Guards as a contribution toward his debts (some, but by no means all, incurred in the service of the Empire) and, in February, returned his house to him.[2]

Then on 28 April, came the great ball which Potemkin gave to celebrate the birthday of the Empress. The interior of the mansion was still unfinished but Gould had turned the Winter Garden into a princely Fairy Land. Three thousand guests waited while Potemkin, in scarlet coat and diamond-encrusted cloak, followed by his be-jewelled hat – too heavy to wear but carried behind him on a cushion – led the Empress Catherine from her carriage. Through Starov's main hall, twenty-one metres high and nearly seventy-five metres long with its double row of thirty-six Ionic columns, until they came to an eight-column rotunda with three columns to the side of it in the shape of palm trees to conceal the heating pipes that nursed the exotic planting. In the

---

[1] Christopher Thacker, *The Genius of Gardening* (London, 1994), p. 215, quoted in *The English Garden* by Charles Quest-Ritson (Penguin: 2001).
[2] The figures for Catherine's contributions to the financing of the Taurida Palace come from the Russian State Archives, quoted by Simon Sebag Montefiore in *The Life of Potemkin* (Weidenfeld and Nicolson: 2000).

centre was a marble statue of Catherine by Shubin (now in the Russian Museum) which Potemkin had adorned with the legend: 'The Mother of Our Country and my Benefactress'. On slightly raised ground beyond the Rotunda was a pyramid of mirrors (Potemkin owned a glass factory) embellished with multi-coloured crystals, jewels, and candles by the thousand. All the candle wax in Petersburg had been commandeered for the occasion. In the depths of the Winter Garden was a grotto made of eleven more mirrors; in the grotto was a pool and, in the pool, a huge marble urn.

Benefactress and guests watched children dance and peoples of the new Empire process, in full national dress; then they all danced to music that included the famous 'Hunt Music' ('*Jagdmusik*', always referred to in its original German), devised by Johann-Anton Maresch. This Russian speciality was performed on thirty-seven horns, ranging from a foot to seven feet long (for extra bass, there was one of twelve feet), each of which could play only one note but which, together, covered the range of a three-octave chromatic scale. The effect was said to be like a full-throated organ and it may have been magnificent to dance to. At 2.00 a.m. the Empress went home. Potemkin was on his knees again; she kissed his forehead, he smothered her hands in kisses; and together they wept. A great love affair and a great partnership was nearing its end.

Three months later Potemkin set off for the wars again and, by October, he was dead. His domestic plans to reconstruct the interior, using Fedor Volkov (the architect who later made the railings round the park, a substantial house in the grounds for Gould and a little port that connected with the Neva), were stalled. A grieving Empress paid off the last lot of debts and provided for his heirs by purchasing the house again (this time for nearly a million roubles) and took possession of it herself. She spent much of the summers of 1792 and 1793 there and then, in December 1795, gave it to Suvorov who stayed for three months, sleeping on

hay which had been laid for the purpose on the inlaid parquet. By November 1796, Catherine herself was dead. Horse
Guards House, since 1792 officially the Taurida Palace, fell
temporarily silent.

Silent before a storm. In 1799, Catherine's son, the
Emperor Paul, was given a bill for its refurbishment. His
reply was to give the Palace back to the Horse Guards, this
time as their barracks. He ordered the Winter Garden and
part of the Hall of Columns to be stripped, the one to
become stables and the other a riding school. Myrtles,
orange trees and jasmine were swept away; stalls were
wedged between the columns of the great hall; the parquet
became thick with manure. Only the small inter-connecting
bedrooms, once occupied by Potemkin and his mother, were
left. So intense was his hatred of Catherine that he could not
bear to touch them but boarded them up instead – and so
they are the only part of the original interior to survive. His
son, Alexander I, restored the house to the status of a palace
(1802–4) but, throughout the nineteenth century, it was
rarely used. Sometimes a furniture repository, sometimes an
exhibition hall (for instance, in 1905, for Diaghilev's exhibition of historical portraits), in 1906 it became the seat of
Russia's first State Parliament (the **Gosudárstvennaya
Dúma**) established so reluctantly by Nicholas II after the
1905 Revolution. The Winter Garden was to change once
more and become the main assembly hall for the Deputies.

So, by February 1917, the Taurida Palace, which began as
lodgings for the Metropolitan, had been a lover's gift to the
conqueror of Russia's southern empire, a cavalry stables, a
furniture depository and the first state parliament of Russia;
the Smolny ensemble, begun as a tar yard, had been a
summer palace, a convent, and a girls' school. Their stories
were now to become intertwined.

On 28 February and 1 March 1917, a crowd invaded the
Taurida Palace and filled the Hall of Columns with *mítingi*
(political gatherings). Later that day, in *Room 13* of the first

floor of the Palace, was held the first meeting of the **Petrograd Soviet of Workers' and Soldiers' Deputies.** This body acquired in a few weeks a national status and was the first to hear the full presentation by **Lenin**, on his return from Finland, of his April Theses which argued the necessity of a socialist revolution to succeed and transfigure the bourgeois-democratic one. (All power must be transferred to the Soviets.) Meanwhile the *Dúma*, watching the power slip from it, continued to meet in the Taurida Palace.

This strange co-habitation – of the *Dúma* and the Soviet – continued until an abortive *coup d'état* by the Bolsheviks on 4 July ended with the occupation of the Taurida Palace by regiments home from the front (led, oddly enough, by Potemkin's old regiment, the Izmailovskiy Guards) and the flight, once more, of Lenin – this time into the countryside around St Petersburg.

At this stage, the Petrograd Soviet moved up the road to the Smolny Institute which gradually became the command centre for the next Bolshevik *coup*, the one that was going to succeed. On 10 October, the Soviet formed a Military Revolutionary Committee (Milrevkom), charged by the Central Committee of the Party with preparing an armed uprising. On 16 October, a steering committee ('Centre') was 'elected'. It included Trotsky (who had just come over from the Mensheviks), his brother-in-law Kamenev, Zinoviev,[3] and Uritskiy (whose name was briefly bestowed on the Taurida Palace), as well as Lenin operating from various hiding places. On the evening of 24 October, Lenin came in from the cold for the last time, made his way by tram across the *Litéyny most* and then on foot along *Shpalérnaya úlitsa* – in heavy disguise, bandaged and be-wigged, looking, some said, as though he had had a hard time at the dentist. Twice he was accosted by patrols along

---

[3] No relation. His real name was Apfelbaum which he changed to Radomyslskiy, Skopin and finally Zinoviev.

the street but they failed to recognise him. On 25 October, he made a brief appearance to welcome delegates to an **Extraordinary Session of the All-Russian Congress of Soviets** which was summoned to declare that the Provisional Government no longer existed (it was, at that moment, still sitting in the Malachite Hall of the Winter Palace). At 3.10 a.m. on 26 October, the Congress heard that the Winter Palace had fallen and the Provisional Government had been taken into custody; at 6.00 a.m. Kamenev adjourned the Congress and Lenin went off to 'rest' in the apartment of Vladímir Bonch-Bruyevich where, far from resting, he drafted the Decree on Peace and the Decree on Land.[4] These he presented, that evening, to the reconvened Congress.

The third decree passed by the Congress that night set up a new government called the **Council of Peoples' Commissars** (*Sovét Naródnykh Komissárov*) with Lenin as its Chairman, which was intended to serve until the convocation of a **Constituent Assembly**. The Assembly was scheduled for the following month but did not in fact meet until 5 January 1918 – and then only after an unarmed crowd, demonstrating in favour of 'power to the Constituent Assembly', had been fired on by Bolshevik soldiers. This takes us back to the Taurida Palace, which was to be the venue for the Assembly. On the evening of 5 January, the square in front of the Palace was filled with 'artillery, machine guns, field kitchens [. . .] cartridge belts piled up pell mell. All the gates were shut except for a wicket on the extreme left, through which people with passes were let in [. . .] Everywhere there were armed men, mostly sailors and Latvians.'[5] Here, in Gould's Winter Garden, in the

---

[4] The Bonch-Bruyevich Apartment is now a small museum, at *Khersonskaya úlitsa No. 5*, between the Smolny Institute and the Alexander Nevsky Monastery.

[5] M. Vishniak, *Vserossíyskoye Uchredítelnoye Sobrániye* (Paris, 1932), quoted by Richard Pipes, *The Russian Revolution 1899–1919* (Harvill/Fontana: London, 1990).

Assembly Hall of the first Russian parliament, the Bolsheviks forced through a vote in which the Constituent Assembly renounced its authority to legislate. Russia had waited nearly a hundred years for such an Assembly (first demanded by the Decembrists in 1825) and now, in January 1918, she lost it.

The Bolsheviks then left and delegates from the other parties were free to make useless speeches. But there was no one to hear them except the Red Guards, who came down from the balcony and filled the seats vacated by the Bolsheviks; many were drunk; some pointed guns at the speakers. At 4.00 a.m. on 6 January, the commander of the Guard, a sailor called Zheleznyakov, put his hand on the Chairman's shoulder and said: 'I have been instructed to inform you that all those present should leave the Assembly Hall because the Guard wants to sleep.' So the one-party state was born.

The Palace became an agricultural college and, after the Second World War, the Higher College of the Communist Party. Now it is the headquarters of the SNG (*Soyúz Nezavísimykh Gosudárstv*), representatives of the Russian Commonwealth.

At the Smolny, Lenin headed the **Government of the Soviet Union**, as Chairman of the Council of Peoples' Commissars, from 27 October 1917 until 10 March 1918,[6] when he, his wife and his cabinet moved to Moscow. His first office, on the second floor of the south wing, was numbered 67 from the days of the girls' school. It became the **Smolny Museum** in 1974. The partitioned room (on the first floor of the north wing) in which he and Krupskaya slept, ate and worked, became a museum in 1927. Krupskaya herself supervised the return of the authentic furniture, including the oil lamp which Lenin had converted to electricity but which, when the power failed, had

---

[6] In February 1918 the calendar changed from Julian to Gregorian.

to revert to kerosene. (Both rooms can still be viewed, on weekdays.) In the same year, 1927, V. Kozlov's life-size statue of Lenin, holding a cloth cap, was unveiled in front of the main portico. With your back to the statue, walking west through the garden towards *plóstchad Proletárskoy Diktatúry* (Square of the Dictatorship of the Proletariat), past the busts of Marx and Engels, you come to a remarkably successful piece of architectural in-fill: the *propiléi*, five-column colonnades placed on each side of the path, framing the view of Quarenghi's Classical façade and connecting the 'Institute' with the railings that enclosed its grounds (1923 by V. Stchuko and V. Gelfreykh). In the square, the British Consulate is to be found.

After Lenin's departure to Moscow, the Smolny Institute became the seat of the **Regional and City Committees of the Communist Party** – in other words, the power base of **Sergey Kirov**, the last major player in this area of St Petersburg. Kirov came to Leningrad as its First Secretary in 1926, chosen by Stalin as a firm pair of hands who would keep control of incipient tendencies towards independence in the Party organisation of the one-time capital. He proved indeed to be a firm pair of hands but, by the end of the decade, he was developing a position in the city which began to look like independence. He tolerated writers, publishers and Old Bolsheviks; he encouraged cultural life; in famine conditions, he demanded – and sometimes obtained – extra food for the workers. He was elected a Secretary of the Central Committee of the Party and a member of the Politburo. It now seems clear beyond doubt[7] that **Stalin** had Kirov murdered – partly to remove a rival but, more importantly, to provide an excuse to remove all potential rivals by implicating them in a non-existent plot to kill Kirov and overthrow the Party.

---

[7] For a summary of the evidence, *see* the latest (1990) edition of Robert Conquest's *The Great Terror* (Pimlico).

In the afternoon of 1 December 1934, Leonid Nikolayev entered the Smolny headquarters. He was not searched; he was carrying a pistol and a plan showing the location of Kirov's office on the third floor. It was his third attempt to meet his victim. A disillusioned young Communist, he had told a friend that he wanted to shoot some senior Party figure; through the friend, the deputy head of the Leningrad NKVD (secret police) planted the idea of Kirov as a target, supplied the gun and caused him to be released on the two previous, unsuccessful occasions. When news of Kirov's death reached Moscow, Stalin left for Leningrad, personally 'to conduct the inquiry' in the Smolny. That same day, he issued, without consultation with the Politburo, a decree under which investigators, judges and the Commissariat of Internal Affairs were to proceed 'without delay or the possibility of pardon' to implement the death sentence against 'those accused of the preparation or execution of terror'. In effect, to suspend the judicial process. The following day, Kirov's bodyguard, Borisov, met with an inexplicable and fatal car accident. By 5 December, thirty-seven people presumed to be enemies of the regime ('White Guards') had been sentenced to death in Leningrad and thirty-three in Moscow. Within a few months, between thirty and forty thousand Leningraders had been deported to Siberia and the Arctic. That was only the beginning.

During the next four years, in ever widening circles of terror, self-accusation and 'confession', literally millions of party members, high and low, were eliminated by Stalin until, by 1938, three former members of the Politburo, the great majority of the Party's Central Committee, the head of the NKVD (he who had helped Stalin arrange the murder) and almost all the higher ranks of the Armed Forces – all were gone, accused of conspiring to undermine the Soviet State.[8] Not to mention some eight million ordinary citizens.

[8] These figures are quoted in Riasanovskiy's *A History of Russia* (OUP: 1963).

If the abortion of the Constituent Assembly in the Taurida Palace ushered in the one-party-state, the murder of Kirov in the Smolny Institute was the consolidation of the one-man Party.

There is a 'branch' of the Smolny Museum (the **Alliluyev Apartment Museum**, *Apartment 20, Sovétskaya úlitsa No. 10*), not impossibly far from the Smolny complex. Its *raison d'être* as a museum is the fact that Lenin Slept Here in July 1917. But it is more moving to go and remember Stalin's second wife, Nadezhda Alliluyeva, who lived here as a girl and to whose father it belonged. Perhaps with foresight of the horrors to come, and certainly in revulsion from the sufferings already being caused by collectivisation, Nadezhda killed herself in November 1932.

Leaving the Smolny by *Tverskáya úlitsa*, until you hit the east side of the Taurida Park, you come to *Tavrícheskaya úlitsa*. At the intersection of the two streets is an apartment house (*Tavrícheskaya úlitsa No. 35*, though it used to be *No. 25*) with a semi-circular tower appliquéd on to the corner, topped by a balcony and a small dome. The apartment behind the balcony was known, all over St Petersburg, as **The Tower** (*Báshnya*). Between 1905 and 1912, it was inhabited by the poet and critic Vyacheslav Ivanov and (until her death in 1907) his wife Lydia Zinoviev (my grandfather's sister).[9] Every Wednesday there gathered here what the 1992 Petersburg edition of the Soviet Encyclopaedia describes as 'the literary *élite* of Russia'. It was a place where sounds were muffled by a remarkable collection of carpets; a place in which calendars and clocks were sternly banished so that Time could not interfere with the arguments, dialogues and monologues, that went on – sometimes for twenty-four hours at a stretch. There were to be no barriers to thought or creativity. Here Diaghilev

[9] She added 'Annibal' to her name in celebration of an ancestor she shared with Pushkin and wrote as Lydia Zinovieva-Annibal.

held meetings of the *World of Art* (*Mir Iskússtva*) group –
composers, choreographers, painters, directors – just to
listen to Ivanov talking; here came the Symbolist poet
Aleksandr Blok, the novelist Andrey Bely, the philosophers
Berdyayev and Bulgakov, Zinaida Gippius and Dimitri
Merezhkovskiy from their own apartment on *Litéyny
prospékt* and Gumilyov, the first husband of the poet Anna
Akhmatova whom he married in 1910 and by whom he
was divorced in 1918.

Among the poets there was much dissension. The
Russian Symbolists declared themselves to be inspired by
the first line from the *Chorus Mysticus* at the end of
Goethe's *Faust*: '*Alles Vergängliche/ Ist nur ein Gleichnis*' (all
things transient / are only a likeness). But Gumilyov, and
another poet called Gorodetskiy, led a reaction: 'we want to
admire a rose because it is beautiful, not because it is a
symbol of mystical purity', which led Blok and his supporters to describe them, satirically, as 'Acmeists' (writers who
concentrated on an isolated point). The arguments went
on, occasionally for days, sometimes (as in the case of the
poet, Kuzmin) for a year and were only silenced by war and
revolution. Gumilyov himself enlisted in the Cavalry – the
only Russian poet to join up – and was twice decorated.
The end of the war found him in Paris from which he chose
to return in the belief that since 'I have hunted lions, I don't
believe the Bolsheviks are much more dangerous'. They
were, though. In 1921 he was arrested on the charge of
conspiring against the Government and, after several
months of imprisonment, was shot by the Cheka.

Ivanov's own centre of interest was religion – and
Classical literature and philosophy, much of which he knew
by heart. But his most extraordinary gifts were his ability to
discourse on practically any subject under the sun, his ability to inspire and his ability to encourage rational thought.
For this he came to be called **Vyacheslav the Magnificent**
and nobody ever seems to have thought the description a

hyperbole. His wife Lydia's clothes were exotic, mannerisms extravagant, books (mostly short stories) second-rate but her conversation appeared to be as inspiring as her husband's. After her death, Vyacheslav married again – in 1910 – this time choosing his step-daughter, my cousin Vera. In the early 1920s, he emigrated to Rome where he converted to Roman Catholicism and died in 1949, leaving a daughter by Lydia and a son by Vera who became a French journalist.

It is difficult now to gauge the real importance of The Tower. But according to the hundreds of their devoted and distinguished visitors, the Ivanovs had an extraordinary influence on the intellectual life of the time. After 1912, the Wednesdays ceased. But the members of the group continued to visit one another until the Revolution finally dispersed them – some to die of hunger, others to be killed or executed, still others into exile.

Carrying on southwards down *Tavrícheskaya úlitsa*, on the southwest corner of its intersection with *Kírochnaya úlitsa* looms the eccentric bulk of the **Suvorov Memorial Museum** (*muzéy Suvórova*). It stands on the site of the Preobrazhenskiy Guards' parade ground, the regiment in those days being quartered further west along the *Kírochnaya* (*Nos. 31–7*) in a building, complete with porticoed hospital, by Volkov (1802–7). Field Marshal Suvorov, perhaps the most brilliant of all Russian field commanders, was tiny – a Nelsonian figure, in whose honour several modern cadet schools are named. Brought back from retirement after his campaigns against the Turks in the early 1790s, he made a celebrated crossing of the Alps in the campaign against Napoleon.

A picture by V. Surikov, on the ground floor of the Russian Museum, shows the Field Marshal mounted and on the brink of a snowy precipice, waving his exhausted soldiers on into the abyss. The same mad light is in his eyes and theirs. They say that, when the going was uphill, he used to get off his horse and dance in front of his troops so that they would follow him over the mountain. The Suvorov Museum, financed by public subscription and designed by A. Hohen and G. Grimm (1901–4), is built in brick in a style that could be described as 'Pseudo-Russian' or 'Neo-Russian'. There is nothing whatsoever 'pseudo' about Suvorov himself – it is claimed that he never lost a battle or a campaign – and anybody with a serious interest in Russian military history should visit his museum. There are fine battle paintings, not to mention fifty thousand tin soldiers – the largest collection in Russia. The building itself was hit by a bomb during the Blockade and required massive repairs (M. Plotnikov, 1950–1).

The way back westwards, to *Litéyny prospékt*, is perhaps best achieved by bus. Along the *Shpalérnaya*, you would miss the Barracks of the Cavalier Guards (*Nos. 41/43*) and the Church of All Who Sorrow (*No. 35a*), both by Rusca (c. 1817). And you would miss, at *No. 25*, the 'House of Preliminary Detention', a remand prison during the last years of the Empire, where many revolutionaries were held awaiting trial including (in 1897) Lenin. It was burned down in the Revolution and rebuilt. You would not miss, because it is on the corner of *Litéyny prospékt* and *Shpalérnya úlitsa*, the massive building called **Bolshóy dom** (Big House), *Litéyny prospékt Nos. 2–4*.

This is on the site of James Bruce's Foundry Works, which were later adapted to house the old St Petersburg Regional Court, scene of many trials of revolutionaries and terrorists (and, also, of the first Russian trials by jury following the reforms of Alexander II). Lenin's brother was condemned to death here; also Zhelyabov and Perovskaya, the assassins of Alexander II. The Court was burned down in 1917 and from its ruins sprang (1931–2, by A. Gegello and N. Trotskiy) the local headquarters of what became the KGB (Committee for National Security). From these head-quarters, the Head of the Leningrad NKVD, Filip Medved, was dismissed two days after the murder of Kirov; here, the mass arrests of Leningraders which followed that murder were planned and implemented. It now houses the current version of the KGB, the FSB (Federal Security Service).

Buses, trolleybuses and trams all go down the *Litéyny*. It is not, in itself, a beautiful street, the present houses dating from after the building of the Liteyny Bridge in 1851 but, in the second half of the nineteenth century, it became a comfortable and fashionable street which ran through other, comfortable and fashionable streets. The first pause might be on the corner of *úlitsa Péstelya*. To the east is *Preobrazhénskaya plóstchad* (Preobrazhenskiy Square) and the regimental church, commissioned by the Empress Elisabeth when the Guards had helped her to the throne in 1741. The present church (the **Cathedral of the Transfiguration**) is by Stasov (1827–9) and the churchyard is surrounded by a fence made of chains and cannon barrels, captured from the Turks in the war of 1828.

On the south-east corner of the *prospékt* (*Litéyny No. 24*), where it meets the square, is an apartment block, bizarre in its architecture and strange in its history. The style of *dom Murúzi* is definitely Eclectic[10] (with a predominance of Arabic, Turkish and Moorish features), built in the 1870s for the son of a Greek in the service of the Ottoman Empire. At least, Muruzi was meant to be in the service of the Ottoman Empire but, his ancestors having been sovereigns of Moldavia, his heart was not really there. Chief negotiators on the Turkish side at the time of the Treaty of Bucharest (23 June 1812), he and his brother provided the Russians with vital information which enabled them to obtain Bessarabia and part of the Black Sea Coast while freeing their

[10] 'Eclectic' as an architectural term is frequently used about late nineteenth-century buildings in St Petersburg. The Yusupov Palace has an 'Eclectic' dining room which includes motifs from 'the French Renaissance', 'Florentine Baroque', 'neo-Gothic' and 'Oriental'. It came to mean 'a little bit of anything that took your fancy and you were rich enough to pay for'. By that time, there was a good deal to choose from.

army to face Napoleon who, on 24 June, crossed into Russia over the Niemen. Alexander I was duly grateful and promised ample reward. Sadly, both brothers were arrested and beheaded, one of their heads being exposed on a pole for three days. But when Muruzi's widow fled to Russia in 1821 (the Greco-Turkish War), Alexander honoured his promise and made her a very rich woman. The family decided to invest in an apartment house of which they would occupy twenty-six rooms on the first floor, decorated with arches, fountains, hanging gardens and other exotic devices (Serebryakov 1874–7). Unfortunately they also brought with them so many relatives that they were eaten out of house and home having, in spite of an extra quarter of a million roubles from the Emperor, to sell the house in 1890.

The front rooms on the first floor became apartments for wealthy tenants, including Aleksandr Pushkin, eldest son of the poet. Into the block, in 1889, there also moved the poet Zinaida Gippius and her husband Dimitri Merezhkovskiy, at first on to the fourth floor and later on to the north front of the first floor. They, too, had a salon, their 'days' being usually Sundays. Their circle overlapped with the Ivanov circle, Blok and Bely featuring prominently in both. But the atmosphere seems to have been more self-indulgent and the effect less lasting. It is hard to imagine Ivanov describing the October Revolution as 'the darkest, most idiotic, dirtiest "social revolution" that history has ever seen', as Gippius wrote on 25 October 1917, '. . . to hell with them all. It's boring and disgusting.' After their departure, the flat was occupied by Socialist Revolutionaries; then by squatters; then by a publishing house run by Gorky. Then, in 1921, just before he was arrested, Gumilyov bravely organised literary evenings and plays there and gave it a last flicker as *dom Poétov* (the House of Poets). Thereafter it succumbed to the mass migration of starving people from the countryside. Rooms were divided by plywood partitions and it became communal flats. In one of these, after the

Second World War, lived Joseph Brodsky who later emigrated to the United States and won the Nobel Prize for Literature.

Westward down *úlitsa Péstelya* and third on the right is **Solyanóy pereúlok** (Salt Lane). It acquired its name from the great warehouses (the *Solyanóy gorodók* – 'salt town'), stretching from the Lane to the Fontanka, that were used from 1782 for a hundred years for the storage of salt, in the days when the monopoly made rich men of salt merchants. (One warehouse remains on the banks of the Fontanka; it was done up in the 1870s by I. Küttner for an industrial exhibition and stretches some 200 yards along the river bank.) In the early-eighteenth century this same area, across the Fontanka from the Summer Garden, was a yacht harbour or marina – created by Peter the Great in 1718 and called the **Partikulyárnaya verf** (Private Wharf). In a characteristic project, everyone who was anyone was instructed to keep a boat – a sloop, a barge, a yacht, a dinghy, no matter what – and use it for getting about town. (The initial vessel was given, free of charge; thereafter, they must maintain it at their own expense.) For Petersburgers were to become proficient at messing about in boats. And to the same end, there were to be no bridges, at any rate no permanent ones, across the Neva. Every so often, the 'Neva Flotilla' set sail together, an Admiral at the head of the fleet and Peter bringing up the rear, along the Neva and back again.

Just before *úlitsa Péstelya* meets the Fontanka, there is a delightful early church (1735–9) with a Baroque belfry and spire, designed by Korobov and dedicated to St Panteleymon (a saint on whose name day the Russians won one of their several victories over the Swedes), which is all that survives of the time when this area was essentially maritime.

After the salt departed, a number of institutions came into the area, of which the Baron Stieglitz School of Technical Design (now the **Stieglitz Museum of Decorative and Applied Arts**) was notable. The present building

(*Solyanóy pereúlok No. 13*), roofed in glass like a massive palm house, was begun in 1885, designed by its first director, M. Messmacher, and houses an astounding collection of Russian and West European artefacts – stoves (eighteenth-century and later), Soviet textiles, tiles of many periods, furniture – as well as the State (Mukhina's) Academy of Art and Industry, with displays of work by its students. The **Blockade Museum** (*Solyanóy pereúlok No. 9*) has a permanent though more modest exhibition, one of several in the city relating to conditions during the Blockade. Two anti-aircraft guns stand guard on the door; inside there is a fine collection of wartime posters and a representation of a wartime apartment – blacked-out windows, smoke-blackened walls and a tiny stove which has consumed most of the furniture. A remarkable feature is the display, round the edge of the hall, of some of the artistic, theatrical and musical events which, starvation and cold notwithstanding, somehow went on.

Returning to *Litéyny prospékt* and still moving south, on the north-east corner of *úlitsa Nekrásova* (*No. 36*) is the apartment from which the poet **Nekrasov** edited *The Contemporary* (*Sovreménnik*, the great rival to *Homeland Notes*, which at another time he also edited). His apartment (and the one next door occupied by his colleague and his wife's lover, Ivan Panayev) is another apartment museum, larger than you would expect and of serious interest to Russian speakers who want to explore the flowering of Russian nineteenth-century journalism. Down the *prospékt* again and, on the corner of *úlitsa Belínskovo* going off towards the Fontanka, is the block which housed the editorial offices of *The World of Art* and the apartment of Sergey Diaghilev (at *No. 45* – not a museum). On the opposite side of the *prospékt* (*No. 42*), a large florid mansion faced with sandstone from Bremen, was built for the Yusupov family (Bonstedt, 1852–8). Creatures called 'Herms', whose size and vulgarity have to be seen to be believed, support the balcony over the main door. *No. 42* is now the editorial offices of the magazine *Znaniye* (Knowledge).

Across *úlitsa Zhukóvskovo* (the Fleet Street of the late Empire), set back from the road and built by Quarenghi in 1803–5, is the Mariinskiy Hospital, *No. 56.*

At *No. 53*, across the road, arrows point you to the back (and currently the only) entrance to the **Sheremetev Palace**, one of the greatest mansions in St Petersburg. The present house stands on a site on the Fontanka given by Peter the Great to Field Marshal Boris Sheremetev after his capture of *Nyenskans* in 1703. It was built for his son by S. Chevakinskiy (1750–5) on the foundations of a slightly earlier building. F. Argunov, a Sheremetev serf who trained as an architect, contributed one floor and some other embellishments. Since then, its exterior has scarcely changed, except for elaborate wrought-iron railings on the Fontanka front (Corsini, 1844) and the one-storey wing with gate and coat-of-arms by N. Benois (1867). The grottos, the hermitage and the fountains which gave the house its original name – *Fontánny dom* – have long since vanished, though a ghost of the garden remains. And the interior has run the gauntlet of the centuries: Voronikhin, Starov, Quarenghi all took a hand and so, after the Revolution, did the State. The Palace and all its contents was 'given' to the Soviet Authorities by its owner, Sergey Sheremetev – whereupon the contents were removed and most of the interiors destroyed. Since 1990, however, the **Museum of Theatrical and Musical Arts** has been slowly restoring the eighteenth-century enfilades and has already moved into them a fine collection of musical instruments which includes an Italian spinet of 1532, a transverse flute from the court of Louis XIV, a Chinese lute with a snake-skin membrane, a Japanese *samisen* and *koto*, and a *biva*. Chamber music is sometimes performed in the evenings.

It is the right museum for this house, whose connection with music and the arts goes back to the early nineteenth century when Boris's great-grandson, Nikolay, at the time the richest man in Russia, married his mistress, Praskoviya Zhemchugova, a singer from his serf theatrical company in Moscow. The marriage received the approval of Alexander I. Their son, Dimitri, made the Petersburg house into a centre for the city's musical and theatrical life – his guests included the composers M. Glinka, A. and V. Serov and Balakirev – though his friends were known to remark on the retrograde attitude he displayed towards his remaining one hundred and fifty thousand serfs.

After the Revolution, the house was converted to communal flats one of which – on the third floor in the south garden wing – was allocated to Nikolay Punin, a distinguished art historian. There were two rooms, one inhabited by Punin's wife and daughter, the other by Punin and his mistress (later, until 1938, his wife), Anna Akhmatova. Between 1925 and 1940, she could publish nothing at all. She wrote about it – the agony of herself and Russia during those years; the arrest (twice) of Punin; the imprisonment and death of the poet, Osip Mandelstam; the multiple arrests of her son, Lev Gumilyov, for news of whom she stood outside the prison every day for seventeen months. What she wrote, she committed to memory destroying the paper it was written on until, late in the 1950s, Khrustchev made it possible for her to speak again out loud. But *Requiem*, perhaps her greatest poem, was not published in Russia until 1987. The six rooms of the **Akhmatova Memorial Museum**, which opened in the south garden wing of the Sheremetev Palace in 1989, tell the story of at least part of her life.

Across the Fontanka (*No. 21*) and slightly to the south, on the corner of *Italiyánskaya úlitsa*, can be seen the bulk of the **Shuvalov Palace**, rather stiff in the neo-Renaissance façade in which it was dressed in the 1840s (N. Yefimov). Built in the 1790s, bought in 1821 by D. Naryshkin who greatly enlarged and embellished it, it became the meeting place of the aristocracy and the literary society of the time (Pushkin, Zhukovskiy, Krylov, the writer of fables, and Gnedich, the translator of Homer). Sold again on Naryshkin's death in 1838 to Countess S. Shuvalov, it lacks the charm of the Baroque Shuvalov mansion further up the street (which was built in the mid-eighteenth century by Chevakinskiy for Ivan Shuvalov). After the Revolution, the house on the Fontanka served as many kinds of institution; then, badly damaged by the bombardment, it was rebuilt over nearly twenty years to become – what it still is – the **House of Friendship and Peace** (*Dom Drúzhby i Míra*). Nowadays this means nothing more complicated than being the venue of foreign receptions and offering the public two restaurants, one of which is excellent, at moderate (in dollars) prices.

Staying on the east side of the Fontanka and moving north, you come to the bridge which ends *úlitsa Belínskovo* and leads out of the square in front of the *Simeónovskaya tsérkov* (the Church of SS Simeon and Anna). The bridge has lost its charm (it once was a drawbridge with four little towers and a brick central section) but the view from it in both directions is a delight. So also is the church, which is one of the earliest in the city (Zemtsov, 1731); the refectory ends in a three-storey belfry and spire, Petrine in style, but its octagonal dome and lantern hint at an earlier and more Russian form of Baroque.

Over the bridge and immediately to the right is the brick red fortress known sometimes as *Mikháylovskiy zámok* (St Michael's Castle), sometimes as the **Engineers' Castle**. With a grim face and a grim history, it was the product of hate and fear: hate by the **Emperor Paul** for his mother, Catherine the Great, whom he (correctly) believed to have condoned his father's murder and to have cheated him of his father's throne; fear inspired by the knowledge that her real desire was to have disinherited him altogether in favour of his son, Alexander (later Alexander I), and that there were powerful people around who shared this desire.

His fear made him decide to build a new palace of maximum security. His hatred made him choose, as a site for
this palace, the place where he had been born and where his
mother, in his presence, was first publicly acclaimed
Empress – the charming, sunny, verdant Summer Palace
(Mark III and IV), built originally for Catherine I and
rebuilt by Rastrelli for the Empress Elisabeth, which was set
among gardens stretching from the Fontanka to what is
now the Griboyedov Canal, and from the Moika to
Italiyánskaya úlitsa. There had been vegetable gardens along
the Moika; rough shooting along the Fontanka; fountains
and cascades and formal parterres in between. On 28
November 1796, one of Paul's first acts as Emperor was to
publish a decree ordering the demolition of this Summer
Palace. The following January, the foundation stone was laid
for his new stronghold. Canals were dug, along *Sadóvaya
úlitsa* and what is now *Zámkovaya úlitsa* and, by 1801, there
was a fortified castle, surrounded by moats, accessed only by
drawbridges. Designed by V. Bazhenov and executed by
V. Brenna (who was pulled off the unfinished third version
of St Isaac's), each façade is in a different style. On the west,
the *Sadóvaya* side, there is a central projection which con-
ceals a church, whose brightly gilded *iglá* can be seen from
the street. The interior has some very fine early neo-Gothic.

In less than five years, Paul's policies had alienated not
only his mother's supporters but a large part of the Russian
military and gentry as well. His enemies were not going to
have to cross drawbridges for many of them were already
inside his castle. Within forty days of his move into his
maximum security stronghold, he was dead, murdered by
conspirators led by the military governor of St Petersburg,
Count Peter Pahlen; other participants included the vice-
chancellor (deputy prime minister), Count Nikita Panin,
and the ubiquitous Aleksey Orlov. Paul's eldest son, the
Grand Duke Alexander, and possibly his wife, knew about
the conspiracy though Alexander insisted that his father's

life should be spared. On the appointed night, some of the conspirators managed to pass the guard at the door of the Emperor's bedroom on the pretext of delivering a report. Sensing danger from the unusual hour and their rowdy behaviour, the Emperor hid behind the fire screen in his night clothes. According to one of the participants, he asked for time to say a prayer. But others, apparently drunk after a celebratory dinner, seized and throttled him with a scarf.

In 1819, the *Mikháylovskiy zámok* became the School of Military Engineering, the first director of which was Paul's second son, the Grand Duke Nicholas (later Nicholas I). Under Nicholas, it became a prestigious and efficient institution attended, among others, by the young Dostoyevsky. It remained in the possession of the Engineers, in one capacity or another, until the Revolution. At the end of 1917, it was briefly the centre of the '*Kadet* Uprising', which was suppressed by the Pavlovskiy Regiment. In 1991, badly in need of renovation and a new purpose, it became part of the Russian Museum which is investing a great deal of energy and money in its rehabilitation (between 1999 and 2001, 280 million roubles – some £70 million – on 'repairs, restoration and reconstruction' of St Michael's Castle alone). The plan is to create Russia's first national portrait gallery.

In front of the castle is a long open space which Rossi, as part of his comprehensive plans for the area, designed as a triumphal avenue (the *Klenóvaya* – Maple – *alléya*). At the north end, Paul had placed an equestrian statue of Peter the Great, originally modelled by C.-B. Rastrelli in Peter's life-time but never previously displayed. On the base he had engraved: *Prádedu Právnuk* ('Great Grandson to Great Grandfather') – a significant inscription in view of the belief that Peter III was not his father. At the south end of the avenue is the *Manézhnaya plóstchad* (Riding School Square), where began the last act of the last murder to be described in this chapter.

It was here that Paul's grandson, the **Emperor Alexander II**, often came to review the parade on a Sunday morning. On Saturday 28 February 1881, it had been discovered that the People's Will organisation were planning to blow him up with nitro-glycerine as he passed over a hole they had dug in *Málaya Sadóvoya*. When, later that day, they arrested one of the leaders of the plot (Zhelyabov), the police recorded him as saying that 'nothing can save the Tsar's life'. The next day, Sunday 1 March, the remaining members of the People's Will were ready. In the morning, the Emperor had an audience with his Minister of the Interior, Loris-Melikov, in the course of which he signed a proposal for constitutional reform which would have involved the surrender of some autocratic power (albeit modest) and the participation in government of some elected representatives. He put the signed document in his pocket, told his wife to have the children ready so that they could all go for a walk in the park on his return and set out for the *Manézhnaya plóstchad*, against the advice of Loris-Melikov who reminded him that Perovskaya, Zhelyabov's mistress and partner in terrorism, was still at liberty.

Alexander left the parade about 1.45 p.m. Six Cossacks rode alongside his carriage and a seventh was on the box, carrying a rifle. On his way home, he made a quick visit to the Mikhaylovskiy Palace to see his favourite cousin, the Grand Duchess Catherine. He left her at 2.15 p.m. and asked the coachman to hurry because his wife and children would be waiting. As they left the palace, they turned right down *Inzhenérnaya úlitsa* and right again northwards up the Griboyedov Embankment. For a minute or two, the Cossack outriders fell behind the carriage, leaving it exposed. Perovskaya, disguised as a woman selling herrings, had been signalling his approach by waving a handkerchief to other young terrorists posted along the possible routes and, at this moment, Rysakov threw his bomb, which exploded, injuring two of the Cossack outriders and a passing errand boy. Carriage and remaining Cossacks came to a halt; the Emperor, ignoring his coachman who sensibly wanted to keep moving, got out to see if he could help the boy and the injured Cossacks saying 'I can thank God for being safe'. Rysakov was heard to mutter: 'It is too early to thank God' – and a second terrorist, Grinevitskiy, threw a second bomb. It blew off the Emperor's legs and, at this eighth attempt on his life, he was mortally wounded. They took him home to the Winter Palace where he died in his wife's arms.[11]

The following year Alexander III decreed that a church should be built on the place where his father was assassinated. The competition for the design specified that the church should be in a style 'purely Russian of the seventeenth century' and was won by Alfred Parland. The result, not completed for many years, is the **Church of the Resurrection**, commonly known as **The Saviour on the Blood** (*Khram Spása na Kroví*), which projects on to the Embankment so that it covers the blood that was spilled. It is indeed in the Neo-Russian style with a profusion of domes and enamelled cupolas and an explosion of mosaics, seven thousand square metres of them, inside and out, by Vasnetsov, Ryabushkin, Koshelyov and Nesterov. After the Revolution, it became something of an embarrassment. It was put to various uses but ended as a store room which was disastrous for the mosaics. In 1970, restoration work began; since 1997, it has been re-opened and reconsecrated (though it is also a museum and is closed on Wednesdays). In the area opposite the church, between the Griboyedov and the Moika, are two streets: *Bolsháya Konyúshennaya* and *Málaya Konyúshennaya* which were renamed, for a time, *úlitsa Zhelyábova* and *úlitsa Peróvskoy*. Years later,

[11] The bomb also killed Grinevitskiy, who died in hospital. Rysakov, unwounded, was arrested, tried and condemned to death.

Stalin was asked whether there should not be monuments erected there to these two leaders of the People's Will. The last man to seek to glorify assassins, he replied: 'On no account'. If Soviet youth was to be brought up in the worship of terrorism, he added, no one would be safe.

Alexander's final journey had begun at the **Mikhaylovskiy Palace** (*Mikháylovskiy dvoréts*) where his cousin, the Grand Duchess Catherine, was living. The Palace had been designed, together with the rest of what is now Arts Square, by Carlo Rossi and executed, by Rossi himself, between 1819 and 1825. It was to be the home of the youngest son of the Emperor Paul (brother of Alexander I and Nicholas I), the Grand Duke Mikhail. After his death, it was occupied for many years by his widow, Elena, and then by their daughter, the Grand Duchess Catherine. As an old woman, she asked her cousin, Alexander III, to witness her will – which he did, without reading it. When she died, he discovered with some irritation that he had put his name to a bequest of the Mikhaylovskiy Palace to Catherine's son, Duke George of Mecklenburg-Strelitz which would mean, he felt, that the property would pass out of the Romanov family. So he sent for his Minister of Finance, Sergey Witte, and told him that he wished to buy out Duke George's interest. (He did – and the Mecklenburg-Strelitz family used the proceeds to buy the Zinoviev house at Fontanka *No. 46, see* p. 196.) He would, further, like the Palace not to be lived in any more but to be devoted to some worthy Romanov project; he suggested the Xenia Institute (another school for well-born girls). He then died in 1894.

Alexander III's son, on his accession as Nicholas II, decided to install his sister Xenia's Institute in the huge and ugly palace on what is now the *Plóstchad Trudá*, where his great-uncle, the Grand Duke Nikolay, had lived until his death in 1881. Witte then told him about the intentions of his father for the Mikhaylovskiy Palace and (according to Witte) himself made the graceful suggestion that it should become **The Alexander III Imperial Museum of Russian Art** – thus honouring Nicholas's father and giving a patriotic boost to indigenous art.

And so it happened: the **Russian Museum** (*Gosudárstvenny Rússkiy muzéy*) was founded in 1895 in the Palace that Rossi had built for the Grand Duke Mikhail. It was much altered which, sadly, involved wholesale destruction of many of the original interiors. All that is left are the hall, the main staircase and the Hall of the White Columns – just enough to tantalise. The public was admitted in 1898. The initial collection was formed by transferring eighty pictures from the Hermitage, one hundred and twenty from the Academy of Arts, two hundred from various royal palaces and an invitation to private donors to contribute.

The exterior remained largely unchanged until the addition on the east of the **Museum of Ethnography** in 1902 (V. Svinyn) and, in 1916, the Benois Wing on the west (designed by L. Benois, executed by S. Ovsyannikov). After 1917, the invitation to private donors took on a new meaning with the 'nationalisation' of major private collections, which enlarged the contents many times over. The other main source of post-Revolutionary acquisition was redistribution within the museum system – so, for instance, there was much exchange between the Russian Museum in Petrograd/Leningrad and the Tretyakóv Museum in Moscow. Tretyakóv was a rich merchant and great collector of Russian art who (in the true sense) had presented his collection to the nation.

There are now some four hundred thousand items (and the number is constantly growing) in the Russian Museum – mostly in the main Mikhaylovskiy building and in the Benois wing. But, given the recent extension of the Museum's responsibilities to St Michael's Castle, the Stroganov Palace and the Marble Palace, given also the great need in all three buildings for repairs and improvements, there is a good deal of turbulence. A floor plan is available at the entrances but is not sufficiently permanent to be worth reproducing here; and a 'Virtual Reality Center' (American-style) is planned which will be based in the western pavilion of St Michael's Castle and will, one of these days, enable visitors to 'plan their own touring route round the complex'. In the meantime, it is possible to make a selection of what you want to see and feed it into the computer system in the **Garden Vestibule,** on the north side of the Ground Floor in the main Palace building, which will indicate its where-abouts. For now, it is probably most sensible for this book simply to give the briefest of indications of the contents, with prompts about some personal preferences.

Icons from the twelfth to the end of the seventeenth century: from the collection it is possible to get an idea of the evolution, and the main schools, of Russian icon paint-ing. There are icons from the Schools of Skov (*Descent into Hell*), Novgorod (*St George and the Dragon, St Paul*), Moscow (particularly Rublyov) and Dionysius (*Our Lady of Odigitria* – The One Who Shows the Way – being the Virgin with the infant Jesus exposed in her womb). And there is Semyon Ushakov (late seventeenth century).

Eighteenth-Century painting: the first of the big Russian portrait painters, I. Nikitin (portraits of *Peter the Great on his Death Bed, A Field Hetman, The Empress Anna, Stroganov*); Argunov (portraits of the *Lobanov-Rostovskiy Family*); D. Levitskiy, a portrait painter in the style of Gainsborough (*The Smolny Girls*); V. Borovikovskiy, who belonged to a sect which demanded deep breathing at Mass to facilitate swallowing the Holy Ghost, breathed too deeply and died – they said – of a surfeit of It (portrait of *Catherine II at Tsarskoye Selo*); A. Losenko, founder of Russian historical painting (from c.1770).

Eighteenth-Century Sculpture: C.-B. Rastrelli (Peter the Great); F. Shubin (Busts of Emperor Paul and Catherine II from the Taurida); M. Kozlovskiy (Hercules on Horseback); I. Martos (Bust of Potemkin).

Early nineteenth-century painting: Historical paintings represented by F. Bruni (*Death of Camilla, Horace's Sister*); K. Bryullov (*The Last Days of Pompeii*); A. Ivanov (*Christ Appearing to the People*). And a developing trend of social realism represented in *Genre* painters such as A. Venetsianov (*Landowner's Morning* – a female landowner gives orders to a peasant girl – and *Sleeping Shepherd*) and P. Fedotov (*A Major's Proposal*). Landscapes, by S. Stchedrin, M. Vorobiev (*Neva Embankment*).

Late Nineteenth and early twentieth-century painting: the full flowering of Realist painters, mainly represented by members of the Society of Travelling Artistic Exhibitions (*Peredvízhniki* – The Travellers), founded in 1871, such as V. Perov and N.Gué (*Peter I prosecuting the Tsarevitch Alexis*); I. Kramskoy, N. Yaroshenko. New realist painters of landscape: G. Myasoyedov (*Harvesting*); I. Shishkin (*Pine Grove* and *Oaks*); Ayvazovskiy (*The Wave*, 1889). The towering figure of Ilya Repin (1844–1930) including some wonderful individual portraits, his *ensemble* of the Council of State (1901), which has a room to itself, the famous *Bargees on the Volga* (1873), and *Cossacks Writing a Letter to the Turkish Sultan* (1891); Repin's distinguished pupil and son of the composer, V. Serov (1865–1911): *Children* (two enchanting boys looking out to sea) and *Princess Orlov* (1911); Leon Bakst – 'I am the best of all Russian painters. I am the Russian Velázquez' – *The Dinner* (1902); B. Kustodiev: *The Merchant's Wife* (1915); Marc Chagall: *The Walk* (1917). The Cubo-Futurist School, particularly M. Vrubel (1856–1911): *The Dance of Toumara*, *Six-Winged Seraph*, *The Swan Princess* and *Princess Volkova* (like a Russian Klimt).

The **World of Art** group (*Mir Iskússtva*): A. Benois, M. Dobuzhinskiy, I. Somov, I. Lanceré. The **Union of Russian Painters** group, which included K. Korovin: *Blue Rose*; M. Saryan: *The Knave of Diamonds*; N. Altman: *Akhmatova* (1915); K. Petrov-Vodkin: *The Mother* (1916). The **Suprematists**, whose king was K. Malevich (1878–1935) – 'I have transformed myself into the nullity of forms and pulled myself out of the circles of things, out of the circle-horizon in which the artist and forms of nature are locked.' – *Flower Girl* (1904), *Black Circle*, *Black Cross* and *Black Square* (1913), and *Suprematism: Yellow and Black* (1917). And those who painted as **Soviet Artists** (including several, like Malevich and Petrov-Vodkin, who had exhibited in previous groups): Petrov-Vodkin: *Alarm* (1919) and *Death of a Commissar* (1927); Malevich: *Peasants* (1932); A. Deyneka: *The Defence of Sebastopol* (1942); E. Moiseyenko: *Victory* (1972).

Sculpture in the nineteenth century: mainly Classical in style by familiar St Petersburg masters such as Pimenov and Demut-Malinovskiy. And **Old Russian Decorative and Applied Art** which includes some early jewellery and some sixteenth- and early seventeenth-century Church silver ware.

The exhibits are spread between the main Palace building (entrance from *Inzhenérnaya úlitsa*) and the **Benois Wing** to the west of it (entrance from the Griboyedov Canal). The two are separated by the Administrative Offices, situated in the **Rossi Wing**.

Behind the Russian Museum are the green and pleasant gardens (*Mikháylovskiy sad*) of the Mikhaylovskiy Palace which, once upon a time, were covered by the old green-houses and forcing frames of the third Summer Palace. One can walk in them right up to the edge of the Moika river in the north, where Rossi's Garden Pavilion (1825) still casts its elegant image on the water. The area in front, fenced off in the Empress Elisabeth's day for forage and gardeners' cottages, became the *Mikháylovskaya plóstchad* (Arts Square – *plóstchad Iskússtv* – as it is still called). The statue of Aleksandr Pushkin, commanding the centre of it, is by Mikhail Anikushin (1957), who was awarded the Lenin Prize for it: 'Pushkin [. . .] was simple in his actions and clear in his thoughts. So I tried to get rid of all the details that might hide that clear image.'

The whole square bears the imprint of Rossi; his unifying design was followed by the architects who executed the other main buildings in the 1830s. Following Pushkin's gesture, on the west of the square (*No. 1*) is the **Small Theatre of Opera and Ballet** (*Mály teátr Ópery i Baléta*), designed by A. Bryullov (1833) to fit behind Rossi's façade. It was reconstructed, in 1860, by A. Cavos (who married into the Benois family and who, in the same year, constructed the Mariinskiy Theatre). The Small Theatre has had many names, starting life as the Mikhaylovskiy Theatre, then from 1918 the Academic Maly Opera Theatre, acquiring its present name in 1964 but adding *im. Moussorgskovo* to it in 1990. Since the early 1930s, it has provided a home for opera and ballet companies which are distinct from the Kirov and from its Imperial predecessor. The most distinguished part of its life was, perhaps, the 1930s when it became a 'laboratory' for Soviet Opera. Here was put on the first performance of Dzerzhinskiy's *Quietly Flows the Don* and Shostakovich's *Lady Macbeth of the Mtsensk District* (which caused so much disapproval that, on its revival in 1963, it was re-titled *Katerina Ismailova*). The tradition continued after the war under the direction of O. Vinogradov.

Plóstchad Iskússtv No. 5, on the south-west side of the square, was built in the 1830s by P. Jacquot as a private house (he was also at work on the Dutch Church on the Nevsky). In the early years of the twentieth century, its cellar – originally used for storing firewood – became a literary/theatrical/artistic club and cabaret called '**The Stray Dog**' (*Brodyáchaya Sobáka*). Run by an actor, B. Pronin, it was dedicated (if that is not too prim a word) to total artistic freedom, freedom to experiment and to improvise. No holds were barred, all egos could trip – painters, designers, producers, actors, dancers, Futurist poets, Symbolists, Acmeists. The queen of it was Akhmatova, then twenty-three or thereabouts, and the king perhaps was Mayakovskiy.

Karsavina used to dance there though it was not, she remembered, for established stars but 'for actors making a precarious living, musicians of prospective fame, poets and their muses who gathered there every night'. 'The Stray Dog' limped its way through the war, dragging out an impecunious existence until 1919. It is alive again now – artists perform there; but some of the spontaneity, what Karsavina described as 'no affectation, no tiresome cliché', is lacking.

No. 2, on the south-east side of the square, is also built by Jacquot (1834–9), also with a façade by Rossi. It is now the **Philharmonia**, the Great Hall of the St Petersburg Philharmonia Orchestra. In the time of the Grand Duke Mikhail, it was the Club of the Gentry (*Dvoryánskoye Sobrániye*). In the long reign of his widow, the Grand Duchess Elena, at the Mikhaylovskiy Palace, she and Anton Rubinstein fostered the Russian Music Society (founded 1859), which was followed in 1862 by the St Petersburg Conservatoire. They arranged for the vast rooms of the Club to be used for the performance, primarily, of Russian music, including Tchaikovsky's Sixth and last Symphony, the *Pathétique*, in 1893 (though Wagner, Liszt and Berlioz were among the foreigners who performed there too). In 1921, the Soviet Union became the state patron and, in 1922, the Academic Philharmonia was established as a resident orchestra. In 1975, '*im. Shostakovicha*' was added to its title.

The Seventh Symphony was written in some sense about, and in every sense during, the Blockade and bombardment of Leningrad. At the beginning, Shostakovich himself was in the city and, as is often told, broke off with appropriate marginal notes in the stave to serve as an air raid warden. By the end of 1941, he was – as were many of the orchestra – in the relative safety of Samara. On 9 August 1942, when St Petersburg had been bombed and blockaded for a year, the Leningrad Radio made an important announcement: 'In a few minutes, Comrades, you will hear the Seventh Symphony by Dimitri Shostakovich [restored, by this time, to the status of 'outstanding fellow townsman'] performed in Leningrad for the first time.' It had been written, said the announcer, while Nazi villains had been showering the city with bombs and while Germans had been shouting all over Europe that the days of Leningrad were numbered. The Radio Orchestra, under Karl Eliasberg, then played their hearts out. From every Soviet radio station, to as many countries in the world as could receive the signal, were transmitted the notes of the Seventh Symphony from the Philharmonia Hall. There were seventeen more months of the Blockade to be endured.

X

South of the Nevsky Prospect

Metro Stations: *Sadóvaya, Sennáya*
Plóstchad / Dostoyévskaya and *Vladímirskaya*

WHEN ARTS SQUARE (*plóstchad Iskússtv*) was still a
kitchen garden and the Philharmonia not even a
gentleman's club but an Imperial flowerbed, **Theatre Square**
(*Teatrálnaya plóstchad*) was beginning to take shape in the
far west of the city on the banks of the Kryukov Canal.
Beyond the Canal, to the west again, was the outer suburb of
Kolómna – until the mid-nineteenth century, a modest area
inhabited by small traders, small businessmen and artisans.

In the beginning, Theatre Square was Carousel Square
which, since the accession of Catherine II, had been associated with public entertainment, most of it in the open air –
fairs, hucksters, merry-go-rounds, *haute école* (where horses
performed the quadrille). Then in the 1770s, on the east
side of the square, Rinaldi built the first '**Stone Theatre**'
(*Kámenny teátr*). For the next forty years, it seems to have
been more than usually prone to destruction by fire. Many
of the rebuilds were supervised by Thomas de Thomon
until he fell off a scaffold and fatally injured himself. Finally,
in 1826, it was taken over by Alberto Cavos who seems to
have understood the requirements of theatrical construction rather better than his predecessors. So the Stone
Theatre became the *Bolshóy teátr* (Great Theatre). And great
it was in many respects – the largest in Europe and Russia's
home for opera and ballet for seventy years. The first performance of the first Russian opera – *A Life for the Tsar* by
Mikhail Glinka – took place here in 1836.

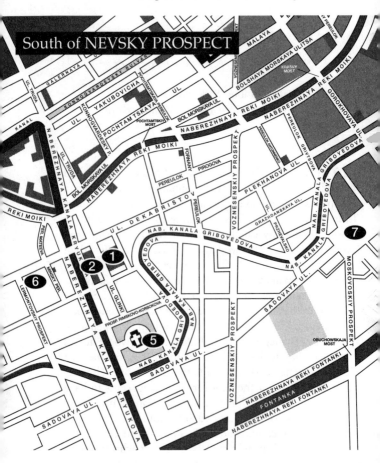

South of NEVSKY PROSPECT

1	Conservatoire	8	Suvorov Military Academy
2	Mariinskiy Theatre	9	Kuznechny Market
3	Theatre Museum	10	Dostoyevsky's Apartment
4	Ballet School	11	Semyonovskiy Platz
5	St Nicholas Cathedral	12	Theatre of Young Spectators
6	Synagogue	13	Rasputin's Apartment
7	Hay Market		

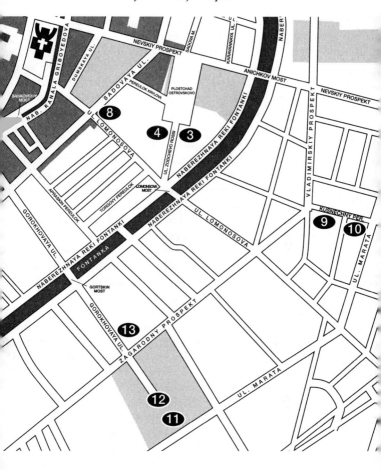

But Russian opera found little favour with the Court and migrated to Moscow where it remained until the 1860s while the Bolshoy and its Imperial sponsors cultivated foreign opera (Italian and French) and ballet (Italian, French and Russian). By the time the curtain came down on the

Bolshoy stage for the last time in 1886 (on Bizet's *Carmen*, as it happened), the Russian Imperial Ballet was in full flower. The first performance of *Coppélia* took place at the Bolshoy in 1884 and of *La Fille du Pharaon* the following year; *Swan Lake* and *Giselle* were familiars in the repertoire.

Then the *Kámenny/Bolshóy* was condemned as unsafe. Perhaps also it was needed for other purposes. And Cavos' Mariinskiy Theatre, which by that time was flourishing on the west side of the square, was ready to take over. At all events, the Bolshoy was more or less demolished and the foundations of what had been a rather elegant, temple-like structure were forced to carry the heavy four-storey bulk of the **Conservatoire** (plans by V. Nicole, built 1891–6) which had been founded in 1862 by Anton Rubinstein and which could now be properly accommodated in a purpose-built home. The Conservatoire (since 1944, the *Konservatóriya im. N.A. Rímskovo-Kórsakova*) still possesses two great concert halls – one with exceptional acoustics – which are in constant use by its own students and by Russian and visiting ensembles. With seven faculties – from Theory and Composition to Opera and Ballet Production, and from vocal to instrumental tuition – it remains the premier music school in Russia, as it was under the Empire and under the Soviet Union.

So the ballet had to move across the square where the outdoor world of the fairground had given way to another building, the Imperial Circus (A. Cavos, 1847–8). In 1860, this had been rebuilt as a theatre (by Cavos again) and named after the Empress Maria Aleksandrovna, wife of Alexander II. The Imperial **Mariinskiy Theatre** was completed in time to greet the return of Russian opera to St Petersburg from Moscow and to capture the outflow of Russian operatic composition (Moussorgsky: *Borís Godunóv* (1874); Tchaikovsky: *Eugene Onegin* (1879); Borodin: *Prince Igor* (completed by Rimsky-Korsakov and first performed, posthumously, in 1890). It became hugely popular.

Thus it was not until nearly the end of the nineteenth century that Russian opera and ballet came under one roof and the Mariinskiy became, what it still is, the (Imperial) Theatre of Opera and Ballet. In 1917, of course, it ceased to be Imperial; and after the murder of Kirov in 1934 it swapped 'Mariinskiy' for 'Kirov', which name was also acquired by its resident opera and ballet companies. Now, though Kirov has gone again and the House has had Mariinskiy restored to it, the Companies continue to use the name of Kirov when on tour abroad.

To complete the architectural story, additions were made in the 1880s to Cavos' restrained and fairly Classical opera-house exterior which, itself, would not have been out of place anywhere from Frankfurt to Prague. There was an extra floor, a heavy loggia at the south entrance, some Eclectic and Neo-Russian embellishments by Schröter (who made similar 'improvements' to Jacquot's Philharmonia in Arts Square). But the interior, and especially the ravishing auditorium, has so far survived in its essentials, decorative and acoustic. The audience still sits in arm chairs which still have peacock blue velvet seats; the Royal Box – and the four Grand Ducal boxes at the sides – are still heavily hung with pale blue silk, while the drop curtain is still painted with layer upon layer of succulent drapery so that 'during those languishing minutes before the performance started', as Alexandre Benois remembered from his childhood visits to the ballet, 'I would literally enter into it'.[1]

If present plans come to fruition, all this may now be radically changed. But the tale of London's Royal Opera House would suggest that the understandable ambitions of the Mariinskiy's distinguished artistic director (Valeriy Gergiev) to expand and modernise his base camp may take some time to be realised. Minor modernisations are already happening; the Wardrobe Department has already

---

[1] Alexandre Benois, *Reminiscences of the Russian Ballet* (Putnam: 1941).

moved out into a house on *Teatrálnaya plóstchad* and others are moving westwards across the Kryukov Canal. Whether these will satisfy the demands of modern opera remains to be seen.

While it may be opera that will force the reconstruction of the Mariinskiy, the story of **ballet** in that theatre has been one of great fruitfulness. At the time of its arrival in 1887, Tchaikovsky had just completed the score of *The Sleeping Beauty*, Petipa was about to choreograph it and Vsevolozhskiy to produce it (1890). People (especially Diaghilev and his group) complained that the Imperial Ballet's décor was over-sumptuous, its clothes stiff and colours crude. The Directorate sometimes complained that royal favourites tied their hands when it came to casting. But it was still able to recruit Cecchetti and Zucchi as new, young dancers from abroad and Fokine as a home-grown ballet master – Fokine, who introduced the revolutionary ideas that music was 'an organic part' of ballet, that the quality of choreography depended on the quality of the music and that dancers should convey character as well as technique.

Nevertheless, the most dynamic developments in ballet were taking place 'off-piste'. Fokine's *Chopiniana* (1908 – later, with Stravinsky's re-orchestration, to become *Les Sylphides* for the *Ballets Russes*) was only permitted as a charity performance. The new stars – Pavlova, Karsavina, Nijinsky – earned their bread and butter at the Mariinskiy but preferred to spend their summers, as soon as their contracts allowed, with Diaghilev and Benois as part of the *Ballets Russes* company in Paris. Stravinsky came into view as the perfect partner for Fokine (*Firebird* 1910, *Petrushka* 1911). But these ballets were not staged at the Mariinskiy; only by Diaghilev in Paris and London and Rome. Then, in 1911, the fissiparous tendency of the Russian ballet accelerated with the dismissal/resignation of Nijinsky from the Mariinskiy. The occasion was the deemed-to-be-inadequate length of his tunic in *Giselle* which Diaghilev, by then his lover, had ordered him to shorten by a couple of inches. By the 1913 summer season of the *Ballets Russes* in Europe, which included Nijinsky's choreography for Stravinsky's *Rite of Spring*, creative energy had really transferred to Diaghilev and left the Imperial Theatre with its increasingly arthritic management. It remains true that, without the Mariinskiy and without the **Imperial Ballet School** which fed it, the *Ballets Russes* could never have come into being.

That School was founded in 1738. When wild boar were still to be hunted in the birch groves off the *Névskiy prospékt*, children of Palace servants were being trained to dance for the Court. So the ballet and the School developed, not only under Imperial sponsorship but under the roof of the Winter Palace. The School found a home of its own in 1836 in the new street, *Teatrálnaya úlitsa* (Theatre Street, now *úlitsa Zódchevo Róssi* – Street of the Architect Rossi), part of Rossi's town plan for the area behind the other great Imperial theatre, the Aleksandrinskiy.[2] It is an exquisite street, ten times longer than the height of its buildings – two hundred and twenty metres long and twenty two metres high – leading from the back of *plóstchad Ostróvskovo* southwards to *plóstchad Lomonósova* on the Fontanka.

As it leaves the square, Theatre Street begins with what used to be two important offices. On the right (*Nos. 1–3*), was the Department of Education. On the left (*No. 2* Rossi Street/ *No. 6* Ostrovskiy Square) was the Office of the Imperial Theatres Directorate and, next door, the Imperial Ballet School. The Directorate vanished with the Revolution and in 1918 its office reopened as the **Theatre Museum** (*muzéy Teatrálnovo i Muzykálnovo Iskússtva*). During the 1920s, it acquired not merely the archives of the Directorate but also private collections which had belonged to leading theatrical figures – Komissarzhevskaya, Petipa, Chaliapin;

[2] When Tamara Karsavina published her memoirs in exile during the thirties, she called them *Theatre Street*.

stage sets by Benois, Bakst, Altman and Akimov; costumes (Chaliapin's for Borís Godunóv, for instance, which the Directorate would not allow him to take to Paris with Diaghilev's production of 1908); portraits. There is also a small branch of the Museum at *Stremyánnaya úlitsa No. 8* (part, in fact, of the complex of the Sheraton Nevsky Palace on the *Névskiy prospékt*) in what was, from 1869, the apartment of the Samoylov theatrical family. (Theatrical costumes are also on display in the Salon at the Mariinskiy. It is meant to bring good luck if you can persuade your escort to complete the round of the room with you during the interval – noting especially the bejewelled tunic of Khan Konchak and the wild red tutu of the Firebird.)

The Ballet School is still, and incomparably, the Ballet School except that, since her death in 1941, it has been called the *Akademícheskoye Khoreografícheskoye uchílistche im. Prof. A. Vagánovoy* in memory of the great ballerina, directress and choreographer, Agrippina Vaganova. She ruled from 1934 and produced a new generation of wonderful dancers which included Ulanova and Lepeshinskaya. After them, still trained in Vaganova's methods, came the dancers who, after the war, began to tour the West and – some of them – to remain there: Plissetskaya, Nureyev, Baryshnikov, Makarova.

Many of the dancers, musicians and artists who worked at the Mariinskiy and the Conservatoire used to live in the streets surrounding Theatre Square. So, like everyone else in St Petersburg, they made much use of their local church. And here they were fortunate for their local church – more gorgeous than St Paul's, Covent Garden but somewhat similar in function – was *Nikólskiy Morskóy sobór* (**the Maritime Cathedral of St Nicholas**) which stands in its own green square leading off the eastern embankment of the Kryukov Canal just south of the theatre. Built (Chevakinskiy 1753–62) as the church of sailors, seafarers, shipwrights and all their associates who inhabited the area south-west of the Admiralty, it later became the theatrical church, which may explain how it managed to keep open as a place of worship throughout the Soviet period. It is approached down a little avenue, past its own, free-standing, four-tiered, Russian-style belfry, turquoise blue and white with triple-angled corners, a multitude of Corinthian pilasters, Rococo window surrounds and the traditional five golden domes, one in the centre and the others set wide on each corner.

In many ways it resembles Smolny Cathedral, which was designed five years earlier. Like but unlike. More welcoming, more open, not so steep, Petersburg Baroque in its last and perhaps most perfect appearance. Unlike Rastrelli, whose pupil he was, Chevakinskiy successfully made the transition from the Baroque style favoured by the Empress Elisabeth to the Empress Catherine's Classicism. So he continued to enjoy Imperial patronage and was able to complete the inside as well as the out of his cathedral. Inside, indeed, is a surprise: two churches, one above the other, and no crypt – for fear of subsidence. The upper church was rendered especially magnificent by a gift from Catherine of ten gold-encased icons, to commem-orate ten naval victories, which embellish the iconostasis. But the overall effect is of charm and grace rather than grandeur.

Turning north out of the Cathedral square, left into the Kolómna District down *prospékt Rímskovo-Kórsakova* and first right up *Lérmontovskiy prospékt*, on the south-east corner where it meets *úlitsa Dekabrístov* is the pied, square building and arched entrance of the **Grand Choral Synagogue**, St Petersburg's centre of Jewish worship. Permission to build was granted by Alexander II in 1869; the site was found five years later; funds were raised largely through donations by the Ginsburg and Polyakov families. Then began a complicated negotiation about how it should look. Such a building was a new departure in the capital of Russia, the great majority of Russian Jews being required to live within the Pale of Settlement;[3] those who, with or without permission, had moved into the city worshipped at a number of meeting houses in scattered locations. So a team was put together, led by the distinguished Russian critic V. V. Stasov (son of the architect) and including the architects I. Shaposhnikov and L. Bakhman, to produce a design acceptable both to the Jewish authorities and to the St Petersburg town planners. The outside is more-or-less Moorish (a style favoured at the time by Jewish communities in central Europe) as are many of the architectural details of the interior. Inside, there was room for a congregation of twelve hundred. The Synagogue was consecrated in 1893.

The date is interesting; the Jewish community in St Petersburg at that time numbered fifteen thousand. Towards the end of the nineteenth century, and for the last two decades of the Empire, there began, in spite of continuing legal disabilities and intermittent, ill-controlled pogroms, a **flowering of Jewish culture** in Russia which paralleled the expansion in the Russian economy. Jews made up over a third of the Russian trading community, provided much of the finance for railways and the shipping industry, owned a major part of the timber and grain business. And they were gaining in confidence.

---

[3] In the eighteenth century, most of the population of Russia had to ask permission to move home. Catherine the Great abolished this requirement, except for the Jewish population (and serfs). Though there were some large settlements in the Baltic States and the Caucasus, in practice most Russian Jews were living in what was then Poland and the Pale of Settlement usually indicated that area (though the restrictions on movement applied everywhere). For a Jew to move without permission, he had to be a woman (no ordinary woman would move alone and so they were often prostitutes), a gold-medallist (on his exit from school) or have a special permit. Many Jews did move – without permission – but, if discovered in a police check, were driven back to the Pale. The law relating to this was abolished immediately by the Provisional Government in 1917.

Their cultural flowering took two forms. On the one hand, there was a purely Jewish manifestation. Hebrew in its modernised form and Yiddish were being fashioned as literary languages mainly (some would say entirely) by Russian Jews: Hebrew poetry (Byalik, Chernykhovskiy and Schneur) and Yiddish story telling (Mendele 1837–1917, Sholem Aleichem 1850–1918, Peretz 1851–1915). On the other hand, there were the Jewish poets, prose writers and painters who began to make their appearance in the mainstream of the Russian intelligentsia, many of them in St Petersburg: the mystical poet Minskiy who, with Merezhkovskiy, started the Religious and Philosophical Society and was one of the precursors of the Symbolists; the Acmeist poet, Osip Mandelstam; the painters Leon Bakst and Natan Altman (who painted the famous portrait of Akhmatova in blue and yellow cubes); the architects Gelfreykh, Levinson and Gevirts – not to mention the extraordinary contribution of Jewish performers and academics to the musical life of the city.

Orthodox Jews remained, however, subject to legal disabilities – of which the greatest was the requirement to seek permission to live outside the Pale. And it was left to the Provisional Government, immediately after the abdication of the Emperor in 1917, to introduce the equality of all Russian citizens before the law. But many of the Russo-Jewish intelligentsia then dispersed – to Western Europe, to America, and some to Palestine. For those who stayed behind, the years of Soviet rule under Stalin proved as punitive as any that had preceded them. Isaac Bashevis Singer, writing in the 1970s' Encyclopaedia Britannica, made the bitter comment that 'the Bolshevik Revolution attracted a number of Yiddish writers [back to the Soviet Union] and later liquidated most of them'. For the Jews who had stayed behind, it was a period of dispersal and secularisation.

So while it is true that the Petersburg Synagogue does not carry on its walls the roll of those who perished in the

Holocaust, it is also true that its congregation suffered greatly. A minor gain has been the current project to refurbish the synagogue (with the aid of private American donors), one objective of which was to restore the original floor plan of the Grand Prayer Hall. This had been modified in 1908 when the authorities ordered all Jewish meeting houses in the city to close and the separate communities to pack themselves into the new synagogue. But the restoration project goes further: it aims to revive the community and to provide not merely Jewish schools and *yeshiva* (already functioning) but a library, lecture hall, first aid room, *matzoh* bakery and 'match-making service'. There are now, apparently, about 100,000 Jews living in Leningrad Province. By providing a marriage bureau in the synagogue – a kind of official version of the old *shiddukh* – the Rabbinate must be hoping that Jews will be encouraged once again to marry Jews.

A tram down *úlitsa Dekabrístov* will pass an apartment where Tolstoy stayed in 1856 (*No. 5*), an apartment occupied by the Mandelstam family in 1899 (*No. 17*), an apartment where Turgenev was arrested for writing in praise of Gogol in 1852 (*No. 28*), a building that contained the theatre where Meyerhold and Komissarzhevskaya put on the first play by Aleksandr Blok in 1906 (*No. 39*), the house where Chernyshevskiy lived in the early 1850s (*No. 45*) until it reaches the junction with the river Pryazhka (*náberezhnaya rekí Pryázhki*). There, at No. 57, was the home of Aleksandr Blok and his wife from 1912 until the poet's death from malnutrition in 1921. They occupied two different apartments in this house: one, relatively spacious, on the third floor until 1920; one which they briefly shared with Blok's mother on the first floor. The **Blok Apartment Museum** was opened in 1980, the centenary of the poet's birth.

It was on the third floor of *No. 57* that Blok wrote his last and greatest poem: *The Twelve*. Not Apostles but drunken revolutionary soldiers stagger through the streets of St Petersburg, shooting at everything and everybody they see, firing shots into the darkness with no aim and no purpose but to kill. They don't want to be shown where to go; they don't want to be led. But they feel something, some human form, is drawing them forward, taking cover behind the houses, always beyond them. And they try to kill that, too. But all that comes back to them are the echoes of their bullets rippling harmlessly through the streets like mocking laughter. The form, unknown to them, is Christ. This is the paradox of revolution. Intended for the betterment of mankind, a Christian act. But the instruments on whom it depends are blind, intent on their own gratification, indifferent to its aims. And in these hands, in human hands, it becomes carnage, debauchery and terror. Blok evokes a haunting image: the bourgeois capitalist stands at a crossroads, shivering, his nose in his coat against the cold and, pressing up against him, tail between its legs, a mangy cur. The bourgeois is as hungry as the dog, uncertain what to do, 'standing at the crossroads . . . speechless like a question mark'. Behind him, seeking protection, cowers the old world – the mangy cur. Blok died, starving and in despair, on 7 August 1921. He is now buried in the *Literátorskiye mostkí* where his remains were re-interred in 1944.

Returning to the Kryukov Canal where it joins **Sadóvaya úlitsa** (Garden Street), we enter very different territory. In literary terms, it belongs to Dostoyevsky who, for six years (1861–7) while he was writing *Crime and Punishment*, lived in *Málaya Mestchánskaya* (now *Grazhdánskaya*) *úlitsa* north-west of *Sennáya plóstchad* across the Griboyedov Canal. Early in the eighteenth century the area south of the *Sadóvaya* was associated with magnificent gardens, running from the street down to the Fontanka and gracing the mansions of grandees – Yusupov, Chernyshov, Apraksin, Vorontsov. It also developed, because it was on the outskirts of town, as a market area – in the first instance for combustible commodities like hay, straw and logs; then for almost any country produce which trundled in to town along the Moscow road to the great market square, *Sennáya plóstchad* (**Hay Market**). The road that is now *Moskóvskiy prospékt* was, in the 1760s, called the Road to Tsarskoye Selo, where the Empress Elisabeth and, later, Catherine II created their country palaces; Catherine personally encouraged the Hay Market. Peasants sold from their carts, or just from the side of the road; meat joined the hay – some on the hoof, some slaughtered; also potatoes, new to Russia and about which Catherine was very enthusiastic, other vegetables, leather, lace and joinery from the villages. The first English shop (proprietor B. Gevsford, as the Russians called him) opened in 1786. The Danish Embassy built a house on the square. So, for a time, market and magnates coexisted and *Sadóvaya úlitsa* prospered. Over all once presided the Hay Market's own church, known locally as the Hay Saviour – *Sennóy Spas* – but, more formally, as the Church of the Assumption (Baroque, built in the 1750s; A. Kvasov and B. Rastrelli both had a hand, being also at work together on Tsarskoye Selo).

But by the end of the eighteenth century, the less inno-cent elements of the market and new speculative building were beginning to turn Garden Street into something more like London's St Giles Circus, Haymarket, Gin Lane and Smithfield rolled into one – eventually, as rural unemploy-ment grew, into something even worse. Turning east into *Sadóvaya úlitsa* from the Kryukov Canal, immediately on the right still stand the 'rows' of St Nicholas Market (*Nikólskiy rýnok*, 1788–9), a long, two-storey rectangle built round a *dvor* (courtyard), arcaded on the ground floor with blind arcading above. In the nineteenth century, people drawn in from the country to seek work in the city would gather in wooden sheds in the courtyard, which acted as a crude labour exchange.

Just beyond *pereúlok Boytsóva* (*No. 50*), in an island of cleanliness and sanity, the Museum of the Ministry of

Transport (now the **Railway Museum**) was built (1901–2) to house the Ministry's collection, begun in 1813, which has models of early track and rolling stock and a history of the Trans-Siberian railway. Then comes the only great garden left – still called the *Yusúpovskiy sad* – with a 'pond' (the English would call it a lake) in the middle of it which serves as a skating rink in winter. The Yusupov mansion, which became the Ministry of Transport when the family left it early in the nineteenth century for the more salubrious banks of the Moika, stands in the south-east corner. It is best seen from the Fontanka. Started in the 1720s, rebuilt by Quarenghi in the 1790s, it still has connections with transport engineers, being the headquarters of their Institute.

Of the Square itself, the centrepiece of *Crime and Punishment*, almost nothing pre-Revolutionary remains. The church of the Hay Saviour was demolished in 1961 when the Metro (*Sennáya Plóstchad*) arrived on its site. (Some years later, the canopy of the Metro station collapsed, killing several people, since when the superstitious have suggested that the church should be rebuilt.) The stalls that sold rotting food, the drunkards, the vagrants, the mutilated beggars and child prostitutes that disgorged into the Square from the lanes around, the courtyards and cellars full of excrement, the rooming houses where seven or eight people slept in one curtained-off corner – these are no longer evident in the modern blocks around. The small Classical building that held the over-worked police station is still there and so, to an extent, are the pickpockets, the prostitutes and the general bustle and smell of cheap food. But the worst of the housing was pulled down in the 1920s and 1930s, when the market itself was abolished.

Perhaps the most terrible aspect of the lanes and tenements, brothels and *kabakí* (pubs) around the Hay Market were the epidemics. The first government commission to investigate living conditions for the poor, in 1844, reported twenty people crowded into single tenements. The crowding grew worse as the century grew older; by the 1860s, the city could claim a mortality rate higher than any in Europe, a greater incapacity to process its own detritus and a greater capacity to consume alcohol. The syndrome was common throughout Europe but peaked later in Russia than elsewhere, perhaps because the exodus from the country came later – after the liberation of the serfs. But it was already evident in the great cholera epidemic of 1831.

One day a crowd gathered in the Hay Market, in front of the police station, intent on killing the doctors who were despatching the sick to isolation barracks and who, they believed, were responsible for spreading the infection. The clergy came out of the church to tell them to stop – and they lynched them, too, while they threw some of the doctors out of the hospital windows. Troops were called out. They arrived, so some historians say, commanded by the Emperor in person (Nicholas I was a professional soldier) standing, alone, in his carriage. He called out, in a voice described as thunderous: '*Na koléni!*' ('On your knees!') and, astounded, they fell as one man to prayer. There is sufficient truth in the story for the incident to be commemorated on the plinth of Klodt's statue in St Isaac's Square and to be described as 'The Knee Riot' – though some say the Emperor arrived on the day after the troops had quelled the peak of the violence.

The worst slums grew up in the second half of the nineteenth century, south of the *Sadóvaya* between *Moskóvskiy prospékt, Gorókhovaya úlitsa* and the Fontanka – as a result of an investment in urban property by Prince Vyazemskiy. He bought two vacant sites running back from the river from a rich, beautiful and extremely disagreeable woman called Poltoratskaya, wife of the Director of the Court Chapel choir, who was in the habit of publicly flogging her serfs and her children. The *Vyázemskaya lávra*, as it was derisively called, consisted of thirteen rooming houses put up in the 1850s and 1860s into which some 20,000 people were said to be packed. So frightening was the reputation of these tenements that the police would not enter the lanes; to recover stolen property, they would frequent a location in the Square called 'The Teahouse' (known to its intimates as 'The Mouse Trap') where half the customers were policemen and the other half were thieves. In the end, the *lávra* frightened even the owners who, in 1912, offered to clear it out and build a road through the middle of it. But, because of war and revolution, the task was left to the Soviet authorities.

Further east along *Sadóvaya úlitsa* are relics of other large markets, including one that developed in the grounds of the Apraksin mansion whose 'rows' (or, rather, the 1863 version of the 'rows', rebuilt by Krakau and Corsini after the regulation fire) are open again for business (junk shops, second-hand clothes, bikes, cannibalised car parts and guns, so they say, if you hang around for ten minutes) at *No. 28* between *Apráksin pereúlok* and *úlitsa Lomonósova*. In the nineteenth century, Stchukin's Rows, just off the Apraksin Market, represented a step-up for Hay Market traders on their way to the *Gostíny dvor*. On the opposite side of the street (at *No. 21*) is Quarenghi's building for Catherine II's State Bank (*Assignatsiónny bank*, 1783–90, now the Financial and Economic Institute), which stands behind handsome railings by Rusca (1817) with its main façade on to the Griboyedov Canal and a bust of Quarenghi (1967) to the west of it.

One of Quarenghi's most delightful creations is the **Maltese Chapel** which he added to the back of the Vorontsov Mansion (1798–1800). The mansion itself, which stands on the south-east corner of the intersection with *úlitsa Lomonósova*, was built for the Empress Elisabeth's Chancellor Vorontsov by Rastrelli (1749–57) and is now the **Suvorov Military Academy**. The Chapel was required when Emperor Paul became (inappropriately for he was neither a Catholic nor a bachelor) Grand Master of the Knights of Malta and presented Vorontsov's mansion to the Order.

In 1810, mansion and chapel became home to the **Imperial Corps of Pages** – one of three privileged schools for boys, the other two being the Emperor Alexander Lyceum (*Litséy*), which moved from Tsarskoye Selo to the *Kámenno-ostróvskiy prospékt* in 1843, and the Imperial Law School (Pravovedeniye) at *náberezhnaya rekí Fontánka No. 6.* All three provided education from the age of ten to post-University level (which is why the top of pre-Revolutionary society in Russia rarely went to university); all three were for children of the élite. The Corps of Pages provided a military education where the boys wore uniforms and senior boys attended the Imperial family on ceremonial occasions; on graduating, they were expected to serve at least three years in the army, preferably in the Guards. In 1917, the building became briefly a club for the Socialist Revolutionary Party; then, for a few years, it was shut down altogether. But, strangely enough, in Stalin's day it was opened again – under new management and a different name but with much the same purpose: to be a military school. The boys, who still wear uniforms, now black and red, enter at fifteen and receive a general as well as a military education; war orphans are given precedence in the selection. The chapel is being meticulously restored and has been opened as a museum.

At this point one could choose to walk down *úlitsa Lomonósova* across the southern end of the elegant *úlitsa Zódchevo Róssi* on to the *most Lomonósova*, whence there are fine views of the Fontanka embankments. If you walk across the little bridge (J. Perronnet, 1785–7), turn back and look diagonally over the river to the **B. D. T.** (*Bolshóy Dramatícheskiy teátr im. M. Gorkovo* – L. Fontana, 1876). It is easy to find: pale green and Classical. Everybody, from the taxi-driver to the professor, agrees that it is the best

theatre in the city as a result of the efforts of its great director, G. Tovstonogov, active there from the 1950s to the
1990s. Since his death there have been various visiting
directors and the company (his 'family') has continued as
an entity, now in the well-respected hands of a Georgian
called Chkheidze. In addition to the *repertoire* of this resident company, it has begun to host plays from the West.

If you prefer to take the Metro (one stop, *Sennáya
Plóstchad* to *Dostoyévskaya*), cross the *Vladímirskaya
plóstchad* to the **Vladímirskaya tsérkov** on the corner. The
church is large, yellow, the last of the great Baroque cathedrals (1761–9, architect unknown) with onion domes set
on high drums and a detached, relatively Classical, belfry
on the north side by Quarenghi (1783), to which a fourth
tier was added by Rusca in 1848. There were also some
additions to the west side in 1831. *Vladímirskiy prospékt*
itself is quite short, a continuation of *Litéyny prospékt* running south from *Névskiy prospékt*; beyond the square it
turns into *Zágarodny prospékt*. In the nineteenth century, it
was lined with second-hand bookstalls and, behind them,
antiquarian booksellers. *No. 12* was The Merchants' Club
(*Kupécheskoye Sobrániye*, 1826–8) which contained a
theatre where Benois and Fokine staged their first collaboration outside the Mariinskiy – a forerunner of *Petrushka*
based on a Harlequinade to music re-scored from
Clementi's sonatas for the piano. It was performed, to no
great acclaim, at the annual students' ball of the Academy
of Arts with Cecchetti as Pantaloon (1908). The building is
now the **teátr imeni Lensovéta**.

Leaving the square eastwards down *Kuznéchny pereúlok*,
on the right is a very up-market market, the **Kuznéchny
rýnok**. Here almost anything can be bought, in the way of
foodstuffs, from anywhere and you might think that supply
was flowing freely across Russia to meet demand. But you
would be wrong. Almost anything can be bought – at a price
that, for most Petersburgers, is prohibitive. If your child

were sick, you might come to buy him a very small piece of fresh fish or some wild honey. But you would not feed yourself from here.

So you cross *úlitsa Dostoyévskovo* and come to the **Dostoyevsky Memorial Museum** (*No. 5/2*), the house that contains the last apartment (*No. 119*) of Dostoyevsky, where he lived for nearly three years from 1878 with his second wife, Anna, and their surviving children. During his twenty-eight years in St Petersburg, he changed his address twenty times (not including his sojourn in the Peter and Paul Fortress), often choosing as here to live on the angle of two streets. If the dramas of *Crime and Punishment* are mostly placed in the lanes around the Hay Market and the Griboyedov Canal, *The Brothers Karamazov* was written in the comparatively comfortable surroundings of *Vladímirskaya plóstchad*. Here Dostoyevsky enjoyed a cheerful and fairly social life: Tuesday evenings at the widow of Stackenschneider, the architect, whose brother (a lawyer) told him what he needed to know about Court proceedings; Wednesdays at the widow of Aleksey Tolstoy, the poet, who gave him a reproduction of a detail of Raphael's Dresden *Madonna*; another evening at Suvorin's, the editor of *Nóvoye Vrémya* (New Times) who published his *Diary of a Writer* and later became Chekhov's friend and publisher. He had fewer fits; he was out of debt; he had given up gambling. And then, one night, working in his study, he dropped his pen on the floor and it rolled under a bookshelf. As he tried to lift the shelves, blood gushed from his throat and in two days, on 28 January 1881, he was dead. The main rooms of the apartment have been re-created, with the help of his descendants who still live in St Petersburg; and there is a display which links the novels to the author's life and to the streets of the city, providing some keys to his topographical *romans à clef*. Perhaps the ardent Dostoyevskian should begin here and then move to the haunted alleys around the *Sennáya plóstchad*.

There is another topographical key to the life of Dostoyevsky in St Petersburg – the *Semyónovskiy plats*. It can be reached by taking the Metro from *Vladímirskaya* to *Púshkinskaya*, which is the station for *Vítebskiy vokzál*. (This was the first train terminal in the city, opening in 1837 to link between St Petersburg and the country palaces of Tsarskoye Selo and Pavlovsk. The present building is asymmetrical *Style Moderne* with an off-centre clock tower – Brzezovskiy and Minash, 1904.) Or it can be approached down *úlitsa Maráta* or *Zágarodny prospékt*. Either way, you arrive at the huge empty space of the Platz that was once the parade ground of the Semyonovskiy Guards and stretched from *Zágarodny prospékt* all the way to the *Obvódny kanál* on the southern outskirts of the city. (It is now mostly occupied by the *Pionérskaya plóstchad* and the *teátr Yúnykh Zríteley* – Theatre of Young Spectators – which opened in 1962).

The Platz, being a good long way away from residential areas, was sometimes used for executions. It was here in December 1849, as the first three condemned men were tied to the posts, that the execution by firing squad of Dostoyevsky and his twenty companions from the 'Petrashevskiy Circle' was cancelled and commuted to four years exile in Siberia – frequently quoted as an example of the gratuitous cruelty of Nicholas I and transfigured by Dostoyevsky in *Notes from the House of the Dead*. Mikhail Petrashevskiy lived in what is now *plóstchad Turgéneva* (and was then *Pokróvskaya plóstchad*) at the far west end of *Sadóvaya úlitsa* and held 'evenings' at which young, reformist intellectuals would gather to discuss the ideas of French Utopian Socialists and admire Belinskiy's attack on Gogol which was read aloud by Dostoyevsky.

Belinskiy had written an open letter to Gogol rejecting the strange *Selected Passages from Correspondence with my Friends* (1847) in which Gogol argued that Russia's moral and material improvement required total submission to the Orthodox Church, the Autocracy and the land owners. 'Yes, I love you,' Belinskiy had written. 'But Russia sees her salvation not in mysticism or aestheticism or piety but in the achievements of education, civilisation and human culture. She has no need of sermons (she has heard too many) nor of prayers (she has mumbled them too often) but of the awakening in the people of a feeling of human dignity, lost for so many ages in mud and filth [. . .] Champion of obscurantism and black reaction, defender of a Tartar way of life, what are you doing? [. . .] The Russian people is right. It sees the writers of Russia as its only leaders, defenders and survivors from the darkness of Russian autocracy, Orthodoxy and nationalism.'[4] Belinskiy's letter was a direct attack on Nicholas I's policies. A police informer had been present on the evening that Dostoyevsky read the letter out to the Petrashevskiy circle and so they were all taken off to the Fortress of SS Peter and Paul.

In this same Platz, six members of the People's Will Party were hanged in April 1881 for the assassination of Alexander II. They included Zhelyabov and Perovskaya. This was the year of Dostoyevsky's death. And the repeated attempts to murder Alexander were much on his mind when he was writing *The Brothers Karamazov*.

Towards the end of the nineteenth century, the Platz became a race track before being adopted by the Young Communist movement. It is one end of *Gorókhovaya úlitsa* – the central leg of the Trident which formed the framework of the early town plan. At the other, Admiralty, end of the street (*No. 2*) is the building that housed the City Police. (After the Revolution it housed Dzerzhinskiy's Cheka which is why the street was later called *úlitsa Dzerzhínskovo*). So it was handy that, in August 1914, **Rasputin** moved into an

---

[4] Vissarion Belinskiy's letter to Gogol quoted by Isaiah Berlin in *Russian Thinkers* (The Hogarth Press: 1978).

apartment at *Gorókhovaya úlitsa No. 64*. There were many reasons why the Imperial police might have wanted to watch him: partly, indeed, to protect him (he had just returned from the country where he had been severely injured in an attempt on his life); partly to see what he was up to. So they hung about in the courtyard of *No. 64*, and compiled a detailed dossier on his activities.[5] A friend, Vera Zhukovskaya, is going to visit Rasputin in *No. 64*:

> After crossing beneath a dark archway into a courtyard poured with asphalt, I approached a reddish-brown three-storey building whose front door opened towards me by itself. A very courteous doorman explained to me in anticipation of my enquiry that Rasputin lived on the second floor and that the door to his apartment was covered with crimson cloth. While the doorman was removing my boots, I gazed suspiciously at a certain personage [. . .] sitting in the corner next to the little iron stove: he would look at everyone entering with excessive attention, then assume a profoundly indifferent expression.[6]

At this (last) stage of his life, Rasputin seems to have spent a good deal of his time drinking heavily and bingeing with the gypsies (in Moscow as well as St Petersburg). But *Gorókhovaya úlitsa* was, of course, also well-placed for urgent visits to Tsarskoye Selo, where the Empress and her children were living.

On 10 January 1916, Rasputin celebrated his forty-seventh birthday in *Gorókhovaya úlitsa*. The police came to the apartment with presents and offered to take the coats of Rasputin's guests. The guests then came with more presents, according to the police: 'a mass of valuable things in silver and gold, carpets, whole suites of furniture, paintings,

---

[5] Published in the *Krásny Arkhív* – Red Archive, No. 24, 1924.
[6] Vera Zhukovskaya in *Memories of Grigoriy Rasputin 1914–16*, quoted by E. Radzinskiy in *The Rasputin File* (Doubleday: 2000).

money'. Then they all got drunk; then came the gypsies and finally, brandishing revolvers, the husbands of two of the ladies who had spent the night in the apartment. The police escorted the ladies out by the back door. But there was a strange hiatus in the police surveillance. Aleksandr Protopopov, who became Minister of Internal Affairs later in the year, wanted, it seems, himself to visit Rasputin on occasion. And for this reason, he ordered that all police agents should be removed from *No. 64* at midnight. After midnight, in the latter part of 1916, Rasputin could be – and in due course was – driven away from his apartment without anyone knowing.

XI

The Embankments of the Moika and the Neva

Metro Stations: *Sennáya Plóstchad / Sadóvaya* and *Névskiy Prospékt*

MY SISTER AND I may be two of the last people still alive to have seen **Rasputin**. It must have been just before his death. It was winter. We were going for a walk with our nurse. And, since we lived at the time on the Moika Embankment, I suspect it must have been somewhere near the *Krásny most* (Red Bridge). A cab on runners came trotting slowly past us. There were two men in it. One of them seemed to me to be very large with a big beard. His hat was off and his head thrown back in uproarious laughter and I could see his teeth gleaming between his black moustache and his black beard. My nurse said: 'Do you know who that is?' We didn't, of course. 'Well, it's Rasputin, that's who it is.' 'Oh!' I said, 'And who's that?' I cannot, for the life of me, remember her answer nor can I imagine how she knew.

But I suppose that, by 1916, everyone in St Petersburg knew what Rasputin looked like. They had heard about his influence over the Empress through his power to palliate her son's haemophilia, about her attempts (in spite of the Emperor's admonitions) to influence appointments to and decisions by the government in line with his wishes, about his disorderly behaviour – and the other factors that led to his murder on the night of 16/17 December. Early on the morning of 19 December, Rasputin's corpse was found in the *Málaya Nevá* on the north side of *Petróvskiy óstrov*. There are many versions of the murder – by those who

277

took part and by those who investigated it. Was there an attempt to poison him? Who fired the fatal bullet? Was he dead before they tipped him into the river? These things only matter if you want to believe that Rasputin was superhuman.

What do we know? We know that from 1915 the Emperor was at the front, having decided in the face of Russian defeats that he personally should command the Russian armies in the field. We know that some – indeed most – of the other members of the Romanov family had come to the conclusion that the partnership of Rasputin and the Empress, left behind in St Petersburg, was in all the circumstances calamitous. We know that Prince Felix Yusupov was married to the Emperor's niece, Princess Irina, who was not only Royal but amazingly beautiful. We know that he and the Grand Duke Dimitri Pavlovich – first cousin of Nicholas II – decided to murder Rasputin, all attempts by the family at persuading the Empress to detach herself from his influence having failed.

They decided to involve three other people: V. Purishkevich, a right-wing member of the *Dúma*, who had denounced the Empress as 'the evil genius of Russia and the Tsar' and Rasputin as heading 'those dark forces and influences' which had 'turned the Tsar's ministers into marionettes'; Lieutenant Sukhotin, a young officer in the Preobrazhenskiy Regiment; and Dr Lazavert who worked with Purishkevich in his military hospital train and was known to be good at driving motor cars. Finally, we know that the plan was to tempt Rasputin to the Yusupov family house at *náberezhnaya rekí Móiki No. 94* (the **Yusupov Palace** on the Moika Embankment) by the prospect of meeting Princess Irina (who was in fact in the Crimea). There he was to be taken by a side door into a basement room, exotically redecorated for the purpose with a bearskin rug, a Persian carpet and a seventeenth-century Italian crucifix. He was to be told that the Princess was

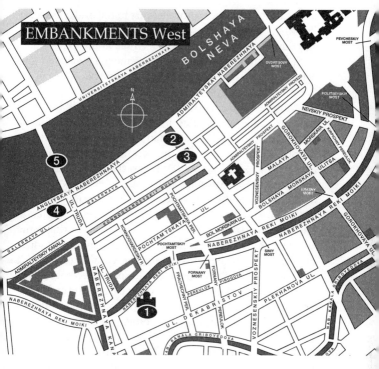

1   Yusupov Palace
2   Senate
3   Synod
4   Rumyantsev House
    (Museum of the History of St Petersburg)
5   Lieutenant Schmidt Bridge

entertaining her friends upstairs where the gramophone
was to be playing but, in due course, would come down.
While he was waiting, Felix was to poison him with cakes
and wine into which potassium cyanide had been introduced by the doctor; his body was to be driven by the doctor

in one of Purishkevich's hospital cars to the bridge between Petrovskiy and Krestovskiy Islands on the outskirts of town and dumped in the river through a hole in the ice.

Shortly after midnight on 17 December, Dr Lazavert and Felix Yusupov arrived at *Gorókhovaya úlitsa No. 64* to collect Rasputin. The police guard had been called off for the night; the Minister of the Interior, Protopopov had paid his usual visit and had warned Rasputin that there was to be an attempt on his life; Rasputin had nevertheless washed and dressed with great care for the occasion and put on some new brown boots. Yusupov, Dr Lazavert and Rasputin go off to *Móika No. 94*. Yusupov and Rasputin enter by the side door and descend to the basement 'dining room'. Upstairs, the gramophone plays '*Yankee Doodle*'. Felix persuades Rasputin, with difficulty, to eat some cakes and drink some wine; he keeps him in conversation, even plays gypsy songs on the guitar, while he waits for the cyanide to work. It appears to have little or no effect. Rasputin becomes impatient to see Princess Irina and Yusupov goes several times upstairs to consult with his co-conspirators. At 2.30 a.m., they decide they must try another means of murder. Yusupov collects a pocket Browning revolver from a drawer in his study and returns to the basement with the gun. Rasputin has another glass of wine and suggests a visit to the gypsies. Yusupov walks across the room and stares at the crucifix so intently that Rasputin goes to look at it too but remarks that he prefers the chest on which it stands. 'Grigoriy Yefimovich, you would do better to look at the crucifix and say a prayer.' Yusupov takes the revolver from behind his back and shoots him in the chest. Rasputin gives a cry and falls on to the bearskin.

Felix was not a practised shot and Rasputin was not dead. He got out of the basement by the same door that he came in by and staggered across the courtyard towards the street. Four more shots were fired but, in all, only three bullet wounds were found in his body. A policeman heard the shots and reported them. Then, at 5.30 a.m., the Grand Duke Dimitri Pavlovich, Dr Lazavert and Lieutenant Sukhotin tied the body up in some material and took it, by car, to the *Bolshóy Petróvskiy most* where, on the second attempt, they succeeded in heaving it and a package of clothes over the parapet into the *Málaya Névka*. One brown boot was left on the parapet and they forgot to add the weights which would have ensured that the body sank. Just after 1.00 p.m. on 18 December, the boot was found and, shortly thereafter, recognised. The body was found two hundred and fifty yards downstream from the bridge.

There we reach the limit of what is known about the murder of Rasputin. We do not know exactly how he died nor who finally killed him. We do not know what took place between him and Yusupov after the first, unsuccessful, shot. There are many versions, including the version that the fatal bullet was actually fired by the Grand Duke. Yusupov's version can certainly not be relied on. Two facts are worth adding: Dr Lazavert, in exile in Paris, later confessed that he could not bring himself to add the cyanide to either the cakes or the wine; and a document, purporting to be based on the coroner's report (the original of which has 'disappeared'), stated that no poison (though a great deal of alcohol) was found in Rasputin's body and no water was found in his lungs when he was taken out of the river. Which seems to suggest that he died, from a shot, before he was dumped in the river, and could not, as some subsequently alleged, have freed his hands and made the sign of the cross as he fell towards the water.

His corpse was taken in a military ambulance to the **Chesme Palace**, some three miles to the south, now surrounded by that part of the city which was developed in Stalin's time. Built in the 1770s by Felten as a staging post for Catherine the Great on her way to Tsarskoye Selo, it had become a convalescent home for wounded soldiers. The coffin rested in the Chesme Church (1777–80) whose extraordinary red-and-white striped face can be seen from the main road, about half-way between the *Park Pobédy* and the *Moskóvskaya* metro stations. At 9.00 a.m. on 29 December, Rasputin was buried in the grounds of a small chapel being built in the Imperial park at Tsarskoye Selo where, as Nicholas II noted in his diary that evening, the family 'assisted at a sad scene: the coffin with the body of the unforgettable Grigoriy, murdered by monsters in the house of F. Yusupov, had already been lowered into the grave. Father Aleksandr Vasiliyev pronounced the eulogy, after which we returned home. The weather was grey with twelve degrees of frost.' His murderers were simply sent away: Yusupov to his estates in the Crimea, the Grand Duke to the army in the Caucasus, Purishkevich, the doctor and the lieutenant back to the front with the hospital train. Some two months later, by which time the Imperial family were under arrest in the Alexander Palace at Tsarskoye Selo, Kerensky (as Minister of Justice but not yet head of the Provisional Government) ordered Rasputin's body to be disinterred and reburied in an unmarked spot in the countryside. In fact, the truck that was carrying the coffin broke down near the forest of Pargolovo, where it was doused with petrol and burned to ashes.

After the Revolution, the Yusupov Palace became – and has remained – a museum, though it is difficult quite to say what of. In the basement is a mock-up of the 'dining room', with wax figures of Rasputin and Yusupov, and another of the room in which the other three conspirators waited anxiously upstairs. There is the staircase and the door into the courtyard and photographs and a death certificate. But somehow the props – particularly the waxworks – seem to usurp the imagination, and the questions that ought to flood into one's mind about the nature of Rasputin and the significance, if any, of his murder, are frozen at source. Then you can also visit the house itself, a House (i.e. Club) for Educational Workers and, more recently, 'a museum', according to the Museum Guide, 'about the lifestyle of the nobility'. It is no such thing.

In the 1730s, the 'palace' was indeed an 'exemplary' timber house of the 'nobility' as prescribed in the town plan. Demolished by the Shuvalov family in the 1760s, it was rebuilt in grander, Classical, style by Kokorinov and finished by Vallin de la Mothe (1766), who gave it a handsome frieze and a six-columned central portico. In the 1830s, it came into the possession of Prince Nikolay Yusupov. His only child, Zinaida, who was Felix Yusupov's mother, was the sole heir to the huge family fortune. (She married Count Felix Sumarokov-Elston who then acquired the Yusupov name and title.) So there was nothing typical about the lifestyle of the inhabitants of *Móika No. 94*. Their investments – in oil, coal, iron, factories and land – have been conservatively estimated at 1914 prices as in excess of half a billion dollars and their annual income in excess of twenty million.

Like many boundlessly rich people, they were not content to leave well alone so the house was assaulted by fashionable architects (not including Stackenschneider) – A. Mikhaylov 'the Second', I. Monighetti, A. Cavos (who refurbished the little theatre where Nicholas II used to take part in amateur theatricals and where the professionals included Liszt, Chaliapin, Pauline Viardot and Pavlova) and Stepanov who re-did the ballroom with its two white pianos and reproduced a Renaissance staircase in Carrara marble, which had taken the fancy of Prince Nikolay in Italy. There is a Red room and a Green room and a Music room (with organ) and a 'Henri II' room and an Oak Dining room and a Rotunda and a copy of part of the Alhambra and a vast, top-lit picture gallery (empty now of any pictures of merit). And all that it says is: Goodness, how rich they must have been.

Of course, it is not even fair to itself – for most of its priceless contents have gone. After the failed Bolshevik coup against the Provisional Government in July 1917, Yusupov began to construct secret rooms and a false ceiling in the house in the hope of concealing the great collections of paintings, books, musical instruments, porcelain and jewels, which it took the Bolsheviks five years to penetrate. (The last Stradivarius was found in a capsule inside one of the columns of Mikhaylov 'the Second'.) Slipping back from the Crimea, Yusupov managed himself to retrieve two great Rembrandts and a portrait of Alexander III which he and Irina took with them to Paris. There they sold them (poorly, through Joseph Duveen) and gave all the money they had to the support of Russian refugees in France and England. The museum now largely supports itself by re-enacting its pre-Revolutionary role: as a venue for entertaining.

Moving north along the Moika under four bridges (if you are in a boat which, in the summer, is the best place to be), you come on the right hand side, just before the Stroganov Palace and the Nevsky Prospect crossing, to a complex of buildings (*Nos. 52, 50, 48*) which now form the **Herzen Pedagogical Institute** (*Pedagogícheskiy institút im. Gértsena*). Like the Yusupov house, they date back to the early town plan of the 1730s; the house which stood on the site was acquired by Kyril Razumovskiy, brother of Empress Elisabeth's favourite, who involved A. Kokorinov, B. Rastrelli and/or V. Bazhenov in expanding and beautifying it with the result that, by the 1770s, with further assistance from Vallin de la Mothe, there were three houses there. These, despite later remodelling, represent a key transitional period in architecture between Elisabethan Baroque and Catherine's early Classicism. Two of the houses subsequently became orphanages and one an educational institute for the orphans so their present role is consistent with their past. Imperial orphanages had something redeeming about them, something which might have put the provision for orphans in nineteenth-century England to shame: they were completely non-judgmental.

There was provision for secret confinements and the care, medical and nursing, provided to the babies was of a high quality by the standards of the time. Though, as one of the doctors described it, it had many shortcomings yet 'it had its origin incontestably in a generous idea'.[1]

Passing under the *Névskiy prospékt* and the former *Politséyskiy most*, currently *Zelyóny most*, the huge, yellow, Classical building on the left is the back of Rossi's General Staff. At the corner of the Moika and the Winter Ditch is a relatively low, rather charming, three-storey pillastered house, the **Arakcheyev House** (F. Demertsov, 1800), owned, but never lived in, by Count Aleksey Arakcheyev, a harsh military disciplinarian who served both as Minister for War and, later, as the administrator of internal affairs for Alexander I.

The river is then crossed by the *Pévcheskiy most*, so called because it leads, on the right hand side (*No. 20*), to the complex of the *Pridvórnaya Pévcheskaya Kapélla*, the Court Choir (now the **Glinka Choir** – *Gos. Akademícheskaya Khorováya Kapélla im. M. Glinki*), the earliest male-voice choir in Russia, dating from 1479. It moved from Moscow in the year that St Petersburg was founded. The present buildings were reconstructed on the original site by L. Benois (1886–9).

Staying on the same side, *No. 12*, with its long river frontage and gateways at each end into the courtyard behind, contains the **Pushkin Apartment Museum** (first opened in 1925). The house (*dom Volkónskovo*), the broad courtyard and the arcaded stables at the back of it, have been almost entirely reconstructed – many times. The last reconstruction, in the 1980s, left only the façade and the stables intact. But the result (recreated with the aid of notes made at the time of Pushkin's death by his one-time

---

[1] In 1900, there were in the towns of Russia 108 illegitimate births per thousand.

mentor, the poet Vasiliy Zhukovskiy) is a delightful version of the place where Pushkin spent the last four months of his life (mid-September 1836 to his death on 29 January 1837). The footprint of the building goes back to the 1730s (the probable date of the stables), the façade to the 1770s, and much of the furniture to the 1830s. The colours are fresh, the rooms full of light; the light fittings particularly delectable – minimalist-Directoire in design with slivers of jewel-coloured glass – the furniture a kind of early Russian Biedermeyer, often in Karelian birch. What a delightful time, one can't help feeling, the people in this apartment must have had.

Almost certainly, they did not. First, they included not merely Pushkin and his wife, Natalya Goncharova, but their four children, all of whom were under five, the youngest only four months old. They also included his two sisters-in-law – Yekaterina and Aleksandra. Somewhere, there must have been some servants, including Pushkin's valet, Nikita. Secondly, Pushkin was deeply in debt – in spite of a loan from the Treasury of 45,000 roubles; he had just (April 1836) launched *Sovreménnik*, which was to become one of the most distinguished journals in Russia, the employer of Belinskiy and Nekrasov. Under Pushkin it did not prosper, while the couturiers' bills of his wife and sisters-in-law would have stretched the purse of a rich man and the rent of the Moika apartment was 4,300 roubles a year. (Pushkin's only regular income, by this time being withheld in payment of the treasury loan, was 5,000 roubles a year from a minor court position. His publishers' royalties, in the 1830s, have been estimated at some 2,000 roubles a year. At his death his debts – paid by Nicholas I – amounted to 76,505 roubles and 12 kopeks, in addition to the treasury loan.)[2] Thirdly, for these and other reasons,

---

[2] Itemised by Kunin, *Posḷédniy god zhízni Púshkina*, and quoted by Robin Edmonds in *Pushkin* (Macmillan: 1994).

Pushkin was in a state not far from a nervous breakdown. Natalya wrote to her brother in July 1836: 'I see how sad and dejected he is. He cannot sleep at night.' and, at the reunion of his old school in October, he broke down and wept. He was reciting a lament for the gradual disappearance of so many of his old school friends; and added: '*Imnítsya ochered zamnoy*' (And now, I believe, my turn is next).

Then there was the agonising, tortuous and, in the end, **fatal affair of D'Anthès**. The museum provides good audio-tapes, in several languages including English, which explain much of the story. In summary: D'Anthès was a French officer who arrived in St Petersburg in 1833 to serve in the Cavalier Guards. Handsome and a great social success, he met the Pushkins probably in the autumn of 1834 and fell in love with Natalya, herself a famous beauty. He paid court to her so often and so blatantly that it was widely rumoured she was unfaithful. On 4 November 1836, Pushkin received a spoof anonymous letter inviting him to a meeting of the Order of Cuckolds. Seven of Pushkin's friends also received a copy. Pushkin is believed to have sent D'Anthès a challenge to a duel but the letter was intercepted by D'Anthès' adopted father, Baron Louis van Hekkeren, the Dutch Minister in St Petersburg, who may at one time have been D'Anthès' lover. He begged Pushkin to call the duel off and appears to have been influential in persuading D'Anthès to deflect the row by marrying Yekaterina (Natalya's sister) which, on 10 January 1837, he did. On 23 January, the two families met at a ball and D'Anthès continued his flirtation with Natalya in a peculiarly offensive manner. On 24 January, Pushkin pawned Aleksandra's table silver and ordered two pistols from the gunsmith. On 26 January, he wrote a letter to van Hekkeren in which he accused him of having 'acted paternally as the pimp of your son'. (He also believed, rightly or wrongly, that the Baron had sent the 'cuckold' letter.) Which left D'Anthès little alternative but to challenge Pushkin. At all events, a duel was inevitable and, at 4.30 p.m. on 27 January, took place in the snow-covered fields of *Nóvaya Derévnya*, on the banks of the little *Chórnaya réchka* (Black Stream) in the northern outskirts of the city. Pushkin was fatally wounded and was brought home to die, on 29 January, in his library on the Moika.

The library is where he is most tangible. His little writing desk is there and the couch on which he lay (indeed on which, no doubt to escape the children, he slept every night). So is his writing table and facsimiles of some of his note-books. Above all, so are his books: 'goodbye, friends', as he managed to say to them, in great pain just before he died. (At least, copies of his books. The originals are in the *Púshkinskiy dom*, the Literary Institute on *Vasíliyevskiy óstrov*.) On the wall is Zhukovskiy's portrait famously inscribed: 'To the victorious pupil from the vanquished master'.

As Pushkin lay dying, Zhukovskiy prepared St Petersburg for his death by bulletins issued from the library, the last of which announced that 'the patient is in an extremely dangerous condition'. Pushkin was attended by his own doctor, Ivan Spasskiy, and by the Court physician, Dr Arendt, who brought with him a message from the Emperor not only forgiving him but undertaking to provide for his widow and children. This liaison with the Palace – to some extent brokered by Zhukovskiy – did not, however, prevent the police from being hyper-sensitive to the possibility of trouble following Pushkin's death. The Requiem Mass, invitations to which specified St Isaac's Cathedral, was switched at the last minute to the local church which is wrapped into the south side of the Imperial Stables, on *Konyúshennaya* (Stables) *plóstchad* – The Temple of the Saviour of the Icon not made by Hands (*Khram Spása Nerukotvórnovo Óbraza*). The church was packed with distinguished mourners and the square was filled with people who came partly to mourn and partly to seek souvenirs – but there was no disorder. At 1.00 a.m. on 4 February, in accordance with the Emperor's orders, the coffin was removed from the church and escorted by one of Pushkin's friends and a police captain to the family estate at Mikháylovskoye. There, it was buried two days later in the grounds of the Svyatogorsk Monastery. D'Anthès was reduced to the ranks and expelled from Russia with his wife, Yekaterina Goncharova. Almost at once, the house on the Moika became, and has remained, a popular shrine.

The curve of the **Court Stables** (*Pridvórnyie konyúshni*) is the last building on the right hand side of the Moika before it reaches the green banks of the *Mikháylovskiy sad* (the gardens of the Russian Museum) and joins up with the Griboyedov Canal. A strange, primitive-looking structure with squat Doric columns set at frequent intervals, archaic Greek rather than neo-Classical, it is in fact, a refurbishment by Stasov (1817–23) of an earlier Baroque building. Stasov was working at the same time on the other side of the river, on the massive barracks for the Pavlovskiy Guards (***Kazármy Pávlovskovo polká***, 1817–19) which occupy practically the entire west side of the Field of Mars. (It was from these barracks in February 1917 that the rump of the Pavlovskiy Guards came down to *plóstchad Vosstániya* and made common cause with the rioting crowds, thus by their mutiny precipitating the Emperor's abdication. Since 1928 they have been the headquarters of the organisation which supplies the city with electricity.)

On the left (north) side of the river, before the embankment opens up to embrace the Field of Mars, is another, much smaller, curved building. This is the **Round Market** (*Krúgly rýnok*) by Quarenghi, architecturally a throw-away line of the 1790s done to tidy up an older, triangular structure. Its main claim to fame is the fact that many of Pushkin's smaller debts were incurred here and were paid off by his friends. It now acts as a kind of reserve store for the traders who operate the souvenir market across the river.

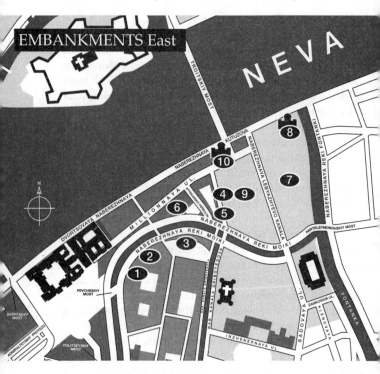

1	Kapella	6	Round Market
2	Pushkin Museum	7	Summer Garden
3	Court Stables	8	Summer Palace
4	Pavlovskiy Barracks	9	Field of Mars
5	Adamini House	10	Marble Palace

At this point you meet with one of the unexpected composite views in St Petersburg. The city can catch you by surprise – partly, perhaps, because it is rivers and not roads that really shape it and rivers flow at unpredictable angles; partly because, when all is done, this is Russia and not

Western Europe. Standing on the west embankment of the Moika, looking over Stasov's stables, you catch a glimpse of the bull's-eye dome rising from the Church of The Saviour on the Blood; to the right of it, the small gold cross floating above the Konyushennaya church; to the left, the tip of the *iglá* and the Maltese cross on St Michael's Church and, through the gap, the northern parapets of St Michael's Castle, pale pink in the sun (rather than the gloomy purple which that building usually gives off); the little iron bridge in the foreground; the blind curve of the Round Market and on, up, to the Classical white portico on yellow walls of the Adamini House (1823–7) on the corner of the Field of Mars. Were you to go into the house behind you, climb to the sixth floor and face north over what, from street level, appears to be the grandest bit of St Petersburg, you would look out over row upon row of rusting steel roofs, with the occasional bright new one – roofs set at crazy angles, roofs over lean-to sheds, crumbling brick-and-stucco chimneys and not a fire escape in sight but, in the distance, the newly gilded dome of the *Kúnstkamera* on the water front of *Vasíliyevskiy óstrov*.

Then comes a magical moment in the course of the Moika. The world each side of it bursts into green (at least, it does in the summer): the *Mársovo Pólye* (Field of Mars) and the *Létniy sad* (Summer Garden) on the left, divided by the little *Lebyázhiy* (Swan) *kanál* which runs straight between them down to the Neva; the *Mikháylovskiy sad* and the gardens round St Michael's (Engineers') Castle on the right. At the beginning of the eighteenth century, the whole area from the Neva southwards was an undrained swamp, particularly deep in the area of the Mikhaylovskiy Gardens. For, in those days, two small rivers wound their sluggish way from there into the Gulf of Finland: the *Krivúsha* (Crooked) and the *Miyá* (now the Moika). The Moika was connected with the Fontanka and provided with a second exit – into the Neva – in 1711. And the *Krivúsha* was slowly disciplined into what is now the Griboyedov (and was then the Catherine) Canal until, in 1800, it acquired its granite embankment. Until roughly the same date, the area to the west of it as far as *Italiyánskaya úlitsa* in the south and the Fontanka in the east were the gardens, kitchen gardens, parkland and birch grove pertaining to the Summer Palace, built by Rastrelli for the Empress Elisabeth in the 1740s and destroyed by Paul when he built St Michael's Castle.

The first part of this area to be tamed was the thirty acres which are now called the *Létniy sad* (**Summer Garden**). Indeed, a Swede called Major Konau had already begun to garden here when the fall of *Nyenskans* to the Russians in May 1703 put an end to his innocent activities. By March 1704, Peter the Great was sending to Moscow for thousands of flowers to plant in what had become 'his' garden, specifying that they should mainly be scented. So began a long tradition of royal gardening in and around St Petersburg. Peter's garden was to be formal, French in style (he involved the French architect Le Blond in its design), edifying in purpose. There were three *allées* – open galleries bordered by small trees and Classical sculptures – along which, in summertime, food and drink were supplied to guests. In the centre was placed a first-century Venus acquired from Pope Clement XI, Russia's first Classical statue which Peter prized so much that a soldier stood on permanent guard over it. (Later it was moved to the Taurida Palace and, finally, into *R. 109* of the Hermitage.)

Peter himself collected about a hundred of these marble figures – some historical, some allegorical, all intended to introduce his Russian guests to the glories of antiquity – but not too many of them had been made before the seventeenth century. His successors collected a further hundred and fifty until, in 1777, the Neva overflowed and swept practically all of them away. Sadly, it also swept away the centrepiece of his garden, an elaborate system of fountains fed from the Fontanka river and powered by a primitive steam engine of Peter's devising, and a large aviary, hot-houses, orangeries and a gazebo where he had been accustomed to sit alone, occasionally inviting guests specially selected with the intention of making them drunk. All other male guests, by the sensible dictat of his wife Catherine, were required to be accompanied by their wives and grown-up daughters. Perhaps the flood was not a total tragedy for Peter's Summer Garden was a dress-rehearsal (one is tempted to say dry-run but has to refrain) for the Great Cascade at Peterhof which he began four years before his death.

His Summer Garden was never restored. It owes its present form to Yu. Felten, who was commissioned by Catherine the Great to design the grand railings and their thirty-six granite columns on the north side (1770–84) as part of his work on the embankment of the Neva; to Rossi who built the Coffee House (*Koféyny dómik*) on the banks of the Fontanka (1826); to the railings on the Moika side by L. Charlemagne who was also responsible for the Tea House (*Chaynyi dómik*, 1827) under the trees just south of the Summer Palace; to the remaining eighty-nine statues (of mixed provenance and quality) which are still protected under wooden wigwams from winter frosts; and to the presiding genius of Ivan Krylov (1855 by Klodt and others) who sits benignly in the centre of it. Krylov told (or rather re-told) fables for generations of Russians; he sits on a plinth round which the creatures of his stories circle in deep relief. The English, for a minute, may be reminded of Peter Pan in Kensington Gardens; but there is nothing emotionally retarded about this fabulist and no hint of whimsy about his animals: lions, elephants, cobras, bears, above all the wicked monkeys. Ah! Those monkeys. And the joke that every Russian parent thought so funny: 'Yes, look, and you are there too.' 'I am? Where am I? Show me.' 'There, can't you see? You see that monkey . . .' They are still at it, so the children tell me.

And, of course, there is the **Summer Palace** (*Létniy dvoréts – muzéy Petra I*) itself. Together with Peter's cabin on the Petrograd Side and Menshikov's Palace on the *Vasíliyevskiy óstrov*, it is the earliest and best-preserved domestic building in St Petersburg (D. Trezzini and A. Schlüter 1710–14). Sitting modestly on the banks of the Fontanka, a few yards south from the first stone bridges in the city – the *Práchechny* (Laundry) *most* over the Fontanka to the east and the *Lebyázhiy* (Swan) *most* to the west – it is also one of the most covetable. Perhaps, for perfection, it is too overgrown by elderly lime trees but it has survived, for three hundred turbulent years, without significant damage to the exterior and remains an almost perfect representation of the house in which Peter lived during the summer, more or less privately, with his second wife, Catherine I and some of his children. Petitioners were received by him on the ground floor (and sometimes detained by him behind a railing in an adjoining room) and there is a room described as a ballroom on the first floor; but formal entertaining took place in the Garden. From the accession of the Empress Elisabeth, the Imperial family did not live in Trezzini's Summer Palace but let it out to various court officials. As a result, many of Peter's personal possessions disappeared and the apartments were constantly redecorated. By the middle of the nineteenth century it was empty. After the Revolution it was given government protection and, in the 1920s, first opened as a museum. The house can and should be visited; a particular pleasure is the pair of Dutch kitchens which you could find any day on the Herengracht or in the canvases of Pieter de Hooch.

Leaving the Summer Garden through Felten's magnificent gate, you step out on to the **Palace Embankment** (*Dvortsóvaya náberezhnaya*) and a view across the Neva which is a sudden reminder that St Petersburg is a great city and also a seaside town. There is salt on the air and small waves on the Neva and the view across to the Petrograd Side is quite distant. Only the domes and spires picked out in gold are easily distinguishable. One can see what terrible floods must have followed when the river, the wind and the tides were in conflict and, in the winter, what acres of ice lay (and of course still do lie) across the centre of the city. From the beginning of December until the second week of April, there was no serious need of bridges until the invention of the tram which is one of several reasons why there were none until 1727. The first bridge was a pontoon – put in place after the spring floods and dismantled in the autumn – that Menshikov erected from his own front door on *Vasíliyevskiy óstrov* to his commercial enterprises on the south bank, next to the first St Isaac's church in what is now *plóstchad Dekabrístov*. Even that had to wait until the death of Peter the Great because, with the exception of the bridges necessary to carry his *Névskiy prospékt* east and south into the Russian hinterland, Peter had forbidden all bridges. Embankments and stone bridges were a novelty introduced by Catherine II and the first stone bridge in St Petersburg (the *Kámenny* – Stone – *most*) was built in 1776 over the Griboyedov (then the Catherine) Canal. The first permanent bridge over the Neva was built at the end of the reign of Nicholas I and cannot be seen from the Palace Embankment; round the corner to the west, it links the English Embankment to *Vasíliyevskiy óstrov* and is now called *most Leytenánta Shmídta*, after a naval hero of the 1905 Revolution.

Immediately to the west of the Summer Garden is the **Mársovo Pólye** (**Field of Mars**) which, as part of the *Tsarítsyn lug* (Tsarina's Meadow) ran down to the Neva once the primeval swamp was cleared in the 1710s. In the early days, it was used for popular attractions: animal baiting, boxing, fireworks, and was known as the *Potéshnoye pólye* (the Amusements Field). It became *Tsarítsyn lug* in 1727, in honour of Peter's widow, Catherine I, who had continued to use the Summer Palace until her death. In the 1740s, an attempt by the town planners (led by the architect,

Zemtsov) to transform the Field into a proper garden was thwarted by the rich, influential and well-connected people who, the moment the Empress Anne adopted Apraksin's house as her Winter Palace, hastened to build themselves houses on this desirable site. From that time on, the Palace Embankment has been the haunt of the rich, the influential and the well-connected. Behind it, the Field continued to be used for a variety of purposes until, at the end of the eighteenth century, it became the favourite venue for the favourite activity of the Emperor Paul who liked nothing better than parading his soldiers (particularly his own regiment, the Pavlovskiy Guards). Hence '*Mársovo*' ('of Mars'), which was the name given to the Field in 1805. It is said of Paul that he once dismissed a regiment whose performance had displeased him 'to Siberia'; obeying orders, they left the parade in full dress and marched as far as Novgorod before being officially forgiven and recalled. On another occasion, a regiment of Cossacks was despatched to conquer India (*Left Turn. Quick March. India*); but they came back safely, too. On neither occasion were they supplied with maps.

After the death of Nicholas I and the change in Imperial preoccupations, the *Mársovo Pólye* reverted sometimes to its earlier role – particularly in Butter Week (during Lent). Then, its empty spaces (nick-named 'the Petersburg Sahara') became filled with stalls, coconut shies and sellers of bad eggs called *tumakí* which were supposed to be a great Chinese delicacy. There were roundabouts and, best of all, *Americánskiye Góry* (American Mountains), switchbacks made from the last of the winter snow for small boys (and girls too, I suppose) to whirl down in their sledges. I was just too young to see the *balagány*. They fell victim to the temperance campaign which gripped St Petersburg at the turn of the century but people still talked of them with nostalgia and delight: covered stages on which sometimes real actors, sometimes puppets, played Harlequinades and masked pantomimes and Russia's version of Punch and Judy, while outside the showman, propped up on a parapet, talked the crowds in with slapstick and a false beard. There was a certain amount of intoxication, of course – on the parapets or squatting under the stage with the puppets – and occasional disorder. So the close of the nineteenth century saw them tidied away to the *Semyónovskiy plats* and, soon, they were forbidden altogether. But they made a triumphant return in the ballet *Petrushka*, where the *balagány* were immortalised by Benois, Fokine, and Stravinsky.

In March 1917, the *Mársovo Pólye* was chosen as the burial place for people who died in the February Revolution and, later, for people who were killed in the October Revolution (*Zhértvy Revolyútsii* – Victims of the Revolution) and the Civil War. In the middle of the Field, a massive wall of red granite (**Pámyatnik Bortsám Revolyútsii**, L. Rudnev) was unveiled on 7 November 1919. (In 1957, on the fortieth anniversary of the Revolution, the Eternal Flame was placed in the centre.) The following year, 1920, it was resolved to provide the monument with a reverential setting and the Petersburg Sahara was laid out (I. A. Fomin) as a garden. Ploughed up for vegetables during the Blockade, it has now returned to grass and beds of lilac arranged according to Fomin's design.

At its north (riverside) end, the hastily constructed houses of Empress Anne's day have been replaced by two huge blocks divided by a narrow square (**Suvórovskaya plóstchad**), in the centre of which stands a wildly improbable statue of Field Marshal Suvorov dressed up like a Roman army commander. It is hard to imagine anything less like the small, wiry, ascetic who willed his troops across the Alps but he has a magnificent view. (The statue, by Mikhail Kozlovskiy, with assistance from Voronikhin on the pedestal, was first unveiled in 1801, the year after Suvorov's death. At that time it stood at the Moika end of the *Mársovo Pólye* but was moved north by Rossi in 1818 to dignify his new square.)

To the Field Marshal's right, the easternmost house (**Betskoy's House**, *Dvortsóvaya náberezhnaya No. 2*) was built, probably by I. Starov, in 1784–7 for Prince Ivan Betskoy, President of the Academy of Arts for thirty years (until 1794), educational reformer, promoter of education for women and (some say) the father of Catherine II. It was remodelled in the 1830s by V. Stasov for the Prince of Oldenburg, whose descendant married the Grand Duchess Olga, sister of Nicholas II, who occupied the house until 1917. The house next door (**Saltykov's House**, Quarenghi 1784–8) had its western façade altered by Rossi when he created *Suvórovskaya plóstchad*. It became first the Austrian and then the British Embassy.

The last representative of Great Britain to occupy it was handsome, gallant and doomed. He was the Naval Attaché, a submarine Captain called Francis Cromie who had stayed behind in the summer of 1918 so that he could organise the sabotage of British merchant ships, embargoed by the Bolsheviks, and thus prevent them from falling into German hands. On 31 August 1918, the crowd forced its way into the Embassy. He drew his sword to chase an intruder from his office, followed him out and was shot dead on the Embassy's grand staircase. In the absence, in prison, of the Anglican chaplain, the Bolsheviks decided to bury him like a criminal. But the Dutch and Swedish consuls successfully protested and organised a funeral cortège along the Neva to the *Smolénskoye kládbistche* on *Vasíliyevskiy óstrov*. As the cortège passed down-river, sailors on the decks of Russian naval vessels, realising whose coffin it was, stood to attention in a spontaneous display of respect. (The Betskoy and Saltykov houses are now occupied by the Krupskaya Institute of Culture, a school for librarians.)

In front of the Field Marshal is **Trinity Bridge** (1903, built for the city's bicentenary), a major engineering feat and the first permanent link across the widest part of the

Neva to the new developments on the Petrograd Side. Without this bridge and the Litéyny Bridge (1875–9 across to the Vyborg Side), there might have been less revolutionary turmoil in the early years of the twentieth century, for they opened the way across the Neva to a huge new reservoir of discontent.

On Suvorov's left are the two great blocks of the Marble Palace, nearest to him the Service Wing (practically entirely remodelled by A. Bryullov, 1841–5, when he redecorated most of the interior of the palace itself further to the west). The **Marble Palace** (*Mrámorny dvoréts, Dvortsóvaya náberezhnaya Nos. 6 and 8*, though its official address is *Milliónnaya úlitsa No. 5*) stands on ground that was once occupied by a Postal Yard (*Pochtóvy dvor*). There was a quay on the Neva where two frigates could tie up and a Post Office which, on Tuesdays and Fridays, despatched packets and letters to Moscow. In 1714, Peter told Trezzini to build a pub (*avstériya*) alongside and temporary accommodation for visitors above it. There was music from a wind band and a good time was had by all, except when Peter wanted to entertain in the pub below when everyone else was thrown unceremoniously out into the snow. When, in 1731, the Empress Elisabeth wanted to put her stables on the site (or, rather, the stables of the Horse Guards of which she made herself the commander), the Post Office moved to St Isaac's Square.

Thereafter, this land was incorporated into the *Tsarítsyn lug* until (1768) Catherine II commissioned Antonio Rinaldi to build a palace there. It was for her lover of the time, Grigoriy Orlov. She owed her throne to him for, with his brother Aleksey, he had conceived and executed the plot to overthrow Peter III and replace him with his wife. This accounts, perhaps, for the palace's huge size, though not for the fact that it appears to have taken seventeen years to build. By the time it was finished in 1785, Orlov was no longer Catherine's lover (a relationship that ended, at

Orlov's initiative, after twelve years, probably in 1772). In 1777, he had married his first cousin, Yekaterina Zinoviev, a marriage which the church condemned because of their consanguinity but for which the Empress bore him no ill will for she continued in her generosity to both of them and made his wife a lady-in-waiting. By 1783, both Grigoriy and his wife were dead – she of consumption in Lausanne and he, two years later, of what was ascribed to insanity brought on by her death (but probably had some other natural cause). It was a sad and early end (he was only forty-nine) to a nearly brilliant life. The only tangible relics of it, apart from the palace in which he never lived, were a son by Catherine (Count Aleksey Bobrinskiy), a two hundred carat diamond (the Orlov) which the Empress had set into the Imperial sceptre and a blood-line of Orlov trotting horses, bred by himself and his brother Aleksey, which are the ancestors of all Russian trotting stock today. These and, one has to say, the reign of Catherine the Great.

Architecturally, the palace is on the cusp between Russian Baroque and Early Classical and has some interesting features: the fact, for instance, that it was the first building in St Petersburg to be faced with stone (when they said 'stone', they usually meant stucco on brick); that parts of it (the pale pink parts) are constructed of a high quality Russian marble which had never been used before; that the main entrance has a 'Transitional' arrangement of windows and a clock gable. But the exterior as a whole (entered from *Milliónnaya úlitsa*) lacks charm. The interior was re-done by Bryullov for the Grand Duke Konstantin, second son of Nicholas I, whose family inhabited the Marble Palace until the Revolution. They included his eldest son, the Grand Duke Konstantin Konstantinovich who, under the initials K. R. (Romanov) wrote very sentimental poetry, some of which was set to music by Tchaikovsky. The palace is being lovingly restored, no expense spared, by the latest owners – since December 1991, the Russian Museum.

It can be visited; there are concerts in the White Room with its rounded windows, neo-Gothic fan vaulting and new chandeliers 'based on historical analogues' at a cost of sixteen million roubles; it has a Greek Gallery and an Oak Gallery, both newly restored; and there is a permanent exhibition of paintings, sculpture, furniture and clocks from the recently acquired collection of the Rzhevskiy brothers. In due course, this will be joined by other permanent exhibits but there are also interesting temporary exhibitions (Russian Abstraction in the Twentieth Century, for instance).

The overall effect has not been improved, perhaps, by the arrival in the forecourt of Paolo Trubetskoy's **equestrian statue of Alexander III** (1909–11). Toppled from its plinth in *plóstchad Vosstániya* after the Revolution, but recognised as a work of originality and power, it was not destroyed but concealed for years behind a fence in the Russian Museum. Trubetskoy had lived in Italy where, together with Rodin, he had been studying sculpture; so he brought a fairly detached eye to his subject and an original approach to the discipline. (He also brought an original approach to his daily walks on the Nevsky when he was accompanied sometimes by his dog, sometimes, more exotically, by a wolf or bear.) When someone commented to him that the style was fashionably *brutale*, he agreed: '*mais oui, c'est une brute assise sur une autre*'. His meaning, apparently, was that it was the image of one solid and powerful figure astride another. As a teacher in the Moscow Art School, he impressed on his students the importance, to a sculptor, of representing not merely the physical likeness of his model but also its significance and the spirit emanating from it. Nicholas II seems to have liked the way in which Trubetskoy represented his father since he gave his approval to his maquette in preference to the other competitors, in spite of the reservations and dismissive criticism of St Petersburg's academicians. There were suggestions at the time that the proper place for the statue, given its mass and the fact that Alexander III was mainly notable for having encouraged the building of the Trans-Siberian Railway, was not in *plóstchad Vosstániya* but in Vladivostók, at one end of the railway, or on top of a mountain in the Urals where Asia and Europe (now connected by the railway) meet. In such a position, it might be rather fine.

Meanwhile in 1937 the Marble Palace had become the main museum of Leniniana in Leningrad; in its forecourt had been installed the armoured car used by Lenin on his arrival at the Finland Station. When the time came in 1994 to remove the car, a new plinth was found for Alexander and he took his present place in front of the palace that his great-great-grandmother's lover never lived in.

Many of the remaining houses westward along the *Dvortsóvaya náberezhnaya* run from the Embankment back to **Milliónnaya úlitsa**, so called because it was a millionaires' row and, to some extent, a Grand Dukes' row too. The entrances are mostly from the south, leaving the view of the imposing façades on the river uninterrupted. *No. 10* was the Imperial Russian Automobile Society. *No. 12* belonged to the Literary and Artistic Circle which used to lease the *Mály teátr* on the Fontanka for the performance of modern Russian plays. *Nos. 14* and *16* were occupied by the English Association (*Anglíyskoye Sobrániye*) – not the English Club but a junior version of the Imperial Yacht club for younger members of the gentry.

No. 18 is another creation (1857–61) by Stackenschneider – for the Grand Duke Mikhail, son of Nicholas I. The **New Michael Palace** (*Nóvo-Mikháylovskiy dvoréts*) was a combination of two existing houses and is a prime candidate for the description Eclectic: neo-Renaissance with neo-Classical porticoes, neo-Baroque caryatids and barely an inch of façade without a frieze, a panel, a *bas relief* . . . no wonder they had to invent *Style Moderne*. The Grand Duke died in 1909 and the palace was owned until the Revolution by his son, the Grand Duke Mikhail Mikhaylovich. On his marriage to Pushkin's granddaughter, he was required by the Emperor to leave Russia. So, when the Revolution came, he and his family were safe in Kenwood House in Hampstead. *No. 26* was the **Palace of the Grand Duke Vladímir**, uncle of Nicholas II (A. Rezanov, 1867–70) who died in 1910; his descendant now claims the Russian throne. He was given permission by Yeltsin to occupy apartments in *No. 26* when he visited St Petersburg.

The south side of *Milliónnaya úlitsa*, the front doors facing the front doors of the Embankment mansions, was also a grand place in which to live. *No. 4*, on the corner of *Aptékarskiy pereúlok* which runs north from the Moika, is a pretty, low house rebuilt by Quarenghi (1789–96) from the 1732 original by Trezzini. It was the Main Pharmacy (*Glávnaya Aptéka*) and gave its name to the lane. *No. 10* was a huge mansion built by Stackenschneider for himself (1852–4) where, after his death, his widow continued to hold crowded cultural evenings.

No. 12, architecturally of no great importance, contained the **apartment of Prince and Princess Putyatin**, friends of the Grand Duke Mikhail Aleksandrovich. The brother of Nicholas II, he was the last (though uncrowned) Emperor of Russia. In this house, on 3 March 1917, he renounced the throne and brought the Romanov dynasty to a close.

On 27 February 1917, his way home from Petrograd to his house at Gatchina south of the city was blocked by Revolutionary troops and the Winter Palace was under fire. So he decided to spend the night at *Milliónnaya úlitsa No. 12* where he and his secretary, Johnson, slept on sofas in the Prince's study. He remained in the house the next day, cars and lorries making a great noise outside the windows, packed with soldiers shouting 'Hurrah!' and carrying red flags. Some were shooting and hand grenades were exploding too but, he concludes, 'the day passed quietly for

us and we were not disturbed'.[3] On 1 March 'we heard of
several murders committed by soldiers in the neighbour-
hood, including the murder of Count Stackelberg. Nicky
[the Emperor] was due to arrive today from Headquarters
but he did not and the whereabouts of his train are
unknown . . . All power is concentrated in the hands of the
Provisional Committee [of the State *Dúma*] which is in great
difficulties due to the pressure on it by the Union of
Workers' and Soldiers' Deputies.'

On 3 March he was woken at 6.00 a.m. by Kerensky, the
new Minister of Justice. Johnson took the call and was
informed that the Council of Ministers would be arriving for
a meeting in about an hour. In fact, the delegation did not
turn up until 9.15 a.m. It then consisted of seven ministers
and five representatives of the *Dúma*, including Lvov, the
Prime Minister, and Rodzianko, Chairman of the *Dúma*.
They were frightened, confused and at odds with themselves.
In the meantime, the Grand Duke had, from other sources,
heard for the first time what Nicholas had decided – which
was not, as most people had expected, to abdicate in favour
of his son and to appoint the Grand Duke Mikhail as Regent
but to abdicate on behalf of his son as well as himself and to
nominate the Grand Duke as his successor. It was a decision
of doubtful validity on two grounds: first, since the Emperor
Paul's decree, sovereigns could not deprive the next-in-line
to the throne of his right to succeed; and, secondly, Nicholas
himself had previously (December 1912) divested his
brother of his obligation (right) to act as Regent (and by
implication his right to the succession) in the event of his
death, as a punishment for his morganatic marriage.

Most of the delegation that arrived in the drawing room
of *Milliónnaya úlitsa No. 12* had already concluded that
their own survival depended on the abdication of the new

---

[3] This and the following extracts are taken from a still-unpublished diary
of the Grand Duke Mikhail Alexandrovich.

Emperor. Their arguments were put by Rodzianko and
Kerensky (who appears to have been in a state of near-
hysteria throughout). Others (Milyukov, the Foreign
Minister) argued that the only hope of re-establishing
order was to maintain a familiar symbol of authority at the
head of the State. The Grand Duke asked for a private conversation with Rodzianko and Lvov. When he returned to
the drawing room, he said that, in the circumstances, he
had to follow their advice. At that stage nothing was written down and there was no form of words. The delegation
returned to the Taurida Palace.

Some time in the afternoon, a telegram arrived at *No. 12*.
It had been despatched from Nicholas's train at 2.56 p.m.
that day. It read:

> To His Imperial Majesty, Petrograd.
> The events of recent days compelled me to decide irrevoc-
> ably on this extreme step. Forgive me if I have grieved you
> by it and also that I did not have time to warn you. I shall
> always remain your faithful and devoted brother.
> I am returning to General Headquarters, whence after a
> few days I hope to arrive at Tsarskoye Selo.
> I fervently pray God to help you and our Mother Country.
> Your Niki

This was the first official intimation received by the
Grand Duke that he was, in theory at least, Emperor of
Russia. And he was well aware of the doubtful validity of
the succession. What he decided to do (unsuccessfully as it
turned out) was to play for time. Late in the afternoon,
with the aid of lawyers acting for himself (Matveyev) and
the Provisional Government (Nabokov, father of the
writer), an agreed statement was drafted and signed by
him. He neither abdicated nor accepted the throne but, in
effect, offered himself as a future constitutional monarch:

> A heavy burden has been thrust upon me by the will of my
> brother, who has given over to me the Imperial Throne of

Russia at a time of unprecedented warfare and popular disturbances.

Inspired like the entire people by the idea that what is most important is the welfare of the country, I have taken a firm decision to assume the Supreme Power only if such be the will of our great people. . .

Therefore, invoking the blessing of God, I beseech all the citizens of Russia to obey the Provisional Government . . . until the Constituent Assembly, to be convoked with the least possible delay, by universal suffrage, direct, equal and secret voting, shall express the will of the people by its decision on the form of government.

Signed: Mikhail.

He then leaves *Milliónnaya úlitsa* and returns to his small villa in Gatchina.

By 2 September, he is back in Petrograd where the doctor comes to visit him; the weather is grey and rainy and the temperature nine degrees but before the evening it becomes a bit brighter. 'In the morning', he wrote in his journal, 'we woke up to hear that Russia has been declared [by Kerensky] a Democratic Republic.' To which he adds a footnote: 'What does it matter what the form of government will be, provided there is order and justice in the land?'

25 October, Gatchina: 'before lunch, started writing a letter to Mama and Xenia [his sister]. We learn by telephone that Kerensky has left in the morning for the station [at Dno] to bring back troops.' (In fact he had not. He had slipped away, leaving his cabinet to be arrested in the Winter Palace.) 'The Winter Palace has been occupied by the Bolsheviks . . . there is occasional shooting in the streets. The whole of the Petersburg garrison has gone over to the Bolsheviks . . . After dinner, we went to the cinema to see *The Oath of Vengeance*, Johnson spending the night with us. The weather is overcast. Temperature three degrees.'

After the Bolsheviks came to power, the Grand Duke and his secretary were arrested, sent to Perm and eventually shot.

Following the *Dvortsóvaya náberezhnaya* past the Hermitage Theatre (*No. 32*), the Hermitage Museum (*No. 34*) and the Winter Palace (*No. 36*), it changes to *Admiraltéyskaya náberezhnaya* (Admiralty Embankment) which, apart from the magnificent twin arms of the Admiralty building at each end of it, is of no great interest. Across *plóstchad Dekabrístov* (Decembrists' Square), the river bank becomes the *Anglíyskaya náberezhnaya* (**English Embankment**).

This acquired its name for a most prosaic reason. Peter the Great had decreed that the only people who could build on the Admiralty glacis were naval employees. On his death, the decree lapsed and, encouraged by the commercial activities of Menshikov in the area of St Isaac's, a large number of (mostly) timber houses began to cluster along the river front – some, indeed, belonging to people with marine connections, some simply opportunist. Three other decrees followed: one obliged those who owned houses on this part of the river to billet soldiers there, as and when required; one (1735) exempted those whose houses were rented to English (and, by the sound of many of the names of eighteenth-century tenants, German as well) merchants from this obligation; and one (1738) said that all timber houses along the Neva were to be abolished and replaced by stone ones. The combined effect was to send those members of the Russian aristocracy who had cash to spare rushing to build handsome stone houses on the river front which they rented out to English (and anyone who could pass as English) merchants. By 1747 there was an English pub with an English publican called Anthony Walters; as early as 1718 there was an English church; and, for many decades, the British Embassy rotated among these houses until it found a permanent home on the Palace Embankment further east.

To begin with, there were restrictions on the sale of land
to foreigners. But, over the years, the freeholds changed
hands – often through long term leases falling in, mort-
gages and pawning arrangements being redeemed by the
wealthy tenants. And, though Imperial consent was
required for any alteration to the riverside façades, most of
the houses suffered many times over from the frequent
attentions of the very rich so that they changed out of
recognition. A few – a very few – bear some resemblance to
their late eighteenth-century appearance.

No. 4, the **Laval House** next to the Senate, built originally
by Menshikov in 1719 as 'chambers' for rent, was rebuilt in
1790 according to designs by Voronikhin, and refurbished
again in the 1800s by Thomas de Thomon for a French
merchant banker of great taste whose daughter married the
Decembrist Prince S. Trubetskoy and was the first wife to
accompany her husband into Siberian exile. The house was
preserved by its last private owner, S. S. Polyakov, banker and
brother of the great dancer Anna Pavlova's natural father.
It is now part of the Russian National Historical Archives
which also occupy the Senate building round the corner
in the square. *No. 24*, together with its two next door
neighbours to the west, was the earliest house on the
Embankment but, of the three, is the only one with an eighteenth-century façade. Bought in 1768 by a James Jackson, it
had a third storey added in 1785 and was thereafter left
alone. *No. 32* was the **Foreign Collegium** (Ministry of
Foreign Affairs), reconstructed by Quarenghi (1782–3) from
two earlier houses. When in 1828 the Ministry was moved to
Rossi's new block on Palace Square, the building on the
English Embankment became the Senior Staff College (later
known as the Nicholas Academy); after the Revolution it
retained a connection with the army and, thus, it too was
preserved. (The Foreign Collegium was a benevolent
employer of liberal-minded young writers, many of whom
had been educated at the *Aleksándrovskiy Litséy*. In 1817,

Pushkin, the poet and Decembrist Küchelbecker and the playwright Griboyedov all went to work at *No. 32*.)

No. 44, the **Rumyantsev House**, now part of the **Museum of the History of St Petersburg**, acquired its present façade in 1835 from the architect V. Glinka who combined two houses to accommodate the books, coins and medals that had been amassed by Nikolay Rumyantsev during the last years of the eighteenth and first years of the nineteenth centuries. The original house, built by Mikhail Galitsin at the insistence of Peter the Great, was divided in the second half of the eighteenth century and passed into the ownership of two English merchants (at which time it contained sixty-seven rooms). Rumyantsev, whose mother had been a Galitsin, bought the site back in 1802. He was Foreign Minister under Alexander I and himself lived in three rooms looking out over the river on the first floor. When he died in 1828, he charged his brother with creating a museum around his great collection (which contained twenty-nine thousand rare books, not to mention prints, paintings and manuscripts). In 1861, it was moved to Moscow where it became the Lenin (now Russian) State Public Library. The house became an apartment building and was extensively changed, many times, inside and out, but the central façade survives. The last private owner was Darya Kochubey, a granddaughter of Nicholas I, who left Russia in 1917 but returned – only to be executed in 1937. The Museum of the History of St Petersburg now uses the house to display exhibits relating to 'Leningrad during the Soviet Years', of which the most significant are mementoes of the Blockade. Across the road, on the Embankment itself, is the stele set up to mark the place in the river where the cruiser *Aurora* anchored in October 1917 and fired its famous 'blank' at the Winter Palace.

Two more houses retain visible links with two hundred years ago: *No. 56*, the **English Church**, was a remodelling (by Quarenghi, again, in 1814) of the original English church hall so that it could hold the 2,700 Protestant worshippers by that time living in St Petersburg. The exterior was tinkered with in 1876 but much of the interior, of varying quality and date, has been preserved and can be viewed. *No. 74*, at the far (west) end of the Embankment, was preserved by the canniness of a Scot, James Wylie, who became Surgeon to Alexander I. There are doubts about his skill as a doctor but none about his business acumen. Wylie was a man who would not dream of wasting good money on refurbishing a house so what you see now is almost what was built in 1738 by Nikita Demidov. Wylie leased his house out in apartments, in one of which Lenin's mother, Maria Blank, was born in 1835. In the 1870s, the house was bought by the Gaush family who planned to reconstruct it 'with fashionable elements in vogue at the end of the nineteenth century'. But something, mercifully, frustrated them.

All the other houses were reconstructed, remodelled, refurbished, redecorated many times over (and, particularly, in the last decades of the nineteenth century) with the enormous riches generated by Russia's economic expansion. They were owned by railway magnates (Derviz), merchant bankers (the brothers Polyakov), the Chairman of the Black Oil Petroleum Company and the President of the first Russian State Bank, Baron Stieglitz whose family lived in *No. 68* in unimaginable splendour until 1887, when they sold it to the Grand Duke Pavel Aleksandrovich. He gilded the lily by employing Maples to do over the billiard room and Meltzer to relay the floors. *No. 20*, early in the nineteenth century, became the Commercial Society (the equivalent of the Rotary Club) which admitted only Merchants and gave the first subscription balls in St Petersburg. In the 1830s it had been bought by Count Orlov-Davydov, the immensely rich descendant of Vladímir Orlov (brother of Grigoriy). The family still owned the house in 1917 and the last of them was still rich enough to have largely financed Russian Freemasonry (dissolved after the Revolution).

No. 28 is now the **Palace of Marriage Ceremonies.** If you
want to have a really smart wedding, these days, you may get
married there (or once again in a church) and leave for your
honeymoon in a speedboat which rocks all the other boats
on the Moika, while your bridesmaids and best man follow
in another. Peter the Great would have approved.

By 1914, many of these mansions were already apart-
ment houses (particularly in their rear wings facing on to
Galérnaya úlitsa), with the owner living on the first floor
front. In flats in these houses lived, at various times,
Dimitri Shostakovich (*No. 20*), Sergey Diaghilev (*No. 22*),
George Washington Whistler and his son, James McNeil
(*No. 34*) and Aleksandr Blok (*No. 40*). During the First
World War, the houses of absent owners tended to be commandeered by the army and treated as the army usually
treats things. Until the Revolution. Then it must have been
irresistible to partition the ballrooms, rip out the Gothic
panelling in the libraries, smash the marble encrustations
of the dining rooms and convert the overblown mansions
into communal flats. No more horses were delivered to the
'equestrian pier' on the New Admiralty Canal. No more
fish restaurants tied up at the steps below the Senate. No
more horn music floated over the Neva from the waters
below the house of Aleksandr Naryshkin. The English
Embankment was re-christened *náberezhnaya Krásnovo
Flóta* (Embankment of the Red Fleet). It got its name back
in 1993. It remains to be seen what kind of identity it will
acquire in the twenty-first century. One thing that can
never be taken away from it is the view across the river to
the southern waterfront of *Vasíliyevskiy óstrov*.

XII

Basil Island

Metro Stations: *Vasileostróvskaya* and *Primórskaya*

A SHORT DISTANCE in space, but the distance in time and culture is vast from the lush palaces of the English Embankment in the late nineteenth century to the first colonisation of *Vasíliyevskiy óstrov* (Basil Island) at the beginning of the eighteenth. So pause, on your way over *Dvortsóvy most* (Palace Bridge), and imagine the house that the second Empress of Russia thought it would be amusing to have built there.

It was January 1740. Prince Mikhail Galitsin had become a Roman Catholic. His punishment was to be made one of the Empress Anne's numerous jesters and compelled to marry one of her Mongol servants. To celebrate the wedding, an **Ice House** (*Ledyanóy dom*) was ordered to be built on the frozen Neva between the Winter Palace and the Admiralty. It was 6.4 m. high, 17.1 m. long and 5.3 m. wide and made entirely of ice. So were the statues on the roof (the Empress was keen on Baroque) and all the furniture and fittings inside, down to the playing cards and the flowers. Outside, it was guarded by two mortars and six pieces of cannon, likewise of ice. At its entrance, two ice dolphins and an ice elephant lit up the night by spouting burning oil while, next door, an ice sauna was heated by burning straw.

The forced wedding was attended by three hundred guests from all over Russia: two (a man and a woman) from each of a hundred and fifty different localities, supplied with national costumes and national musical instruments. Since little or no attempt was made to harmonise the music,

1	Menshikov Palace	7	Exchange (Naval Museum)
2	Palace of Peter II	8	*Strélka*
3	University ('Twelve Collegia')	9	Customs House *(Púshkinskiy dom)*
4	Academy of Sciences	10	Academy of Arts
5	*Kúnstkamera*	11	Mining Institute (and Museum)
6	Zoological Museum		

it must have sounded like the braying of many asses as it accompanied the wedding procession, headed by an elephant – a live one – with a small pavilion on its back in which sat the bridal pair. A good time was had by all except, presumably, the bride and groom whose nuptial bed was also made of ice. It is not surprising that the ordeal nearly cost them their lives. But they recovered and, though the bride died about two years later, the groom lived on for thirty-five more years until the ripe old age of seventy-five. They even managed to produce a son whose descendants continued until the middle of the twentieth century. The Ice House lasted until April, when it finally melted into the waters of the Neva. But it, too, lived on – as the subject of nineteenth-century Russian novels and of learned articles. In Soviet times it was (unconvincingly) argued that it was not merely an Imperial whim but a serious experiment which tested the elasticity and resilience of ice and thus contributed to the foundation of glaciology as a modern science.

From the beginning, it was on **Vasíliyevskiy óstrov** that Peter the Great intended his new city to be. He saw it primarily as a port, Russia's new import and export facility on the Gulf of Finland which, once he had concluded his war with the Swedes, would replace the ice-locked outlet at Archangel. He appointed his closest companion and collaborator, Menshikov, Governor-General of St Petersburg and made him a present of *Vasíliyevskiy óstrov*. This island had acquired its name from the Representative (*Posádnik*) of the Republic of Novgorod, Vasiliy Selezen, who had administered it at the end of the fifteenth century; but only the eastern end was populated – by river pilots and ferrymen whose job it was to guide vessels through the tricky waters of the Neva estuary and to ferry occasional passengers from one bank of the river to the other. The western end – which became known as the *Gávan* (haven or port) – was a huge, uninhabitable, swamp, the lowest-lying land in the area of St Petersburg and the most subject to flooding. It remained so, indeed, until after the Revolution. E. M. Almedingen, who lived on the island at the beginning of the twentieth century, described a flood in 1903 and another in 1909: 'Even as a child I felt puzzled why all those fragile timbered houses had not been replaced by stone buildings better fitted to withstand that savage onslaught of the swollen waters . . . Looking out of the window I saw boats plying up and down the wide street.'[1] Hundreds of those timber houses would be smashed, she remembered, and the actual number of casualties never came to light.

Menshikov did not bother himself much with the western end of his island but, by 1714, had built himself a handsome palace towards the eastern end, complete with gardens, green houses, stables and windmills. Nothing so grand had been built on the Petersburg islands before. But, in spite of this ostentatious example, it was some time before Peter's ambition to develop *Vasíliyevskiy óstrov* was realised – and never in his life time. Before his death in 1724, he had issued sixteen decrees making it obligatory for people to live there – everyone who was not involved in work at the Admiralty or the dockyard or with the fleet. Nobody took any notice. In 1721, there was another decree: all those who had not moved to *Vasíliyevskiy óstrov* would have the roofs removed from their houses. Still they did not move and nor, probably, did their roofs. They knew – what Peter strangely omitted to notice – that the most perilous crossing of the Neva was between *Vasíliyevskiy óstrov* and the south bank where the dockyard was developing. Here, in spring and autumn, the currents were fastest and the flood waters most unpredictable.

Then there was the question of the **canals**. In 1714, a Major Lepinas was ordered to survey the island. Architects, including Trezzini and Mattarnovi, were invited to submit plans. But nothing happened until August 1716 when a French architect – Jean-Baptiste Le Blond, whom Peter had

[1] E. M. Almedingen, *I Remember St Petersburg* (Longman: 1969).

met on his travels in Western Europe – submitted a plan
for the development of St Petersburg which (although
Peter was still abroad and Le Blond had not yet visited
St Petersburg) was adopted as the official blue print. The
new city was to be defended by a system of canals and locks.
No architect was to build anything without Le Blond's
counter-signature. In 1717, Le Blond arrived in St Petersburg
as architect-in-charge. There grew up a legend, so powerful
that it was reported as fact by Kurbatov[2] at the beginning of
the twentieth century, that Menshikov and Le Blond had
executed the latter's plan and that, when Peter returned
from his travels, he had declared the canals to have been dug
too narrow and too shallow so he stopped the work and
beat Menshikov with his stick. The legend was reinforced,
perhaps, by the Makhayev plan of St Petersburg, engraved
and printed in 1753 on the commission of the Empress
Elisabeth to celebrate the fiftieth anniversary of the
city's foundation. There, on the Empress's instructions,
Vasíliyevskiy óstrov appears criss-crossed with canals as
Le Blond had designed it. But good evidence supports the
view that the canals were never dug. (In 1727, well after
Peter's death, decrees were still being issued about the
necessity to start work on them.) The truth was simpler and
less picturesque: Le Blond had not realised that, from mid-
October until April, the Petersburg climate meant that no
canals could be used for any purpose, commercial or military. One or two ditches were dug, more for drainage or as
approach roads – one, for instance, along the line of the
present *Filologícheskiy pereúlok*, down the eastern side of
Menshikov's estate, and one parallel to what is now
Mendeléyevskaya líniya.[3] But the rest, including Makhayev's
plan that was sent to the Western chancelleries, was fantasy.

---

[2] V. Kurbatov, *Péterburg: Khudózhestvenno-Istorícheskiy Ócherk* (1913).
[3] For this use of *líniya* to indicate a street, *see* Appendix on Practical
Information, p. 436.

Menshikov, meanwhile, made himself comfortable. The south-eastern part of the island, including the *Strélka* ('spit' or 'point'), had belonged to a Swedish General of French origin called Jacob de la Guardie. He owned a farm there and a hunting lodge from which he enjoyed fine duck shooting. Menshikov took over the farm and, by 1709, had laid it out as a magnificent park. In place of the hunting lodge there was an imposing timber mansion. But, once the Battle of Poltáva in the same year guaranteed Russia's permanent presence in the Gulf of Finland, why stop at timber mansions? By August 1710, he had hired the Italian architect Giovanni Fontana to start on a stone palace: the **Menshikov Palace** (*Ménshikovskiy dvoréts*) at what is now **University Embankment** (*Universitétskaya náberezhnaya*) *No. 15*. By 1 October 1712, building operations had advanced sufficiently for a house-warming party. But by that time the Court, the Royal Family and all the officials of the Government had moved from Moscow to St Petersburg. Menshikov gave his party but lost his island. Peter took it back into the possession of the Crown, though he left his collaborator his new stone palace and his much-embellished farm. Immediately to the east of the palace was the entrance, by water, to another of Menshikov's projects: some chambers (in timber and long since vanished) where distinguished visitors from abroad could be accommodated in great grandeur, to be wined and dined and impressed by the burgeoning civilisation of Peter's Russia and the bottomless wealth of Menshikov. To the east again was a timber church and, next to that, the house of Menshikov's estate manager, Solovyov.

By the standards of only forty years later, the early eighteenth-century Menshikov Palace seems trim and restrained. But it was a great deal more splendid than anything available to the Tsar (or anyone else in St Petersburg) until Mattarnovi completed the third Winter Palace in about 1720. So, not having his own palace, Peter often stayed there. Part of it was used – by Peter and Menshikov – as administrative offices; and Peter used it, almost invariably, for his own entertaining – diplomatic receptions, celebrations (the Russian naval victory at Hangø, for example, when the fleet saluted in front of Menshikov's landing stage), the weddings of his friends, relations and collaborators. It was, in fact, never finished but constantly altered and enlarged (by Gottfried Schedel, assisted by Trezzini and Mattarnovi) until after Peter's death in 1725 and Menshikov's downfall in 1727. Perhaps the last embellishment was added in the autumn of 2002 with the unveiling of a bust of Menshikov created by Litovchenko, the widow of the sculptor Anikushin.

Weddings were a particular speciality – not as cruel as the Empress Anne's for Galitsin but almost as elaborate. When Peter's niece Anne (later the Empress Anne) married the Duke of Kurland, the cake had no sooner been placed on the table than two dwarfs, male and female, burst out of it and proceeded to dance a minuet. (The guests, presumably, ate a different one.) And there was another, more sophisticated innovation: what Peter called '**assemblies**' (*assambléi*). They took place in the late afternoon (not earlier than 4.00 p.m. and not later than 10.00 p.m.). Of a piece with his earlier social reforms such as the compulsory shaving of beards and the instructions on 'how to pay compliments in correspondence' (translated from the German) and on not going to bed with your boots on, the intention was to 'Westernise' – in this case, the role and status of women in Russian society. On 26 November 1718 the assemblies were introduced by decree and accompanied by rules of conduct which would 'eventually become customary', written out in the Tsar's own hand. The public was informed in which house the *assambléya* was to be held, and the owner had little option but to host it (or pay for it). Often it was Menshikov but the choice sometimes fell on others.

Their purpose was 'not only for entertainment but for business as well' and they included not merely husbands but wives and grown-up children who would spend their time playing games (chess was the favourite), dancing to Western music (Peter had learned to dance on his trips abroad and was determined that his subjects should share his passion) or, if so minded, discussing business. Western dress was to be worn and, most revolutionary of all, men and women were to talk to each other. A Queen of the Ball was to be named from the ladies present and everyone, including Peter and his family if they were present, was to do her bidding. Those who failed to turn up, male or female, were punished by being forced to drink a huge bowl of vodka. There were those who said the whole idea was ungodly; but it was the beginning of a tradition in Imperial Russia in which women were offered an education – and the chance to work – equal to that of men and superior to any that was available in Western Europe.

It was given a further impetus, no doubt, by the accident of a great female sovereign in Catherine II, who was also something of a blue stocking, supported by her reforming Minister of Education, Betskoy. More surprisingly, Catherine's son, Paul (a sovereign not noted for reformist zeal) placed his wife, Maria Fedorovna, in charge of Catherine's Institutes for girls at Smolny. Maria created another school, the Catherine Institute (Quarenghi 1804–7) on the Fontanka Embankment (*No. 36*). Later again, in 1894, the Grand Duchess Xenia founded the 'Xeniinskiy' Institute in Stackenschneider's *Nikoláyevskiy dvoréts* (Nikolay Palace) in *plóstchad Trudá* at the invitation of her brother, Nicholas II (*see p. 245*).

But the **education of Russian women** owes its beginning to Peter the Great. In the year before his death, on the advice of Leibnitz and other West European *savants*, he approved the foundation of a University in St Petersburg. It was to educate all Russians, women as well as men, in the sciences and applied sciences that were the necessary implements for Russia's enlightenment. And because – unlike most academic foundations in the West – its inspiration was scientific rather than religious, there was no obstacle in principle to the entry of women. In fact, about a third of the students in scientific subjects were at the outset female. More than one hundred and sixty years later, the nineteenth century caught up with Russian universities and the higher education of women became, in theory, separate from that of men. They were required to attend 'Bestuzhev Courses' outside the mainstream. But neither the curriculum nor the professional staff appeared to change in any respect and things went on much as before.

Since 1981, Menshikov's palace has been open to the public as a museum under the auspices of the Hermitage. This followed twenty-five years of meticulous restoration in the course of which the rooms were returned to their original appearance and appropriately furnished – largely with seventeenth-century furniture. Three rooms have kept (or regained) their Delft tiles which cover not only walls but ceilings too, where they are set into fine plaster mouldings. There are Menshikov's and Peter's tools and a turning lathe, cooking pots and ovens. Altogether it provides a comprehensive vision of early eighteenth-century life-at-the-top and a sober reminder of how modest – compared with everything that came after – that life was, even when lived by one of its most corrupt and indulgent practitioners. It is also enormously charming.

Having murdered his son by his first wife and lost, in infancy, the sons born to him by his second, Peter passed a law of succession (1722), substituting choice by the sovereign on the basis of merit for the principle of birthright. In February 1725, dying and in great pain from an obstruction of the urinary tract, he told his daughter Anne to bring pen and paper – according to her husband's secretary Count Bassewitz – but managed only the words:

'leave everything to . . .' before the pen dropped from his
hands. Menshikov was not far away and nor were the
Preobrazhenskiy Guards, arriving almost simultaneously at
the death bed. Peter's widow, Catherine, who in earlier days
had been handed on from Menshikov to Peter, was
declared Empress and Menshikov became, until her death
a mere two years and three months later, the effective
sovereign of Russia – a position that he had no intention of
abandoning when she died. Catherine appointed as her
successor the grandson of Peter I by his first wife (the son
of the murdered Tsarevich Aleksey), who succeeded to the
throne at the age of eleven as Peter II. The Supreme
Council, of which Menshikov was the most powerful
member, was nominated Regent and Menshikov made two
important moves: he planned to marry the young Emperor
to his daughter; and he began to convert the house of his
estate manager into a palace for him. It was, after all, right
next door.

This is how the **Palace of Peter II** came to be built at
Universitétskaya náberezhnaya No. 11. It was begun in
1727 but, at Peter II's death in 1730, building stopped.
Furthermore, Menshikov was in disgrace, stripped of all
his possessions and exiled with his family to Siberia where,
within two years, he himself was dead. For Peter II had disliked Menshikov and did not fancy his daughter. Instead,
he turned to Prince Ivan Dolgorukiy and, in 1729, became
engaged to Yekaterina Dolgorukaya. He moved his residence to Moscow where, a year later, he died of smallpox.

Menshikov's palace became (1732) a military school, the
First Cadet Corps. A wing was added (1764) at right angles
to its western end, along what is now *S-yézdovskaya*
(Congress) *líniya* but was once *Kadétskaya líniya*, to accom-
odate the Cadets; the drawing room on the first floor,
where Peter had held his *assambléi*, became their chapel and
Peter II's palace was adapted (1759–61) to provide classrooms. In the narrow space between the two palaces, at

Universitétskaya náberezhnaya No. 13, was placed the
Manézh – Riding School – of the First Cadet Corps (1757–9,
designed by the 'building master' attached to the school,
I. Burkhardt).

It was a civilised and distinguished school; Field
Marshal Suvorov was one of its graduates; others included
the dramatist Aleksandr Sumarokov (some of his plays
were specially written to be performed by the boys) and the
father of Russian acting, Fedor Volkov, as well as the poet
and leading Decembrist, K. Ryleyev. In the latter part of the
nineteenth century, Peter II's Palace became part of the
University of St Petersburg, the wing behind Menshikov's
Palace serving as a library and museum. After the February
Revolution, part of it was used as a conference hall. Here,
in early summer, there was held the first All Russia
Congress (*S-yezd*) of the Soviets of Workers' and Soldiers'
Deputies in the course of which a Menshevik deputy
voiced the general feeling of despair when he said that in
the current crisis there was no single party able or willing
to assume the totality of power. 'There *is* such a party',
came a voice from the body of the hall. And, later, from the
tribune, Lenin made his interjection explicit: his party, the
Bolshevik party, was 'ready to assume total power at any
moment'. In honour of that moment, *Kadétskaya líniya* was
re-named *S-yézdovskaya líniya*.

Between *No. 11* and *No. 7* on the Embankment is a small
house with an eighteenth-century façade, built in 1834–5
(Stchedrin) but in the style of the much earlier building to
its east. In the **Rector's Wing** (*Réktorskiy flígel*), Aleksandr
Blok was born and spent some of his childhood in the last
years of the nineteenth century, his maternal grandfather
being Rector of the University. (At the age of twenty-three,
Blok married – unhappily, as it turned out – the daughter
of the great chemist, Dimitri Mendeleyev, who had lived
and worked round the corner in the main University building, on what is now *Mendeléyevskaya líniya*.)

So we come to the second building still standing on the University Embankment which was begun (though not finished) in the life time of Peter I: at *Universitétskaya náberezhnaya No. 7*, the **Twelve 'Collegia'** (*Dvenádtsat kollégiy*), started by Trezzini between 1722 and 1734 and finished by Schwertfeger and Zemtsov, who went on working there until 1742. It is odd that it should now be the main building of a university because originally it had nothing to do with things academic. As part of his fundamental reform of the old Muscovite institutions of government, Peter abolished the old *prikázy* (offices of state) which had grown haphazardly over the centuries. (By 1700, there were fifty of them.) And he replaced them by nine (subsequently twelve) 'Collegia' or boards, each with a chancellery, a president, a secretary and ten other members including, often, a foreigner. The model was largely Swedish, the theory that it assured greater variety and interplay of opinion, the perceived advantage (by Peter, at any rate) that, since he did not have enough trustworthy collaborators to be placed in full charge, it would be safer to rely on boards the members of which would keep a check on each other. (The 'Collegia' were founded in 1717 and lasted until the early years of the nineteenth century when Alexander I gradually transformed them into Ministries, headed by a single minister.)

Trezzini was ordered to design a building which would reflect both the independence of each 'collegium' within its area of competence and the community of their tasks in the wider context of the state. At right angles to the river and looking eastwards over the Spit of the island, he built twelve attached houses, each one distinguished by a projection marked by four pilasters and topped by a Dutch gable, joined together by a single roof line four hundred metres long. (When first they were built, each house had its individual roof and only the façade was continuous.) As the main part of the city developed on the south bank of the Neva, the difficulties of the river crossing from *Vasíliyevskiy óstrov* to the Admiralty side meant that, gradually, the agencies of government migrated southward. And, by 1819, the University – which by that time had outgrown the Academy of Sciences next door – was ready to move in behind them. So the Colleges became Faculties.

The **Academy of Sciences** (*Akadémiya Naúk*) at *Universitétskaya náberezhnaya No. 5* was the heart of Peter the Great's University and perhaps the most beautiful of all the buildings on the south bank of the island. Having received his approval in 1724, it did not acquire its present casing until sixty years later when Catherine II commissioned Quarenghi (1783–9) to create it. Until then, it was contained within the *Kúnstkamera* next door to the east; it was there, and not in Quarenghi's lovely, simple, Classical mansion, that Lomonósov, chemist, physicist, astronomer, grammarian, artist and poet, became professor of chemistry in 1745 and, eventually, Rector of the University of St Petersburg.

So it is right that the **Lomonósov Museum** (opened in 1949) should be housed in the *Kúnstkamera* (*Universitétskaya náberezhnaya No. 3*) – the third and last of the buildings on the Embankment that were begun in the reign of Peter I. By the time of Peter's death, only the walls had been completed (G. Mattarnovi, 1718–25). The tower and circular hall which linked the two halves of the building, also the interior decoration, were not in place until 1734 (Harbel, Chiaveri and Zemtsov). The building, at that stage, was intended to house the Academy of Sciences, the Library (originally Peter's collection), the 'Observatory' and the growing scientific collection of which Peter's *Kúnstkamera* (donated by him to the new Academy) was the nucleus – it was to be, in other words, a dynamic scientific and educational complex.

By a piece of extraordinary serendipity, Mikhail Lomonósov appeared over the horizon less than twenty years after its foundation. No country would have been entitled to expect him, a Renaissance figure arriving at the beginning of the eighteenth century in a backward country that was just awakening. Born in 1711, the son of a fisherman in the Province of Archangel, he consumed learning as other men consumed food. He took himself to Moscow and from there to St Petersburg where the patrons of science sent him to study metallurgy at Marburg. On his return, he wrote – in Latin – important works on the 'Cause of Heat and Cold', the 'Elastic Force of Air' and the 'Theory of Electricity'. But he also laid the foundations of modern Russian, both verse and prose. Without Lomonósov on the principles of prosody (the art of versification), it is doubtful if we could have had Pushkin; and Lomonósov's principles of Russian grammar were still taught in Russian schools when I was a boy. Without Lomonósov, though perhaps this is less important, we would not have recovered the art of mosaics. And without him, the University of St Petersburg would not have become the eminent European institution that its founder dreamed of. He was not always an easy man to deal with. (In this, as in many other respects, he resembled the founder.) He quarrelled, on occasions, with both the Empresses under whom he served. But when the Academy's first President threatened to expel him from the Academy and the University, he was merely stating a fact when he replied: 'I think it would be better if you expelled the Academy and the University from me.'

The museum which is dedicated to him is contained in the circular hall and tower of the *Kúnstkamera*. In addition to the Lomonósov exhibits – how hard to 'exhibit' such a man – it contains the round table at which the first meetings of the Academicians took place and a replica (the original was destroyed by fire in 1747) of the Great Academic Globe presented to Peter I in 1713 by his son-in-law (and father of Peter III), the Duke of Holstein-Gottorp. Twelve people can sit inside and rotate through the heavens.

Nowadays, the rest of the *Kúnstkamera* building is devoted to the **Museum of Anthropology and Ethnography** (*muzéy Antropológii i Etnográfii*) which, over the centuries, has grown from a sub-group of Peter's original collection. It includes material brought back from many scholarly expeditions in the nineteenth century – to Siberia and Kamchatka, to New Guinea and Polynesia, to the Antarctic and elsewhere. It also includes some early specimens bought by Peter from a Dutch anatomist and the oddities from Peter's own collection. These last, so we were told by our guide, include the relics of Peter's personal servant; the man, she said, was two metres thirty-five centimetres tall and his penis (which is in the collection) measured forty-five centimetres.

The **Zoological Museum** (*Zoologichéskiy muzéy*), which developed from another sub-group of the *Kúnstkamera*, has, since 1896, been housed at *Universitétskaya náberezhnaya No. 1*. This is one of two converted warehouses which were built, each side of the great Exchange on the Spit of *Vasíliyevskiy óstrov*, by G. Lucchini (1826–32) within an overall plan by Zakharov. This museum, too, was the recipient of discoveries by great Russian expeditions. Of the forty thousand animal species on permanent display, the unique exhibits include the wonderful Berezevo Mammoth, a gigantic ram from Komodo Island, a baby mammoth from the Magadan region, and the extinct 'Southern Elephant'. It is all rather beautifully displayed.

Before we leave the University Embankment, two more museums should be mentioned. The first is the **Apartment Museum of Mendeleyev** at *Mendeléyevskaya líniya No. 2*, just back from the Embankment in the building of the Twelve 'Collegia'. Mendeleyev (1834–1907) was a great chemist. His discovery of the 'periodicity' of the properties and inter-relationships of the elements is central to a great deal of modern chemistry and physics. He was also a figure in the cultural life of St Petersburg (the painters Ivan

Kramskoy and Ilya Repin used to attend his 'Wednesdays') and, politically, a progressive. As a result he was never elected a full member of the Academy but, in 1890, was retired from his Chair for transmitting to the authorities a request from his students for the remedy of perceived injustices. His stance was significant for it indicated the end of the island's isolation from developments on the south bank of the Neva. There was a permanent bridge, now, across the treacherous river (the *most Leytenánta Shmídta*, formerly known as the *Nikoláyevskiy most*, built in 1855); there was the Baltic Shipyard at the west end of the island and important new factories (including Siemens & Halske) in the north-west; and there was working class housing in the *Gávan* and around *Mály prospékt*. It was natural for students and workers to find common cause and, in any event, students themselves were becoming revolutionaries. In the 1870s, Georgiy Plekhanov was studying at the Mining Institute on the Lieutenant Schmidt Embankment. Lenin and his brother, Aleksandr Ulyanov, both attended the University of St Petersburg. In 1887 Aleksandr was executed for his part in an attempted assassination of Alexander III; four years later Lenin, a new recruit to the Marxist Party, took a first class degree in Law. These and similar incidents may well explain why the authorities acted so nervously in the case of Professor Mendeleyev. Mendeleyev himself went off to work at the Central Chamber of Weights and Measures (now the Institute of Metrology) at *Moskóvskiy prospékt No. 19*. 'Science', he famously remarked, 'begins with measurement.'

The remaining museum on this Embankment is the great building to the west of Menshikov's palace next to the garden, at *Universitétskaya náberezhnaya No. 17*. The **Museum of the Academy of Arts** (*Akadémiya Khudózhestv*) was founded in 1757 by the Empress Elisabeth, under the Presidency of Ivan Shuvalov. It was conceived both as a museum – for the preservation of works by outstanding students – and as a centre for teaching and research. In 1947, the Academy moved to Moscow and the Petersburg building now houses the museum and the Repin Institute of Painting, Sculpture and Architecture ('the three noblest arts' as the Academy's charter described them) which is one of the largest art schools in the world. It still contains the casts made of Classical and West European sculptures for teaching the gifted young sculptors, such as Demut-Malinovskiy, Martos, Pimenov, Stchedrin and Terebenyov, who flourished in St Petersburg in the first half of the nineteenth century; I. Starov, A. Voronikhin and A. Zakharov studied architecture here; Repin, Serov, Surikov and Shishkin all studied painting. And so did a school of painters without whom much of St Petersburg would no longer exist: they called themselves 'Painters of Interiors' and they developed a technique of drawing as it were with a wide-angle lense which made it possible to reproduce the interiors of houses and palaces as though you, the viewer, were standing in them. Their water colours were often clearer (and sometimes more beautiful) than the real thing, whether of the distant vista down a gallery or of the chintz and carpets in the foreground. As a result, they became an invaluable and infallible source of reference. Should the inside of the Winter Palace be destroyed by fire, it could be redecorated exactly as before; should the Germans blow up Tsarskoye Selo or Peterhof, should the Soviet Government pull out the guts of the Marble Palace, there was the meticulous record of how the White Room used to look. This group of painters included M. Vorobiev (1787–1855), Edward Gué (1807–88), Luigi Premazzi (1814–91) and Konstantin Oukhtomskiy (1818–81).

The Academy building was designed for Catherine the Great at almost the same time (1764) as the Small Hermitage and by the same architect (J.-B. Vallin de la Mothe). It was executed, over more than twenty years, under the supervision of A. Kokorinov. Because of its monumental scale, it has the appearance of being much later than it is. It is strange to think that it was begun almost twenty years before Quarenghi's Academy of Sciences – though it was completed only a year earlier (1788). The quay in front, however, dates from over forty years later and was designed by the man who built the Moscow Station, K. A. Thon. The Sphinxes, brought with great labour to St Petersburg in 1832, were found at Thebes and are said to date from the thirteenth century BC.

On the other side of the island, in the north-east corner between the *Birzheváya líniya* and the *Birzhevóy most*, are the earliest beginnings of **Peter the Great's port**. The *Málaya Nevá* turned out to be too shallow for big ships which was why, in the early-nineteenth century, the main commercial activity shifted eastwards and came to rest right on the Point (*Strélka*) of the island. In 1713, Peter first decreed that goods for export from the interior of Russia should pass out through St Petersburg and no longer through Archangel. The first 'Exchange' (*bírzha*) was on the *Tróitskaya plóstchad* on the Petrograd Side where there was also a *Gostíny dvor* for merchants. The build-up was rapid and, five years later, one third of all Russian trade was leaving the country down the Neva. In 1728 port activity moved from the Petrograd Side to *Vasíliyevskiy óstrov* and, in 1731, the Empress Anne pursued Peter's first intention by ordering that a wooden 'Exchange' be built on the bank of the *Málaya Nevá* (now *náberezhnaya Makárova*). Anne was married to a German. So perhaps she had in mind a Petersburg version of the *Fondaco dei Tedeschi* on the Rialto in Venice. At all events, the *bírzha* and *Gostíny dvor* that grew up along the bank of the *Málaya Nevá* were, by any standards, enormous and a mansion, which Naryshkin had bought from Menshikov in the early days, was converted to serve as a customs house. If old prints are to be believed, the *Gostíny dvor* alone had at least fifty arches. Early in Catherine's reign, a storage facility for hemp was added to the complex – the Tutchkóv Warehouse (*Tutchkóvskiy buyán*, Rinaldi and Dedenev, 1764–70) across the *Málaya Nevá* at the end of the *Tutchkóv most* on the Petrograd Side. Though much altered, it is still standing. So *Vasíliyevskiy óstrov* became – and remained until the twentieth century – a haunt of foreign, mainly German and British, merchants, who came to live there fairly modestly with their families. It has been said that by the middle of the eighteenth century it already resembled a provincial town in Germany.[4]

As trade through St Petersburg grew, yet more space was needed. Early in her reign, Catherine II commissioned Quarenghi to build a new and grander Exchange (the *Novobirzhevóy Gostíny dvor*). But only the first two floors were completed and it is now incorporated into the Library of the Academy of Sciences (*Bibliotéka Akadémii naúk*). By 1786 it became clear that the navigational difficulties of the *Málaya Nevá* outweighed its other advantages and Catherine and Quarenghi started again, this time some way away from the *Gostíny dvor* on the very point (*strélka*) of the island. The Turkish war intervened, money ran out, and Catherine died without her new Exchange. In 1805 Alexander I and Thomas de Thomon returned to the new site, demolished Quarenghi's walls and, in a mere five years, built the massive temple of commerce that stands there still today. It was officially opened in 1816, at the end of the Napoleonic Wars.

Thomas de Thomon's *Bírzha* (now *Voyénno-Morskóy muzéy* – the **Naval Museum**) was based on the mid-sixth century BC Temple of Hera at Paestum, a settlement of *Magna Graecia* in Southern Italy and a model that gave a new twist to neo-Classicism as hitherto practised in St Petersburg. The temples at Paestum were archaic, built by *émigré* Greeks before the flowering of fifth-century

---

[4] P. Stolpyanskiy, *Kak Vozník, Osnoválsya I Ros Sankt-Peterburkh* (Petrograd: 1918).

Athens; they used only Doric columns and derived their effect from massive simplicity. These temples were, like the new *Bírzha*, designed to be approached from the sea. The sense of the archaic carries through into the '**Rostral Columns**' (*Rostrálnyie Kolónny*) which Thomas de Thomon placed each side of his temple – this time, archaic Roman, for they are modelled on third-century BC Roman symbols of victory at sea. The Romans used to decorate such columns ('rostral' means literally 'decorated with beaks') with the prows of Carthaginian ships captured in the Punic Wars. (The victorious Roman galleys were fitted with hinged gangplanks and grappling irons to provide a boarding ramp for the Roman marines.) Painted Etruscan red, the columns on the *Strélka* appear primitive and even savage; but their function as conceived by Thomas de Thomon was entirely beneficent: hemp oil, burning in bronze bowls thirty-two metres from the ground, was to provide navigational beacons for ships as they approached the docks.

The **ensemble of the** *Strélka*, including the granite embankment which slopes down to meet the river, was conceived in part by the Russian architect, A. Zakharov, who was at the time working on the new Admiralty building across the river. Zakharov's scheme was completed by warehouses (*pakgáuzy*, designed by G. Lucchini, 1826–32) which flanked the main *Bírzha* and also by a re-working of the eighteenth century Customs House (*Tamózhnia*) on the bank of the *Málaya Nevá* round the corner (same architect, same date). The dome of the latter was intended to balance the dome of the *Kúnstkamera* on the south side of the island and provided a look-out from which a signal was sounded when ships approached.

Gradually the emphasis shifted from the exchange of goods to the financial operations associated with it. From the 1830s, stocks and shares began to be quoted on the *Bírzha;* and by 1900, dealing in commodities and paper were separated, both in the same building but in distinct sections.

Much of the cargo began to be directed to the new port south-west of the city. When the Revolution put an end to the market in stocks and shares and the quotation of commodities on the open market, it was inevitable that the *Bírzha* should lose its role. As early as 1896, the southern warehouse had become the Zoological Museum. The northern warehouse now houses the Soil Science Museum; the *Bírzha* itself has, since 1939, accommodated the Naval Museum; and the Customs House became the Institute of Russian Literature, which also contains the Literary Museum.

The **Naval Museum** has its origins in the chamber set up by Peter I as a repository for models and working drawings of naval vessels. Now it tells the story of the Russian Navy – in models, paintings, blue prints, weaponry, navigational equipment and personal effects, including its operations in the Second World War and beyond. In particular, it contains Peter's original boat, the one that is made of sixteenth century English oak and is too fragile any longer to live in the Boat House built for it in the Fortress (*see* p. 37); it also contains Russia's oldest surviving submarine, photographs of the Kronstadt mutineers and a dug-out said to be three thousand years old.

The **Customs House** (*Tamózhnya*), which occupies the site equivalent to the *Kúnstkamera* but to the north of the Exchange, became in 1927 the **Institute of Russian Literature** of the Academy of Sciences (housed since its foundation in 1905 in the main Academy building). It is often called the *Púshkinskiy dom* (Pushkin House) because Pushkin's manuscripts are kept there. (The editing of these manuscripts has, incidentally, been funded mainly by the Prince of Wales.) The Institute is an important centre for the study of Russian literature from the twelfth century (*The Lay of Igor's Host*) to the present. The rather grand Classical interior includes rooms set aside for a **Literary Museum** where photographs, portraits, manuscripts and first editions relating to Tolstoy, Lermontov, Gogol, Blok and Gorky are on display. Some of the furniture from Gorky's apartment on the *Kronvérkskiy prospékt* is there; also the original volumes from Pushkin's library.

Leaving the *Strélka*, the *Bírzha* and the buildings associated with it, and returning westward along the southern bank of the island, a tram will take you along the river from the *Shevchénko plóstchad* to the Mining Institute. In the *Shevchénko plóstchad* itself is an obelisk (1799 by V. Brenna) in memory of the defeat of the Turks by Field Marshal Rumyantsev. Passing the Academy of Arts on your right and the *most Leytenánta Shmídta* (Lieutenant Schmidt Bridge) on your left, you come to a busier, less formal part of the Embankment where small ships still come up the river to do business. Lieutenant Schmidt must have had nerves of steel. During the revolutionary year of 1905, as a member of the Naval Soviet he assumed the leadership of the mutiny of the Black Sea Fleet by hoisting a signal on his own ship, the cruiser *Ochakov*, which read: 'Am Commanding the Fleet'. It is hardly surprising that he was court-martialled and shot by the Imperial Government. Nor is it surprising that the Soviet Government in 1918 decided to re-name in his honour the *Nikoláyevskiy most* – the first permanent bridge to have been built (1855) across the Neva.

Not only the bridge but the Embankment too. At the bridge, *Universitétskaya náberezhnaya* becomes *náberezhnaya Leytenánta Shmídta*. At *No. 1* there is the **Apartment House of the Academy of Sciences** (1808–9, Zakharov), remodelled from an earlier building by Chevakinskiy, where twenty-six bronze plaques record some of the distinguished Academicians who lived there; *Apartment No. 11* was occupied from 1918–36 by **Ivan Pavlov**, best known by non-scientists perhaps for his work on conditioned reflexes though in 1914 he was awarded a Nobel Prize for research on the physiology of the digestion. On the river bank opposite *No. 11* is a prominent statue (Schröder 1873) of the first

Russian to circumnavigate the globe, **Admiral Krusenstern**. He was a scientist as well as an admiral and some of the fruits of his voyage (1803–6) are displayed in the Museum of Anthropology and Ethnology.

At *No. 17* is the **Higher Naval College** (before the Revolution, the Naval School, *Morskóy kadétskiy kórpus*). Like other buildings in this part of the island, it was a re-modelling in Classical style of several earlier buildings, unified by a many-columned portico (F. Volkov, 1796–8). Past graduates include Admiral Krusenstern (who became its Director), Admiral Nakhimov (one of the defenders of Sebastopol during the Crimean War), Mikhail Lazarev (member of the expedition that discovered the Antarctic in 1821) – and Lieutenant Schmidt.

The **Mining Institute** (*Górny institút*), which was founded in 1773, is a long way west, between the *21-ya* and *23-ya líniya*, at *No. 45 náberezhnaya Leytenánta Shmídta*. Here five earlier buildings were combined and unified by a massive twelve-columned portico and pediment by Voronikhin, who began work on it five years after he began Kazan Cathedral but finished three years earlier (1806–8). Perhaps in sympathy with Thomas de Thomon, this time he used Doric rather than Corinthian columns and his inspiration was Greece rather than Rome. Each side of the entrance steps are groups of statuary by Demut-Malinovskiy and Pimenov – one of the Rape of Proserpina (as mining rapes the earth) and one of Hercules struggling with Antaeus (a giant who was invincible until Hercules lifted him off the ground). The statues and heavily symbolic frieze which circles the building were designed by Voronikhin. The magnificent interior (by A. Postnikov) houses a **Mining Museum**, founded at the same time as the Institute. It contains, among many other marvels, the gemstones used in the map of the Soviet Union dismantled from the Throne Room in the Winter Palace (*see* p. 143).

Running the length of the island from east to west are three avenues: the *Bolshóy* to the south, the *Srédniy* in the middle and the *Mály* to the north. E. M. Almedingen describes them in the early 1900s:

> *Bolshóy prospékt*, whatever its social gradations, was lovely from end to end because of its trees and its nearness to the great river. *Srédniy* brushed close to slumminess . . . pick-pockets sprang up like mushrooms after a rainy night and some were bold enough to snatch a handbag or a shopping basket. The shout 'stop thief' sometimes produced a policeman but the public seemed oddly indifferent. Yet it did not lack pretensions and boasted two of the very first cinemas on the island . . . *Mály* had no restaurants but many *cháyneiye*, tea rooms where the very poor could get a kettle of hot water for nothing and those slightly better off could quieten their hunger by pickled eels, fried potatoes and a sausage for five kopeks, with a glass of tea thrown in. *Mály* had many pubs, *traktiry*, from which workmen, small bottles of vodka in their hands, would come out, break the seal and empty the bottle in one or two gulps.[5]

At the eastern end of **Bolshóy prospékt**, *No. 1* is the **Lutheran Church of St Catherine**, now a recording studio, an early Classical Western-style church by Felten (1768–71) with stairway towers added at the entrance in 1903. Another relic of the German community is the neo-Gothic Lutheran Church of St Michael on the corner of *Srédniy prospékt* and *2–3-ya líniya*, now back in the hands of Lutherans who hold Sunday services in both English and Russian.

At the northern corner of *Bolshóy prospékt* and *6-ya líniya* is the Orthodox **St Andrew's Cathedral** (*Andréyevskiy sobór*) built from 1764 to 1779 by A. Vist (whose only other known building in St Petersburg is the Boat House in the Fortress).

---

[5] E. M. Almedingen, *I Remember St Petersburg* (Longman: 1969).

It is based on an unusual plan with a sanctuary in the shape of a trefoil, an exceptionally tall central octagonal drum and dome, four small domes on two-tier drums and a belfry with a spire. The belfry is joined to the church by a refectory that was widened in 1850. To the north of this church, up the *6-ya líniya*, is the small and rather earlier **Church of the Three Holy Men** (*tsérkov Tryokh Svyatíteley*). It is believed to have been begun in 1740, though not finished until 1760, and it was heated. It came to be used as the winter annexe to St Andrew's. Just north of this again is an even earlier building – *dom Troyekúrova* (Troyekurov's House) – which follows a 'standard plan' as specified, probably by Le Blond, in the 1720s and which, most unusually for St Petersburg, retains most of its original features including its rusticated corners and Baroque-shaped windows.

On the south side of the *Bolshóy prospékt*, also on *6-ya líniya*, is the open arcade of **St Andrew's Market** (*Andréyevskiy rýnok* (1789–90), the exact contemporary of St Nicholas Market on *Sadóvaya úlitsa*. (Next door is a thriving modern market, *Vasileostróvskiy rýnok*.) Further down the same street towards the river, but on the opposite side at *7-ya líniya No. 12*, is another very early, 'standard plan', house: the **Guest House of the Alexander Nevsky Monastery** (*Aleksándro-Névskoye podvórye*), where Church dignitaries would stay when visiting the *lávra*. Construction was supervised by Trezzini and Schwertfeger (1720–6) following a design laid down by Le Blond as appropriate for houses of distinguished citizens (*imenítyie*) – a grander category than Troyekurov's House. If Peter I had lived longer, much of the island would have looked like these two houses. Only after the great fire of 1737, and the establishment of the Building Commission, were new 'standards' set.

On the north side of *Bolshóy prospékt*, right down at *No. 83*, is the **Kirov Palace of Culture** (*dvoréts Kultúry im. Kírova*, architect N. Trotskiy, 1930–7). It stands in an area which, until the 1920s, was virtually uninhabited – the

Smolénskoye pólye (the Smolenka Field), stretching roughly from the *20/21-ya líniya* to the *28/29-ya líniya*. There, on the edge of the city, public executions of political prisoners were carried out until late in the nineteenth century. A. Karakozov, one of several unsuccessful assassins of Alexander II, was hanged there in 1866 and A. Solovyov, another, as late as 1879.

The *prospékt* ends in the Sea Terminal (*Morskóy vokzál*) where passenger ships come in to the city – not too many of them now, rather removing the point of the *Hotel Morskáya* and *plóstchad Morskóy slávy* (Marine Glory Square). *Sredniy prospékt* ends in the *Gávan*, where the permeable timber housing that used to be washed away by the floods has been replaced by building of the 1930s and 1950s much of which, some say, might be better washed away. North of *Sredniy* and south of **Mály prospékt**, a desolate industrial area is dissected by the *24/25-ya líniya*. Several of the factories date back to the end of the nineteenth century and the people employed there were massively involved in the 1905 and 1917 Revolutions. North again, but south of the Smolenka, is the **Smolénskoye kládbistche** (**cemetery**), one of the oldest Orthodox burial grounds in the city. Many Leningraders who died of hunger and cold during the Blockade were buried here in mass graves.

Across the Smolenka River, *Vasíliyevskiy óstrov* forms a sub-island of 4.1 square kilometres. In the eighteenth century, it used to be called Goloday Island, a corruption of the name of the British Dr Thomas Holiday who owned a factory and a plot of land here. Now it has come to be called *óstrov Dekabristov* because it is believed that the bodies of the five Decembrists, executed on the *Kronvérk* in 1826 (*see* p. 61) were buried here. In this belief, a black granite monument inscribed with their names (architect A. Bobrov) was erected in 1926 at the western end, within walking distance of *Primórskaya* Metro. Further east, just north of the Smolenka, are the **Lutheran** and **Armenian**

Cemeteries. Here, because it was a place where the non-Orthodox could receive a Christian burial, are the graves also of some British families – the most recent being the East Anglian yachtsman, Greg Palmer, who helped to build, and train the crew of, the *Shtandárt*. (This is a replica of Peter the Great's flag ship, built by its young and inexperienced crew, most of whom were unemployed, now on a world tour.)

Since the late 1880s, the intention has been to develop this part of the island. The architect I. A. Fomin was commissioned to draw up a plan for New Petersburg, which he did, and the area was even marked as such on maps of 1903. But nothing much was built. After the Revolution, the idea of a comprehensive plan seems to have been dropped and attention shifted to the south of the city. Now, much of the necessary infrastructure is in place, with the embanking and in-filling of the coastline here and on Petrovskiy Island, the canalisation of the western end of the Smolenka and the arrival of the Metro at *Primórskaya*. New Petersburg may yet be built in the twenty-first century.

XIII

The Other Islands

Metro Stations: *Krestóvskiy Óstrov* and *Petrográdskaya*

TO THE NORTH of *Vasíliyevskiy óstrov*, across the *Málaya Nevá*, is a small, slim island barely separated from the Petrograd Side by the little River Zhdanovka. In the nineteenth century, the German community of *Vasíliyevskiy óstrov* had their weekend *dáchas* here, on *Petróvskiy óstrov* (Peter's Island). In 1895, a retirement home for old actors was built towards the western end. Rather surprisingly – sign, perhaps, of the high esteem in which Petersburgers hold the theatre – it has survived all the intervening turmoil: *dom Veteránov Stsény* (The House of Stage Veterans) on the north-eastern side of the *Petróvskaya plóstchad*. Right on the western tip, the Central Yacht Club has a large marina from which boats can be chartered to sail round the Gulf of Finland.

The island has always had a mixed history of industry and holiday-making. Peter I took it for his private property for no better reason, it seems, than because it was the lowest-lying land in the estuary and totally uncultivated. This meant that it was difficult to cultivate and he could not resist the opportunity of showing what could be achieved 'with a little energy'. After his death, it became the property of his sister-in-law, the Tsaritsa Praskoviya (widow of Ivan V). It presumably remained Crown property, though by the 1740s warehouses and shops began to be built there and, in the 1750s, a factory which must have generated a vast revenue. It made wax candles and was the only source in St Petersburg – a good investment, one

THE OTHER ISLANDS

BOLSHAYA NEVKA

YELAGIN ISLAND

SHREDNYAYA NEVKA

KRESTOVSKIY ISLAND

MALAYA NEVKA

PETROVSKIY ISLAND

MALAYA NEVA

N

DECEMBRISTS' ISLAND

M	Metro Station	7	Lopukhin's Garden
1	Kirov Stadium	8	Institute of Experimental Medicine
2	Yelagin Palace	9	Botanical Gardens
3	Flag Pavilion	10	Popov Memorial Museum
4	*Strélka*	11	Chaliapin's Apartment
5	Kamenny (Stone) Island Theatre		(Museum of Russian Opera)
6	Kamenny (Stone) Island Palace		

cannot help thinking, given the millions of candles that all those theatres, all those altars, all those chandeliers in all those palaces, mansions and grand houses must have consumed during the next hundred years.

Catherine II liked the island so much that she commissioned Rinaldi to build her a summer palace there, in timber.

Her grandson, Alexander I, gave it to the Free Economic Society which established an experimental agricultural institute on the island. Her other grandson, Nicholas I, took it away again (in 1836) and gave it to his eldest son (later Alexander II), after which it was slowly covered over with factories, mills and *dáchas*. But Catherine's wooden palace survived until it burned down in 1912. A sports stadium was built (1924–5) towards the eastern end; this was reconstructed (1957–61) and named the Lenin Stadium (now called the Peter Stadium).

The three islands to the north of *Petróvskiy óstrov* were given the collective name of the '**Kirov Islands**' after the murder of Sergey Kirov in 1934. The southernmost of them, *Krestóvskiy óstrov* (Island of the Cross), can now be reached by Metro – which brings all three islands within easy reach even for those without a car. They remain predominantly green (in summer) and predominantly dedicated to enjoyment (winter and summer), a watery pleasure-ground comparatively free of traffic which Petersburgers surely deserve. A branch of the Neva, the *Bolsháya Névka*, wanders among them calling itself sometimes under its own name, *Bolsháya* (the Great), sometimes *Málaya* (the Small) and sometimes *Srédnyaya* (the Middle). Nowadays, there is a growing amount of water traffic and the speed boats are getting speedier. But on the whole Kirov's islands are good for the spirit.

Though not his stadium, built on the western end of *Krestóvskiy óstrov*. Between 1933, not long before his murder, and 1941 when the Blockade stopped everything, a million cubic metres of earth were dredged from the bottom of the Gulf of Finland, to which were added a million and a half cubic metres of sand, and all this was deposited on the western point of *Krestóvskiy óstrov* to create an artificial hill. Inside the hill, there was to be a depression around which grandstands would be placed, while the seaward slopes of the artificial hill would be so landscaped that they would appear like a natural sea front. The project was actually completed in 1950 (architects A. Nikolskiy, K. Kashin and N. Stepanov) but the Gulf of Finland is not California, so there are certain difficulties in making full use of the **Kirov Stadium**, which is in effect made of mud. At the main entrance stands a statue of Kirov (sculptor V. Pinchuk), behind which are two pavilions, connected with the playing field by tunnels, designed to accommodate visiting teams. Two grand staircases, decorated with statuary, a fountain and water cascades, lead to the top of the artificial hill. Looking down into the 'bowl' from a balcony round the top, there is a view of row upon row of benches (end to end, they would measure thirty-two kilometres) – room for 80,000 seated spectators and standing room for twenty thousand more.

To the east of the stadium lie over four hundred acres of the **Maritime Victory Park** (*Primórskiy park Pobédy*), bisected by the *Morskóy prospékt*, in the middle of which is the **Monument to the Heroes of the Great Fatherland War** (*Pámyatnik Geróyam Velíkoy Otéchestvennoy Voyný* 1941–5), the twin of the Moscow Victory Park in the south of the city. Before the Revolution, most of this area was also a park – but a private one designed for the Beloselskiy-Belozerskiy family, who had bought the whole island in 1803 and, fifty years later, had Stackenschneider build them a house there (now destroyed). There was also a sailing club, as there is now, at the end of the *náberezhnaya Martýnova* in the north-east. Just before the First World War, the Beloselskiys sold the island to a British company – but the deal never went through and the family continued to live there until 1918.

The next island to the north, *Yelágin óstrov* (Yelagin Island), can only be reached on foot or by bicycle and is the most beautiful of the three. The arms of the Névka are never far away and nor is the smell of the sea, yet there is none of the turbulence and crippled, windswept landscape that usually accompany the sea. Happy days can be spent here in summer, wandering through woods of tall oaks and birches and Scots pine, picking marguerites in the Buttercup Meadow, eating a modest-looking ice cream which turns out to be delicious – and everywhere scented with lilac. In winter there are other treats: skating (and music to skate to), ski touring, roast chestnuts.

When the Russians first landed on Yelagin Island, they heard a great noise in the woods and thought they had fallen into a Swedish ambush. But what came lumbering towards them was not a Swede but a bear and so they called the island Mishkin (the name Russian children give to bears). Peter I gave the island to a Dutch Jew called Shaphiro whom he had baptised, to whom he stood godfather and who became Peter's Chief of Police. So it was Russified as Shafirov Island. Then Ivan Yelagin, secretary and theatre administrator to Catherine II, acquired it at the end of the 1770s, built himself a house at the sheltered eastern end, a great earth dyke as a defence against the river, on which an avenue of trees still grows to this day, and a granite quay on the north-eastern point from which twelve cannon and an orchestra saluted the arrival of important guests. Then, for a short time, Yelagin's house became the property of one of the Orlov brothers (Vladímir) who sold it, in 1817, to Alexander I for his mother, Maria Fedorovna, the widow of the Emperor Paul. Alexander gave Carlo Rossi his earliest important commission in St Petersburg, to remodel Yelagin's eighteenth-century house and appropriately to colonise the rest of the island.

This took Rossi four years and one has the impression that Maria Fedorovna rather lost interest – if she had ever had any. (She was already magnificently housed at Pavlovsk.) But Alexander's brother, Nicholas (shortly to become Nicholas I) adopted the new house as his official summer residence and thus began a great partnership between sovereign and architect which, over twenty years, was to transform the public face of St Petersburg. What Rossi did to Yelagin Island was very delicate; he touched it – with the house, the kitchens, the stables, the orangery and the pavilions – but it remains a country island, fairly simple and fairly wild. The house is open as a museum and is, usually, a delightfully informal way of exploring a Classical interior without crowds or lectures. On the second floor is an exhibition of furniture and decorative objects, many of them made from Karelian birchwood. The western steps are guarded by a pair of lions, each patting a ball with his paw, which provide a valuable insight into the nature of St Petersburg lions (or, at any rate, Rossi lions). They recur, these lions, at various significant points in the city – and they are able to do so because they are not stone but cast iron (the Yelagin ones were cast in 1822), produced on demand by a Petersburg foundry. Lions from the same cast guard the steps of the Russian Museum (date-marked 1824) and the Embankment by *plóstchad Dekabrístov*, looking over to Menshikov's Palace.

The other buildings are dotted about – how did they get the food from the vast kitchens (never mind about them facing inwards so the odours did not escape) to the dining room in the house without it becoming stone cold? – but each has its points of interest. Perhaps the grandest is the **Flag Pavilion** on the north-eastern point facing down the *Bolsháya Névka*, which has just been restored by the World Monuments Fund. The flag, which had (and will soon have again) a pole on the roof of Rossi's small temple, replaced Yelagin's twelve cannon as a salutation for important guests as they approached from the east down the long straight stretch of the river. From the river, this temple with its solid Doric columns must, like the Exchange on *Vasíliyevskiy óstrov*, look extraordinarily Greek.

The far end of Yelagin Island, facing westwards out to sea, has since the 1840s been a favourite place from which to watch the setting sun. Several paths take you there from the palace, one along the banks of the *Bolsháya Névka* and one through the centre of the island. On the very point (*strélka*), are lions. But these ones, beware, are not cast iron. They are stone, carved in the late 1920s.

You can leave Yelagin Island by the First Yelagin Bridge (*1-ya Yelágin most*) and cross back into a half-real world on *Kámmeny óstrov* (Stone Island), passing two more of Rossi's creations: the Music Pavilion (which is really two little pavilions connected by a colonnade, with a semi-rotunda and a convex staircase leading to the park); and the Guardhouse, a small arcaded wooden building that stands near the bridge. The combination of this and the Ionic portico of the (also) wooden *Kámenno-ostróvskiy teátr* (Stone Island Theatre), just over the bridge, makes you wonder whether you have not wandered by accident into a film studio – Hollywood not Ealing – where they are setting up to shoot the early sequences of *Gone with the Wind*. And the impression does not leave you as you get deeper into Stone Island, which is spattered with large country villas, set in their own estates, eccentrically designed. Perhaps, after all, not Hollywood but the east end of Long Island.

First, though, the theatre (at *Krestóvskaya náberezhnaya No. 10*). Built as a summer theatre in 1827 (S. Shustov), it was demolished and replaced in 1844 by one designed by the master builder of all theatres in St Petersburg, A. Cavos. There were no more plays there after 1914 (though it has now been restored and, for the moment, is used as a television theatre). But on 20 June 1920, there was a mass theatrical event on *Kámmeny óstrov*; the whole place was decorated and transformed into a huge stage (by the architects I. A. Fomin and N. Trotskiy) for a play called *The Blockade of Russia* to be performed in the open air; for the island was to be re-christened 'Island of Toilers' (*óstrov Trudyástchikhsya*) by official decision of the Petrograd Soviet. The holiday homes left behind by the idle rich had been confiscated and were now to be converted into Houses of Rest for the workers of the Soviet Union. Some of them were; some, of course, eventually found their way into the hands of state enterprises, including the security services; some of them are still in those hands; one is now being extensively refurbished for the President of Russia (whose native town is St Petersburg). In 1989, this time without ceremony, the 'Island of Toilers' became once again Stone Island. Nobody seemed to notice; when had it ever been anything else?

At the beginning of the eighteenth century, Peter I gave this island to his Chancellor, Count G. Golovkin and it was removed from his son by the Empress Elisabeth. The son was a supporter of the Regent Anna Leopoldovna, whose baby, Ivan VI, was taken from her at the age of eighteen months and imprisoned by his cousin Elisabeth, who then assumed the crown. Golovkin was tried, condemned to death, reprieved at the foot of the gallows and banished to Cherman in north-east Siberia, where the average winter temperature is minus 40 degrees centigrade and the respite between the last frosts of the old year and the first ones of the new is thirty-seven days. The (by this time) Empress Elisabeth invited his wife, who was one of her ladies-in-waiting, to stay on in *Kámmeny óstrov* – but, bravely, she chose to join her husband. So the island was acquired by A. Bestuzhev-Ryumin who built himself a wooden country house set in an elaborate, formal park on the eastern point. In 1765, Catherine II bought the site – one of the loveliest in the estuary, facing up the long stretch of the *Bolsháya Névka* and cradled in its arms. She replaced the timber house with a stone one and developed the whole point as a summer residence for her son Paul. Unappreciative, he is said to have visited it only twice in his life. But his eldest son (later, Alexander I) adopted the house that Catherine built and made it his own. There he lived and worked for much of the summer time throughout the Napoleonic Wars.

The *Kámenno-ostróvskiy dvoréts* (Stone Island Palace) was built between 1776 and 1781 by an unknown architect, under the supervision of Felten. It follows a fairly standard pattern for a mid-eighteenth-century Russian country mansion, two-storeyed with shallow projections at each end and a central flight of steps leading to a six-columned portico and pediment in the centre. It is not possible to visit it – nor even to gain a clear view of the exterior though it can be glimpsed – as it is now a military sanatorium; but photographs of the interior suggest a strictly Classical treatment, the three central rooms having curved ends, *bas reliefs* of Classical subjects on the walls and statues in niches all around. The grounds, which are now intersected by the northern extension of *Kámenno-ostróvskiy prospékt*, contain a little neo-Gothic brick chapel (the Church of St John the Baptist at *Kámenno-ostróvskiy prospékt No. 7*) with which Felten must have amused himself while supervising the building of the palace. It is more ordinary and modest (almost like a mid-Victorian chapel) than his so-called neo-Gothic Chesme church in the south of the city; but it was a very early essay into Gothic revival and pre-dates Chesme church by a year. (It is open again for worship.) In 1810, Thomas de Thomon was commissioned by Alexander I to re-design the park and add an archway into the garden; for his archway, he used Doric columns which echo his Exchange.

At the same end of the island, on the *nábarezhnaya Máloy Névki*, a number of substantial country houses began to cluster near the Imperial palace. At *No. 11*, is the *dácha Dolgorúkova* (Dolgorukiy's House, 1831–2, by S. Shustov), built in timber in the style of a Palladian villa with a central rotunda but decorated by Stackenschneider in the 1840s. Though the rotunda and hall were badly burned in the 1930s, they have been restored. Further west along the same embankment is an example – again in timber – of a neo-Russian *dácha* (the *dácha Buturliná*) with elaborately carved window frames and over-hanging eaves (V. Sobolstchikov 1860–70). Later still, on the other side of the island, I. A. Fomin (who began as a fashionable neo-Classical architect in the last years of the Empire but maintained a flourishing practice under the Soviet Government) created the large, cold, be-columned, essentially urban *dácha Pólovtsova* for Aleksandr, son of the historian, Senator Polovtsov, and the adopted daughter of Baron Stieglitz – a curious time to be building such a huge mansion but Polovtsov (Junior) had been in some disfavour and only returned to St Petersburg just before the war. He was later to be instrumental in preserving the palace at Pavlovsk from post-Revolutionary depredations (*see* p. 420) and in establishing a tradition of extraordinary reverence for palace 'museums' among the post-Revolutionary public which still amazes foreign visitors.

Meanwhile, his *dácha* was the first to be converted by the Petrograd Soviet into a House of Rest (*dom Ótdykha*) and was visited by Lenin on his last visit to Petrograd in July 1920 (commemorated in a plaque on the wall). Now it has the forlorn look of a house in search of inhabitants and is rented out, from time to time, for corporate entertaining. Among the great variety of extravaganzas on *Kámmeny óstrov*, particularly along the *allées* which cross the interior, there are one or two examples which are not to be found anywhere else in the world – though they are faintly reminiscent of the houses in which *New Yorker* cartoonist Chas. Adams used to torture his captive family. They are built, often in timber, in a style which has been given the untidy name of 'Northern Moderne' and look rather like the hooded crows which haunt the island. They are currently much in fashion with Russians who can afford them.

The way out of *Kámmeny óstrov* at its eastern end is by the Prospect and bridge which bear its name. Almost immediately, you return to urban St Petersburg at the northern end of the Petrograd Side. But to the left (north-east) of the Prospect, between the bank of the *Málaya Névka* and *úlitsa Akadémika Pávlova*, is **Lopukhínskiy sad** (the garden of the Lopukhin *dácha*). In that *dácha*, now vanished, lived the French Ambassador – from 1807 until 1811, the year before Napoleon invaded Russia. From his study, he commanded a perfect view (it can be commanded from the same spot today) of those who came and went across the pontoon bridge which linked the city to the Emperor's country residence – ministers, senior military commanders, foreign representatives.

Yet the **Marquis de Caulaincourt** was more than a careful observer. He was a European statesman. The relationship between him and the Emperor of Russia was long, complex and of world importance. First posted to Russia for a year in 1801 as a *protégé* of Talleyrand, his return as ambassador in 1807 was welcomed by Alexander I. On his recall to France in 1811, he fell on his knees to implore Napoleon not to invade Russia; the result, he correctly forecast, could only be disaster for France. As every child knows, Napoleon ignored his advice and taunted Caulaincourt with having become 'Russian'. He did, however, grant his request to be posted far away to Spain. When, at the end of the disaster, the defeated Napoleon was escorted back to Paris, Caulaincourt was a member of the small entourage which accompanied him. In March 1814, Alexander himself made a triumphant entry into Paris; in April, he negotiated and signed the treaty which exiled Napoleon from France and made him King of Elba. The man who led the negotiations on the French side was the French Foreign Minister – by that time, Caulaincourt. When Napoleon returned from Elba and was defeated at Waterloo, it was Alexander who ensured that the newly restored Bourbon monarchy allowed the ex-ambassador to retire quietly and without recrimination.

You are now on *Aptékarskiy óstrov* (Apothecary Island), cut off from the rest of the Petrograd Side by the Kárpovka

River and named after the oldest establishment on it, the Apothecary (now the Botanical) Gardens in the south-east corner. These were established in 1714 by Peter the Great as a garden for medicinal herbs (*Aptékarskiy ogoród*); and it was, no doubt, for the preparation and dispensing of these remedies that Trezzini was instructed to build the Main Pharmacy (*Glávnaya Aptéka*) on the corner of *Milliónnaya úlitsa* and *Aptékarskiy pereúlok*.

On this island, called by the Finns *Korpi saari* (Spruce or Crow Island), Peter forbade anyone to build or otherwise interfere with the cultivation of his herbs. Indeed, building was forbidden by decree by all sovereigns until Paul – though, as usual, small attention was paid to the decrees and, in the justified belief that the authorities would not notice, people did build country homes and *dáchas*. The island was very agreeable and near the Imperial palace. Right into the twentieth century many of the houses were in timber, most of them were clustered along the *Kámenno-ostróvskiy prospékt* and almost all of them were pulled down in the 1950s and 60s to make room for blocks of flats.

Continuing through Lopukhin's Garden, *úlitsa Akadémika Pávlova* leads eventually to the **Institute of Experimental Medicine** (at *No. 12*) where **Ivan Pavlov** had his laboratories from about 1890 until his death in 1936. It was here that he conducted his most famous experiments – on the conditioned reflexes of dogs – and it is fitting that he commemorated his eighty-fifth birthday with a statue of a dog, placed in the courtyard of the Institute. What is less well-known is his collaboration, in old age, with Stanislavsky, the actor and founder of the Moscow Arts Theatre and the originator of the Stanislavsky school of acting. Stanislavsky was in search of a 'Method' by which the emotions implicit in a role could be aroused by the actor at will, rather than thought and played through the intellect. He believed that Pavlov's work on the brain's higher nervous activity might hold the key. Pavlov, in return was interested in the responses that Stanislavsky could conjure from his actors. The collaboration was ended only by Pavlov's death. The result of it is to be seen on stages and screens throughout the world.

Following the Embankment of the *Bolsháya Névka* southwards from the Institute, one comes to what is now called *úlitsa Proféssora Popóva*. Here, at the eastern end of what was then simply Sand Street (*Pesóchnaya úlitsa*), one of Imperial Russia's greatest statesmen, **Peter Stolypin**, had his weekend *dácha*. Minister of Internal Affairs and, later, Prime Minister in the early years of the twentieth century, he pursued two policies in parallel: on the one hand, to raise the income and standard of living of Russia's peasant population, transforming them into farmers on the West European model through the expansion of their ownership of land and livestock; on the other, forcefully to suppress the terrorist campaign which followed the collapse of the 1905 Revolution. Both policies aroused violent opposition, particularly by the revolutionary parties, making Stolypin the target of several attempts on his life.

One of the earliest was on 12 August 1906 when three men arrived for a Saturday afternoon session where Stolypin was accustomed to receive petitions. These men came not with petitions but with brief cases; when guards attempted to inspect them, all three threw their cases on the floor and shouted revolutionary slogans. They killed themselves and twenty-four other people instantly, wounding seventy more including Stolypin's three-year-old son and one of his daughters who nearly lost both her legs. Stolypin and his wife by some miracle escaped unhurt although the top was blown off Stolypin's desk and the inkpot hit him in the neck; when the Minister of Finance arrived on the scene shortly after the explosion, Stolypin said simply: 'This shall not alter our programme. Our reforms are . . . Russia's salvation.' Five years later, in 1911, there was another – and successful – attempt on his life when he was shot and killed in a theatre in Kiev.

Lenin judged Stolypin's agricultural reforms to be 'revolutionary' and was bitterly hostile to them on the grounds that, if successful, they would render his own plans for an agricultural revolution 'superfluous' – possibly another way of saying that they might, indeed, have been 'Russia's salvation'. The agricultural census of 1916 suggests that Lenin's fears were well-founded: it showed that 89.4 per cent of Russia's sown area and 95 per cent of the livestock by that time already belonged to the peasants. In fact, as was later pointed out by the distinguished Soviet agricultural academic, Professor A. N. Chelintsev, on the eve of the Revolution almost the entire agricultural production of Russia belonged to the peasants.[1] The 1917 Revolution swept away these reforms and cancelled their effect on the peasant population when Lenin introduced the decree which nationalised all land and thus ended the prospect – perhaps for ever – of the Russian peasant becoming a West European farmer.

At the same end of *úlitsa Proféssora Popóva* but on the opposite side of the street, lie the **Botanical Gardens** (*Botanícheskiy sad*) which, in one form or another, have been on the same site for nearly three hundred years. As Peter I conceived them, their original purpose was strictly medical. Scientific horticulture was conducted, from 1735, on *Vasíliyevskiy óstrov* under the auspices of the Academy of Sciences. But in 1823, the medicinal and the horticultural functions were merged and, in the following year, Joseph Charlemagne was commissioned to build a house on the Apothecary site for a Director of the Botanical Gardens – eighteen years before the gardens at Kew were handed over by Queen Victoria to the Department of

---

[1] Professor A. N. Chelintsev, *Rússkoye sélskoye khozyáystvo péred revolyútsiey*, 2nd edition (Moscow, 1928), pp. 10–11.

Woods and Forests and became a scientific institution. Contact between Kew and the St Petersburg Botanical Gardens had begun in the eighteenth century, when Kew was the personal property of George III and his German Queen, Charlotte. At that time, the passionate gardener in the Russian Royal family was Maria Fedorovna, the German wife of Paul. In 1795, George III sent Maria Fedorovna 126 plants which had recently been discovered in the South Seas and developed by his gardeners at Kew. Including their pots, they weighed over three tons and were delivered to Paul's palace at Pavlovsk, complete with a gardener called Mr Noe, in fifteen carriages. When Maria Fedorovna died in 1828, she left her collection of rare plants, including those that had survived among King George's gift, to the Imperial Botanical Gardens which, by that time, were consolidated on *Aptékarskiy óstrov*.

Charlemagne's house for the Director is still there, at *úlitsa Proféssora Popóva No. 2*, to all outward appearances exactly as it was built – a modest timber *dácha* with a tall arched window supporting a small pediment, looking out over the gardens. Charlemagne also provided orangeries and a hot house. In the 1840s, K. Thon, who built the Moscow Station, added some more greenhouses and, in the 1890s, came the Palm House. The glory of the garden is usually said to be its early association with the largest water lily in the world: the *Victoria Regia* from South America, whose leaves are sometimes six feet across and whose flowers may be eighteen inches wide. (They float on an underside which looks like uncooked tripe.) The first *Victoria Regia* to flower in Europe is said to have flowered in Riga and, from there, to have been transferred to the *Aptékarskiy óstrov*.

There were, however, some eccentrics among the early directors of St Petersburg's Botanical Gardens. Professor Siegesbeck was particularly notable for his determined refusal to accept the conclusions of the eighteenth-century Swedish botanist, Linnaeus, whose accounts of plant reproduction seemed to him not merely abhorrent but impious. God, and certainly not the true Christian God of the Orthodox Church, would never have allowed such blatant immorality among plants, which were free of original sin. It was fortunate, one feels, that this Director never came face to face with the founder of the Apothecary Gardens.

A short distance to the west of the Gardens, at *úlitsa Proféssora Popóva No. 5* on the north side, is the curious building that gave its name to the street – the Electro-Technical Institute where Aleksandr Popov was professor and head of department. A strange, rather ugly building put up in 1890 in an Eclectic mix of styles, it now contains the **Popov Memorial Museum** – the laboratory in which he worked and the flat in which he lived from 1901 until his death in 1906. Popov himself was concerned with ship-to-shore radio communication and developed such a system for the Russian Navy as early as 1898. To his posthumous misfortune it was claimed by the Soviet Government that he, not Marconi, had invented radio. The claim has since been quietly withdrawn and should not be a discouragement to visiting a carefully conceived museum at *Apartment No. 33*.

Where *úlitsa Proféssora Popóva* meets *prospékt Médikov*, it is worth turning left (south) to the Embankment of the Kárpovka River (*nábarezhnaya rekí Kárpovki*) to see a much-admired and very elegant building by Ye.Levinson and I. I. (son of I. A.) Fomin, 1931–5. The characteristic of the **Lensoviet Apartment House** (*zhilóy dom Lensovéta*) is its lightness – a rare commodity in St Petersburg. Six storeys high, it has a long, curving façade, a recessed gallery along the first floor, recessed balconies and two end-pavilions. (Levinson was also involved, 1930–4 with V. Munt, in the Lensoviet Palace of Culture on the west side of *Kámenno-Ostróvskiy prospékt* at *No. 42*, on the other side of the Kárpovka – a Constructivist building to which nobody would think of attributing lightness.)

Resisting the temptation to make for home at the *Petrográdskaya* Station and turning north up the *Kámenno-Ostróvskiy prospékt*, there is one pilgrimage more to be made on *Aptékarskiy óstrov*. The third turning on the right after the Kárpovka Embankment is *úlitsa Gráftio* where, at *No. 2b*, Chaliapin lived from the beginning of the First World War until 1922, when he finally left for Paris. His apartment, after much repair work, was re-opened to the public in 1997 as the **Chaliapin Apartment and Russian Opera Museum**, a branch of the Museum of Theatrical and Musical Arts. Perhaps nobody has combined theatricality and musicality to such a high a degree. It is interesting that, in his volumes of autobiography, he writes about himself more as actor than singer.

He arrived on the operatic stage in Russia from Kazan at a time when Italian opera dominated the scene. Italian singers regarded the voice as all and acting as superfluous; the greatest Italian tenor of the day, Mazzini, never even gave it a thought. One evening in St Petersburg, when the libretto required the soprano to sing a long lament over the body of the dying tenor, Mazzini simply got up and walked away in the middle of her *aria*, returning only when it was time for him to sing again. At which point he came back, lay down on the spot where he had been lying before and they carried on singing. It was in protest against such performances that the Musical Drama Theatre of St Petersburg set out to reform operatic productions and that Chaliapin decided to become – and became – as great an actor as he was a singer.

But that should not be allowed to obscure his greatness as a singer to which anyone who has heard him sing in the West will testify. Borís Godunóv, yes, but also Leporello and Mefistofele (in Arrigo Boito's opera of that name.) In his apartment on *úlitsa Gráftio*, hear his voice; see some of his costumes, his furniture, his props. There is also an exhibition based around the history of Russian opera and the St Petersburg opera scene at the turn of the nineteenth and twentieth centuries, including the work of the Diaghilev designers and of some delightful painters. It makes one remember, with a smile, Chaliapin's own story about himself and Gorky – both penniless, both needing a job. They hear about a vacancy in a church choir. They go in and apply. Gorky is accepted; Chaliapin is turned down.

There is another island, lying some way off-shore, of vital importance for the defence of St Petersburg and an integral part of Peter the Great's original concept. It is **Kotlin Island** (*Rotu saari*, to the Finns), which, with the fortress of **Kronstadt**, is the main base of Russia's Baltic Fleet and has been so since Russia began to acquire a Baltic Fleet in 1703. It lies twenty miles west of the city of St Petersburg in the Gulf of Finland, ironically referred to by Russian sailors as the Marquis's Puddle from the time when an early nineteenth-century Minister of War (confusingly called the Marquis de Traversé) restricted the deployment of the Baltic Fleet to the waters round about. To the north, between Kotlin Island and the Finnish coast, the sea is too shallow for boats drawing more than fifteen feet; to the south, a sandy spit projects from Oranienbaum on the Russian mainland. The guns of the Kronstadt fortress easily command the navigable channel.

Its strategic significance would not have been lost on Peter the Great even if he had not come across a Welshman called Edward Lane, who enlisted in the Russian Navy as an ensign in 1702. To Lane he entrusted the task of making the first plan of Kotlin Island (though he drew the line at Lane's suggestion that all he needed in the way of a new city could, and should, be accommodated there). By 1704, the first fortifications were in place on the south-east of the island and the fort was christened Kronshlot. Over the next few years, Lane produced his plan with enviable precision: there was room, he suggested, for 7,272 houses, ranged along 62 canals, the site for each house being 46.5 metres long and

8.3 metres wide (a good deal wider than the standard house in Amsterdam). Somehow, none of this happened, though Lane was promoted to Junior Captain in 1711 and to Captain, First Rank, 'for his particular services in harbour works', in 1715. In 1719, work started on building a system of docks and canals, some of which are still in use. In 1722, as Captain-Commodore with the pay of a Rear Admiral, Lane became Officer Commanding the Kronstadt Ports and, in September 1723, the central fortress was constructed to which the name of Kronstadt was given. Ensign Lane had come a long way. The man in overall charge of the development of Kotlin Island was Menshikov, who found time to build himself an 'Italian Palace' overlooking the harbour.

Like all naval towns, **Kronstadt** is a mixture of old and new, decay and modernisation, the beautiful and the utilitarian. Any resident of Portland or Portsmouth would be at home there, for sailors tend to keep tidy ships and untidy towns. There are some rather handsome monuments: one to Peter the Great (1841 by Jacques, undoubtedly romanticised); one to Admiral Makarov, the inventor of ice breakers, who commanded the Pacific fleet at the beginning of the Russo-Japanese War but who was sunk, in his flag ship, by the Japanese at the Battle of Tsusima. And there is the *Morskóy sobór* (the huge Maritime Cathedral by Kosyakov, 1903–13) which is based on the plan of Santa Sofia in Istanbul, much-prized by the local community (it was built with donations of sailors) but hard to find a good use for in the twenty-first century. There has been a concert hall on the ground floor, a sailors' club on the first, and a Museum of the Fortress including a diorama of its role during the Blockade; in 1967, they even tried to blow it up but had to desist, in the face of local opposition. It seems to be used nowadays for occasional divine service.

But the saddest story of Kronstadt is the story of the **mutiny** which took place there between 1 and 18 March 1921 and was directed against the policy of the young Soviet

Government. The sailors at Kronstadt were objecting, specifically, to the Government's policy of 'War Communism' and the deployment of 'barrier units' (*zagradítelnyie otrády*). These last were special units developed by Trotsky (by this time Commissar for War). Their role was, literally, to place a barrier against front line troops trying to retreat from the front.

The Communist movement up to this time had relied to a considerable extent on the revolutionary ardour of the Navy: 'the beauty and pride of the Revolution'. The sailors were famed for their ferocity and the cruelty with which they despatched their enemies. So the Kronstadt mutiny was in no sense reactionary or counter-revolutionary. If anything, it was an anarchistic reaction to the increasing intolerance by Lenin's Government of free expression and free association. It took place against a background of terrible civilian hunger and industrial strikes. 'Power', said the manifesto of the Provisional Revolutionary Committee published in the Kronstadt *Izvestia* of 8 March, 'has passed from a monarchy based on the police and gendarmerie into the hands of usurpers – Communists – who have given the toilers not freedom but the daily dread of ending up in the torture chambers of the Cheka . . . In this sea of blood, the Communists drown all the great and bright pledges and slogans of the toilers' revolution'[2] – 'Communism without Communists' as the mutineers' slogan went. The Provisional Revolutionary Committee arrested some 450 Communists, including the Fleet Commissar, Kuzmin, and demanded: freedom for the peasants to deal with their own land; free trade unions; freedom of action for the Socialist parties 'of the Left'; the dismissal of political commissars (who were responsible for the political reliability of Soviet citizens, particularly in the armed forces).

---

[2] Quoted by Richard Pipes in *Russia under the Bolshevik Regime 1919–24* (Harvill/Harper Collins: 1994).

Kronstadt at the beginning of March is surrounded by ice. The first attack on it, ordered by Trotsky and commanded by Tukhachevskiy (later Field Marshal, shot by Stalin on the eve of the Second World War), was made from the north-west shore of the Gulf across the frozen sea. Behind the Government soldiers were Cheka machine-gun detachments with orders to shoot any one who ran away. In front of them were the batteries on the fortress. Some soldiers refused to charge; a few went over to the mutineers; many were killed. Trotsky ordered the execution of every fifth soldier who disobeyed orders. But the final assault, ten days later, was from the south – from Oranienbaum and Peterhof – by fifty thousand troops against a garrison of less than twenty thousand.

Official statistics list a thousand of the garrison killed (though that seems likely to be an underestimate), two thousand wounded, two thousand five hundred captured and sent, on Lenin's specific instructions, to concentration camps on the White Sea from which few, if any, returned. About eight thousand made their way across the ice to Finland where some of them, twenty years later, were discovered, brought back and executed. An official (but by that time entirely posthumous) pardon was issued to the mutineers by the Russian Government in 1994.

Trotsky was completely successful – and, no doubt, he discouraged others who might have had similar action in mind. But it has been suggested that his association with the suppression of the Kronstadt mutiny weakened his position so that it was Stalin, as General Secretary of the Party, who was in pole position eventually to succeed Lenin. Ironically another slogan of the Kronstadt mutineers was: 'All power to the Soviets but not to the Party'.

XIV

The Blockade

Metro Stations: *Plóstchad Múzhestva, Moskóvskaya* and *Moskóvskiye Voróta*

THE GERMAN ATTACK on the Soviet Union in the summer of 1941, after a period of alliance and apparent friendship between the two countries, took Stalin's Government completely by surprise and found it completely unprepared. The possibility of such an attack had been suggested to Stalin by a number of sources including Churchill, who even supplied the date: 22 June. But the information had been received with total disbelief. Furthermore, the Soviet army, navy and air force had just been decimated in the Purges.

By 1940 the Purges had resulted in the following losses from the élite of the General Staff:

3 out of the 5 Marshals
13 out of the 15 Army Commanders
8 of the 9 Fleet Admirals and Admirals Grade I
50 of the 57 Corps Commanders
154 out of the 186 Divisional Commanders
16 out of the 16 Army Commissars
25 out of the 28 Corps Commissars
58 out of the 64 Divisional Commissars
98 out of 108 members of the Supreme Military Soviet[1]

---

[1] Figures given in the Soviet publication *Ogonyok*, No. 28, 1987, quoted by Robert Conquest in *The Great Terror* (Hutchinson: 1990), reprinted by Pimlico, 2000.

And the mayhem did not only occur at the top. At Regimental Commander level, there was no one left who had been through Staff College. According to Khrustchev, speaking many years later, the cadre of leaders who had gained military experience in Spain and the Far East was almost completely liquidated. And, as Khrustchev also pointed out, the fact that officers of all ranks and even private soldiers had been taught to 'unmask' their superiors as hidden enemies had 'a negative influence on the state of military discipline'. As a result, even when the German invasion was on the point of being launched it was doubtful 'whether any consistent plan for the defence of the Soviet Union existed'.[2] Ilya Erenburg, writing in 1964, noted that Stalin 'suspected his own closest comrades but trusted Hitler'.

As late in the day as Friday 13 June 1941, the Soviet Government authorised the news agency, Tass, to issue the following statement:

> In the opinion of the Soviet Government, the rumours of the intention of Germany to break the [non-aggression] Pact and to launch an attack against the Soviet Union are completely without foundation.

At dawn on Sunday 22 June Germany attacked the frontiers of the Soviet Union, from the Baltic to the Black Sea, with 175 divisions and the support of Finnish, Rumanian and other units. Though the Russians had substantial superiority in numbers and equipment, German intelligence had estimated that it would take the Red Army four years to regain the level of efficiency that prevailed in 1937.[3] So the German strategy was to defeat the Russians within two

---

[2] John Erickson, *The Soviet High Command* (London, 1962), also quoted by Robert Conquest in *The Great Terror* (Hutchinson: 1990), reprinted by Pimlico, 2000.

[3] John Erickson, *op. cit.*

or three months or, in any case, before the winter. It was to be another *Blitzkrieg*, a lightning war.

In the north, the German advance towards Leningrad across the Baltic States was, indeed, lightning. By the end of August, the last rail link between the city and the rest of the Soviet Union had been cut (at the rail junction of Mga) and by 8 September the Germans had passed around the south of the city and captured Schlüsselburg on Lake Ladoga. (They captured the town but the fortress itself, on an islet in the middle of the river, was never captured. It was the target of continuous bombing and eye witnesses reported a permanent red cloud of fine brick dust hanging over it. From the islet the Russians were able to direct anti-aircraft fire against German planes trying to blow up the key points on the only route into the city.) The fall of Schlüsselburg was the end of all overland communication and the beginning of the Blockade. The experienced German commander of 'Group Nord', General Halder, believed, so he told his journal, that the fall of Leningrad was imminent. 'Leningrad: very good progress. The enemy begins to soften on the front of Reinhardt's corps. It would appear that the population does not want to take a hand in defence.'[4]

At 6.55 p.m. that evening, the Germans dropped over six thousand incendiary bombs and started nearly two hundred fires, including one that set the freight yards of Vitebsk Station alight and another which burned down the Badayev warehouses near the Warsaw Station. In these wooden sheds, packed within thirty-five feet of each other over an area of some four acres, was kept a significant part of Leningrad's food reserves – meat, grain, flour, butter, oil and two and a half thousand tons of sugar which melted and flowed into the cellars. The fire was still burning in the morning.

---

[4] Quoted from *The Halder Diary*, ed. A. Lissance, in *The 900 Days* by Harrison E. Salisbury (Pan: 1969).

There was food rationing in Leningrad but, until that day, it was sufficient for more-or-less normal living. On 9 September, the State Defence Committee in Moscow despatched to Leningrad Dimitri V. Pavlov, a senior administrator of food supplies for the Defence Secretariat. His arrival was in response to a telegram – sent before the hit on the warehouses – from the city's mayor which informed the State Committee that Leningrad had less than a month's supply of food. On the night of Pavlov's arrival, another air raid hit the zoo and killed Betty, the elephant, who died noisily and in great pain. The following night, a bomb hit the main creamery.

The situation at Pavlov's arrival was as follows: the only route into the city was across the southern end of Lake Ladoga where there were no adequate boats, no piers or warehouses to handle substantial shipments. The population of the city, which had barely been reduced, was 2,887,000 civilians (including nearly half a million children) and some half a million troops.

Pavlov made an inventory of all food supplies, everywhere – under the floor boards of the breweries, in the sugar-soaked earth beneath the warehouses, in barns and military sheds and still on the fields. He sent factory workers and clerks into the area between the suburbs and the German lines to harvest the last of the potatoes and vegetables before the frosts. He set the scientists to work discovering how to extract yeast from cellulose and how to mix soap, engine oil and water as a substitute for vegetable oil. He ordered flour to be adulterated with cotton seed cake, chaff, hemp and hydrolised cellulose. And he issued new ration cards with a drastically reduced ration entitlement. For children, adolescents and non-working adults, there was to be: 200 g of bread a day; and 400 g of meat, 3/4 lb of fat, 3 lb of (poor quality and adulterated) pastry/confectionery per person per month. Workers were to get 400 g of bread and soldiers 800 g a day.

On 12 September, the bombardment began – from heavy guns mounted on railway trains and from six artillery emplacements around the southern side of the city. Meanwhile, the German troops continued to advance, though more slowly. On 18 September, General Halder was more cautious:

> The ring around Leningrad has not yet been drawn as tightly as might be desired and further progress after the departure of the 1st Panzers and 36th Motorised Division from the front [to the Moscow front] is doubtful . . . the situation will remain tight until such time as Hunger takes effect as our ally.

On 19 September came the worst air raid yet. They came over in six waves, two hundred and eighty planes; the hospital east of *Suvórovskiy prospékt* and the *Gostíny dvor*, on the Nevsky, received a direct hit and burned for several days. Ninety-eight people were killed and one hundred and forty-eight were wounded. But Shostakovich and some friends ignored the raids as they stood round the piano in his flat, for he was playing to them the two movements that he had just completed of his Seventh Symphony. (He was shortly to be evacuated to Kuybishev – now again Samara – where he completed the third movement in time for it to be performed in Moscow in March and broadcast from Leningrad on 9 August 1942.)

Then, on 22 September, came the first serious indication that the *Blitzkrieg* was over, so far as Leningrad was concerned. The new tactic was to be attrition without mercy.

Hitler's Headquarters issued the famous secret directive No 1a 1601/41:

> The Führer has decided to wipe the city of St Petersburg from the face of the earth. After the defeat of Soviet Russia, there will be no reason at all for the further existence of this large inhabited area . . . It is proposed to blockade the city closely and by means of artillery fire of all calibre and ceaseless

bombardment from the air to raze it to the ground. If this creates a situation in the city which produces calls for surrender, they will be refused.

And, on the ground, the Germans could be seen to be digging in.

Strangely, and almost simultaneously, Stalin too had decided that Leningrad should be razed to the ground, if the German advance continued into the city. In Kronstadt, there were two battleships, two cruisers, thirteen destroyers, forty-two submarines, two hundred and eighty-six planes and eighty-four thousand sailors. On 15 September Admiral Tributs, commanding the Baltic Fleet, relayed Stalin's order that not a ship nor a supply dump nor a cannon was to fall into enemy hands. All were to be mined and, before the ships were finally scuttled, the personnel was to be taken ashore, formed into ranks and marched to the front.[5] In the city itself the new Chief of Staff, General Khozin, and the Military Council, operating from the General Staff building in Palace Square, ordered that forty tons of explosives be released by the army to '*tróiki*' headed by the First Secretaries of the party organisations in the main Leningrad regions.[6] The *tróiki* were, in the greatest secrecy, to mine the southern approaches to the city, including what remained of the Kirov (formerly the Putilov) heavy engineering works and the *Elektrosíla* (formerly Siemens-Schukert) electrical engineering works (the one on *prospékt Stáchek* and the other on *Moskóvskiy prospékt*). Four days later, the centre of the city was similarly mined through its inner rail system so that, at the command, a plunger could activate the explosives. It was to be the twentieth-century version of the burning of

---

[5] V. F. Tributs, *Podvódniki Báltiki Atakúyut* (Leningrad, 1963), quoted by Harrison E. Salisbury in *The 900 Days* (Pan: 1969).
[6] M. Khozin, *Ob Odnóy maloisslédovannoy operátsii*, published in *Voyénno-Istorícheskiy Zhurnál*, February 1966, quoted by Harrison E. Salisbury.

Moscow in 1812, with the peculiarly twentieth-century twist that no serious attempt had been made to evacuate the population and it was now too late. Whether or not Stalin's orders permitted it, some attempt was made by Leningrad Party leaders to save the most historic buildings by the removal from their premises of all military installations (such as anti-aircraft or machine gun emplacements) and, thus, all excuse (if any was needed) for the Germans to destroy them.

Sometime between 19 September and the end of the month, the Germans ran out of momentum, the Russians re-organised their defence under Marshal Zhukov and the front line was stabilised. On the south, it ran from **Strelna** (east of Peterhof), through **Dáchnoye** (where the Germans controlled the railway to the Baltic States and Pskov), across the **Púlkovo Heights** (where it ran within yards of the Observatory and within eighteen kilometres, just over eleven miles, of the Winter Palace), through **Kólpino** (which controlled the railway to Moscow) to **Ivánovskoye** (on the Neva half way to Lake Ladoga), along the Neva to Schlüsselburg (Shlisselburg) and round the southern shore of Lake Ladoga to **Lígovo** on the eastern bank. In the north, the line was drawn several miles south of the Russo-Finnish border from Sestroretsk on the Gulf of Finland across to Nikolskoye on the west bank of Lake Ladoga. In strategic terms, it was hardly significant that the German lines, thus drawn, had enveloped four of the five great country palaces of Petersburg – Peterhof (Petrodvoréts), Gatchina, Tsarskoye Selo (Pushkin) and Pavlovsk. But culturally it may have been important. The German army destroyed them; and the fact that they had been so destroyed made the surviving population of Leningrad revere and restore them with an extraordinary passion.

General Halder's ring may not have been as tight as he would have liked but the only gap in it was (as the crow might fly) a hundred and thirty-five kilometres across the southern bulge of Lake Ladoga – in the winter, by lorry; in the summer by boat – and thence, by a very rough road, south-west into Ókhta on the eastern outskirts of the city. **The Road of Life** (*Doróga Zhízni*), it came to be called. On the north-eastern outskirts of the present City of St Petersburg in the region of Rzhevka, through miles of marshland and obsolete factories, past brick-built arms dumps along the roadside, over the crowded level-crossing which serves as a staging post for long-distance lorry-drivers, through a fresh green birch wood, you come on to the *Ryábovskoye shossé* (Highway). There, at the beginning, they have placed a memorial milestone marked with a star (the symbol of war) and inscribed *Doróga Zhízni*. 'That was a long time ago', said our companion. 'It wasn't even my father's war but my grandfather's.' Memories are beginning to fade.

On 9 November 1941, the total supply of food in Leningrad was flour for seven days, cereals for eight, fats for fourteen, sugar for twenty-two – and no meat at all, except for what might be supplied by such dogs and cats and rats as had chosen to remain. On 20 November, Dimitri Pavlov cut the bread ration to 125 g (about two slices) a day, of which a quarter consisted of 'edible' cellulose. Many people, including a large proportion of the young, would die on those rations. Furthermore, all ration cards had to be renewed, in person, each month, to prevent the cards of the dead being used by the living, and if a card was lost in the course of the month, even if it was stolen at the point of a knife, you had to wait for the renewal date. In the course of November, something like 11,000 people did die – of starvation (described as dystrophy) or dysentery; in December it was 53,000 and in January/February 1942, 200,000 – of hunger alone. (Deaths from air raids and bombardment during the entire Blockade were some 17,000 with 34,000 wounded.)

The first snow fell on 14 October but it was not until 22 November that Lake Ladoga finally froze hard enough for lorries, loaded with supplies, to cross the southern bulge. During that winter of 1941–2, some half a million people were evacuated on the reverse journey. But, meanwhile, all public transport ceased in early December; electricity generators and central heating ran out of fuel; sewage disposal stopped. (At the end of December, temperatures dropped to minus 40 degrees centigrade and you could throw the sewage out of the window but, in the spring, it had to be cleared up again.) In March, there were two direct hits on the main water towers and starving people had to carry every drop of water in buckets from holes in the Neva, the Moika, the Fontanka and the canals. The water could not be boiled and the holes were surrounded, like water holes in the desert, by the bodies of those who had died. The only form of heating was a *burzhúyka* (a little tin stove which would burn furniture, house timbers, waste and was equipped with a flue pipe to stick out of the window). The *burzhúyki*, however, were a severe fire hazard; in January 1942 alone there were two hundred and fifty fires and they burned for days as there was no water to quench them.

Such circumstances gave rise not only to courageous endurance and death but, inevitably, to great temptation and wickedness too. It was the second time in twenty years that the inhabitants of Petrograd/Leningrad had suffered a terrible famine – though, on the first occasion, they had been sharing the fate of the rest of the country, when the droughts of 1920 and 1921 and the consequences of the early Communist economic policies had dried up the supply of food.

So the Hay Market came back into its own, as the black market: by 1942, prices had soared. Things fell, as they always do, off the backs of lorries; there were stories of whole boxes of butter and chocolate for sale; and a few people got fat while most got thin. Gangs appeared who killed for ration cards, for loaves of bread being carried feebly home from the bakeries. And there was – there seems to be no doubt about it – trade in human flesh. Whether it was all cut from corpses, or whether some of it came fresh from kidnapped children, no one now will ever know. But people did fear for their children.

The winter of 1941–2 turned out to the coldest of modern times. And as mortality rose and enfeeblement spread, the disposal of the dead became a growing problem. To begin with, they used coffins. But soon coffins were for burning and people wrapped the corpses of their families in sheets, tied them on to their children's sleds and dragged them through the snow-bound streets. Already they began to rely on the army to dynamite common graves or scoop them with steam shovels from the frozen earth. At the Piskaryovskoye Cemetery on the Vyborg Side, some way out of town, bodies lay waiting for communal burial in heaps so large on each side of the road that two cars could not pass on it nor could they turn round. Pavlov, writing sixteen years later, still found himself reproached by the memory: 'Let the dead forgive the living for, at that desperate time, they were unable to fulfil their duty to the end though the dead were worthy of far better burial rites.'[7]

Summer came, and with it some improvements in the lot of those who were still alive. The bread ration had been slightly increased as supplies came through the Road of Life. Now, in June 1942, an oil pipeline was laid beneath Lake Ladoga, in spite of German air raids, and the power supply returned. There would be terrible hunger in the coming year but less need to freeze. Every spare inch of ground – the Field of Mars, the Summer Garden, any small plot of earth – was put down to potatoes and cabbages; in the meantime, weeds and herbs – nettles, chervil, cow parsley, anything green – were eaten at home and in the fields.

---

[7] Dmitri V. Pavlov in *Leningrad v Blokáde* (Moscow, 1958), quoted by Pavel Kann in *Leningrad, A Guide* translated by Raduga Publishers (Planeta Publishers: Moscow, 1990).

Several hundred thousand more people were evacuated. The population shrank, because of those who left and those who died, and there were fewer to feed; but they returned to work in the armaments factories and, amazingly, to act, to paint, to write (this they had never stopped), to read and to make music. (By the end of the Blockade, in January 1944, 620,000 people remained in Leningrad, 80 per cent of them working, three quarters of them women. Those who had been evacuated amounted to 1,376,000. The dead – the vast majority of whom had been killed by starvation – numbered over 800,000.)

Then, between 12 and 30 January 1943, the Russian army succeeded in recapturing Schlüsselburg and a corridor, some ten kilometres wide, along the southern shore of Lake Ladoga. Units on the Leningrad front met, and clasped the hands of, units fighting on the Volkov front to the east. And now, less than five kilometres from the German lines, the Russians built a railway and a road for thirty-three kilometres along the lakeside which opened once again a land route into the city. Many of the supplies that came in by this new route could now be delivered by train to the Finland Station on the Vyborg Side. Until then, they had travelled by lorry from Ókhta over the *Ókhtinskiy Bolshóy* – now Peter the Great – *most*. It must remain one of the mysteries of the war why the Germans did not succeed in blowing up this bridge.

General Halder's ring was prised open but the Blockade still had another year to run. On 14 January, 1944, the 867th day, the Russians opened an artillery barrage on the German lines and advanced about two miles. The following day, after delivering half a million shells in two and a half hours, they advanced another six miles. And the German army was in retreat. Eight hundred and seventy-two days after they had captured Schlüsselburg, twenty-four salvoes were fired from three hundred and twenty-four guns as a prelude to the announcement by the Russian High

Command that 'the city of Leningrad has been entirely liberated from the enemy's Blockade and his barbaric artillery bombardment'. It was the evening of 27 January 1944.

Although the war continued, Leningraders wasted no time whatever in starting to rebuild their city, in which almost every building had been damaged to some extent and almost every family had been decimated. The damage included the destruction of five and a half million square metres of housing as well as major damage to the Anichkov Palace, to the Russian Museum, to the Winter Palace, the Admiralty and to many buildings along the *Névskiy prospékt* (particularly the *Gostíny dvor* and *No. 30*, the Lesser Philharmonia Hall). In the southern suburbs along *prospékt Stáchek* (Strike) and *Moskóvskiy prospékt*, in the Kirov and Moscow districts, half of all the dwelling units had been destroyed. Art treasures rumbled back into town, buried statues were dug up and reinstated. By the end of 1945, one-third of the damage had been restored; within another four years, there was no ruin left in the city. (There were still ruins outside it but they belong to the next chapter.) And in the reconstruction there was a conscious policy not merely of restoring what had been destroyed but of returning each historic building so far as possible to its pristine state, as created by Trezzini or Quarenghi or Voronikhin, stripped of nineteenth-century accretions.

In April 1944, only three months after the end of the Blockade, an exhibition was opened in part of the old salt warehouse on the Fontanka, at *Solyanóy pereúlok No. 9*, entitled '**The Heroic Defence of Leningrad**'. But there was a strange and still mysterious hiatus in the history of this little museum. In 1949, it was closed – as the museum's own promotion literature explains – in connection with 'the Leningrad Affair'. Its 37,000 exhibits were destroyed or dispersed and its Director, Major Rakov, sent to Siberia. Elsewhere, the blue-and-white signs that had appeared all over the city centre warning people which side of the street was liable to be shelled were painted over. And though Leningrad was awarded the Order of Lenin and declared to be 'The Hero City' in 1945, most of the monuments to its heroism had to wait until the sixties and seventies. (The museum re-opened in 1989, in the same premises and with some – but not all – of its original exhibits and is now called the **Blockade Museum**. Other material relating to the Blockade is displayed in the **Rumyantsev Museum**, on the English Embankment, as part of the Museum of the History of St Petersburg.)

Perhaps for reasons also connected with 'the Leningrad Affair', work on the **Piskaryovskoye Memorial Cemetery** (*Piskaryóvskoye Memoriálnoye kládbistche*) did not begin until 1955. (Stalin died in 1953.) Sixteen years after the Blockade was lifted, on 9 May 1960, the Cemetery (architects Ye. Levinson and A. Vasiliyev) was formally opened.[8] Four hundred and seventy thousand, more than half all those who died during the Blockade of Leningrad, are buried here. Mass graves have an ugly ring about them; yet the architects, the poets, the gardeners, the relatives of the dead have created, with extraordinary reticence, a mass grave for nearly half a million people which is, if anything could be, completely appropriate – sixty-five acres of mounded grass surrounded by a girdle of limes and poplars, with a distant view from the raised entrance over the long, unmarked mounds that spells both peace and desolation. It is, strangely, a great monument, which relies neither on religion nor architecture for its effect. The people involved in its creation had suffered with the people who were buried there and this must be what it relies on: a catastrophe shared in common between the living and the dead.

At the end of the view is a statue (Vera Isayeva and Robert Taurit), six metres high with arms outstretched.

---

[8] Reached by Metro to the *Plóstchad Múzhestva* station; then by bus eastward down *prospékt Nepokoryónnykh* (Avenue of the Unsubdued).

It represents 'The Motherland' holding out a garland of oak and laurel leaves towards the graves. Behind her is a wall, inscribed with a funeral oration by Olga Bergholts, a poet who had lived in Leningrad and broadcast throughout the Blockade: 'Know as you look at these stones that no one is forgotten, nothing is forgotten.' Twenty-first century St Petersburg has not forgotten. But it is hard for it to continue to share the catastrophe with the first intensity. When I first went to Piskaryovskoye Cemetery, people were still bringing offerings to the mounds (the mounds have no names, of course, but they are marked with the year and with either a star, for soldiers, or a hammer and sickle for civilians) that their relatives would have longed for when alive – a small loaf of bread, some potatoes, a cabbage. Now the personal chain is broken and the occasional bunch of plastic carnations lies there from one season to another. But the collective memory has not died; the grass is perfect (nowhere else in Petersburg is there perfect grass – it grows very badly because of the climate and the sandy soil); the paths are weedless, the piped music relayed from the trees (when I was last there, the *Dies Irae* from Verdi's *Requiem*) sympathetically calibrated, the eternal flame still burning. School children come in buses and stand, reverentially, in front of 'The Motherland'. Only the little pavilions at the entrance, which used to contain a museum in miniature, have been emptied of everything but photographs. Hitler's infamous command, the diary of eleven-year-old Tanya Savicheva who recorded day by day the deaths of her family until, on 13 May 1942, only she was left – these are now back in the city, for safer keeping perhaps.

On the other side of town, some eleven kilometres out along the main road due south from the Hay Market, the second monument was erected.[9] At this point in its journey out of the city, the *Moskóvskiy prospékt* forks, the left hand

---

[9] Reached by Metro to *Moskóvskaya* station.

road continuing to Moscow. The right hand becomes the highway to Pulkovo (*Púlkovskoye shossé*) on its way to the airport, the Observatory and Tsarskoye Selo (Pushkin). From the airport, this monument and the twenty-two storey towers that flank it on each side of **Victory Square** – *plóstchad Pobédy* – act as the modern gateway into St Petersburg. The memorial faces south, towards the German lines that had hovered around the Pulkovo Heights.

On 9 May 1975, the thirtieth anniversary of the end of the war, the **Monument to the Defenders of Leningrad** was unveiled. And, if the Cemetery is full of sorrow and reticence, this is fierce and triumphalist. Like the Victory Park (*Moskóvskiy park Pobédy*) that was planted further north along the Prospect in 1945, it was created largely with the donations and by the volunteer labour of Leningraders themselves. 'The Square' is in fact an oblong, in the centre of which is a broken ring; in the centre of the ring is an obelisk one hundred and sixty feet high (higher than Alexander on Palace Square), made of pink granite blocks and inscribed in gold; '1941–1945'. At its base are two monumental bronze figures – a Worker and a Soldier – representing 'The Victors'; on either side of the broad staircase which rises from the south are three more huge groups of toiling statuary: sailors, partisans, builders of the defences on one side, soldiers, salvage workers and volunteers on the other. Beneath is a Memorial Hall where various incidents of the Blockade are recorded in bronze and mosaics and there is a bronze memorial diary on a granite pedestal. The metronome beats, like the one that was broadcast in the intervals between live programmes during the war; there is a violin on display that took part in the relayed concert of the Shostakovich Seventh and a recording is played of the Symphony itself. The architects, this time, were V. Kamenskiy and S. Speranskiy, the sculptor, Anikushin (whose Pushkin stands in *Mikháylovskaya plóstchad*); all three won the Lenin Prize.

That, looked at one way, is the end of the road out of St Petersburg. But, having got there, it is perhaps important to travel back – in time as well as space – towards the heart of the city. The first sight you come to, on the right or east of *Moskóvskaya plóstchad* (Moscow Square), is a declamatory statue of Lenin (1970, Anikushin and Kamenskiy) with, behind him, one of the largest and most threatening buildings in St Petersburg, the **House of the Soviets** (*Dom Sovétov*). This was built just before the war by an architectural collective headed by N. Trotskiy for the new administrative and Party headquarters of the city; additionally, it was packed partly by secret organisations and partly by secret laboratories. The secret organisations have gone, replaced by commercial enterprises, but they say that the secret laboratories – or some of them – have remained.

This complex (though not the statue of Lenin) was part of the 1935 General Plan for Leningrad which set out to shift the centre of the city southwards, away from its Imperialist roots by the river (and, later, away from the front line of the Russo-Finnish War) into the area of heavy industry with which Stalin wished to associate its future. It was to have linked westwards across the industrial area to the 1930s grandiose town planning of Narva Square and Kirov Square (where the murdered Sergey Kirov is commemorated – V. Pinchuk, 1935 – in a statue of somewhat misleading benevolence).

This was to be '**Stalin's Leningrad**', some of which was completed – roughly between Moscow Square and the Moscow Triumphal Gate – before the Germans attacked in 1941. The Plan was taken down from the shelves and put back into practice in the early 1950s, when elaborate designs were made to transform the newly planted 170 acres of Victory Park into a park for the glorification of Stalin; there was to be an overwhelming statue of him in the centre and, at his back, something like the Palace of Culture in the centre of Warsaw with a central citadel and great wings on the lower floors – Bolshevik Baroque, out-Smolnying Smolny. They were about to embark on the serious work – on the plans they had re-named *Moskóvskiy prospékt* as *prospékt im. I. V. Stálina* – when Stalin died.[10] The Palace of Culture, or whatever it was going to be, was never built; the Moscow Prospect kept its name and, at the distant east end of Victory Park now glitters a Sports and Concert complex, dedicated to Lenin and seating 25,000 spectators. (It was completed in 1980 and features wonderful events on ice.) Between Moscow Square and the northern end of Victory Square is an extensive area of residential flats, built in the late 1930s and designed by one of the chief planners of Leningrad during the 1930s, L. A. Ilyin. They are tall and grey and by no means beautiful; but, de-communalised and with private money spent on them, they are said to be comfortable and have become much sought after by richer Russians.

North of Victory Park begins an area of heavy industry that came to St Petersburg at the end of the nineteenth century. The furnace chimneys are still there and some may still be operating. Certainly the huge *Elektrosila* works, greatly expanded during the twenties and thirties, still producing during the bombardment of the forties and expanded again in the fifties to produce turbo-generators, can trace their origins back to 1911. They spread both sides of the Prospect and, like most of the major factories in the city's inner suburbs, still have their own railheads with links to the rest of Russia.

North again, and we come to another structure which, in the reign of Nicholas I, used to mark the entrance to the city of St Petersburg – the **Moscow Triumphal Gate** (*Moskóvskiye voróta*), at the junction of *Moskóvskiy prospékt*

---

[10] The architects' drawings and impressions of the finished buildings are contained in the 1953 edition of *Arkhitektúra Leningráda* published by the Akadémiya Arkhitektúry USSR.

and what was once the Ligovskiy Canal but is now the *Lígovskiy prospékt* (*see* p. 212). Hitler had planned his victorious entry into Leningrad through this arch with a review of his troops in Palace Square before his ceremonial banquet in the Hotel Astoria. In fact the arch had been dismembered and lumps of it used in the defences of the city. And the soldiers who, early in 1944, marched through the space where it had been (and was to be again) were not victorious troops but German prisoners of war.

XV

The Country Palaces

IT IS A TIRESOME JOURNEY by road out of St Petersburg to the west – down the *Voznesénskiy prospékt*, over the Fontanka to the Obvodniy Canal, where the industrial area begins, west along the Canal to pick up *prospékt Stáchek* (Strike Avenue), south through the Narva Gate and then follow your nose to the *Petergófskoye shossé* (Peterhof Highway). There are problems: some chronic, like the railway crossings leading into the biggest factories (it can take half an hour for a freight train to collect or deliver from the Kirov works), some acute (a visiting dignitary, bridge repairs, taking tramways up or putting them down), some endemic (too many vehicles, though road improvement schemes are beginning to come on-stream). So it may be quicker (but not easier) to go by train from the Baltic Station – *Baltíyskiy vokzál* – or, best of all in summertime, by hydrofoil from the pier on the Winter Palace Embankment (*Dvortsóvaya náberezhnaya*).[1]

Along this coast road, on the southern shore of the Gulf of Finland, are three once-Imperial palaces: at Strelna (whose name has not changed); at Petrodvoréts (whose name was changed to remove its German connotations) where the palace, but not the little town, has now reverted

---

[1] The only disadvantage of the hydrofoil is that it goes to Peterhof only. But maybe that's enough. Peterhof can fill a whole day with one kind of delight or another. You can eat there or, like most of the world in summer, take a picnic. Frequent tourist coaches leave from the *Gostíny Dvor* Metro Station. Minibuses (*marshrútki*) for Peterhof and Oranienbaum leave from *Kírovskiy zaród*, *Léninskiy prospékt* and *prospékt Veteránov* metro stations.

to its original name of Peterhof; and at Lomonósov (where the same has happened – the palace has again become Oranienbaum but the town has kept the new name). And because the road was much travelled by the court from 1703 until 1917, scattered along it were the country residences of courtiers and associates. At *prospékt Stáchek No. 45* is the *dácha* of Princess Dashkova – '*Kiryanova*' – now the Kirov Palace of Weddings (probably Quarenghi 1783); and at *No. 162*, the *Aleksandrino* estate (1770s, architect unknown, destroyed in the war and rebuilt in 1960) which had belonged to Count Peter Chernyshov. Just beyond this mansion, the road to Peterhof forks right, hugging the coast, and there at the fork was a resting place (*privál*) for troops and others on their way to and from the palaces. During the Blockade, a common grave was dug here for those who died defending the city.

Strelna

It all began, this royal development of the south coast of the Gulf of Finland, with Peter the Great feeling that he must keep a close eye on his new navy. Being built at the dockyards of the Admiralty, the finished vessels were handed over to admirals at Kronstadt who appeared to be in constant need of being supervised, stimulated and led by practical example. So a small house must be built on the coast in which Peter could rest and entertain. The first such house was built at Strelna (probably early 1700s, architect unknown) in timber, on high ground surrounded by coombs or deep hollows falling away to the shore. It is still standing there, the earliest known example of a Russian Baroque timber building (the proto-typical *dácha*); titivated[2] by Rastrelli in the 1740s at the command of the

[2] 'Somewhat enriched', according to the *Architectural Monuments of Leningrad Suburbs* (Stroyizdat: 1985).

Empress Elisabeth who thought it looked shabby; taken apart and rebuilt in the 1830s; used as a kindergarten after 1917; damaged by the Germans; in 1979 it was restored and refurbished by the Peterhof Museum-Preserve. The house itself, with its decoration and seventeenth-century furniture is practically perfect. So is the setting which does not include the normal public amenities.

After 1709, when the Battle of Poltáva had made the Gulf a securer proposition, Peter began to sketch some improvements to his small house. There were to be fountains and a canal to the sea (the latter was dug north-west of the house and is still there, much overgrown). And there was a complete *usádba* (everything that a house needed for its support – apiary, orangery, fish ponds, kitchen garden, orchards) and a little church which stood on the slope of the hill to the east of the house and was burned down by the Germans. But in a year or two, Peter had greater things in mind – a show piece on his newly pacified Gulf, complete with fountains up to Western European standards, a 'regular' garden interlaced with canals and 'water parterres' and a formidable palace in stone. In 1716, Le Blond won the commission and started to build, some way to the east of the timber house; the water garden was installed and the ground floor laid out when in 1719 he died.

N. Michetti took over but by this time Peter's interest was waning and his enthusiasm had moved westwards down the coast. The stone palace at Strelna was not worked on again until the 1730s, by Zemtsov, and in the 1750s by Rastrelli. In 1797, it became known as the *Konstantínovskiy dvoréts* when it was given by Paul to his second son, Konstantin, who involved Voronikhin and Rusca. Its huge carcass, much pecked at over the years, is still to be seen though (perhaps because so many people have had a go at it) strangely characterless, standing in a wild park above its ruined water garden. Now, however, it is acquiring a new identity – for which $170 million have been allocated – as the maritime

residence of the President of the Russian Federation, to be
known as **The Palace of Congresses** (*dvoréts Kongréssov*).
The exterior is being restored; guest villas are being built or
refurbished in the park; undesirables are being cleared out
of the locality. The interior will be modernised, with the
exception of a small suite of rooms which will include the
library; here it is hoped to gather together again the library
of the last Romanov to occupy Strelna, Grand Duke Dimitri
Konstantinovich, who was shot in the Fortress of SS Peter
and Paul in 1919.

Peter I lost interest in Strelna after he visited Versailles
from which he returned with the conviction that he must
have bigger and better fountains than the king of France.
The problem at Strelna was the local water supply which
did not provide adequate pressure for world class fountains. So he gave the whole estate to his daughter, Elisabeth,
and concentrated on a site further west along the coast
where Braunstein and Le Blond were already building him
a *pied-à-terre* which was to be called Peterhof.

Peterhof
(Nearest Metro for the Baltic Station: *Baltíyskaya*)

The site at Peterhof is split-level, on high ground (to the
south, away from the sea) falling steeply away to sea level
on the north. **The Great ('Upper') Palace** (*Bolshóy dvoréts*)
and the little ('Lower') **Palace of Monplaisir** (*dvoréts
Monplezír*) were begun almost simultaneously in 1714. For
two years, Johann Friedrich Braunstein worked on the
centre block of the Great Palace, on laying out the Upper
Park which lies to the south between the palace and the
main road and on the canal which was to link the lower
park to the sea. But though he wanted to impress – and, to
that extent, be formal – Peter's personal predilection was
always to be by the sea and, while wanting his grander
schemes to out-shine the French, for his personal use he

preferred Dutch. So, down on the coast to the north-east of the Great Palace, he himself designed a small 'Dutch House' to be made of brick pointed Dutch-fashion in lime, full of glass and light (also Dutch-fashion), washed by the sea on its north side and approached through five fountains and a little garden on the south. The fountains were Peter's own creation – a Wheatsheaf in the centre and four Bells (the names relate to the shape made by the fountains, not to the statues giving rise to them). For the house by the sea, he enlisted the help of Andreas Schlüter, who had worked with him on the Summer Palace in the city. Thus was built (1714–23) the central block of the 'Lower' Palace of Monplaisir.

It is important to know that Braunstein was the pupil and associate of Schlüter. Their style, though always described as Baroque, has much more in common with Holland (their use of glass) and the Baltic (the restraint of their façades) than with Italy and southern Europe. At Peterhof, Braunstein's Great Palace (*Bolshóy dvoréts*) was later swamped by the huge additions of Rastrelli. Catherine II, writing fifty years later, describes a visit by her and her husband to Peterhof in 1748. They were 'quartered in the upper rooms of the palace that Peter I had built. It still existed at the time but they had begun to build on both sides of it the two enormous structures of stone which now seem to crush the little house.'[3] (In fact, it was not quite crushed because the form of it can still be detected in the central seventeen windows of the present block – and, of course, it was not as little as all that.)

Monplaisir was also enlarged – on the east, running southwards, by a series of service annexes (bath houses, kitchens, pantries); and on the west, by a building that was later known as 'the Catherine block' (*Yekateríninskiy kórpus*).

---

[3] *Memoirs of Catherine the Great of Russia*, translated by Katharine Anthony (Alfred Knopf: London, 1928).

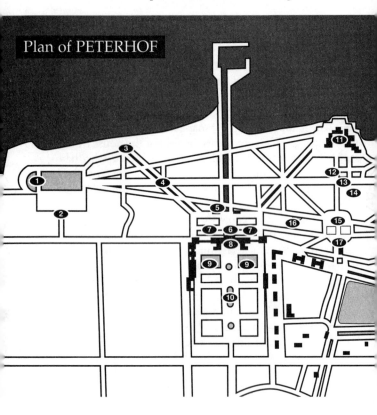

Plan of PETERHOF

1	Marly Palace	12	Sun Fountain
2	Golden Hill Cascade	13	Monument to Peter I
3	Hermitage	14	Umbrella Fountain
4	Eve Fountain	15	Roman Fountains
5	'Favourite' Fountain	16	Triton Fountain
6	Samson Fountain	17	Dragon Cascade
7	Great Fountains	18	Pyramid Fountain
8	Great Palace	19	Gothic Chapel
9	Fountains of the Square Ponds	20	Farm Palace
10	Neptune Fountain	21	*Kóttedzh*
11	Monplaisir Palace		

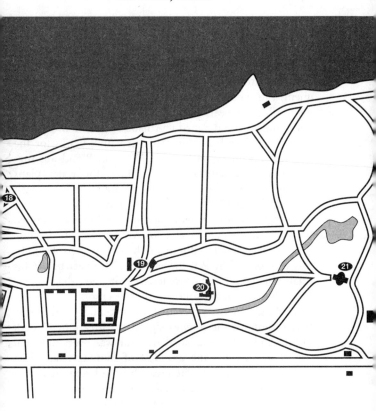

Rastrelli had a hand in both; so (on the west) did Quarenghi and so, also, did a number of others in the nineteenth century. But the central block of Monplaisir, on its lime-shaded terrace above the sea, now looks much as it did in 1721, as planned by Schlüter and implemented by Braunstein. So also does the interior which, given the fact that in the Second World War the Germans treated it with particular barbarity (using it as a soldiers' barracks and burning practically everything that could not be crudely converted to their use), is a miracle of restoration.

Within two years of work being started at Peterhof, Le Blond was sent for (rather late in the day) to strengthen the foundations of the Great Palace (1716) and, subsequently, to take charge of all operations at Peterhof until his death three years later. In that time, he organised the main underground aqueduct (made of wood), broadened the sea canal and organised the structural works for the **Grottos** and the **Great Cascade**. When Le Blond was succeeded by Michetti, fresh from Italy, the water plans became even grander (stimulated, no doubt, by Peter's visit to Versailles in 1717), the projected fountains even larger but, and this seems rather remiss, no one had yet identified the *source* that would be able to provide adequate pressure to make it all work without mechanical pumps. Happily, this was located by Peter when, in 1720, a year before his final subjugation of the Swedes, he visited Ropsha, twenty-five kilometres to the south-west of Peterhof.

Hydraulic activity reached a crescendo in the next twelve months: the Swedes signed the Treaty of Nystadt (1721) and the Great Northern War was over; sufficient water pressure for the grandest of fountains had been found and harnessed. The great Russian hydraulic engineer, Vasiliy Tuvolkov, was retained to run a live trial of the Great Cascade and what was to become the Samson Fountain at its feet. Michetti created two colonnades at the north end of the Samson pool (replaced, in 1800, by Voronikhin's elegant versions with fountains on their roofs). Tuvolkov laid out an 'English Park' in the east of the estate while Braunstein was to produce two more small palaces in the west near the sea to balance Monplaisir: the Marly Palace, floating on one great pond and four small ones, fed from the south by the Golden Hill Cascade which tumbles glitteringly down to it; and the Hermitage, set apart by a small moat and entered, by Peter's invitation only, over a drawbridge. (Both have been perfectly restored and refurbished.) Now it was time to go gardening.

Having out-Frenched the French with fountains, Peter set out to out-Dutch the Dutch with parterres, knots, *allées* and formal plantings. He hired a Dutch master-gardener and sent for labourers from his personal estates near Moscow – between three and five hundred of them – and they began on the 'lower' park. But not fast enough. After 1721, the army being less in demand by the military, regiments of the St Petersburg garrison were co-opted. At the peak, in the five years between the Treaty of Nystadt and the return of the Court to Moscow after Peter's death, five thousand people went daily to work on shifting earth and creating the formal gardens at Peterhof.

So it was in every sense the house that Peter built and, in all its essentials, it was built before he died. The next major development was the arrival of Zemtsov (in the 1730s), with a variety of commissions from the Empress Anne, and Rastrelli (1745–55) with a commission from the Empress Elisabeth to make the buildings bigger and the statues more golden. (Peter's statuary had been in lead. Elisabeth's was gilded.) Catherine's 'two enormous structures of stone' were added by Rastrelli to Braunstein's 'upper palace' and, beyond them again, a long gallery with a wing (*flígel*) at each end – westernmost for the military and easternmost for the Church. On the roof of the western wing was placed a weather cock in the shape of a double-headed eagle; but, lest the wind should blow him in a direction which rendered only one of his heads visible from the ground, he was given three. And so the wind was defeated.

The odd thing is that nobody much seems to have wanted to live in the Great Palace. True, it was not well built and Catherine reports trouble with the floor joists as early as the 1740s. Even the Empress Elisabeth, chiefly responsible for its aggrandisement, seemed to prefer Monplaisir and used the little palace by the sea as her private quarters. But by that time, Zemtsov had added an Assembly Hall on the east of it and Rastrelli had added (1748–9) another range on the west where Peter had once had a vegetable patch.

Monplaisir was also, both before and after her accession, the favourite residence of Catherine II. While her husband was still Grand Duke and heir-apparent, he was given the palace at Oranienbaum, some seven kilometres further west along the coast, as his country estate. But their son (later Emperor Paul), removed from Catherine on the day of his birth and brought up in Elisabeth's Court, used to spend his summer holidays at Peterhof. So Catherine was in the habit of spending the night there on a visit to him. Preferring the 'lower' palace, but so as not to be under the same roof as the Empress, she used to sleep in the 'tea house' (*Cháyny dómik*) on the south-west corner of the Monplaisir *ensemble*.

By 1762, with Elisabeth dead and Peter on the throne, relations between Catherine and her husband were such that she rarely went to Oranienbaum, leaving that role to his mistress and preferring herself to stay at Peterhof. On the night of 27/28 June 1762, 'I was in Peterhof. Peter III lived and got drunk at Oranienbaum . . . He wished to change the faith, marry Yelizaveta Vorontsov and lock me up in prison' (or, alternatively, send her to a convent). There had, for some months, been a plot to force him to abdicate. On 27 June, news of this plot broke and forced the plotters' hands. So 'at six o'clock on the morning of the 28th, I lay quietly sleeping [in the tea house]. It had been a very restless day for me because I knew what was under way. Then Aleksey Orlov [younger brother of Catherine's lover Grigoriy] entered my room and said with great calmness: "It is time for you to get up; everything is ready to proclaim you."' Having found out the cause of the urgency, she dressed herself 'as quickly as possible without making a toilette' and got into the carriage that Aleksey had brought with him. Meeting Grigoriy on the way, they drove into town to the Izmailovskiy Regiment where the soldiers (twelve men and a drummer) had been alerted to swear the oath to her on a cross conveniently provided by a priest who was conveniently present. Within a few hours, Catherine was acclaimed Empress by the Senate and the Synod, both of which had conveniently been assembled to meet her at the new Winter Palace. The precipitate beginning of a long and, on the whole, successful reign had gone more smoothly than any one could have expected.

At ten o'clock on the following evening, 29 June, Catherine, 'after I had had myself named Colonel amid indescribable jubilation', put on Guards' uniform, mounted her white horse and marched all night back to Peterhof, to complete the unfinished business of her husband's future (*see* p. 397).[4] It is the portrait of her at this moment (Vigilius Eriksen, 1762) that hangs in the throne room of the Great Palace.

Nearly twenty-five years later Catherine, as Empress, adopted the tea house and the Rastrelli wing of Monplaisir, commissioned Quarenghi to redesign the complex and used it as the venue for formal dinners and for annual balls for the graduates of the Smolny Institute. The décor (of great elegance and simplicity), the furniture (Russian late eighteenth- and early nineteenth-century *Directoire*) and the porcelain (from the Imperial Porcelain Factory in St Petersburg 1809) are delectable. Small wonder that the **Yekateríninskiy kórpus** (**Catherine Block**) of Monplaisir became, in turn, a favourite place for her grandson Alexander I (whose taste must also be reflected in the furnishings). If it is too difficult to see everything at Peterhof in a day, be sure to see Monplaisir – Peter's house, Catherine's house and Alexander's house by the sea.

---

[4] This description comes from a letter from Catherine to Count Poniatowskiy, in Warsaw, 2 August 1762.

After that, the nineteenth century set in with extraordinary rapidity. **The Cottage** (*Kóttedzh*), on a hill in the eastern corner of the Peterhof estate, was built (1826–9) on the orders of another of Catherine's grandsons, Nicholas I, by a Russianised Scotsman called Adam Menelaws. It must, in its way, have been in advance of its time – an outsize *cottage orné* which took Strawberry Hill Gothic into early Scottish Baronial, capturing on the way something essentially Russian which reappears less elegantly in some of the 'Northern Moderne' villas on *Kámmeniy óstrov*. The furniture, too, was created after drawings by Menelaws in the Gothic taste, carried to extremes in the dining room (but think of Pugin and this looks modest). At all events, it was where a complicated, in many ways reactionary, in others deeply romantic, early Victorian autocrat who was not without some instinct for chivalry thought his wife, the Prussian-born Aleksandra Fedorovna, would like to spend her summers.

The Cottage was Menelaws' last commission and, perhaps, his most important; one of the earliest embodiments of Russian Gothic Revival, it is a bridge between the pure Classicism of Cameron and Voronikhin and the Eclectic architectural vocabulary that characterised Imperial taste for the rest of the nineteenth century. Indeed, Menelaws' own life (a long one – c.1750–1831) was such a bridge. He came to Russia as a master vaulter, to help Cameron build the Cold Baths under the Agate Rooms in Tsarskoye Selo (*see* p. 406). He then worked for twenty years with N. Lvov, sometimes building in the Palladian idiom, sometimes prospecting (successfully) for coal. Finally, he met up with yet a third Scot (William Hastie), who had arrived in St Petersburg as a bridge builder but stayed to become chief architect to Alexander's Court and of the town of Tsarskoye Selo (1808). At Tsarskoye Selo, Menelaws built the Egyptian Gates, the Arsenal, the ruined Chapel and the Llama House for Alexander I. In St Petersburg, he worked with Carlo Rossi on the gardens of the Anichkov and Mikhaylovskiy palaces. At Peterhof, he not only built the Cottage but also designed the park (**Alexandra Park**) in which it stands. He and his new royal patron, Nicholas I, seem to have discovered a shared affinity for the settings of mediaeval knighthood and the novels of Walter Scott – to great architectural effect.

Another beleaguered Emperor spent a great deal of time in the Alexandra Park. Due north of the Cottage, overlooking the sea, Nicholas II built the **Lower Dacha** (*Nízhnyaya dácha*), which was damaged by the Germans and then obliterated on the orders of Khrustchev in the early 1960s. Here in 1904 the *Naslédnik* (the Heir, Tsarevich Aleksey) was born and Khrustchev is said to have detected a tendency among the visiting public to turn it into a place of pilgrimage. But times have changed. Two years ago, the Peterhof Museum placed a statue of the Tsarevich on the site of his birth – the only statue of him anywhere – and now there is talk of reconstructing the house itself for its historical as well as its sentimental association. The Court Journals for the period, recently released into the public domain, make it clear that Nicholas spent about a third of his time in the Lower Dacha, often when the official communiqué indicated that he had left St Petersburg for Tsarskoye Selo. He liked Peterhof better and it was relatively easy to protect him there. It was in the Lower Dacha that in 1905 he signed the October Manifesto which granted a Constitution and, in 1914, the order to mobilize the Russian armies.

So who, one wonders, lived in the Great Palace.[5] To be sure, the present enfilade includes a 'Royal Bedchamber' (based on some 1770 drawings by Felten for a different room) and a 'Dressing Room' (five rooms further on) which

---

[5] The State Museum-Preserve 'Peterhof', in association with Abris Publishers in Finland, have produced for sale at the Palace an exceptionally fine illustrated guide, in the *Treasures of Russia* series. There are conducted tours in many languages, including English.

contains some silver given by Louis XV to the Empress Elisabeth before her succession, when there was an idea that she might marry him. But, essentially, the Great Palace was for show and for formal entertaining. When Alexander II succeeded his father, Nicholas I, his coronation was to be in Moscow in the late summer of 1856. But the foreign delegations arriving to attend the ceremony were received by him at Peterhof – in such state that one of the British delegation, Colonel George Ashley Maude, wrote with a note of English-Victorian disapproval to his wife: 'Where the Russians get their money from is a puzzle, but they certainly spend enormous sums.'

The delegation arrive in a steamer from the city and are driven to 'a sort of summer villa' (probably the Marly Palace) to dress and have lunch. 'On our landing at the wharf we found no end of carriages waiting for us, all the servants in state liveries of a curious old fashion with very large cocked hats.' Refreshed and re-clothed, they are picked up again in different carriages and taken to the Great Palace where they encounter the Austrian delegation, 'Esterhazy at their head, all blazing in diamonds and precious stones'. Lord Granville has quarter of an hour alone with the Emperor; then the Empress and two other ladies ('both very plain') were conducted into the room. She, 'very delicate-looking and tall', was 'well-dressed, some very handsome diamonds all over her train which was light blue'. With a polite exchange in French about the extent of the Colonel's recovery from losing an arm to a Russian sniper at Balaclava and a swish of the train, the audience is over. More protracted is a two-hour drive round the estate – in yet another set of carriages, low-slung for the view; then at six o' clock they sit down for dinner, 'sixty of us, the Austrians, Sardinians, Americans and ourselves'.[6]

---

[6] From the unpublished letters of Colonel George Ashley Maude to his wife.

The slightly cold eye of Colonel Maude did not seem to have taken in much of the *mise en scène*. No mention of Rastrelli's gold and white staircase by which he must have approached the Audience Chamber nor of the marvellous parquet in Felten's Throne Room, nor of the Divan Room with its Chinese wall paper where Catherine II and Prince Potemkin are said to have lounged during the day, nor even (which might have been more to Mrs Maude's taste) of the Drawing Room whose walls are covered in ravishing silk partridges from Lyons. But, though he was unaware of it, Colonel Maude was fortunate. He saw Peterhof before the Germans destroyed it.

In the first two or three rooms in the Great Palace there is an exhibition of how it (and the fountains and other palaces in the Lower Park) has been recreated. The skill, patience and imagination with which this has been accomplished – and the speed – is as much to be marvelled at as the Great Cascade itself. Some objects – statues, urns – were buried when the enemy were seen to be coming; a lot of furniture and pictures were taken inland to relative safety, care being taken even in the rush to secure at least one of everything. But there was not much time and a great deal could not travel at all. Everything left was damaged; much of it was destroyed – some deliberately, as the German army left, some by rough usage.

It is impossible to do justice to the team that has restored it but a few examples may illustrate their achievements: on Rastrelli's staircase, only one of the nymphs was left and the rest have been copied from drawings; for the painted ceiling in the Ball Room, there was nothing left to copy so they went back to Venice, found the original, purchased the right pigments and did it all over again; in the western Chinese lobby, the inlaid floor of *Bois des Îles* has been replaced, rare wood by rare wood, from the original island sources. In Monplaisir, there is among many other marvels a Study lined with ninety-four panels lacquered in the Chinese style by the

Russian icon painters of Palekh. The Germans used these panels for firewood or for lining trenches; three were found – in trenches – and, from these, latter-day icon painters in Palekh have reproduced the missing ninety-one. Most famous of all the fountains, perhaps, is Samson, wresting open the mouth of his lion to release its huge jet of water at the foot of the Great Cascade. (The Battle of Poltáva was won on St Samson's day, 27 June.) The Germans stole Samson and never brought him back. The group was designed by Rastrelli and the stolen version was made in 1801 by M. Kozlovskiy; no drawings were left. But by the end of August 1947 Samson, with his eight dolphins and his four smaller lions on their mound of stones, was being trundled down Nevsky Prospect on his way home to Peterhof while cheering people hung out of the windows and soldiers fired a salute; V. Simonov and N. Mikhaylov had not only created him but scientifically calculated how he must have been.

Human beings, however, cannot be replaced. On 5 October 1941, the Naval Cadet School at Kronstadt despatched five hundred boys aged seventeen and eighteen to intervene in the German occupation of Peterhof. Four hundred and ninety seven of them were killed as they landed. Three miraculously escaped by hiding under the pier. One of the boys who was killed saw what was about to happen and scribbled, on a scrap of paper which he pushed into a cartridge case: 'Those who are alive, sing of us.' The Russians knew of the disaster but no traces of it were found until sixty years later, when museum staff were tidying up the foundations of Monplaisir; then they uncovered the body of an Officer Cadet, identifiable by his boots, a button from his uniform and a set of cleaning tools for his revolver. In the summer of 2001, he was buried with full honours and a march past of Kronstadt Cadets. A small monument has been erected over the grave.

During that year, 2001, one million people (most of them Russian) tramped through the enfilade of the Great

Palace. Six million had been to marvel at the fountains in the parks, upper and lower. Perhaps what they came to marvel at was not primarily the gold and crystal of the fountains nor the grandeur of the grottos but the sparkling gaiety of the place – the gaiety and the humour. The Sun, the Pyramid and the Basket make you smile with delight. So do the furious Chinese dragons spouting all over their chessboard. But the best fountains make you laugh out loud: they souse you when you sit on the wrong bench or try to grab the fruit from the bowl or shelter under the mushroom. Few royal palaces can claim such good or enduring jokes.

Oranienbaum
(Nearest Metro for the Baltic Station: *Baltíyskaya*)

Forty-one kilometres west of St Petersburg, further along the Gulf of Finland, Oranienbaum is short on jokes though it has some surprising splashes of great beauty. It was begun at much the same time as Peterhof, when Peter gave the land to Menshikov and Menshikov, as was his wont, commissioned Fontana to build him a mansion on it (1710). In 1713, Schlüter and Schedel arrived in Russia and, shortly thereafter, Fontana left Russia; Schedel then took his place. There was a suite of rooms where Peter the Great could stay and, in the Great Hall, a Musicians' Gallery. But, as things were liable to with Menshikov, building took some time. Oranienbaum was eventually finished after Peter's death, Menshikov by this time being the effective ruler of Russia.

Not for long, however. His mansion was completed by the consecration of the church in its western pavilion on 3 September 1727. Five days later, Menshikov was arrested, sent into exile, his property confiscated. The estate at Oranienbaum was taken over by the Imperial Ministry of Works which eventually decided to convert it into a Naval hospital. Then, in 1743, it was presented by the Empress Elisabeth to her heir and nephew, the Grand Duke Peter.

What the Grand Duke (later Peter III) acquired was the Petrine mansion of Fontana and Schedel, modified inside by Zemtsov and Yeropkin to accommodate the Naval hospital and modified again by Rastrelli to make it fit for Imperial habitation. It may not have been much to the Grand Duke's taste but, rather than modify it, he did what most Russian sovereigns did after him – built a new palace more to his taste alongside the old one. The result in this case is the fortunate survival of the exterior of the Petrine building, almost without modification. It sits, as it has always sat, on a bluff with terraces descending to a large formal garden which lies between it and the road to *Kopóriye*. On that road, are two lodges or 'lower houses' (*Nízhniye domá*), built between 1710 and 1720. Though Rastrelli made major alterations to the terraces and grand staircase, the façades of the **Great Palace**, with their hipped roofs and princely coronet in the centre, still appear much as they did when Fontana/Schedel created them for Menshikov – perhaps a unique example of Petrine architecture on the grand scale. Whether it is as charming as Petrine architecture on a smaller scale is another matter.

In 1756, a new architect arrived on the scene to participate in building the Grand Duke Peter's own palace – Antonio Rinaldi, fresh from Italy and appointed architect to the Grand Duke's Court. Rinaldi's palace took the form of a miniature (well, fairly miniature; it covered five acres) fortress with five bastions and twelve cannon, to the southeast of the Great Palace on the banks of the River Karest. Inside the bastions were a stone Gateway (*voróta kréposty Peterstadt*, 1757, recently restored), a small stone palace for Peter known as **Peterstadt** (*dvoréts Petra III*, 1756, also restored, with some lovely, relatively simple, eighteenth-century plasterwork) and barracks for the Holstein troops by whom he surrounded himself and with whose repetitive drilling he amused himself. Peter, as his wife Catherine was fully aware, was a case of arrested development – arrested at the moment when he was brought from his native Holstein, at a time in life when small boys used to play soldiers, to Russia as the chosen heir of the Empress Elisabeth and then neglected. He went on playing (German) soldiers until his dying day.

Then in 1762 the second owner of Oranienbaum was taken into custody. Catherine had returned to Peterhof, acclaimed Empress by Guards, Senate and Synod, in the early hours of the morning of 30 June to arrange for the future of her husband and displaced Emperor. He, it is said, had come looking for her at Peterhof and, failing to find her, looked in vain under the bed in the Tea House. Now it was (or so Catherine says) her intention to hold him in suitably modified accommodation in Schlüsselburg, until she could negotiate his safe and harmless return to Holstein. But, while 'decent and suitable quarters' in Schlüsselburg were fitted up for him (and no doubt made more secure), she arranged for him to be taken to the small palace at Ropsha to the south of Oranienbaum and Peterhof. 'He had incidentally asked (in almost incomprehensible French), for his mistress, his dog, his negro and his violin; but in order to avoid a scandal and prevent increasing the excitement of his guards, I had only sent him the last three.'[7] There is no evidence that Catherine intended him to be murdered and some that she regarded it as a misfortune for herself that he was. No sensible woman wants to start her reign as a regicide as well as a usurper. But killed he was, whether accidentally or on purpose, within a few days of his arrival at Ropsha in the course of a drunken brawl with his guard which involved Aleksey Orlov and Prince F. Baryatinskiy. 'My dear Lady, merciful Sovereign! How can I explain or describe what has happened. Never will you believe your

---

[7] Letter from Catherine II to Count Poniatowskiy, 2 August 1762.

faithful servant but I shall speak the truth before God. My dear Lady, I swear by my life I know not myself how that misfortune happened. My dear Lady, he is no more . . .'[8] In a different letter, Aleksey describes the guard-master at the time as Petty Officer Potemkin, 'who is serving without pay'. (Potemkin at the time was twenty-three.)

For about twelve years after Peter III's abdication and death, Catherine and Rinaldi worked together on Oranienbaum with wonderful effect. Like Peter, they did not significantly alter the Great Palace (though Rinaldi could not resist leaving his own mark on the grand staircase and on the interiors of the two pavilion wings). But in the Upper Park, to the north of the Great Palace, they joined in creating what has been described as 'the most miraculous palace of eighteenth-century Russia'.[9] It must certainly be one of the most unapologetically self-indulgent. In the **Chinese Palace** (*Kitáyskiy dvoréts*) they seem to have dared each other to greater and greater visual extravagances – the farewell, for both, to Baroque and the beginning of their Classical period.

There is not much that is Chinese about this palace except the excuse for it which was to house a fashionable collection of Chinese artefacts. The ceilings were purchased in Italy and originally included a Tiepolo in the **Light Blue Hall**, which was taken for safety to Peterhof at the beginning of the war whence it was stolen by the Germans. (It was replaced, in 1980, by one painted by Torelli.) The walls are covered sometimes in chinoiserie, sometimes in sheer Rococo, sometimes (as in the *Steklyárusny Kabinét*) with pale silk velvet embroidered with bugle beads. The floors – Rinaldi's designs – have to be seen to be believed. In the great **Dining Room** (*Bolshóy zal*) are some rare *bas reliefs* in marble of Peter the Great and the Empress Elisabeth

[8] Letter from Aleksey Orlov to Catherine II, 6 July 1762.
[9] I. Grabar, the distinguished Russian art historian, in *Peterbúrgskaya Arkhitektúra v XVIII i XIX vekákh*, reprinted by Lenisdat: 1994.

depicted by Marie Collot, who modelled the head of Falconet's 'Bronze Horseman'. And, miraculously, most of it escaped the attention of the German army whose advance by-passed the coastal projection on which the township of Lomonósov is sited. All they inflicted on Oranienbaum was the theft of the Tiepolo and a direct hit on Peter III's bedroom in Peterstadt. Worse was done to it by Stackenschneider, Bosse and Bonstedt in the nineteenth century who lumbered the Chinese Palace with an extra storey and a heavy entrance hall and converted Rastrelli's Stone Palace into a Lutheran Church.

For a short period, Catherine must have wanted to make a home in the Chinese Palace for she commissioned Rinaldi not only to build her a range of housing for her maids-of-honour (converted in 1852 and 1853 by Bonstedt into the **Chinese Kitchen** – *Kitáyskaya kúkhnya*) but also to design a suite of rooms, on each side of the lakeside entrance, for herself and her son, Paul. These were done in the Chinese style and have kept their original decorations.

As a final flourish there was the *Katálnaya górka*, a Russian invention which in the next century the Americans picked up and turned into the Roller Coaster. It is no longer there, having been stopped in 1801 and finally demolished in 1860. All that remains is the Pavilion (*Pavilión Katálnoy górki*), built between 1762 and 1774, which displays on its first floor a model of Catherine's version of the roller coaster.

In twelve years (1762–74), Catherine spent less than two months here. In April 1792, she gave the whole place to the Naval Cadet Corps and much of the interior decoration, including the floors, was removed. On his succession, Paul, wanting no doubt to get his mother's creation off his hands, gave it to his eldest son, who became Alexander I. But Alexander, after commissioning Rusca, Rossi and Stasov to alter some apartments in the Great Palace, decided to live elsewhere. Thus, in 1831, it came into the possession of the youngest brother of Alexander and Nicholas, the Grand

Duke Mikhail Pavlovich (whose town house was the Mikhaylovskiy Palace, later the Russian Museum) and his heirs. In the course of the century all the formal gardens disappeared and various reconstructions took place, some but not all of which were removed during reconstruction work after the Revolution. Restoration started again immediately after the end of the Second World War with the parks (1946), Peterstadt and the Pavilion in 1952–3 and, finally, the Great Palace. Perhaps rightly, Oranienbaum is treated by the museum authorities as a minor, rather than a major, site, the Chinese Palace open only in the summer and guided tours in Russian only.

Tsarskoye Selo
(Nearest Metro for the Vitebsk Station: *Púshkinskaya*)

Tsarskoye Selo is reached by taking the south-bound road out of St Petersburg, the Moscow Prospect, and following it beyond Victory Square up on to the summit of the Pulkovo Heights where you come to a crossroad. These heights were never captured by the Germans but, if you take the road straight ahead, you come to a mass grave of Leningraders who died defending them; if you take the road to the right, you come to the Airport. For the town of Pushkin (and the palaces at Tsarskoye Selo), turn left. Here on the hillside is a pavilion known as the 'Old Man' (Voronikhin 1809) placed there when the hill was still part of the park. On the right are the restored buildings of the Pulkovo Observatory (still functioning). Cross the River Kuzminka, which formed the front line of the Leningrad defence throughout the Blockade, into territory that was held by the Germans, pass through the Egyptian Gates (Menelaws, 1829–30) and you have arrived.[10]

---

[10] Alternatively, take the train from Vitebsk Station ('*Kúpchino*' platform) to Detskoye Selo.

The problem at Tsarskoye Selo is how not to be overwhelmed. Like Peterhof, it has become the way it is by
an accretion of owners and architectural exhibitionism
throughout the eighteenth century. Like the Winter Palace,
the result is that the main building – the Catherine Palace –
is immensely long, three hundred and twenty-five metres,
and without any significant features in depth, relying even
more than the Winter Palace on the gross Baroque/Rococo
detailing of the windows and its colonnaded segments. Its
beauty lies in three constituents: the interior; the parks and
lakes; and the Cameron wing. Its main interest lies in the
Litséy (Pushkin's old school, now a museum) and the
Alexander Palace (where Nicholas II and Alexandra spent
most of their time after 1905 and to which, after February
1917, they were confined).

Tsarskoye Selo is not so-called because the words mean
'royal village' (though they do) but because it was called
Island Farm by its original Finnish owners. *Saari* being the
Finnish for island which the Russians adapted as *Sáarskaya*
and *Mýza* being the Russian for farm, it became *Sáarskaya
Mýza*. Once it became Royal – which it did when Peter I,
having as usual given it to Menshikov, got cross with him,
took it back and gave it to his wife, Catherine – it was irresistible not to corrupt the Finnish name still further and
turn it into Tsarskoye Selo. This sequence of events also
explains the fact that the Catherine Palace at Tsarskoye Selo
does not mean the Palace of Catherine the Great but the
Palace of Catherine, the wife of Peter the Great and his
successor as Catherine I.

In August 1724, **Catherine I's Palace** (*Yekaterininskiy
dvoréts*) was finished. Braunstein had taken six years to build
a neat two-storey house; Jacob Roosen (presumably from
Holland) had laid out the upper garden (now the terrace on
the north-west side of the palace); there was a party for hundreds of guests and Tsarskoye Selo was christened. During
the next thirty years, there was more or less continuous

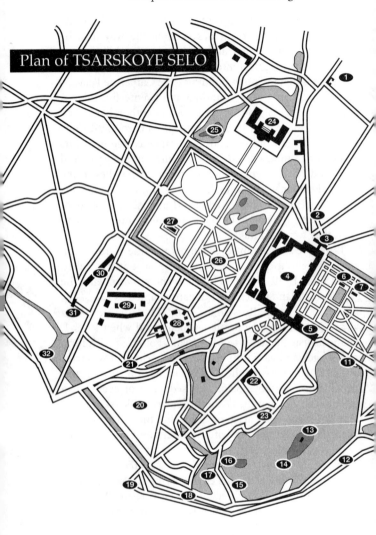

Plan of TSARSKOYE SELO

The Country Palaces

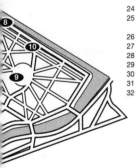

activity: the Empress Anne commissioned Zemtsov, together with his two assistants, Kvasov and Chevakinskiy, to make a grand Baroque entrance courtyard on the north-west and to add a Chapel and a 'Hall' on to each end of Braunstein's house; then bits were pulled down and galleries added until, finally, rather as with the Winter Palace, the Empress Elisabeth sent for Rastrelli and ordered him to transform the pieces into an organic whole. He did – and the result was the present *kórpus* (building), largely complete on the outside in the 1750s.

The next phase of activity came with Catherine II who brought in the Russian Neyelov father-and-son to liven up the formal gardens (the two **Bath Pavilions**, the pseudo-Gothic **Hermitage Kitchens**, the redbrick **Admiralty**, the **Great** and **Small Caprices**) and, in 1779, the English (they came from Hanover *via* Hackney) father-and-son team of John and Joseph Bus(c)h to 'anglicise' the park. At the edge of the park, on the road to Gatchina, she commissioned Rinaldi to design the **Gatchina** or **Orlov Gate** (iron work by Quarenghi in 1787) to celebrate Orlov's return from successfully quelling a plague riot in Moscow; and on the lake Rinaldi was to build the **Chesme Column**, in celebration of a Russian naval victory in the Aegean. (The designs for these were done in 1772 and 1771 respectively and were the first examples in Russia of the triumphal arch and victory column.) So the **Catherine Park** was, in a true sense, the park of Catherine II.

She did not touch the outside of Rastrelli's gorgeous building – but she did not like it. So she changed some, but not all, of its interiors and added (as though she needed one) yet another new wing just a few steps away to the south-west of the great palace, in the purest of pure Classical styles. It was built by the Scottish architect Charles Cameron but the idea was Catherine's own. In 1772, she sent a letter to Falconet, with whom she had often discussed the question of artistic style, to thank him for sending her his sketch book of furniture and mural designs based on Roman ruins. She wrote:

> I should like a design for an antique house laid out on the antique plan. Each of its rooms would have to be decorated according to its particular purpose and furnished in the style of the decorations. The house should not be too large nor too small. I could build a Graeco-Roman house of the sort in my park at Tsarskoye Selo, provided it were not too large . . . I desire all this and need your help to indulge my fancy, for which I will naturally pay.

Falconet suggested Clérisseau and Clérisseau suggested a giant pseudo-Roman palace and a giant fee; there was a row – and a pause in Catherine's planning. By 1778, she was on to **Charles Cameron**, by what route no one has yet discovered. He let her believe that he was a Jacobite by sympathy and related to the last Stuarts. But, more importantly, he built her the house she had described to Falconet, perhaps the most enchanting building in Tsarskoye Selo.

Little is known about Cameron, before he started to work for Catherine in 1779.[11] He is unlikely to have been connected to anyone connected with the Stuarts but did spend several years in Rome around 1768, where he may have met Clérisseau, and he published a 'subscription' volume of drawings of '*The Thermae of the Roman Emperors*' in 1770. There is no record of anything he built before he was employed in Tsarskoye Selo. And, once there, he did not get on with Catherine's other Classical practitioners, particularly Quarenghi and Felten. But his partnership with the Bushes was entirely successful, to the extent that he married

---

[11] For information about Charles Cameron, we have relied largely on material gathered together for the Arts Council exhibition of his work in 1967–8. Also on *Charles Cameron: An Illustrated Monograph on his Life and Work in Russia* by Georgiy Loukomskiy, adapted into English by Nicolas de Gren (Nicholson & Watson: London, 1943). In the last few years, the *Dictionary of National Biography* has carried an entry on Cameron.

one of Bush's daughters, which may account for the miraculous way in which the Cameron Gallery (*Kamerónova galleréya*), small as it is, is allowed to dominate the 'English Park' below and to be so wonderfully grafted on to the meadows by the Hanging Gardens at its side. On grounds partly of skill but partly also of economy, Scottish stone masons at the time earning a great deal less than Russian ones, Cameron imported about seventy craftsmen and their families from Leith, many of whom settled in Russia for the rest of their lives – much to the chagrin of the British Ambassador who thought that Scotland could ill afford to lose them.

What astonishes about the **Cameron Gallery** and the **Agate Rooms** attached to it is the way in which they combine the dour and puritan nature of Cameron with the aesthetically sensitive but self-indulgent nature of Catherine. ('I deserve it', she had written to Falconet.) Thus the vaulted ramp of the **Hanging Gardens**, architecturally so elegant, was created to help the by this time corpulent Empress to pass through sweet-smelling meadows to a viewpoint from which she could survey her burgeoning park without being troubled by steps; the **Cold Baths** beneath the Agate Rooms, with Menelaws' vaulting (until Menelaws arrived from Scotland, they had failed several times to keep the ceiling up), their fine, under-stated *bas reliefs*, marble detailing and gilded taps were designed to provide a swimming pool for her refreshment. And, should the water really be cold, it would be heated with metal balls.

In the main **Agate Hall** itself, the fireplaces, of which there are several, are slim and delicate, each one like a series of cameos, while the walls are decorated with Grecian urns of various stone (agate) from the Urals – porphyry, jasper, malachite, labradorite and lapis-lazuli. (The floors and elaborately inlaid doors, by the way, were brought from the Petersburg house of Aleksandr Lanskoy, one of Catherine's lovers who had died early of fever. It was through these floors that the German officers, who during their occupation used these rooms as their Mess, chose to drive the waste pipe of their lavatory.) The Sleeping Room for *siestas* has its private library; the Oval Room has a curved fireplace like the inverted side of a vase; the cantilevered Spiral Staircase from Baths to Hall spires on an oval not a circle; the Gallery, suspended high above the Park and lined with bronze busts of ancient philosophers, was available for walks or card-playing should the weather be inclement, and incidentally provided a great stimulus for the bronze-casting industry of St Petersburg. It is hard to think of any respect in which refined taste and personal comfort could have been better satisfied.

When he worked outside, Cameron remained careful to cosset his Imperial patron. In the Catherine (Lower) Park, he built the **Pyramid** (1781) as a mausoleum for Catherine's dogs including Sir Tom Anderson, her favourite greyhound. But, for the rest, he seems to have confined himself to implementing the plans of others – in particular, rescuing the **Chinese village** (1782) and octagonal pavilion-pagoda from a certain confusion in which it had been left by the Neyelovs and Rinaldi in the early 1770s.

When he worked on the interior of the Catherine Palace itself, the puritan in Cameron seems to have been suppressed perhaps by the challenge of having to compete with Rastrelli. Cameron designed two distinct areas inside the long building which are separated by Monighetti's white **State Staircase** (*Parádnaya léstnitsa*, 1860s): the private apartments of Catherine II (not yet restored) at the south-west end within a convenient stroll to her Gallery and the apartments of her son Paul and his wife, Maria Fedorovna, towards the north-eastern (Church) end. To reach either, visitors (as they did in Catherine's time) have to pass through Rastrelli at his most ebullient. The southern wing is still under restoration but Rastrelli's **Great Hall** or **Ballroom**, preceeded by the dining-room of the *Kavaléry* (holders of Orders), is not only open but restored to the point where you can see your face in its walls a thousand times over. Forty-seven metres long and seventeen metres wide, it is the ultimate demonstration of the power of glass to magnify and multiply; two tiers of windows on each side and at the ends with, between them, pier glasses illuminated by miniature chandeliers. Rastrelli's patron was the Empress Elisabeth and he was providing for her passion for fancy dress balls. As an exercise in interior decoration, it is hard to beat.

So, too, is his **Amber Study** (*Yantárnaya kómnata*), five rooms down on the other (north) side of the entrance staircase. Frederick I of Prussia gave the original panels (of mosaics executed entirely in amber) to Peter I in 1716 and they were delivered to St Petersburg by their creator, the architect and sculptor Andreas Schlüter (who stayed for many years to work with Peter in his Summer Palace and in Peterhof). Peter installed them in his Winter Palace and, in return, presented Frederick with 248 soldiers, a wine cup he had made himself and the lathe on which he had made it. When Peter's daughter, Elisabeth, demolished her father's Winter Palace to make room for her own, she required Rastrelli to remove the amber panels to Tsarskoye Selo and install them there. And when the Germans left Tsarskoye Selo in 1944, they took the opportunity of recovering their amber panels and removing them. They have never been found. But the museum authorities have not allowed the matter to rest. For fifty years or so, they collected amber from the beaches of the Gulf of Finland. By the year 2002, they had been able to replace all but two of the panels and those two were expected shortly. The return of the Amber Study has been achieved by a fine alliance between Russian craftsmen and German money, donated by Ruhr-Gas.

Through the Picture Hall (114 of its 130 pictures were successfully concealed from the Germans), past its magnificent Delft stoves, through two other rooms, and one arrives at Cameron's suite for the Grand Duke Paul and his wife, Maria Fedorovna. There was much at stake for Cameron in this commission for, in 1780, he had been 'lent' by Catherine to the young couple to build them their own palace at Pavlovsk. Each room is breath-taking and, in its own way, extravagant; Cameron has no Ballroom but he has a **Green Dining Room**, a **Blue Drawing Room**, a **Chinese Blue Drawing Room**, a **Choir Ante-room** (*predkhórnaya*), still swathed in the original silk swans and peacocks which were woven by a secret process in a remote village and hidden throughout the war, a **Bedroom** (*opochiválnya*) with no less than eighty-four porcelain columns and eight concealed doors, and several service rooms. Who wins, Rastrelli or Cameron, is a matter of taste but it is a magnificent contest.

Leaving the Palace courtyard by the north-facing side gate ('Dear visitors, Administration of the State Museum at Tsarskoye Selo offers apologies for troubles caused by the restoration works' – to which one is moved to propose a speech of humble thanks), on the right is the **Memorial Museum of the Lyceum** (*Litséy*). The building was commissioned by Catherine II from Ilya Neyelov (1789–92) as a new wing for her grand-children beyond the Church (to which it is attached by a flying bridge so that the Empress could pass from the *piano nobile* of the Great Palace without having to negotiate stairs). In 1811, one of her grandchildren having been Emperor for ten years, the Imperial schoolroom was reconstructed by V. Stasov and opened (19 October) as the Tsarskoye Selo *Litséy* which removed in the 1840s to the *Kámenno-ostróvskiy prospékt No. 21* and, under the name *Aleksándrovskiy Litséy*, continued until the Revolution to provide a liberal education to boys aiming mostly at the Civil and Foreign services. Pushkin was among the first intake of thirty boys in the heady years of 1811 to 1817; many of his generation became Decembrists or, at the least, supporters of the movement. Between 1966 and 1974, the building has been returned to something like its original appearance, including the Newspaper Room, Great Assembly Hall, classrooms and library on the first floor and sleeping quarters (each boy had his own cubicle with his name above the door) on the second. Like the main palace, and the little town around it, the *Litséy* was gutted in the War; the first glass window to be replaced in the town of Pushkin was in Pushkin's dormitory.

Immediately on the right of the *Litséy* as you leave the Palace is the small, very early (1734) **Church of the Sign** (*Známenskaya tsérkov*), designed by Zemtsov and built by I. Blank. Except for its bell tower, it looks more like a New England chapel than a place of Russian Orthodox worship and it replaced an even earlier wooden church, burned down after being struck by lightning, at whose consecration Peter I and Catherine had been present in 1717. It is extraordinary to think that Rastrelli was designing his golden Ballroom only twenty years after Zemtsov's little church was built at the Palace gates.

A little further on is a small garden (A. Menelaws, 1818), which had been given to the *Litséy*. In the centre of it, to mark the hundredth anniversary (1899) of the poet's birth was placed a **statue of Pushkin**, pensive on a bench, by Robert Bach. Pushkin always said that he needed to be in the country if he was to compose and, though Tsarskoye Selo is only modified country, this statue of him has a curious power; it could be Keats' 'foster-child of silence and slow time /. . . Fair youth beneath the trees, thou canst not leave / Thy song, nor ever can those trees be bare'[12] – though it is doubtful whether Bach had ever heard of Keats. Before the Germans arrived in 1941, 'Pushkin' with his song was buried six metres deep and survived the war.

On down towards the Egyptian Gates and St Petersburg, but not very far, is the **Alexander Palace** (*Aleksándrovskiy*

[12] *Ode on a Grecian Urn* by John Keats, first published in London in 1820.

dvoréts), on the left of the road. Catherine II commissioned the new building from Quarenghi (1792) for her grandson, Alexander, on his marriage to Princess Louise of Baden but, though the interior was finished in the year of Catherine's death (1796), the exterior was left unfaced until 1800 and one has the impression that nobody took much care of it until the accession of Nicholas I (1825), who used to bring his family here in the spring. Once again, the Imperial family had turned their backs on the huge palace of their predecessors, leaving it for pomp and receptions, trying, in vain of course, to create a private house (which was almost as huge). Alexander III did not live in either palace after his accession, though his eldest son (Nicholas II) was born in the west wing of the Alexander Palace while his father was still Tsarevich.

In fact, if the Alexander Palace 'belonged' to anyone, it was to Nicholas II, his wife and their children who came there intermittently from 1896 onwards and based themselves there all year round, rather than in the Winter Palace, after the Revolution of 1905. So there began again the process of 'personalising' someone else's palace, regardless of the merits of what was being replaced with what. Out went Quarenghi's interiors (or such of them as Nicholas I had left); in came the mahogany panelling and furniture to match of Messrs Meltzer & Co (1903–6), most notably in the Billiard Room which connected, through its balcony, with the Empress's private apartments and where, so her critics maintained, she used to listen unseen to her husband's discussions with his ministers; on the newly-stripped walls of the east wing were erected black-painted deal panels; stuffed Edwardian sofas, brass bedsteads and many, many, icons appeared in the bedroom; in the private sitting room, two rooms along, the pride of place went to a Pre-Raphaelite *Annunciation* presented by Queen Victoria to 'Alix'.

This was the room where, on 3 March 1917, Alexandra heard the news of her husband's abdication, while Nicholas

was being shunted in his military train back and forth
between Bologóye and Mogilév. Five days later, General
Kornilov arrived to place her and her children, who were
suffering from measles, under arrest – as a precaution, he
explained, to protect them from the excesses of the Soviet
and the revolutionary guards. And the following day they
were joined by Nicholas.

For the next five months, the family were confined to
the Alexander Palace, the 'Children's pond' to the west of it,
and the immediately surrounding ground. Nicholas read
and smoked, read aloud to his children, shovelled snow
and sawed wood. At the end of the month, Kerensky came
to see them, as nervous as they: in the Drawing Room in
the south-west corner, 'the Imperial family . . . were standing near the window, in a small perplexed little group.
From this cluster of frightened humanity, there stepped
out somewhat hesitantly a man of medium height in military kit who walked forward to meet me with a slight,
peculiar smile . . . I told them not to be frightened but to
have complete confidence in the Provisional Government.'
He probably meant it. But he was not in control of events.
After the 'July Uprising' of the Bolsheviks, Kerensky
decided that he had better remove the family from the
vicinity of St Petersburg. On 31 July, the day after the
Tsarevich's thirteenth birthday, they were despatched by
train across the Urals into Siberia where they were to stay
at Tobolsk. They were on their final journey to
Yekaterinburg and in less than three months Kerensky, too,
was a fugitive.

Now in that Drawing Room there is an exhibition of
pathetic objects: the uniform worn by the Tsarevitch when
he used to join his father at the front; a photograph of them
all with the man who (as his biographers tell us) did nothing to save them, Nicholas's first cousin, George V. Visually,
it is nothing very much – even Quarenghi's great exterior.
Few people seem to visit, though the west wing is now open

to the public.[13] But as a historical site, with all its sad echoes, it is perhaps the most important building in Tsarskoye Selo.

Four hundred metres due north, and about the same distance to the west of the main road to St Petersburg, is the 'Cathedral' of St Fedor (1910–12 by V. Pokrovskiy), built because the Empress felt the family needed a personal church. Next to it is a monument (perhaps the only one?) to Nicholas II, a bust on a pedestal signed by Niktopolion, which was unveiled in July 1997. To the east, Pokrovskiy constructed a miniature Kremlin (*Fédorovskiy gorodók*) in Early Russian style, intended as a barracks for the Emperor's bodyguard. (The bodyguard went to war and the barracks became a hospital where the Empress and her two eldest daughters worked as nurses.) So the compulsion to build only stopped with the Empire itself.

Gatchina
(Nearest Metro to Baltic Station: *Baltíyskaya*)

Gatchina, overlooking a wonderful stretch of water called the White Lake, is perhaps the least sympathetic of the country palaces; it is also the furthest away from the centre of St Petersburg. Nor was its beginning particularly propitious. In 1765, three years after giving birth to his son, Catherine II gave a small house which had belonged to Peter I's sister to her lover of twelve years, Grigoriy Orlov.

Rinaldi finished the **Palace of Gatchina** (*Gátchinskiy dvoréts*) in 1781. Orlov never lived there although he remained close to Catherine, in spite of his marriage, until his final illness in 1783, when Catherine gave this palace to her son, Paul – a curious move in the light of his resentment of her lovers. But, far from rejecting it, he adopted it with a strange passion and made it the centre of his intense

---

[13] Details of the Alexander Palace, and the opening times, are available on *www.alexanderpalace.org*.

military life – both before and after his accession. It is often said that Paul was not the son of Peter III but of an early lover of his mother's, Sergey Saltykov; but when one pictures him drilling his Russian soldiers, forced miserably into German-style uniforms, up and down the square at Gatchina, it is tempting to detect a genetic connection with the second owner of Oranienbaum and his much-drilled Holsteins.

At the time Paul acquired it, Rinaldi's Gatchina consisted of a three-storeyed centre block with two symmetrical single-storey wings, one for the kitchens and one for the stables (the Orlov brothers being distinguished breeders of horses). Rinaldi had also made a park, part of which was for hunting, and laid out lawns in front of the house. From 1793, Paul employed his favourite architect, Brenna, to make the place more to his taste: some of Rinaldi's interiors went; the open galleries on the first floor of the central block were filled in; the single-storey wings became heavier with another storey added; the lawns were covered with gravel and turned into a parade ground, the whole being surrounded by a moat and entered by drawbridges. By the time he had finished, the exterior of Gatchina looked much as it does now and very different from the Gatchina of Orlov/Rinaldi.

Following Paul's election as Grand Master of the Maltese Order, N. Lvov built for him (in 1790) a second palace (the **Priorate Palace** – *Priorátskiy dvoréts*) on the banks of the smaller but still beautiful Black Lake, to the south-east. A strange building, like a large North German farm house, it has a Gothic spire sprouting from the middle of it. After Paul's death it became the property of his wife who, in 1828, gave it to her second son, by that time Nicholas I. Nicholas made Gatchina his headquarters for a short time every year when he attended the Autumn Manoeuvres at Krasnoye Selo. In the mid-nineteenth century, Nicholas brought in the architect Kuzmin to raise the wings again and add a floor to the signal tower (1844). In 1857, the Hunt was transferred from Peterhof to the park at Gatchina which resulted in various buildings associated with it being erected in the park, including huntsmen's lodges and accommodation for the animals to be hunted: deer, wild boar and European bison. Sixty years later, the Hunt had become a game reserve but there was still a wolf in the park at Gatchina which was killed by the Grand Duke Mikhail on leave from the front in 1915.

Nothing much happened to Gatchina during the reign of Alexander II, who does not seem to have stayed there at all. But, after his assassination in 1881, his son and successor, Alexander III, went to live at Gatchina for the next two years, giving Karl Marx the opportunity to describe him as 'the P.O.W. of the Revolution'.[14] (Later, he returned to St Petersburg for official duties but, even then, he and his wife preferred the Anichkov Palace where they had lived before their accession.) From 1881, until his own death thirteen years later, it remained the preferred country house of himself and his wife, Maria Fedorovna (sister of the British Queen Alexandra). This meant that, for their two youngest children – the Grand Duke Mikhail (*see* p. 303) and his sister Olga – Gatchina was the place they always associated with home.

When Rinaldi built the wings, they had one floor. When Brenna built them up, he added a second floor, as it were of maids' bedrooms; he also renamed the 'Stable' wing as the 'Arsenal' wing in recognition of Paul's minimal interest in horses and total preoccupation with soldiers. Kuzmin added a third, rather grander, floor. The result was that the country apartments of Alexander III and his family were the maids' bedrooms, slightly improved, of Brenna's Gatchina. Mikhail was three and his sister not yet born

---

[14] The comment appears in the 1882 Russian edition of the Communist Manifesto.

when they moved into them. Mikhail as a bachelor went on having rooms there in almost Spartan conditions except for the attentions of a fleet of servants that continued to occupy the palace right up to the Revolution. When he married the twice-divorced Natalya Wulpert (who became Countess Brasova) in 1912, he was banished (to England) by his brother Nicholas II and his wife forbidden to live on Imperial premises. This is why, on his return to Russia at the beginning of the First World War, he, his wife, his son and step-daughters went to live in a small wooden villa in the town of Gatchina, Nikolayevskaya Street *No. 24*, which he had bought for Natalya before their marriage and exile. It was here, and not in the palace, that he was living when he became Emperor of Russia for a day.

Early on 25 October 1917, Kerensky abandoned his cabinet in the Winter Palace and fled to Gatchina where General Krasnov, commander of the Third Cavalry Corps, had fallen back in front of the Bolshevik forces with a few hundred Cossacks still loyal to the Provisional Government. By 8.00 p.m. on the evening of 1 November, the Bolsheviks were in control of Gatchina, sailors arrived at Nikolayevskaya Street to confiscate the Rolls Royces and Kerensky went into hiding in a peasant cottage.

Three days later, the Grand Duke and his family were arrested and taken into Petrograd; Kerensky vanished (he eventually left Russia in May, the following year); and a mob, mostly revolutionary sailors looking for Kerensky, had invaded the palace and started to loot the contents.

Another person was intermittently involved in the palace at Gatchina at this time: Count Valentin Zubov, descendant of the brother of Catherine the Great's last lover and an art connoisseur. Together with Aleksandr Polovtsov and the art historian Peter von Weiner, he had decided in March that the only way of saving the artistic heritage of St Petersburg from present and future turbulence was without delay to transform the most important Imperial palaces into museums that were the property of the nation, cataloguing their contents, beginning the process of conservation and, at the same time, opening them to the crowds of people who wanted to see how the emperors of Russia had lived. By June 1917, they had co-opted a number of students from the city's art institutes and started work on the multitudinous contents of Gatchina. (They were later to do the same for the Winter Palace and Pavlovsk, *see* p. 420.) The local Soviet at Gatchina, however, proved too much for Zubov. It encouraged crowds to force their way in, break the windows, pull down the curtains and tapestries and to appropriate anything that was portable. The situation eventually stabilised and Gatchina was a museum, of a kind, until the Second World War.

If it suffered at the hands of the Bolsheviks, it was nothing to what it suffered from the Germans. In January 1944, the Germans set fire to the palace before they left, entirely destroying the interior and leaving the walls. I myself saw the message they left behind for the Russians: we're leaving, it said, and you won't enjoy what you get back. But within eighteen months, the park (which perhaps is the loveliest part of it) was open again to visitors; in 1977, with the aid of old plans and detailed watercolours by the 'Painters of Interiors' school, work started on the inside which can now be seen throughout the year. Views of Gatchina in the eighteenth century are displayed in the Yellow Drawing Room.

Pavlovsk
(Nearest Metro for the Vitebsk Station: *Púshkinskaya*)

Pavlovsk is different. It is personal rather than Imperial, in the sense that it was created by the Grand Duke Paul and his second wife, Maria Fedorovna, before their accession. It stems from a single vision; the last person to make any significant changes was Maria Fedorovna herself who spent much of her widowhood there and who left it to her

Plan of PAVLOSK

The Country Palaces

1 Round Hall *(Designed by Cameron, late 1790's; built by Brenna 1799-1800)*
2 Venus Pond
3 Island of Love
4 River Slavyanka
5 Apollo's Colonnade *(Architect: Cameron 1783, altered 1817)*
6 Cold Bath
7 Centaurs' Bridge *(Bridge by Cameron 1799; Centaurs introduced by Voronikhin 1805)*
8 Temple of Friendship *(Designed by Cameron 1779)*
9 Iron Bridge with Vases *(Designed probably by Rossi, c.1823)*
10 Visconti's Bridge *(Designed probably by Voronikhin 1808, executed by Visconti)*
11 Pill-Tower *(Architect: Brenna 1795-7)*
12 The Three Graces Pavilion *(Designed by Cameron 1801)*
13 Aviary *(Designed by Cameron 1782-3)*
14 Gazebo *(Designed by Rossi)*
15 Monument 'To my Parents' *(Architect: Cameron 1786-7. Sculptor: Martos)*
16 Apollo in Temple *(Designed by Cameron 1780)*
17 Mausoleum of Paul I *(Designed by Thomas de Thomon 1805-10. Sculptor: Martos)*
18 Rose Pavilion *(Architect: Voronikhin 1805 for Prince Bagration)*
19 Deers' Bridge
20 The Palace *(Architects: Cameron 1782-89, Brenna 1789-1796)*

youngest son, Mikhail, as his family home (though he chose to live in a *dácha* in the park). It has been adored by everyone connected with it. Maria Fedorovna's grandson, Konstantin Nikolayevich, loved it and wrote a history of it to mark its centenary. Her great-grandson, Konstantin Konstantinovich, poet, pianist and one-time President of the Academy of Sciences (who died in 1915), sorted its archives and, in 1903, allowed it to be extensively photographed. His sister, Queen Olga of Greece, and the family of his eldest son, Prince Ioann, were the last people to live in Pavlovsk. So it escaped the attentions of reigning royalty, of Stackenschneider and all the 'improvers' who came after him.

Thanks to **Aleksandr Polovtsov** and the man whom Lenin appointed to be the first Commissar of Education, **Anatol Lunacharskiy**, it more or less escaped the attentions of the Red Guards too. Polovtsov went to find Lunacharskiy in a room in the Winter Palace, surrounded by known and unknown artists, 'dirty and hirsute', who 'seemed to be debating grave questions'. When they drifted off to another meeting, Polovtsov got hold of him and told him that Pavlovsk must be saved. He remembered that Lunacharskiy replied: 'Yes, I think it should be saved. What needs to be done?' And he answered: 'Name me commissar of the palace.' So he arrived at Pavlovsk, early in November 1917; he persuaded the Queen to leave, invited the chairman of the local Soviet to come to a meeting at the 'new house of the people' and began to reconstitute the rooms exactly as Maria Fedorovna had put them together. The records were still in her library. With Lunacharskiy's continuing goodwill, but with a great many hazards from other quarters, in June 1918 Pavlovsk was opened to the public 'two or three times a week'; long lines of people queued to put on *tápochki*[15] and shuffle respectfully round. Pavolvsk was 'nationalised' but safe.

---

[15] The new curators invented these, made of old rugs, to protect the inlaid floors, for which purpose they are still used today in almost all museums.

Two or three weeks later, Nicholas II, his family and his servants were assassinated in the basement in Yekaterinburg. The next day, in Alapayevsk in the Urals, three sons of Konstantin Konstantinovich, together with several of their cousins and the Empress's sister, the Grand Duchess Elisabeth, were thrown alive into a disused mine shaft and after them were thrown hand grenades and heavy timbers. Peasants who heard them crying out in pain and singing hymns reported that some took several days to die.

By the end of October, it was time for the Polovtsovs to leave too. The 'dangers and disappointments of the Bolshevik regime' were, by now, such that, 'if I had stubbornly stayed, I could easily have put in jeopardy the work to which I had devoted myself for more than a year. So, by the end of October, without a passport or any papers . . . almost as if we were criminals, we crossed the frontier to Finland.'[16]

If it had not been for the German invasion, Pavlovsk would have come down to the Russian public as a perfectly beautiful, almost perfectly preserved, vast but not outrageously so, late eighteenth-century country house, built over a period of thirty-four years – from the arrival of Cameron in 1780 to the death of Voronikhin in 1814. But the Germans not only came but left; and, as they left, poured petrol over the floors, placed explosives in strategic places, and set the palace on fire. The returning Russians found a hulk that had been burning for ten days; the roof was gone; the premises were mined; the walls were scorched and every valuable object that had been left in it, down to the door knobs and the butterfly collection, had been taken away or destroyed.

When in the summer of 1941 the museum staff at Pavlovsk had seen the Germans coming, they started to pack. Through July and into August, they packed thirteen

---

[16] A. Polovstov, quoted by Suzanne Massie in *Pavlovsk, The Life of a Russian Palace* (Hodder and Stoughton: 1990).

thousand objects which were despatched inland with meticulous care: 'Two curators . . . took time to draw diagrams of how the bronze rims and crystal garlands on the chandeliers were positioned before they were carefully taken apart and packed; the crystal in cotton, the bronze in hay.' The original designs and historical documents were sent to safety. From each set of furniture, several examples were taken; the rest were left behind and duly broken, sawed, dismembered by the German occupiers. Objects too heavy to transport were buried – Greek and Roman antiquities were dragged on carpets to the far corners of the cellars, walled in and disguised, so that they avoided destruction. Other statues, in the park and the pavilions, were buried several metres deep below their plinths and they too escaped. The result was that, at Pavlovsk, more than at any of the other country palaces, it was possible to return to the reconstructed palace the majority of the objects and decorations with which Paul and Maria Fedorovna had filled it. It took many years and involved training new craftsmen as well as curators and restorers. (A special school for this purpose was opened in Leningrad in 1943, while the city was still blockaded.) It also involved searching for stolen pieces, in Russia and in Germany. It is not finished yet.[17]

What did they restore? The main body of the house was designed by Cameron – planned in 1780, foundation stone laid in 1782, habitable in 1783, not finished (and then by Brenna) until 1796. It may have been inspired by Palladio's unfinished Villa Tressino, which was also used by Thomas Jefferson as a model for the University of Virginia – three storeys high, built on a rectangle around a central hall and crowned with a rotunda which is supported by sixty-four slender Doric columns. The interior is mainly the work of three people: Cameron himself; Brenna, who was put in

---

[17] For this account of the evacuation and return, we have relied mainly on Suzanne Massie.

charge of the work by the Royal couple after 1786 though Cameron continued to design for the park; Voronikhin, who was called in by Maria Fedorovna (by this time Dowager Empress) to help repair the ravages of a fire in 1803 and stayed to make his own exquisite contribution. Quarenghi worked there (though mostly on the floors); so, mostly on the ceilings, did Pietro di Gonzaga who employed a sort of *trompe l'oeil* which enlarged and enhanced the spaces created by Cameron and Brenna; Carlo Rossi returned two or three times (he had worked as Brenna's assistant in the early years) and importantly in 1824 to create the Library. But the theme remained Cameron's, taken direct from the early years of Rome.

When Paul acquired Gatchina in 1784, he gave Pavlovsk to his wife and from that time onwards, her taste predominated – in the gardens, in the pavilions of the park and in the house itself. Unlike her mother-in-law, she, with her husband, had travelled in Europe (for fourteen months between 1781 and 1782), staying at Versailles with Louis XVI and Marie Antoinette (who loaded her with gifts and of whom she made a real friend) and in Rome, where they bought fireplaces (much to Cameron's chagrin), pictures (including Hubert Robert and Salvatore Rosa) and antiquities (rather better quality than those bought by Peter I and Elisabeth). Four of the more important pavilions in the park are the **Temple of Friendship** (Cameron, 1782), the **Monument to my Parents** (sculptor I. Martos, 1807), the **'Mausoleum' of Paul I** (who was buried in the Cathedral of SS Peter and Paul but whose mourning family is depicted in this pavilion by Thomas de Thomon, 1808–9) and the **Rose Pavilion** (built by Voronikhin originally for Prince Bagration but acquired by the Dowager Empress in 1811. It became the centre of her life at Pavlovsk.) The statue of Paul (I. Vitali) in the courtyard, facing down the lime avenue, was put up in 1851 by his grandson Alexander II, many years after Maria Fedorovna's death. It is a sympathetic portrait and reflects the fact that the man who lived here may, for a few years, have been happy – at all events, a less tormented character than the one who later occupied Gatchina and the Engineers' Castle.

Pavlovsk can be seen in a day – though do not hurry; in fine weather, the river and the park, which was once part of a hunting forest, are as delightful as the house itself. Almost every room is beautiful (with the possible exception of the Egyptian Hall). But two quite small ones have a claim to be called the most beautiful of all: **Maria Fedorovna's Boudoir** (Brenna and Voronikhin), next to her Library, which includes a 1774 *forte piano* made in London; and the **Little Lantern Study** ('*Fonárik*'), with its half-domed bay window, cool green walls and warm, spinning floor panels. Almost every detail in this room is designed by Voronikhin who reminds one, sometimes, of how fat men dance – with exceptional lightness. The man who designed Kazan Cathedral here takes your breath away with the elegance of his waste paper basket.

All these palaces around St Petersburg, built outside the city as a retreat and a rest from it, are nevertheless an integral part of it. What binds them together is the unreality of the whole ensemble, the city equally with the princely holiday homes around it. Many writers have likened it to the drop curtain of a giant theatre, painted on canvas. Looking across the Neva from either bank and closing one's eyes, it would be no surprise to open them again to find the curtain raised and nothing left in view but grey skies, a vast expanse of river and a few bleak cottages belonging to Finnish fishermen scattered about some islands in the estuary. But the visitor will take away three different and vivid impressions: of the superhuman energy and foresight of St Petersburg's creator, of the magnificence of its appearance and of the fortitude of its inhabitants.

Appendices

Some Important St Petersburg Architects

Sovereign	Prevailing Style	Architect	Born/Died	Principally active in St Petersburg
Peter I 1682*–1725 * Effective sovereign from l696	Petrine Baroque	Jean-Baptiste Le Blond	1679–1719	1704–1719
		Dominico Trezzini	1670–1734	1706–1734
		Georg Mattarnovi	?–1719	1710–1719
		Giovanni Fontana	?	1710–1714
		Gottfried Schedel	1680–1752	1710s
		Andreas Schlüter	1655–1714	1710s
		Theodore Schwertfeger	?	1713–1733
		Johann Braunstein	?	1714–1723
		M. Zemtsov	1688–1743	1718–1743
Anne 1730–1741 Elisabeth 1741–1761	High Baroque	M. Zemtsov	1688–1743	1718–1743
		I. Korobov	1700–1747	1730s
		Bartolomeo Rastrelli	1700–1771	1740s–1761
		S. Chevakinskiy	1713–1780	1750–1760s
		A. Kvasov	1718–1772	1750s–1760s
		M. Rastorguyev	1725–1767	1756–1767
Catherine II 1762–1796	Early (Russian) Classical	S. Chevakinskiy	1713–1780	1750–1760s
		A. Kvasov	1718–1772	1750s–1760s
		A. Kokorinov	1726–1772	1762–1772
		Antonio Rinaldi	1710–1794	1756–1785
		J.-B. Vallin de la Mothe	1729–1800	1761–1788
		Yu. Felten	1730–1801	1764–1780s
		I. Starov	1745–1808	1776–1780s
		Charles Cameron	c.1740–1812	1779–1811
		N. Lvov	1751–1803	1780–1790s
		Giacomo Quarenghi	1744–1817	1782–1814
Paul I 1796–1801 Alexander I 1801–1825	Classical	V. Bazhenov	1737–1799	1798–1799
		Vincenzo Brenna	1745–1820	1785–1802
		A. Voronikhin	1759–1814	1790s–1814
		L. Rusca	1758–1822	1800–1818
		A. Zakharov	1761–1811	1800s
		Thomas de Thomon	1760–1813	1800–1811
		Adam Menelaws	c.1750–1831	1787–1831
		A. Mikhaylov II	1773–1849	1802–1830s
		V. Stasov	1769–1848	1811–1843
		Carlo Rossi	1775–1849	1816–1834

Sovereign	Prevailing Style	Architect	Born/Died	Principally active in St Petersburg
Nicholas I 1825–1855	Classical	Adam Menelaws	c.1750–1831	1787–1831
		V. Stasov	1769–1848	1811–1843
		Carlo Rossi	1775–1849	1816–1834
	Late Classical	Charlemagne Brothers	1782–1861	1820s–1830s
		Auguste de Montferrand	1786–1858	1817–1858
		Paul Jacquot	1798–1852	1829–1840
		A. Bryullov	1798–1877	1831–1845
	Theatrical	Alberto Cavos	1801–1863	1840s–1860s
	Eclectic	Yefimov Brothers	1799–1864	1839–1853
	incl. Neo-Renaissance;	K. Thon	1794–1881	1843–1851
	Neo-Russian;	Harald Bosse	1812–1894	1840s–1860s
	Neo-Gothic;	A. Stackenschneider	1802–1865	1833–1860s
	Neo-Moorish	N. Benois	1813–1898	1850s–1860s
	and Oriental	Ludwig Bonstedt	1822–1885	1847–1858
Alexander II 1855–1881	Eclectic including *Style Moderne*	A. Stackenschneider	1802–1865	1833–1860s
		N. Benois	1813–1898	1850s–1860s
		Ludwig Fontana	1824–1894	1870s
		Maximillian Messmacher	1842–1906	1880s
		P. Syuzor	1844–1910	1880–1910
Alexander III 1881–1894 **Nicholas II** 1894–1917	*Style Moderne* incl. Eclectic, *Jugendstil* and *Art Nouveau*	P. Syuzor	1844–1910	1880–1910
		L. Benois	1856–1914	1890–1914
		A. Hohen	1802–1865	1833–1860s
		F. Lidval	1870–1945	1902–1914
		G. Baranovskiy	1860–1920	1901–1915
		M. Peretyatkovich	1872–1916	1908–1912
	Neo-Classical	I. A. Fomin	1872–1936	1912–1930s
Lenin/Stalin 1918–1953	Various incl. Proletarian Classical; Constructivist; Historicist; Functionalist and International Modernist	I. A. Fomin	1872–1936	1912–1930s
		V. Stchuko	1873–1939	1910–1923
		A. Gegello	1891–1965	1925–1932
		G. Simonov	1893–?	1920s–1930s
		L. Ilyin	1880–1942	1920s–1930s
		A. Nikolskiy	1884–1953	1925–1953?
		N. Trotskiy	1893–1940	1930s
		D. Krichevskiy	1892–1942	1930s
		Ye. Levinson	1894–1968	1930s–1950s
		I. I. Fomin	1904–1989	1930s–1985
		V. Kamenskiy	1907–1975	1950s–1970s
Currently practising in St Petersburg		N. Yavein, M. Reinberg, O. Kharchenko, V. Popov and J. Zemtsov		

Practical Information

The City Tourist Information Centre (Городской Туристско-Информационный Центр) is to be found on the south side of *Névskiy prospékt* at *No. 41*, the old Beloselskiy-Belozerskiy Palace just east of the Anichkov Bridge. Telephone: 812 (St Petersburg) 311 2843; it has a web-site: www.tourism.spb.ru and an e-mail address: tourism@ctic.spb.ru

The Centre provides free information including: visa support; hotel reservations; rent-a-car; guide and excursion services; books and maps. It also provides a seasonally updated *Guide* in English and Russian which includes: opening times of museums; details of the main Orthodox churches and (where applicable) times of services; addresses, booking office opening times and performance times for the main concert halls and theatres; restaurants 'listed by cuisine'; information about 'nightlife' and casinos. It warns you, very sensibly, not to get drunk in public and to beware of pick-pockets.

During the celebrations of the tercentenary of the foundation of the city, an 'official jubilee web-site' provides current information on festivals, exhibitions, theatres and concerts on www.300.spb.ru Information is updated monthly.

Getting About

Traffic is bad and getting worse. Tour groups, large or small, will most of the time be conveyed in buses, large or small. And, in spite of the traffic, this is a great convenience. But for individual travellers whether taking a day off from the tour or making an independent visit to the city, the most reliable way of getting about is to walk (therefore comfortable and, in winter, warm, shoes) and/or to use the Metro.

The **Metro** is modern (the first line opened at the end of 1955 and lines are still being extended), quiet, reliable and architecturally interesting. A Metro map is on p. 430 of this *Guide*. There are four lines: *Kírovsko–Výborgskaya* (Кировско–Выборгская),

Moskóvsko–Petrográdskaya (Московско–Петроградская), *Névsko–Vasileostróvskaya* (Невско–Василеостровская) and *Pravoberézhnaya* (Правобережная). They interchange at six points: *Tekhnologícheskiy Institút 1/2, Sennáya Plóstchad/ Sadóvaya, Névskiy Prospékt/Gostíny Dvor, Plóstchad Vosstánya/ Mayakóvskaya, Plóstchad Aleksándra Névskogo* and *Dostoévskaya/ Vladímirskaya.* (The reader will note that the transliteration system used differs marginally from our own.) To enter a station, you must buy a counter (for one trip) or a plastic card (for multiple trips) from the station hall. The Metro opens at 5.45 a.m. and closes at 0.15 a.m.

But the Metro will not get you everywhere you are liable to want to go. In particular, it does not go to the Smolny area; the area round the Hermitage and the Admiralty, including the Mariinskiy Theatre, is also badly served. For these, you can go by bus or tram but a taxi may be preferable.

So individual tourists, who do not have the facilities of organised tours and tour buses, will almost certainly need on occasion to take **taxis**. In theory there are some official, yellow, taxis but they are rarely to be seen. The simplest thing to do is choose an occasion which is not important and a destination that is not very distant, stand on the edge of the street and flag down an ordinary car with no passengers in it. If it stops, it will be a taxi; if it doesn't, get out of the way quickly. If all goes well and you find a way of communicating with the driver, take his mobile number and use him/her as you would a local hire-car – always having agreed a price first. It will not, relative to other things, be expensive. Even a day out at Tsarskoye Selo will be bearable if you split the fare four ways. Good hotels will certainly have similar arrangements which they will lay on for you but they are liable to be more expensive.

The other form of transport that is useful – and delightful – is on the water. For getting your eye in, during the summer months take a **boat** round the waterways. Regular boat tours leave every half hour from the Fontanka Embankment (*náberezhnaya rekí Fontánki No. 44*), near the Anichkov Bridge. These are cheap, with a Russian commentary. Individual **water-taxis** can easily be hired from moorings at various points along the Moika, between the *Zelyóny most*

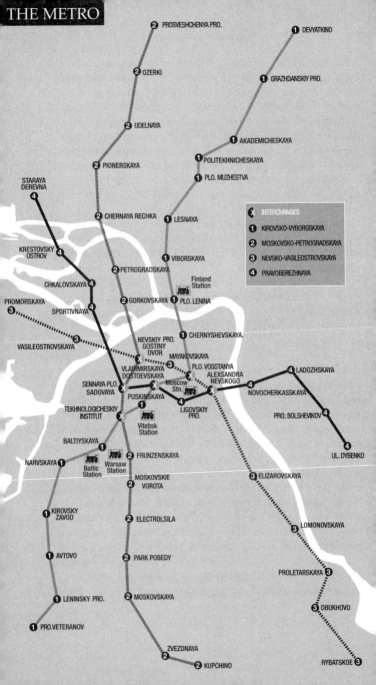

THE METRO

PROSVESHCHENYA PRO.

DEVYATKINO

OZERKI

GRAZHDANSKIY PRO.

UDELNAYA

AKADEMICHESKAYA

PIONERSKAYA

POLITEKHNICHESKAYA

PLO. MUZHESTVA

STARAYA
DEREVNA

CHERNAYA RECHKA

LESNAYA

KRESTOVSKY
OSTROV

VIBORSKAYA

PETROGRADSKAYA

CHKALOVSKAYA

Finland
Station

PROMORSKAYA

SPORTIVNAYA

GORKOVSKAYA

PLO. LENINA

CHERNYSHEVSKAYA.

VASILEOSTROVSKAYA

NEVSKIY PRO.
GOSTINY
DVOR

MAYAKOVSKAYA

VLADIMIRSKAYA
DOSTOEVSKAYA

PLO. VOSSTANYA
ALEXANDRA
NEVSKOGO

LADOZHSKAYA

SENNAYA PLO.
SADOVAYA

Moscow
Stn.

NOVOCHERKASSKAYA

PUSKINSKAYA

TEKHNOLOGICHESKIY
INSTITUT

LIGOVSKIY
PRO.

PRO. BOLSHEVIKOV

Vitebsk
Station

BALTIYSKAYA

UL. DYBENKO

NARVSKAYA

FRUNZENSKAYA

Baltic
Station

Warsaw
Station

ELIZAROVSKAYA

MOSKOVSKIE
VOROTA

KIROVSKY
ZAVOD

LOMONOVSKAYA

ELECTROLSILA

AVTOVO

PROLETARSKAYA

PARK POBEDY

LENINSKY PRO.

OBUKHOVO

MOSKOVSKAYA

PRO.VETERANOV

ZVEZDNAYA

RYBATSKOE

KUPCHINO

INTERCHANGES

1. KIROVSKO-VYBORGSKAYA
2. MOSKOVSKO-PETROGRADSKAYA
3. NEVSKO-VASILEOSTROVSKAYA
4. PRAVOBEREZHNAYA

(more usually referred to by its former name, *Politséyskiy most*) and its junction with the Griboyedov Canal near the *Mársovo pólye*. Journeys by water-taxis can, within limits, be bespoke; you can ask to cross the Neva to the Fortress and the Petrograd side. Depending on the route, they will take between an hour and an hour-and-a-half and cost in the region of $50 (or its rouble equivalent).

Hydrofoils (*strélky*) leave, in summer, at frequent intervals from the Palace Embankment (*Dvortsóvaya náberezhnaya*), in front of the Winter Palace. They go direct to Peterhof (taking about half-an-hour) or up and down the Neva.

Alternative ways of getting to the **Country Palaces** are:

* Strelna and Peterhof (Petrodvoréts) – frequent excursion buses from the *Gostíny Dvor* metro (parked between the station exit and the department store)
* Tsarskoye Selo (Pushkin) – suburban train from the main-line Vitebsk Station (Витебский Вокзал) to Detskoye Selo (Детское Село- г. Пушкин), having taken the metro to *Púshkinskaya* (a particularly elegant metro station)
* Pavlovsk (Павловск) – this is the next train stop on the main line after Detskoye Selo. The station at Pavlovsk, one and a half kilometres from the Palace, was built originally in 1837 and in the 1850s became famous for the concerts in its restaurant. It was called Vauxhall, after the London pleasure gardens, which became the Russian name for 'station' (*vokzál*–вокзал). Orchestra conductors included Glinka and Johann Strauss, who came for nine successive seasons and took not just Pavlovsk but Petersburg by storm, conducting his own music, including 'The Pavlovsk Polka', themes from the new operas of Wagner and, in 1865, some dances by the very young Tchaikovsky.
* Oranienbaum (Ораниенваум- г. Ломоносов) – train from the suburban-line Baltic Station (Балтийский Вокзал), having taken the metro to *Baltíyskaya*
* Gatchina (Гатчина) – train, also from the Baltic Station.

Resorts on the north coast of the Gulf of Finland, such as Repino, are reached from the main- and suburban-line Finland Station (Финляндский Вокзал) on the Vyborg Side (*Výborgskaya*

Storoná). The station surroundings have been reconstructed
several times since Lenin's famous arrival there at 11.10 p.m. on
3 April 1917; the first occasion was to make room for the monument to Lenin (V. Stchuko and V. Gelfreykh, sculptor S. Yevseyev,
1924), the last occasion being the end of the 1950s when the station itself was rebuilt (N. Baranov, P. Ashastin and I. Lukin, 1960)
and a granite landing stage erected on the embankment.

Churches, Worship and Choral Singing

Many, though not all, the main churches of St Petersburg are open
again for worship. Some, like the Cathedral of SS Peter and Paul, the
Smolny Cathedral, St Isaac's and the Church of the Resurrection of
Christ (Saviour on the Blood) are open only as museums.

The following are the most important churches to hold daily
Orthodox services:

- Kazan Cathedral (собор во имя Казанской иконы Божией
  Матери, usually referred to simply as Казанский собор) on
  Névskiy prospékt
- Vladímir Cathedral (собор Владимирской иконы Божией
  Матери) on *Vladímirskaya plóstchad*
- St Nicholas Cathedral (николо-богоявленский морской
  кафедральной собор) on the Kryukov Canal.
- The Preobrazhenskiy Cathedral (Преображенский собор)
  on *plóstchad Preobrazhénskiy*
- Trinity Cathedral (троицкий собор) in the Alexander Nevsky
  Monastery which has an exceptional choir.

A popular place for Sunday services is the Temple of the Icon
not made by Hands (*Khram, Spása Nerukotvórnovo Óbraza*), the
church where Pushkin's funeral was held, inside the Imperial
Stables facing on to *Konyúshennaya plóstchad* off the Moika.

A fine choir can be heard at the **Armenian Gregorian** Church,
at *Névskiy prospékt Nos. 40–42*.

Lutheran services are held in:

- St Catherine's Church in *Bolshóy prospékt* on *Vasíliyevskiy
  óstrov*

- St Peter's Church at *Névskiy prospékt Nos. 22–4*
- The Evangelical-Lutheran Church of St Mary on *Bolsháya Konyúshennaya No. 6.*

Roman Catholic services are held in:

- St Catherine's Church at *Névskiy prospékt Nos. 32–4*
- The Church of the Holy Mother of Lourdes at the former French Embassy on *Kóvenskiy pereúlok No. 7*
- The Cathedral of the Assumption of the Holy Virgin on *1-ya Krasnoarmeyskaya No. 11*, south of the Fontanka and east of *Moskóvskiy prospékt.*

There is choral singing at the **Synagogue** on *Lérmontovskiy prospékt*. The **Mosque**, on *Kronvérkskiy prospékt No. 7*, is open for daily worship. There is a **Buddhist Temple** on *Primórskiy prospékt No. 91*, not far from the little footbridge between Yelagin Island and the north shore of the Gulf of Finland.

For singing, there is most importantly the **Kapella** (капелла имени М. Н. Гдинка) on *náberezhnaya rekí Móiki No. 20*. This is not a church but the college of the oldest professional choir in Russia. It performs sacred music with organ and choir but also works from the classical repertoire. There is a booking office, open midday to 7 p.m.

Museums
It is best to confirm their opening times at the City Tourist Office. The important thing to check is the days of the week on which they are open/shut. In particular, the Country Palaces have all their sites open only on a few days in the week. (At Tsarskoye Selo, the Catherine Palace is closed on one day, the Alexander Palace on another, the *Litséy* on a third and the Cameron Gallery on a fourth; the same is true, *mutatis mutandi*, at Peterhof.) There will almost certainly be three days when they are all open. Good multi-lingual (including English) audio tapes are available in the Pushkin Museum, the Russian Museum, the Hermitage and the Fortress Museum.

The latest information on museum opening times is contained in the seasonal *Guide* given out by the Tourist Office. Information

on the opening times of the Country Palaces is contained in a separate section at the back of the *Guide* under 'Suburbs' or
'Outskirts'. But beware weekends. All tourist sites are massively
more crowded on Saturdays, Sundays and public holidays and this
is particularly true of ones with an open-air ingredient like those
mentioned in the chapters on the 'Other Islands' and the Country
Palaces. With big urban museums such as the Hermitage and the
Russian Museum, you can often avoid queuing if you go at 'off-
peak' times like mid-morning or mid-afternoon.

The Tourist Office can also supply the details and addresses of
at least three, first class, **Chess Clubs** – the Chigorin City Club, the
St Petersburg State University Club and the Prometei Club; three
Yacht Clubs – The River Yacht Club of Trade Unions, the Navy
Yacht Club and the Water Motor Club; and the largest **Ice Hockey
Stadium** in Russia on *prospékt Pyatilétok*, near the *prospékt
Bolshevikóv* metro in the *Málaya Ókhta* district, where matches
are played all year round.

Food and Water

Do not drink water from the tap. And boil, very thoroughly, the
water in which you wash fruit and vegetables. Never put ice in
your drinks unless you have made it yourself from boiled or bot-
tled water.

The main food store of the city is **Yeliséyev** (Елисеев) at
Névskiy prospékt No. 56. It has been housed in its present *Style
Moderne* quarters for a hundred years. (In Soviet times it was
re-named *Gastronóm No. 1*.) A cross between Fortnum and Mason
and Harrods Food Halls, it is perhaps more elegant than either.

More modest food shops in the centre of town are usually to be
found in the bottom (semi-basement) of apartment houses. They
are open early and late and you can buy – in a limited range – more
or less anything from wine, through fruit and vegetables, salami
and eggs to soap powder. They are not cheap. Better quality,
though not necessarily cheaper, food is to be found at up-market
markets like the *Kuznéchny rýnok* on *Kuznéchny pereúlok*, near
Vladímirskaya metro, the *Nekrásovskiy rýnok* at the junction of
Lígovskiy prospékt and *úlitsa Nekrásova* near *plóstchad Vosstániya*

metro, the ***Sennóy rýnok*** off the *Moskóvskiy prospékt* near the *Sadóvaya/Sennáya plóstchad* metro and the ***Sýtninskiy rýnok*** off the *Kronvérskiy prospékt*, (fairly) near the *Górkovskaya* metro.

There is increasing choice – and an increasing range of prices – for meals in restaurants. In general, good value for money seems to be available in ethnic Georgian, Azerbaijani, Armenian, Caucasian and Ukrainian restaurants, often to be found on the lower-ground floors of nineteenth-century buildings.

Weather

The best weather is from late May until the end of August, when the days are long and average temperatures range between 15 and 18 degrees. The 'White Nights' begin at the end of May when it is light enough to read at midnight and the air in the *Mársovo pólye* is heavy with the scent of lilacs. This is the loveliest time. But it is also the time when tourists choose to visit and, for the moment, St Petersburg is short of hotel accommodation. So you may decide to go in the winter – from December through until mid-February – when the days are very short and very cold (minus 8.5 degrees centigrade average temperature which may drop to minus 30 degrees or below). It is bitter but there are people who like frost and snow; for them, there is skating, indoors and out; and the Country Palaces look like the second act of the *Nutcracker*.

It is usually wise to avoid October/November and March/April. In late autumn, it rains and there may even be floods (though the days of catastrophic floods from the Neva are probably over); in late spring, the thaw is neither one thing nor the other and is thoroughly disagreeable.

Currency

Most people in St Petersburg, including restaurants and water taxis, now expect to be paid in roubles. To which end, it is probably most sensible to take sterling travellers' cheques (as British banks still do not buy or sell roubles). There seems to be less trouble changing sterling, as opposed to dollar, cheques. Sterling or dollar notes are still acceptable and, occasionally, preferred to roubles. But this now tends to be the exception.

Health Care

Twenty-four hour emergency health care is provided by the British American Family Practice at *Gráfskiy pereúlok No. 7*, telephone 327 6030, by the American Medical Center at *Serpukhóvskaya úlitsa No. 10*, telephone 326 1730, and by the Euromed Clinic at *Suvórovskiy prospékt No. 60*, telephone 327 0301.

Maps

Whatever aids your guide book may contain, you will still be happier with a pocket map. The best available in good map and travel shops in this country (and perhaps any other) is in our experience the Insight Flexi-Map of St Petersburg; laminated and virtually indestructible, it can be bought separately from the Insight Guide.

On *Vasíliyevskiy óstrov*, a street running north and south across the main prospects is called a *líniya* (line). Each side (or line of houses) is allotted a different number; thus a street may appear on the map as *2-ya–3-ya líniya* (2nd–3rd line). Elsewhere, streets whose names begin with *1-ya, 2-ya* etc were usually part of an old military *slobodá*; it simply means first, second etc.

Dates

Until mid-February 1918, the calendar in use in Russia and the USSR was the Julian Calendar. In the nineteenth century, this was twelve days behind and, in the twentieth century, thirteen days behind, the Gregorian Calendar in use in the West. The dates in this book, like most of the dates quoted by museums and commentaries in St Petersburg, conform to the calendars in use i.e. they follow the Julian Calendar up to mid-February 1918 and, thereafter, the Gregorian. With well-known dates – such as the defeat of Napoleon at the Battle of Waterloo, the outbreak of the First World War or the October 1917 Revolution – this may produce surprises and apparent inconsistencies. But any other approach is probably even more confusing.

Alphabet

All street names, station names and other directions are given in the Cyrillic (Russian) alphabet. Travellers in St Petersburg will find it a great help if they can learn the letters before they arrive. (*See* The Russian Language, opposite).

The Russian Language

The Russian Alphabet

Аа(Aa)*   Бб(Bb)   Вв(Vv)   Гг(Gg)*   Дд(Dd)   Ее(ye)*
Ёё(yo)*   Жж(Zz*)   Зз(Zz)   Ии(Ii)*   Йй(*)   Кк(Kk)
Лл(Ll)   Мм(Mm)   Нн(Nn)   Оо(Oo)*   Пп(Pp)   Рр(Rr)*
Сс(Ss)*   Тт(Tt)   Уу(oo)*   Фф(Ff)   Хх(kh)*   Цц(ts)
Чч(ch)*   Шш(sh)*   Щщ(stch)*   Ыы(*)   Ээ(Ee)*   Юю(Yu)*
Яя(ya)*

Ьь (soft sign, only follows consonants and adds an almost inaudible 'i' to them).

Ъъ (hard sign, follows consonants only in the middle of a word, separating the sounds of two letters).

* See transliteration table below:

Russian / English Transliteration

In transliterating Russian into Latin characters, we have adhered basically to the Library of Congress system but have allowed ourselves a few changes. The table below includes those Latin characters whose substitution for their Russian equivalent needs some explanation.

Latin character	Russian equivalent
A	А а A short open sound pronounced as in French or Italian. Never as in English 'act' (short, closed) or 'father' (long, open).
Ch	Ч ч as in 'church'. Never as in 'loch' or 'character'.
E	Э э as in 'set'.

G	Г г Hard as in 'get', never soft as in 'George'.
I	И и 'Ee' as in 'deep' or 'leak'.
Kh	Х х as in 'loch'.
O (stressed)	О о Short as in 'not'.
O (unstressed)	О о More like 'u' as in 'but'.
R	Р р Pronounced hard as the Spanish 'r'.
S	С с Always 'ss' as in 'seek' but never as in 'measure'.
Sh	Ш ш as in 'sheet' or 'bash'.
Stch	Щ щ We spell it 'stch' to distinguish it from the German 'sch', which corresponds to the English 'sh'. Hence *plóstchad* (square), often spelt *plóshchad*.
U	У у Short 'oo' as in 'took'. Never long as in 'loom' and never as in 'fury'.
Y	Ы ы / Й й as in 'boy' i.e. corresponding to the German 'j', as in *junker*. But in the middle of words, more like 'i' just before you add an 'l' as in 'bill' or 'build'.
Ya	Я я as in the German *ja*.
Ye	Е е as in 'yet'.
Yo	Ё ё as in 'yonder'.
Yu	Ю ю as in 'union'.
Zh	Ж ж as in 'measure' – or 'j' in French *janvier*.

Russian / English Vocabulary

In pronouncing Russian words, the stress is all-important. In the wrong place, it may change the meaning altogether e.g. zámok = castle, zamók = lock.

Below are a number of Russian words used in this guide, together with their transliteration and their meaning:

English Transliteration	Russian Original	English Translation
Bírzha	биржа	Exchange (of commodities or stocks)
Bolshóy, -áya, -óye	большой, -ая, -ое	Large, Great
Dom	дом	House
Dvor	двор	Yard
Dvoréts	дворец	Palace
Flígel	флигель	Wing, Annexe
Gávan	гавань	Haven, Harbour
Gostínitsa	гостиница	Hotel
Gostíny dvor	гостиный двор	Merchants' Yard, Department Store
Iglá	игла	Needle, Spire
Kadétskiy kórpus	кадетский корпус	Military Cadet School
Kámenny (adj.)	каменный	Stone
Kanál	канал	Canal
Kanávka	канавка	Ditch, Small Canal
Kazármy	казармы	Barracks
Kládbistche	кладбище	Cemetery
Krépost	крепость	Fortress
Kórpus	корпус	School, College, Body (of a building)
Lávra	лавра	Important Monastery
Létniy (adj.)	летний	Summer
Líniya	линия	Line, Row (of stalls; in some streets, of houses)
Lug	луг	Meadow
Mály, -áya, -óye	малый, малая, малое	Small, Little
Morskóy, -áya, -óye	морской, морская, морское	Maritime

Most	мост	Bridge
Náberezhnaya	набережная	Embankment
Óstrov	остров	Island
Pámyatnik	памятник	Monument
Park	парк	Park
Passázh	пассаж	Arcade
Pázheskiy kórpus	пажеский корпус	Corps of Pages
Pereúlok	переулок	Lane
Plóstchad	площадь	Square
Pólye	поле	Field
Prospékt	проспект	Prospect, Avenue
Réchka	речка	Stream, Little river
Reká	река	River
Rýnok	рынок	Market
Sad	сад	Garden
Sobór	собор	Cathedral
Storoná	сторона	Side
Teátr	театр	Theatre
Tsérkov	церковь	Church
Úlitsa	улица	Street
Vkhod	вход	Entrance
Vokzál	вокзал	Station
Voróta	ворота	Gate
Výkhod	выход	Exit
Yeliséyev	Елисеев	Yeliséyev's food emporium
Zal	зал	Large room, Hall
Zámok	замок	Castle
Zímniy, -yaya (adj.)	зимний, знмняя	Winter

Internationally-known names, which have acquired an accepted spelling, are spelt as they are normally spelt even when this does not conform to the above, e.g. Tchaikovsky (who would have been spelt Chaykovskiy if we had followed the rules above), Chaliapin (Shalyapin), Galitsin (Golitsyn).

Further Reading

We have found the following **Guides** more useful than most.

Blue Guide: Moscow and Leningrad, ed. Evan and Margaret Mawdsley (Ernest Benn Ltd: London, 1980). There is a 1991 edition which is out of print.

The Environs of Leningrad, Pavel Kann, translated by Barry Jones (Progress Publishers: Moscow, 1981)

Leningrad: A Guide, Pavel Kann, English text edited by Alexandra Buyanovskaya (Planeta Publishers: Moscow, 1990)

Saint-Pétersbourg, ed. Mastelinck et Baubault (Guides Gallimard: Paris, 1995). Text in French but highly – and brilliantly – illustrated.

Literary Russia: A Guide, Anna Benn and Rosamund Bartlett (Papermac: London, 1997)

The Museums of St Petersburg: A Short Guide, initiated by the Union of Creative Museum Workers of St Petersburg and the Leningrad Region (EGO Publishers: St Petersburg, 2000)

Travel Guide for Saint Petersburg, approved by the Committee for Culture of the Administration of Saint Petersburg (Fregat: St Petersburg, 2000)

St Petersburg, The Hermitage, The Russian Museum and *Peterhof, Pavlovsk, Tsarskoye Selo, Gatchina, Oranienbaum*. Illustrated guides, English edition, in hard or soft covers (P-2 Art Publishers: St Petersburg, 2000. E-mail: *info@p-2.ru*)

The Rough Guide to St Petersburg, Dan Richardson (Rough Guides Ltd: London, 2001)

The following **Reference Books** are excellent source material.

Péterburg: Khudózhestvenno-Istorícheskiy Ócherk (St Petersburg: An Artistic and Historical Sketch), V. Kurbatov (St Petersburg, 1913). Text in Russian.

Panorama of Nevsky Prospekt and Supplement, 1740s–1970 (Aurora Art Publishers: Leningrad, 1974). Text in Russian, French and English. Illustrated.

Architectural Monuments of Leningrad (Stroyizdat, Leningrad Branch: 1976). Text in Russian but title and some captions also in English.

Architectural Monuments of Leningrad Suburbs (Stroyizdat, Leningrad Branch: 1985). Text in Russian. Title in English and Russian.

Moscow and Leningrad: A Topographical Guide to Russian Cultural History, Vol. I, Charles A. Ward (K. G. Saur VG & Co: Munich, 1989). Text in English. Subsequent volumes never published.

Sankt-Peterburg, Petrograd, Leningrad Encyclopaedia (Nauchnoye Izdatelstvo: St Petersburg, 1992). Text in Russian.

The following may be useful **Further Reading**. We mention here only books of general application. The details of some other books relating to specific aspects of the city, its buildings or its history are given in footnotes to the text.

Berlin, Isaiah, *Russian Thinkers* (The Hogarth Press: London, 1978)

Grabar, Igor, *Peterbúrgskaya Arkhitektúra v XVIII i XIX Vekákh* (*Petersburg Architecture in the Eighteenth and Nineteenth Centuries*), reprinted by Lenisdat: 1994. Text in Russian.

Gray, Camilla, *The Great Experiment: Russian Art 1863–1922* (Thames and Hudson: London, 1962)

Hughes, Lindsey, *Peter the Great. A Biography.* (Yale University Press, 2002)

Lincoln, W. Bruce, *Sunlight at Midnight: St Petersburg and the Rise of Modern Russia* (Originally published in the United States by Basic Books, 2001. British edition by The Perseus Press: Oxford, 2001)

Madariaga, Isabel de, *Russia in the Age of Catherine the Great* (Weidenfeld and Nicolson: London, 1981)

Pekarskiy, P., 'Peterbúrgskaya Stariná' ('Bygone St Petersburg'), published in *Sovreménnik* (*The Contemporary*), St Petersburg: 1862

Further Reading

Pipes, Richard, *Russia under the Old Regime* (Weidenfeld and Nicolson: London, 1974)

———— *The Russian Revolution 1899–1919* (Harvill/Fontana: London, 1990 by arrangement with Alfred A. Knopf Inc.)

———— *Russia under the Bolshevik Regime* (Harvill: London, 1994 by arrangement with Alfred A. Knopf Inc.)

Punin, A., *Arkhitektúra Peterbúrga seredínye XIX Veka (Petersburg Architecture in the mid-Nineteenth Century)* (Lenisdat: 1990). Text in Russian.

Riasanovsky, Nicholas, *A History of Russia* (OUP: New York, 1963)

Salisbury, Harrison E., *The Siege of Leningrad* (Secker and Warburg: London, 1969; published in paperback by Pan as *The Nine Hundred Days*)

Sindalovskiy, N. A., *Legéndy i Mífy Sankt-Peterbúrga (The Legends and Myths of St Petersburg)* (Norint: St Petersburg, 1997). Text in Russian.

———— *Peterburg. Ot Dóma k Dómu. . .Ot Legéndy k Legénde (St Petersburg: From House to House . . . From Legend to Legend)* (Norint: St Petersburg, 2001). Text in Russian.

Stolpyanskiy, P., *Kak Vozník, Osnoválsya i Ros Sankt-Peterburkh (How St Petersburg Arose, was Founded and Grew)* (First published in Petrograd 1918, reprinted by Nega: St Petersburg, 1995). Text in Russian.

Vyatkin, M., ed., *Ócherki Istórii Leningráda 1703–1941 (Sketches of the History of Leningrad 1703–1941)*, four vols. (Akadémiya Naúk: Moscow-Leningrad, 1955–64). Text in Russian.

The following **Web Sites** are worth consulting:

www.hermitagemuseum.org
www.rusmuseum.ru
www.museum.navy.ru
www.alexanderpalace.org
www.peterhof.org

Index

gives *Petróvskiy óstrov* to Free
Economic Society, 342
heads European coalition
against Napoleon, 113
marriage to Louise of Baden, 411
occupies house on Stone
Island, 347
occupies Winter Palace, 124, 146
Oranienbaum given to by
Paul, 399
and plot against Paul, 241
portrait, 143
relations with Caulaincourt, 350
restores Taurida Palace, 224
stays at Monplaisir, 389
succeeds to throne, 240
transfers 'Twelve Collegia' to
university, 323
Alexander II, Emperor
apartments in Winter Palace, 130
assassination attempts on and
death, 130–1, 146, 188–9,
214, 243–4, 274, 337, 415
coronation, 134, 392
and Decembrists, 85
grants permission to build
Grand Choral Synagogue, 261
marries Yekaterina
Dolgorukaya, 146
presents elephants to Sophie
Ter-Regan's zoo, 60
reforms, 85, 116, 130, 172, 233
Alexander III, Emperor
assassination attempt on, 28,
327
avoids Tsarskoye Selo
palaces, 411
death, 195
lives at Gatchina, 415
monument, 204–5, 301–2
occupies Winter Palace, 146
raises church on site of father's
assassination, 244
removes Mecklenburg-Strelitz
family from Mikháylovskiy
Palace, 196

reverses Alexander II's
reforms, 85
witnesses Grand Duchess
Catherine's will, 245
Alexander Column
(*Aleksándrovskaya kolónna*),
112–13
Alexander Nevsky Monastery, 6,
37, 136, 198, 205–10
Guest House, 336
Alexander Nevsky, St (Prince
Alexander of Novgorod), 37, 63
Neva victory, 6, 206
remains and reliquary, 136–8,
207–8
Alexander Nevsky Square *see*
Aleksándra Névskovo, plóstchad
Alexander Palace (*Aleksándrovskiy*
dvoréts), Tsarskoye Selo, 410–13
Alexander Park
see Aleksándrovskiy Park
Alexandra, Empress of Nicholas II
arrest, 411–12
at Peterhof, 390
confined at Tsarskoye Selo, 401
marriage, 50
murdered, 421
and Rasputin, 277
Alexandra Park, Peterhof, 391
Alimov, A., 204
All Who Sorrow, Church of, 233
All-Russian Congress of Soviets:
Extraordinary Session (October
1917), 226
Alliluyeva, Nadezhda, 230
Almedingen, E.M., 315, 335
Altman, Natan, 263
Amber Study (*Yantárnaya*
kómnata), Tsarskoye Selo, 408
Amigoni, Jacopo: *Peter the Great*
accompanied by the Goddess of
Glory (painting), 140
Amsterdam: influence on
St Petersburg, 1, 3
Anastasia Nikolayevna, Grand
Duchess, 34n

Index

Index

Index

Index

Index

Index

Index

LIBRARIES
INVCLYDE